THE SOCIAL STRUCTURE OF VALUES

Some other Books by Dr. Radhakamal Mukerjee

The Foundations of Indian Economics (1916)
Principles of Comparative Economics (1923) (2 Vols.)
Borderlands of Economics (1925)
Ground Work of Economics (1926)
Democracies of the East (1923)
Civics (1926)
Rural Economy of India (1926)
Regional Sociology (1926)
Introduction to Social Psychology (with N.N. Sen Gupta) (1928)
The Land Problems of India (1933)
Migrant Asia (1935)
The Theory and Art of Mysticism (1938, 1960)
Horizon of Marriage (1937)
Food Planning for Four Hundred Millions (1938)
The Regional Balance of Man (1938)
Man and His Habitation (1940, 1968)
The Institutional Theory of Economics (1940)
The Political Economy of Population (1942)
Economic History of India 1600-1800 (1946)
The Indian Working Class (1945)
Planning the Country Side (1946)
Races, Land and Food (1946)
Social Ecology (1940)
The Social Structure of Values (1949)
The Dynamics of Morals (1951)
The Symbolic Life of Man (1959)
Lord of the Autumn Moon (1957)
The History of Indian Civilization (2 Vols., 1956)
The Culture and Art of India (1959)
The Philosophy of Social Science (1960)
The Philosophy of Personality (1963)
The Dimensions of Human Evolution (1963)
The Destiny of Civilization (1964)
The Flowering of Indian Art (1964)
The Dimension of Values (1964)
The Sickness of Civilization (1964)
The Cosmic Art of India (1965)
The Oneness of Mankind (1965)
The Way of Humanism: East and West (Bombay: Academic Books, 1968)
Astavakra: The Song of the Self-Supreme (Astavakragita) (Delhi: Motilal Banarsidas, 1971)
Fundamental Unity of India (Bombay: Bharatiya, 1977)
Society and Community in India (Ajmer: Sachin Publications, 1979)

Collected Works of

Dr. Radhakamal Mukerjee

THE SOCIAL STRUCTURE OF VALUES

General Editors

Dr. G. R. Madan/V. P. Gupta

Under the auspices of

Radhakamal Mukerjee Memorial Society, New Delhi

RADHA PUBLICATIONS

New Delhi - 110 002

First Edition 1949

Second Edition 1965

Third Edition 2005

Reprint 2023

ISBN : 81-7487-369-4

RADHA PUBLICATIONS

4378/4B, Ansari Road, Daryaganj

New Delhi-110 002

Phone : 23261839, 23254306

Published by Nitin Garg for Radha Publications and printed by R.K. Printers, Shahadra, Delhi.

Editorial Note

Radhakamal Mukerjee (1889-1968) has been one of the few multidisciplinarians of our age who wrote with equal ease, originality and authority on a large variety of areas including economics, sociology, ecology, mankind, democracy, civilization, art, psychology, personality, population, values, morals, philosophy, evolution and mysticism. He authored about fifty books on various subjects.

Professor Radhakamal Mukerjee, the father of Indian sociology, is universally acclaimed for his encyclopaedic treatment of social values. In a pre-publication comment on Mukerjee's "*The Social Structure of Values*", Karl Mannheim remarked correctly that prior to this book there was no systematic work on the sociology of values although there were various articles and a great interest in the subject. As a matter of fact, among the many stimulating contributions to theoretical and empirical social science, to which Professor Radhakamal Mukerjee devoted his life, none is more provocative to the sociologists than his theory of value. Mukerjee dealt with the nature and scope of values in most of his writings, but his classic works on the subject are mainly two: "*The Social Structure of Values*" (1949), and "*The Dimensions of Values*" (1964).

In this book Dr. Mukerjee has assigned a very important position to universal values in society. Without universal values, ideals and symbols understood, interpreted and fostered by sociology, the coming world society cannot be built up. Groups and institutions rise and disappear and obtain their true meaning in the flux of values. The supreme values of individuals are those of profound communion—love, sharing and solidarity. These values build up the most harmonious group. Civilisations come to grief by compartmentalising values and human relations within the boundaries of specific groups, roles and obligations. Such segregation of values is an obstacle to social efficiency and personality adjustment.

The human community maintains its solidarity through participation of its members in certain common traditions and values. Such participation involves an integration of the activities of individuals in the social structure in terms of some scheme, values or ends. Changes in social gradation in all societies reflect changes in the invariable world of values. Dr. Mukerjee has cited the example of Hindu society to prove his point. According to him Hindu society expanded across the centuries in India through a gradual process of social assimilation of aboriginal and forest folks rather than through subjugation and expropriation. These were included in the Hindu fold as they gave up impure animal foods, abandoned nomadism and pillage in favour of agriculture, tanning, leather work, or farm labour and adopted certain customs in respect of marriage and worship. But in this process of absorption many lagged behind. These were gathered into castes that were regarded as low and unclean in the Hindu social scale.

The scales of values of the different social strata always coalesce or clash, depending on the process of social integration. In a society where certain social groups are superimposed upon others, their superior attitudes give rise to counter-values. Society in such a case becomes split up into discordant groups. The results of such a situation are social disintegration and personal disorganisation. Society is a changing compound structure in various levels of social cohesion. Its scales of values constantly shift and intermingle. There are always individuals and groups who rise and fall in the social scale. Besides the social classes, such primary groups as the family, the neighbourhood and the rural community, and such associations as the club, the university and the sports ground set their own patterns of values. In a harmonious society the sale of values of the elite groups become representative of the whole community. It provides an orderly framework of cooperation and coordination between the different groups.

Professor Mukerjee further adds that the most important function of culture is of course the ranking of values and imperatives as embodied in the scheme of stratificatory status, social mobility and distance that guide both personality integration and social reciprocity. The highest prized values are those of the dominant prestige and power groups and institutions in every social culture. It is the dominant and central groups and institutions of a social cultural milieu that mould sovereign values, ethos and personality types. All the while the superior men, artists, poets and mystics, as they seek self-fulfilment, create ideal values that establish the widest society and the most intimate communion—the perfection of social living.

Between man and society, the floating wick and the deep oil, there is a never-ending give-and-take, producing the bright, steady flame of value experience that eternally radiates light and warmth on our bleak, dreary universe. Man, society and values cannot be understood separately. Each can be understood operationally only in terms of others in the personality-value-group, and man (organism)-culture (function)-environment "field". The social "field" and man's adjustment to it should both be considered as dynamic processes in which change constantly take place, in which new social roles and statuses arise on the outer side, and social values, ideals and norms on the subjective side. The structuring of society, of values and of self is inseparable, with old articulations being superseded by new and apparently more adequate and satisfactory ones, these in turn constantly responding to external events, technological changes, cultural developments and chronic, subjective tensions. Values are the only stable realities that may constitute a frame for the ordering of these complex, intermeshed phenomena of the social "field".

Sociology should now see the individual, society and values, the wick, the oil and the flame—apiece, the indivisible unity of the inner and the outer, of the microcosm and the macrocosm. The perception of this unity would also accompany a reorientation of methods of study that should combine scientific and empirical with normative and philosophical approaches integrated together for the adequate interpretation of Man and Society that comprise both biopsychological and spiritual levels of reality, and of values, that are both empirical facts as social uniformities and normative judgments as directing Man and Society to determinate goals.

—*General Editors*

G.R. Madan, *President*
V.P. Gupta, *Secretary*
Radhakamal Mukerjee Memorial Society

PREFACE TO THE SECOND EDITION

A revised edition of the volume has been overdue. During the last two decades the naive social Darwinism, naturalistic psychologism and cultural determinism in which the social sciences formerly rooted themselves have encountered serious challenges. The methodology of all social sciences is undergoing transformation with a view to give guidance to man for his life, values and fulfilment. The dualism between facts and values, individual and society, egoism and altruism, community and cosmos, self-actualization and self-transcendence that has thwarted sociological analysis and synthesis is now fading away. The unity and openness of society, values and the human person are emphasized from various angles. From psychology comes the important finding that dichotomizing marks a low level of personality development and of social and psychological functioning. All this is having its impact on the core of sociological theory. Interdisciplinary studies that are characteristic only of the last two decades expose the unwisdom of the previous emphasis of the closedness and relativity of values and social systems and treat the system of values on a par with language, technology and material culture. "Experiments with groups," has aptly remarked Kurt Lewin, "will lead to a natural integration of the social sciences and it will force the social scientist to recognise as reality the totality of factors which determine group life."

To discover values, whether intrinsic and ultimate or instrumental and immediate, as historical and workable theories pragmatically and programmetically; to appreciate the continuity between the intrinsic and the instrumental values in all means-ends-scheme; and to clarify, harmonise and adjust values—the laws or uniformities in the social cosmos—as dynamic expressions of the richness and uniqueness of the human personality and of social integration and harmony are essential features of the new outlook in sociology. This will bring about a Copernican revolution in the field of social science, shifting the stress from the method of Aristotle to that of Galileo with reference to social phenomena: the former dealing with the *properties* of objects, the latter dealing with the *relations* of objects to the whole sociological situation. Like man's own nature, dispositions and possibilities, like his ever changing and enlarging social milieu, values change, extend and co-ordinate themselves as dynamic *inter-relations* in a functional on-going whole—the social order.

On the one hand, we increasingly discern greater integration and co-ordination of the various social disciplines as there is acknowledgement of the unity and wholeness of values and personality and the integralness of the social order. On the other hand, there is stress of the general trends of man, society and values towards the enlargement of their boundaries—the recognition of humanist, universal and transcendent values and frames of reference.

In Western civilization the successive scientific, technological and industrial revolutions are responsible for a competitive conflictful, aggressive pattern of selfhood. The modern thought-pattern, derived from Descartes, also stresses the thinking of the discrete, solitary self as the ground of the certitude of existence of the cosmos. From these springs the basic Western emphasis of the *value-subject* with its relativistic and calculable dispositions and interests rather than of the *value object* with its imponderable and universal claims that stem from a metaphysical or transcendent dimension or order given for the self and the neglect of its interchanges and continuities with the cosmos. The Western way of living and thinking discount the openness, wholeness and transcendence of the human self and values. We need today to replace the prevalent empirical bio-social theory of mind or self by a multi-dimensional theory that can do justice to the self's deep and expansive cosmic affinities and transactions shaping themselves into man's intrinsic and ultimate values and norms.

Reflection on the nature of values and self that enable man to live and act simultaneously in different dimensions of his cosmos, and on the terrible costs of closedness, disharmony and conflict rather than openness, balance and integration of his values and personality in human affairs will increasingly justify the use of social intelligence and imagination for his achievement of the universal values and the unlimited society of mankind and cosmos. His finite society is the replica of this infinite, transcendent community of cosmos, whence he finds universal and perennial love, goodness and justice that hallow his transitory and arbitrary human relations, values and institutions. His social adventure embodies this grand transformation simultaneously with his own metamorphosis into *Homo universalis*. Since the Pleistocene period *Homo sapiens* is becoming "turce born" as *Homo universalis*. Openness, universality and transcendence must be recognized as necessities of his adaptations to his unlimited and refined social environment. *Homo sapiens* may be yet adolescent as *Homo universalis* but there is no doubt that he is on his way to full maturation and completion with his new moral and spiritual equipment.

Releasing itself from the old assumptions and procedures of physicalism, behaviourism and determinism that die hard and perpetuate a false view of human nature, society and values, sociology should focus the image of man as *Homo universalis* and define and clarify the cultural universals appearing as part of the human career and providing for human growth, wholeness and transcendence beyond the biological and the social dimensions everywhere. Thus can sociology gain openness and universality so far lacking, and formulate fundamental principles of solidarity at the successive dimensions of the family, social stratification, state, law, morality and religion. Without universal values, ideals and symbols understood, interpreted and fostered by sociology, the coming world society cannot be built up.

University,
Lucknow

RADHAKAMAL MUKERJEE

PREFACE TO THE FIRST EDITION

This is a systematic attempt to present sociology from the viewpoint of valuation as the *primum mobile* in the social universe, the nexus of all human relations, groups and institutions. Contemporary sociology, in spite of the dissent of a growing body of able writers, endeavours on the whole to eschew valuations and keep to 'hard facts', but too often becomes "heavily loaded with static and fatalistic valuations in its hidden ethos." Its effort to remain value-free is rooted in its derivation from the ideology of the Great Enlightenment, political liberalism, *laissez-faire* and social Darwinism in Western culture. The movement for a positive methodology to come out in the open with an explicit presentation of values and full analysis of their moral presuppositions, deductions and consequences is, however, now gaining ground. We may mention only two path-finders in this direction, *viz.*, Lynd and Lynd's dual study of the attitudes and value-patterns of the Middletowners and Myrdal's monumental report on the Negroes in American society. Our aim in this volume is an analysis of the structure and dynamics of values that underlie the unity and stability of culture and the continuity and uniformity of groups and institutions. Values are embedded in the dominant status scheme and insititutional pattern of a social culture; but these are not sacrosanct, requiring confirmation as these do in terms of the need and experiences in the objective social situation. These are both facts, *i.e.,* social uniformities or laws that govern actual social relations and behaviour as well as norms that guide individuals and societies to certain coherent and common standards and ideals of behaviour.

Man's behaviour and values are interrelated as part and whole. His values and roles of life weave sacial bonds and make groups; and the social groups interacting on the values, roles and consciences of the growing individuals make morals, ideals and personalities. Human urge, behaviour and value thus comprise a unity. Similarly man's conscience, reason and sensibility and his exterior code of morals, culture, laws and institutions are inseparable and continuous. These interpenetrate with one another and make an integral whole—the world of values in which he lives and moves, which is interjected into his consciousness, and at the same time embodied in his external social heritage. The latter patterns his needs and roles and canalises his feelings, beliefs and ideals. Groups and institutions rise and disappear and obtain their true meaning in the flux of values; while they also mould and stylise his various roles, oriented towards a variety of socially sanctioned values, and fuse his many group-selves. Society achieves the miracles of transformation of ego-centric desires into values, of impulsive behaviour into social roles, of fluctuating attitudes and sentiments into perennial ideals and symbols, of biological individuality into social personality. It is the central concept of valuation that comprises the thread, tying together the beads of individual happiness, personality adjustment and social and institutional adaptation in their togetherness.

As long as we cannot discern human values, morals, personality, social roles and forms of social control in their interlocking and interpenetration in the group-environmental "field", and in terms of the on-going processes of man's social living, self-enhancement, and communion, we cannot do justice to the meanings and dynamisms of both personality and society.

Recent trends in *Gestalt* psychology, psychoanalysis, psychiatry and personality study have contributed towards development of the conception of the social group as a dynamic, structural-functional whole, 'that is superseding the older nineteenth century concept of 'society' as either an exalted super-individual entity or an amorphous mass of free, uninstitutionalised individuals. These trends have modified contemporary approaches in cultural anthropology, as in the works of Malinowski, Benedict, Mead, Bateson and Linton. The cross-fertilisation of the methods and materials of clinical psychology and cultural anthropology is of outstanding significance in the development of structural-dynamic analysis of human values and relationships and types of personality in relation to the functional needs of a social culture. Basic to the functional analysis of any social system are the notions of the level and scale of values or ethos, and of the major statuses and roles of individuals and institutions, that serve to maintain the social order and keep the various interpersonal relationships, groups and institutions geared in with one another.

The structural-functional relationships of values thus provides the central, integrating core of theory of sociological science, values being linked to the individual's roles and statuses, and social roles and statuses to the multiple group structuring of both society and personality. No society is ever unorganised, without its stable values, groups and institutions, its well-settled social roles and statuses. No individual is ever unattached or anarchic. His behaviour is neither isolated nor unrelated. It is stylised, patterned, geared to repeatable situations in a stable, cosmic frame or routine in which he lives and matures. Thus is behaviour transformed into role. Morally, man has only one single, inescapable role ordained for him, of doing what is to him perfectly, unqualifiedly good and right. Socially, he has usually several fluctuating roles, full of differences according to his age-group, sex-group or class and the principles of *quid pro quo*. Such differences in roles, indeed, stop short of criminality and abnormality. It is laughter and ridicule at the outset, folkway and public opinion later and law and medicine finally that take charge of grave, intolerable differences between legitimately expected and actual roles of men, all in the background of the process of acculturation, the learning of values, roles, and expectancies by the individual in his group. The unit of sociological theory is the person-in-group and culture that in their ramifying and proliferating values, roles, and patterns of thought and action produce and nurture the personality, and maintain the stability of society and of its intimate everyday relationships that are the moulds and vehicles of his valuation and conception of himself and of his statuses and obligations in society.

A realistic role-and-status psychology—rooted in the ethos, the eidos, the central value system and theme of primitive and peasant culture configurations—which is on the way is influencing the analysis of both the structuring of personality and patterning of roles statuses and value-systems. The study of contemporary urban culture, its dominant social classes, status-prestige system, social control and growth of insecurity and impersonality is likewise obtaining its anchorage point from the self-maintenance mores, ethos or value scale of the community. Each culture, tribal, rural-communal or urban-industrial, from the functional social-psychological viewpoint, is a creative synthesis of group values and ideals, a system of interrelated statuses and a framework of rights-and-duties for each role, position and status that mould personalities and govern character and virtues.

Comparative sociology is little developed and needs much attention today. Its systematisation rests on the study of the functional differentiation of values and cultural and institutional patterns on a regional and comparative basis. It is the divergent patterns of social values that underlie differences in typical behaviour in social roles in different cultures. Each social culture with its distinctive cultural and institutional norms shows also typical social deviations that may be considered as the foci of new values. There will always be found in any social system certain groups that through their challenge of the given institutional patterns, and of the status-power system supporting these, often reveal new strivings, meanings and values.

Neither the patterns of human urges and strivings, nor values, virtues and morals, nor groups and institutions are fixed and unchangeable. It is the lags, distortions and discontinuities of their dynamic reciprocity that are the root causes of man's tensions, neuroses and group and institutional conflicts and maladjustments. This has obtained recognition in psychotherapy that is now including group analysis and treatment of frustrations and aggressive behaviour.

The development by sociology of a sound theory of values rests on the examination, *inter alia*, of the stages and levels of valuation as embodied in the categories of goals, ideals and norms; the gradation and interrelationships of values and their relation to social roles; the ordering, augmentation, protection, equalisation and transmission of values by the vast ramifying framework of traditions, institutions, laws, morals and education; and the functional interdependence between the type of group participation, the depth-level of personality and the quality of moral consciousness. Such treatment will contribute towards establishing sociology as the philosophy of social sciences, and giving both impetus and orientation to various structural-functional social investigations by a central frame of reference.

Finally, the analysis and clarification of social goals and values and of groups and institutions intended to foster these will materially help in distinguishing, first, between individual urgings and satisfactions and social values, and, second, between normal or adequate and diseased, unorganised or frustrative groups and institutions with their expressive or repressive forms of control and their fateful conditionings of, and reactions on, the personality patterns.

The antithesis between true and false social values is that of comprehension and exclusion, creativeness and constraint, reality and fantasy, ideal and idol. It also underlies the contrast between education, morals or devotion to truth and righteousness and propaganda or manipulation of goals and values with their wholesome or pernicious influence upon public opinion and mass action. Values and ideals, idols and fetishes are the social medium in which man's life is lived and matured. The same medium produces, communicates and manipulates truths or lies, right or wrong valuations, and appeals to build up goodness and love or aggressiveness and hate, that have compulsive power over him and explain his fulfilment or emotional tension. True or false values pervade his theoretical beliefs, faiths and the entire organisation of his world of purpose and action. These produce and sustain conscience, virtues and loyalties or their opposites, goodwill, impartiality and disinterestedness or pride, fanaticism and power complex, transcendence of self, role and group interests or preoccupation with biological and social contingencies and lust after the absolutes of a class, nation, state or race.

Yet the self, though largely group-determined and comprising the needs of other selves, groups, classes and values, defines and integrates in the same process *his* group and class, *his* values. The common denominator of most meanings, values and loyalties is self-status and self-enhancement. The self constantly develops in the course of adjustment to the social milieu new ideals and norms, new strivings for goodness and justice that are essentially his own and that spell out his own duties and allegiances. Man's moral venture rests finally on the autonomy of self, mind and values that refuse to be entangled by the contingent limitations and fluctuations of life and society. It may be religious not because of its concern with values, but because it may recognise the value and obligation of adjustment to an extra-human source and order of values, permanent and independent of the evolutionary process of the movement of individuals and societies. Value like logic, from this viewpoint, depends neither upon the minds that appreciate it nor upon the life and society to which it responds. The value-lover, like the philosopher of Plato, becomes a "spectator of all time and all existences".

The sociological examination of values, symbols and fetishes, saturated as it is by the practical objectives of alteration of anticipated social and institutional trends, is indispensable for social planning or 'engineering'. Such a practical programme based on an analysis of social goals and values, their assumptions and their causal interrelations as well as their internal contradictions should guide the direction of theoretical research in sociology coming to grips with practical problems. Thus 'social engineering' will march hand in hand with both evaluative and theoretical sociology.

Values, ideals and norms form a coherent and harmonious hierarchy, comprising the basic common knowledge of the human situation and the right principles of behaviour of individuals and groups. Clarification of the scale of values and ideals provides the standards for the measurement of social progress—the goals and norms by which groups, societies and civilisations can be judged. Such scaling of values, of course, proceeds not from the evolving world-stuff or the social process that are in fact determined and regulated by the former, but from the developing individual insight and vision. It is the new order and dimension of man's being and not merely the methods of science, whether biology, sociology or psychology, that reveal the total and perennial human situation and super-human source of values and norms. Knowledge that man's goals and values are true and harmonious aids in their mass adoption and diffusion, in overcoming the bias, partiality and resistance of individuals, classes and institutions. Suspicion that certain pressure groups and institutions seek to misunderstand, distort and manipulate goals and values in their own local particular interests is preventive of their dissemination in society. 'Social engineering' rests on the proper scaling of values and the recognition of man's dignity, creativeness and freedom of participation in the major values of life, and resists the use of fellowmen as pawns or as objects whose loyalty and credulity are exploited for selfish ends. As the art of planning intellectual and moral production and distribution, 'social engineering' not only re-establishes the most significant of human hierarchies—the hierarchy of values and the ordering of life, mind and society—but also re-institutes techniques and symbol-devices of social control and evocation that are less dependent upon coercion and fear of sanctions, and more upon understanding, sympathy and goodwill for the elimination of all kinds of evil and deviant behaviour and education and participation of larger and larger sections of the community in the higher values of life.

In the stratified industrial communities of Europe and America the disruption of long-established, customary groupings in which men have their proper roles and statuses and enjoy self-respect has had its effect in emotional insecurity and dissemination of false values and idols, collapse of moral restraint and increase of social coercion. As the Industrial Revolution takes the whole of agricultural Asia and Africa within its ambit, the structure of values resting upon the interpersonal relationships, roles and Statuses in families, village communities and occupational groupings will disintegrate, producing social and moral problems much more quickly and for much larger populations. In the reciprocal adjustment of technology, human relations and values that 'social engineering' has to deal with now on a global scale, the dispersal of industrialisation, reorientation of neighbourhoods and recovery of personal relationships and values are equally essential.

Three principles emerge that serve as the basis of 'human engineering.' First, the moral and intellectual qualities of a culture are proved not by ideological cliches and formulae but by the basic dimensions and quality of human relations and group participation these connote. Values emerge neither as eternal essences in a cosmic frame nor as attributes of personality that are later applied to the social situation, but in the structure of concrete group relationships, and largely require for their nurture and development the constant support of such relationships. Second, it is only deliberate adoption and pursuit of social and industrial policy that can maintain a dominant group and institutional pattern producing the highest values, personal interrelationships and personalities. Third, in the dynamics of culture both the community with its dominant ideology and arrangement and the individual in his uniqueness become foci of new values, new conceptions of human relationships that may lead to an overall reconstruction of society.

While society and its major institutions and roles play the leading part in the definition, ordering, conservation and sharing of the major values through its arrangements, traditions, laws and freedoms, it is the knowledge, love and creative imagination of individuals that constantly create new sensibilities and values, bring these into the ever-expanding common pool, and compel society to make these a part of the social living and experience of all. The supreme values of individuals are those of profound communion-love, sharing and solidarity. Such are the values that also build up the most harmonious and the most extensive group. This may be called Commonalty. The progression from Crowd through Interest-group and Society to Commonalty—the four "ideal" types of human associations that cover in a successive functional series all possible social bonds in the dialectic of human communion—measures at once the increase of group participation or mutuality, depth of the self or dominance of its universal or transcending aspects over those that are immediate or restricted, and moral responsibility and creativeness. Man is a creature and creator of many groups in which his several selves are embedded, and his roles, values and moral norms shift as he belongs to one or other of these basal categories of groups in the daily routine of life. Both man and society show accordingly fluctuating schemes of roles, values and norms that remain distinct and supreme within each type or grouping, each level or phase of social integration, but also sometime invade other spheres of group life to the detriment of the whole culture. No culture can survive the incursion, for instance, of the standards of reciprocity and contract from the Interest-group, like the class or work 'association, into familistic relationships, normally governed by the values of love, sharing and service. Mankind has developed its sense of moral obligation from the bonds of long-settled, customary famitistic groups. The permanence and solidarity of the family as a Commonalty group in the Orient are due mainly to the intellectual reconstruction and aesthetic symbolisation of the major family loyalties and intimacies that have become seats of universal and eternal values and virtues, emotionally charged symbols of approach to the deity. Thus aesthetic and religious ideology and symbolism import into "human nature's daily food" the transcendence of the absolute. The symbols and norms of the Universal Person in the Oriental world add a new dimension to human relationships and experience, and play no small role in building up a wholeness and integrity in social life.

In the concrete social situation we find groups changing from one basic kind of social participation and bonds to another with profound transformation of values and of quality of social life and behaviour. Interest-groups like the social classes, trade-unions and political parties through a lop-sided development of normal factors of the social structure disrupt those human-relationships upon which the individual personality is most intimately dependent. These easily and recurrently regress into crowds and mobs that challenge established social values, habits and standards of conduct. From this springs indeed the greatest menace to the higher values and social stability in the industrialised, depersonalised interest-group world of modern civilisations. True Commonalty seeks solidarity of the species; but spurious. Commonalty fosters exclusive familism, communalism, nationalism; sectionalism or partisanship, creating disvalues that block higher social integration and bring about emotional instability and unbalance of judgment. It is the sense of insecurity and threat of isolation of groups and individuals that lead to the collapse of moral responsibility and understanding under the impact of emotional stress, and account for what Durkheim called 'social anomie,' and for frustration, neurosis and disorganisation.

Evaluative sociology works on the basis of a generalised, telic evolution theory providing the dynamic framework for the ordering and organisation of the phenomena of values and of social relationships with which these are intermeshed. There will be a great progress in the social studies if there be a scientific understanding of the quality of various types of social relationships, levels of group participation and the valuations, sensibilities and controls that keep them moving.

Civilisations come to grief by compartmentalising values and human relations within the boundaries of specific groups, roles and obligations. Such segregation of values is an obstacle to social efficiency and personality adjustment. What Bougie calls 'conjunction of values' makes for social sanity and goodness and wholesomeness in interpersonal relations. The most important function of culture is of course the ranking of values and imperatives as embodied in the scheme of stratificatory status, social mobility and distance that guide both personality integration and social reciprocity. The highest prized values are those of the dominant prestige and power groups and institutions in every social culture. It is the dominant and central groups and institutions of a social cultural milieu that would sovereign values, ethos and personality types. All the while the superior men, artists, poets and mystics, as they seek self-fulfilment, create ideal values that establish the widest society and the most intimate communion—the perfection of social living.

Between man and society, the floating 'wick and the deep oil, there is a never-ending give-and-take, producing the bright, steady flame of value experience that enternally radiates light and warmth on our bleak, dreary universe. Man, society and values cannot be understood separately. Each can be understood operationally only in terms of others in the personality-value-group, and man (organism)-culture (function)-environment "field". The social "field" and man's adjustment to it should both be considered as dynamic processes in which changes constantly take place, in which new social roles and statuses arise on the outer side, and social values, ideals and norms on the subjective side. The structuring of society, of values and of self is inseparable, with old articulations being superseded by new and apparently more adequate and satisfactory ones, these in turn constantly responding to external events, technological changes, cultural developments and chronic, subjective tensions. Values are the only stable realities that may constitute a frame for the ordering of these complex, intermeshed phenomena of the social "field."

Sociology should now see the individual, society and values — the wick, the oil and the flame—apiece, the indivisible unity of the inner and the outer, of the microcosm and the macrocosm. The perception of this unity would also accompany a reorientation of methods of study that should combine scientific and empirical with normative and philosophical approaches integrated together for the adequate interpretation of Man and Society, that comprise both bio-psychological and spiritual levels of reality, and of values, that are both empirical facts as social uniformities and normative judgments as directing Man and Society to determinate goals. Neither the interpersonal roles and group relationships and institutions in society nor the human values, ideals and norms can be understood without a simultaneous dual reference: an empirical theory of social relationships, values and institutions that takes recognition of the widest range of knowledge concerning the bio-psychological nature of Man and Society, and permits of verification by the methods of natural science; and a normative theory denning an "ought" for society, which introduces preferences and moral values and ideals, resolves the ideological and ethical conflicts of Man and Society, and obtains its verification by taking care of the most extensive range of ethos and eidos of the world, together with their basic postulates and premises in respect of the nature of man, society and universe. Thus would social philosophy bridge the gulf between biological and mcral man and society, between the philosophy of science and the science of values.

I have utilised in this volume lectures which I have been privileged to deliver in various Departments in the Harvard University, the Columbia University, New York, the University of Maryland and the University of Washington in the U.S.A., the School of Economics and Political Science in London, and the Graduate Institute of International Affairs in Geneva, during my brief sojourns for attending certain international conferences in Europe and America in 1947 and 1948. I am grateful to Professors Sorokin, Zimmerman and MacIver, and particularly to Professors Robert Ulich and Gordon Allport, for the stimulating discussions arranged in the Seminar and Colloquium in the Departments of Education and of Human Relations respectively in the Harvard University. Certain materials of the book have appeared as articles in the American Sociological Review, Sociology and Social Research and Social Forces in the U.S.A. and the Sociological Review in Great Britain. My thanks are due to my pupil, Mr. Sushil Chandra, M.A., for the Index.

University,
Lucknow

RADHAKAMAL MUKERJEE

CONTENTS

1

SOCIOLOGY AS SCIENCE AND AS PHILOSOPHY

Man, the Value-seeking Animal

Society has both its visible and invisible aspects. The patterns of social behaviour and institutions are visible. It can be seen and even measured to some extent how men interact towards one another or play their roles in society, and how institutions, that have always a visible focus, work in the direction of orienting the behaviour of groups of men towards certain definite ends and values. Man's role, position and mobility in the visible or spatial field of his interaction and relationships come under the scope of social ecology as quantitative sociology, regarding status and mobility as primary units of analysis and classification. But there is another more significant aspect of society—the subjective and invisible one, which is usually taken-for granted, and which underlies all human relationships, viz. values, ideals and norms that define, maintain and regulate the visible social structure and interaction, give them cohesion and stability so that they cross the boundaries of time and space. The infinity and universality of values, ideals and norms can never be visible; but the social structure and institutional life render a part of these visible by patternising and stereotyping these through symbols, and by so doing make it possible for man to understand and experience these, and live and act in society.

The phenomena of the natural world can be explained with reference to other physical phenomena preceding these. Man's life and activity cannot be explained except with reference to future potentialities and happenings or goals, values and norms. McDougall stressed that it is the knowledge of "certain great natural goals" towards which man strives which gives the key to his conscious activities and behaviour. Such goals and values, while these stabilise man's relationships and interactions, themselves obtain a relative permanence like the laws of physical causation through the instrumentality of society, the scene and medium of value consciousness, referring all his behaviour to a future consummation—value, ideal and norm.

Man's social nature and society are responsible for his being the value-seeking animal. His desires, habits and interests are so transformed in social Jiving that remote values stimulate instead of depressing his mind. Goals and values, spontaneous, pervasive and compulsive, and value-seeking processes of both men and groups are the primary data of sociology. The realm of values is the field in which sociology unites with psychology, ethics and philosophy. For values have a relative permanence and universality ; while social activities, relationships and institutions in which the values embody themselves, though not wholly, clearly or invariably, pass through constant change or adjustment. Values are in truth the stabilities and uniformities of group interaction, and have the same significance for the social sciences as the natural laws have for the positive sciences.

Values as Emergents in Group Situations

Sociology as a science, concerned with the analysis of values operative in social life and with the consideration of the limitations and methods of their fulfilment, finds ethical principles and norms inherent in social groups that, indeed, constitute the frame-work of all value meaning and realisation. It can furnish for empirical ethics a classification of groups that provides the necessary socio-psychological basis for the ordering and organisation of moral values and experiences as social data. Man's basic moral attitudes and obligations are founded on the degree of cohesion and unitive feeling as represented by four "*ideal types*" (in Max Weber's sense) of group life and relations" *viz.* Crowd, Interest-group, Society and abstract Commonalty that constitute a successive functional series according to the intimacy of human bonds. These embrace all possible kinds of associations and social relations in human culture.[1] In so far as man arises from the level of Crowd to Society and from Interest-group to abstract Commonalty, he not only achieves greater closeness and solidarity in actual social living, but also greater depth and aspiration in his moral consciousness in ideal and in fact. On the other hand, the moral creativeness and aspiration towards ideals of the personality sustain appropriate group and institutional patterns.

Moral values are derived from and differ according to such group patterns. Norms and ideals are "emergents" in these basic group relations. These are not remote nor abstract, but are part to the group process, functions of the social situation. The imperatives belong to the social situation itself. The means of control which impose order spring from the group relations themselves, and from the problems which these call for solution. The social situation in this sense is "autonomous", each individual evaluating and behaving in such manner that he fully realises its value potentialities by establishing a definite pattern of human relations, whether in the family, the factory organisation, the class or profession, the church and the nation. Each type of social participation provides the medium for the creation and realisation of specific intrinsic and instrumental values. At the same time, according to the maturity or immaturity of the individual consciousness and the presence of rational or impulsive factors of the personality, coercion, shame, honour and conscience play their role separately or together in the imposition of order and organisation. Order, if it be imposed by coercion, fear and insecurity, is repressive, and does not fulfil the value potentialities of the situation. The spontaneous forms of control, as represented by man's conscience, reason and faith in values, establish a natural order and organisation in and through which the ideal values can be completely realised as the nature of the group permits.

The Need of a Functional Social-Psychological Outlook

Man's group and institutional relations and his moral habits and ideal values are, to be sure, interdependent. Society, personality, values or moral cannot be adequately treated except from this integrated viewpoint. None can be understood except in the terms of the others in the on-going processes of man's social living and dialectic of communion. Outside these processes values and meanings are meaningless or arbitrary. And yet how little ethics profits from the advances in social psychology, as represented by the writings of Dewey, Cooley and Mead still grounding itself on metaphysical individualism, hedonism, or idealism! How strong and deep, too, is the conviction of modern sociology that accommodation of conflicting interests and values of groups and individuals is a matter of institutional arrangement, of laws and procedures that will automatically evolve the "justness" of social relations through the coordination of interest to interest and of right to right! It is too often forgotten that a higher sociality involves integration rather than accommodation, interpenetration rather than interdependence, equality and solidarity rather than equity and justice, and an appreciation of common manings and values and of commonness or commonalty as a value in itself rather than a rational weighing of interests and values.

As a matter of fact the challenge in modern civilisation between liberal individualism and totalitarianism and the social crisis it has brought about in the West can be solved less by institutional technique and control or the multiplication of new social and economic rights, laws and administrative procedures, and more by moral transformation based on the recognition of spheres of values which are outside both the individual and the state, and from which are derived both the unassailable liberties of the individual on the one hand, and the destiny of society and the state on the other.

An even more unsatisfactory and perhaps more dangerous view held in the social field is that as man's ethical problem shifts from personal relationships to the relationships of groups and collectives, egoism and selfishness dominate, demanding aggressive and exploitative policies of classes, states, and empires. The mutual relations among these, it is contended, are determined by coercive rather than moral or rational factors that guide that department of morality which belongs to the individual. Such a view of morals is one-sided. There is no dichotomy between individual and social morality; for the capacity for moral conduct is the same in the individuals, classes, and the Great Society. Consciousness and moral life, in modern psychological analysis, comprise the constant reciprocal interplay between self and others in the social milieu, that indeed defines the meaning of the symbol, the word and the gesture in man's ideas, and the experience of the value and the norm in his responses to fellowmen. The false social analysis referred to is undoubtedly an outcome of the profound maladjustment of individuals, groups and institutions in modern capitalistic-society and its unfavourable reactions upon moral relations, dissipating the medieval legacy of primary groups, feudalism religion.

The Theory and Planning of Values

The problem of social values is the core of social theory. The logic-tight dichotomy of the world of facts and the world of values has been in great measure the result of the philosophical and ethical atomism and the constricting biological naturalism of the nineteenth century. It is responsible for the profound cultural crisis in the modern age; a faulty methodology in the social sciences contributing towards the dissociation of values from economic and political institutions, and distrust and perversion of the values themselves. In the midst of the present clash of ideologies, it is necessary for sociology to develop a central theory of norms and values as basic units in the description and explanation of social relationships and behaviour, and to clarify tools of analysis relevant to the full development of human personality on the one hand and of social solidarity and commonalty on the other. This will restore and amplify the heritage left by the great founders of the science—Comte, Herbert Spencer, Lester F. Ward, Wundt, Schelerand Hobhouse — although it will demand a breakaway from prevalent methods .and cherished postulates.[2]

Modern civilization prepared itself in the ordeal of the two world wars for the practical task of planning. Man is indeed passing from an unplanned to a planned society; and there is great danger that in the swift, perplexing march of events the values attributed by the elite or interest-associations to outworn traditions and institutions will be tacitly accepted without discussion; or the system of values reduced to uncertainty and chaos due to institutions working at cross-purposes; or, again, only the biological and economic values that are favoured by the masses fostered. Liberal Democracy, Socialism and Communism comprise today contrasted crystallized sets of values and ways of living for mankind that require clarification, analysis and appraisal so that new institutions and types of individual relations can be developed with the growth in awareness of new values or changes in value scaling. Even more essential is to find the unity of the value system under varied patterns of social institutions, rights and freedoms. There are different dimensions of values in each social system and the intrinsic or ultimate and the instrumental or immediate, the higher and the lower values must be reconciled, integrated and coordinated. The major goals and values of man, society and culture arrange themselves in a fairly definite scale for mankind as the basis of the principles of preference and urgency. Mankind's fundamental dispositions and acquired habits are such that a value scale precedes judgment of comparative values, being "organic" rather than "conscious", according to Dewey. But the social sciences show an inadequate appreciation not only of an acknowledged gradation of values in relation to human living and growing, but also of the inhibiting or constraining and stimulating or enhancing influences of the institutional and cultural situation. The higher needs and intrinsic or ultimate values of life require better environmental conditions, familial, economic and political, to make them possible, while their pursuit and fulfilment safeguard and fortify man's enlarged social roles, institutions and culture. Such higher needs and intrinsic values may, indeed, be regarded as more uniquely human, more specifically conducive to the realization of human resources and potentialities. Planned society rests on value-planning. Where there is value planning, the higher cultural values will not be monopolised by the elite groups but there will be systematic endeavours through rights, laws and institutions as well as through education towards a diffusion and sharing of these. No special values of institutions will be created and manipulated for class advantage, nor will these predominate over human nature values. The ancient and widely diffused primary-group intimacy and idealism will not be sacrificed to efficiency and power of the complex, anonymous, secondary interest-group world of today, with its characteristic large-scale industrial and economic institutions; nor will the new insistent values of economic security accrue by causing individuals to lose the stimulus of their internal value system, their personal freedom and moral responsibility. Old institutions that actually thwart, stultify, or bring the values they have created and stood for into disrepute will be given up; and new values and ideals will give rise to new institutions, freedoms, rights-and-duties.

The generation that is passing built its traditions and institutions on the values of freedom and sense of responsibility of the individual on the one hand, and the efficiency and power of industrial organization and ambition for empire and world domination in the organised state-society on the other. The new generation is inclined to build on the basis of the values of personal association, social security, and equality in the sharing of great values. It is also groping after total and human (world) values into which regional and national values maybe integrated, an ethical system that is universal for mankind, and that achieves order and solidarity on a global basis by world-wide institutions and practices. New attitudes and norms are bringing about new institutions; new social situations and institutions are fostering new attitudes and norms. The principle of integration and coordination of institutions and norms, set in the conflicts and harmonies of the social system, is represented by the ordering of values that is again to be determined by the closeness of their bearing upon the development of personality and the harmony and solidarity of community life. In this exciting social transition an adequate theory of values in sociology can alone provide the much-needed key to more balanced group and institutional patterns, more cooperative and integral ways of living and action. It is the structure of the values of collective living at its best, stressed for fulfilment and enhancement, that is the final measure of, and lends true meaning to, the system of planning and the progress of society.

Amidst the battle of values that was fought out by tanks and aeroplanes, could not sociology have enabled humanity to find a rational way to judge which values shall prevail without resort to violence or coercion and so guide social orientation? The task was and still is by no means easy. For the norms and principles of sociology are less exact and more susceptible to error than the laws and formulae of the natural sciences. But it can be successfully undertaken if, following the methods of science, sociology grounds its analysis and formulation of norms and values in the data of social situation, need and experience, and inquires into values and social policies with the same independence and detachment as the scientists showed in their inquiries into natural phenomena and laws when they rebelled against scholasticism three centuries ago.

Scientific and Normative Sociology

Sociology in its *scientific* phase regards values on a par with language, technology and material culture. Values are mechanisms of man's social orientation and guidance; they are tools of adjustment of human groups and individuals to the physical and social milieu, and are sifted and tested out in actual social experience by the three-fold criteria: (1) how far the dominant values that men hold lead to the full poise and integration of the personality, achieving freedom and control of the environment; (2) how far the present system of values with whose aid men create and maintain groups, institutions, laws and rights-and-duties successfully guides society in intra-group struggle and survival; and (3) how for the present system of values promotes the creation and maintenance of intimate, enduring and ideal social bonds and relations and an ideal solidarity of humanity. Scientific sociology measures values and also institutions, regarded as shelters and nurturers of values, according to the three-fold criteria of man's social adaptation that show different phases with corresponding value-levels.

Following up what may be called the natural history of values and institutions, sociology essays the task of directing the planning of values and institutions. This is sociology in its *normative* phase. Normative sociology or social axiology tests and checks values and norms against social need and experience, and also checks social need and experience against values and norms in the formation and mutation of cultures.

Accepting the present social order and institutional set-up to a point like the natural order in the physical sciences, normative sociology would ask, are the groups and institutions fulfilling the standards and values ascribed to them? Certain social experiments always go on in every society in the fields of industry, business, government, education and group organisation, striving towards new goals and leading to a different social order. Their programmes and consequences would be objectively studied with reference to both value-seeking, and value-achievement. Thus a set of social goals or values could be posited and tested as hypotheses, with precise analysis of all their social premises and moral pre-suppositions and full logical development of the premises, deductions and consequences.[3] The present phase of social disintegration in the world focuses the attention on the relativity of values and points of view as well as on the social origins and uses of modes of thought. Both unconscious motivations and conscious ideals and norms share in their formulation, as so admirably analysed by Karl Mannheim.

A Comparative Theory of Social Values

The relativity of values and ideals in a dynamic social context stresses the special need of a comparative theory of values, dealing with the hierarchy of values and the logical structure of value systems in contemporary societies that sociology can usefully undertake. For normative sociology or social axiology there are four major types of value problems: (1) Values are peculiar to divergent types of social participation, relations and groups (as represented by the qualitative "ideal types" of Crowd, Interest-group, Society or community and abstract Commonalty). Their structuralisation in a complex dynamic society should demand the attention of sociology studying each kind of group or social system as the locus of values. The dominance of a particular type of social grouping gives the complexion to a culture, and governs the trend of social progress. (2) Each social culture has its distinctive ethos or structuralisation of value systems. The ranking of values is divergent in different cultures, giving rise to distinctive status-power-prestige systems that nurture divergent personality traits and virtues of peoples. This has to be conceived in the context of changing circumstances. The social culture constantly revises its value patterns. A religious, social or political movement or revolution is the product of a new social valuation, often accompanied by a change in the social stratification, in the interrelationship between institutions, and in the codes of rights-and-duties, laws and even morals. Sociology should discern in what measure new value systems make themselves felt in the social consciousness, forecast social trends and make the social transition smoother through the clarification and criticism of new values of organised groups, institutions and individuals. Thus sociology would show how the institutional set-up could integrate or accommodate new values and ideals with the old value system, pouring new wine into old bottles. (3) In spite of such divergent value systems there are certain universal values common to mankind. Comparative social anthropology and sociology reveal certain specific as well as universal values of peoples and cultures, certain distinctive trends of valuation as well as similar transformations in values and gradations of values associated with economic and cultural development of communities.[4] The modern Western sense of relativism of values is linked with the dominance and expansion of the civilization of Europe and the accompanying contempt of backward and oppressed societies and cultures in other continents. The studies of Macbeath, Ginsberg and Kluckhohn show, however, universal moral principles and regularities of human behaviour. Ginsberg particularly finds that a common moral denominator can be found in the moral codes of primitive peoples.[5] Universal values arise due to both common humanness and commonness in human situations. The current doctrine of the relativism of values has at least two baneful intellectual consequences. First, since values are dogmatically confined to restricted cultural frames there is a tendency of values being considered as without objectivity, as elusive or distorted having no power over or concern for man and society. Secondly, there is a tendency to reduce, deny or banish all absolute values and foster intellectual superficiality and arrogance.[6] (4) Values are peculiar to individual consciousness, experience and social action. There are differences in individual mental set-ups and temperaments due to which value appreciation and experience become different. Social conditioning factors such as the interest and bias of economic class, social habit, education and religion also influence valuations. There is also a shift in values with the ageing and acquisition of new experiences in the various stages of life span of the individual, and also with change in his social and economic roles and milieu.[7] On the whole the distinction between the introvert and the extrovert, the dominant and the recessive, the egoistic-aggressive and the social-sympathetic types of individuals is superficial. It is man's social and economic setting which is basic in the differentiation of goals, purposes and forms of behaviour. The-economic and political system with its characteristic institutions, laws and social attitudes sometimes fosters, sometimes discourages the cooperation and harmony of the various social groups of which the individual is a member. The individual's, value adjustment and experience are a composite process arising out of his identifications with the various types of values and experiences of groups. But often two or more groups become so dominant and highly organised that their traditions, attitudes and ways of action restrict or warp the development of individuality. On the other hand, the individual, even though conscious of the selfishness and arbitrariness of the traditions and limitations of the groups, cannot easily free himself from these.. For social cultures differ in their repressive and compulsive characteristics, permitting different scope to the individual's moral initiative and ideal creativeness to modify the socially approved schemes of values.

Dewey rightly protests against the idea of fixed and eternal values and insists on the empirical validation of judgments of values; but, as Mitchell points out, his is a "theory of valuation" rather than a theory of values that he summarily rejects. Out of the studies of normative sociology along the four major lines, indicated above will emerge a comparative theory of values, dealing with the interrelationships and ranking of values, the social structuralisation of value systems and the conflict, integration and enhancement of values. Such a science of values would avoid the notion of fixed and eternal values as readily as biology discards the notions of entelechies and fixed species, and have, as is rightly observed, the same relations to the theory of valuation that the science of morphology has to the theory of growth and evolution.[8]

Sociology in relation to Value Conflicts

A theory of values in the contemporary world would no doubt especially turn its attention to the social background in which value conflicts now arise, and values change for the worse instead of for the better, with the persistence of pathological groups, institutions and social policies. Conflict of economic and political interests related to the special, limited goods of life of vast aggregations of classes and pressure groups can be mitigated or abolished less through the individuals' revising their value schemes and devising their own techniques, and more through organised groups, and institutions becoming conscious of the more universal and humanitarian values of life. No doubt most of personal maladjustments, tensions and neuroses arise today out of social-cultural disvalues destroying the sanity and corroding the morals of the individual. Social disagreements constantly arise out of ignorance, disharmony of special limited goods and values and difference in moral attitudes and valuation. Conflicts in valuation are inevitable, but just as valuations arise only in the social situation and as social facts, so do value disagreements. These emerge largely as conformity to, or divergence from, existing traditions, institutions and laws, and are resolved by cumulative discussion and criticism in the social context. In fact, it is the continuous deliberation and criticism of the community—essentially social processes—that eliminate subjective caprices or class attitudes and sentiments from valuation. Social intelligence, ever vigilant and persistently operative, leads to the approximation of both a valid moral attitude and a scientific hypothesis towards objectivity. Normative sociology as it deals with value experiences and value expressions will accordingly have a dispassionate, objective attitude towards disagreements in valuation, neither taking for granted any ideology and becoming narrow and opinionative, nor fighting shy of value conflicts and confusions that sometimes accompany the overthrow of social and political organisations and deadly social and political struggles in actual life. It will apply alternative hypotheses in respect to social values and public policies for dealing with social situations and consequences, and adopt these as procedures for experimental use in social action, gradually eschewing the role of tradition, dogma and chance in the direction of social affairs. Human skill and experience can thus be effectively utilized for the achievement and enhancement of social values and improvement and control of human relationships and institutions as these have been hitherto applied for the improvement and mastery of the physical environment.

Having investigated various social values and moral ideals as functions of specific social situations and structures, and discovered a consistent basis of judgment and improvement of social relations and institutions, consonant with a scale of values completely analysed and validated, normative sociology assimilates its concepts of social planning and control into the ethical meliorism of the modern age, and harnesses a constantly improving social intelligence in the service of planned society. In order that the higher values of life may be conserved and enhanced, and direct progress, normative sociology clarifies, refines and rectifies both the scale of social values and the instruments and techniques of social control. Coercion, repression, mass propaganda, advertisement and slogan are to be divested of their gross features. Sociology studies and calls forth the progressive mental adaptation of men and groups so that through the social processes of reasoning, criticism, and evocation the struggle for values and progress may be rational and orderly. The struggle between values easily deteriorates into blood-letting. This can be counteracted only by social intelligence and imagination, freedom of communication and discussion, and collective resolve to maintain the integrity of ideals and culture as an enduring heritage in what is a disillusioned world.

Philosophical Sociology

Sociology in its *philosophical* phase presents an imaginative formulation of social relations and values, logically coherent and not incompatible with what is factually observed and analysed. It integrates the conclusions of the various social sciences into a whole by the nexus of value treatment. Thus alone can it rise to a synoptic or synthetic discipline, a subdivision of general philosophy, enabling man to assume an enlightened attitude in the experience of values and disvalues in the social-cultural environment. Sociology as philosophy is basically concerned with the reciprocity and interdependence of economic, political, legal and spiritual values and norms that influence the behaviour patterns of particular cultures. It goes beyond the surface of social phenomena to the realities of man's social self and enduring and imperative goals and values in different spheres of social relations, and thus its comprehensive knowledge of person and society directs progress according to authentic and compelling norms and ideals. It substitutes the notion of the social self or "person" for the notion of the atomic individual as its basic concept, and regards the relation of the person to groups and institutions as that of function to structure. It rejects metaphysical individualism and posits that groups and persons are inseparable parts of the same processes of social living. Neither the person nor his goals, values and morals exist apart from groups and institutions; groups and institutions represent the core of meanings and values, actual and possible, that the notion of the social self or person stands for. Thus philosophical sociology offers suggestions how the functioning groups and institutions of society are to be organised into an integral and complete whole within which the person's life-function embodies itself and obtains its true meaning. It is only social philosophy that can invest the facts of institutional life and change with a rationally assimilable meaning and significance and redefine the system of ethical and legal principles and norms upon which the social structure rests for the guidance of man and society according to the system of ultimate ideas and values.

The False Metaphysical Individualism in the Social Sciences

No doubt the present institutional maladjustment and perversion of values are largely aided by inadequate or false theories and concepts in the social sciences. The foremost among them, economics, still pictures the individuals, as isolated from his social and institutional milieu, motivated by single atomic drives, and feverishly engaged in the production of "goods" that bears little relation to his social impulses or moral aspirations. Philosophical sociology integrates economic goals with the unified system of goals and values that alone make society possible, and relates the analysis of prices and volumes in the market process to the entire background of group and institutional relations that define and regulate the former. It rediscovers for economics the true clue to the economic proceses which is found less in the rationality and responsibility of the "economic man", and more in the person's social contacts, institutions and values that constantly modify and are modified by the economic proceses. It accordingly presents the economic system as means to an integrated system of social values and the economic values as symbolic and not causal of the social relations. Grounded as the economic processes are on a variable institutional framework of social values and incentives, laws, freedom and property distribution, philosophical sociology will precisely define such framework of norms, institutions or outlooks as are now subsumed under vague general names, such as individualism, Jiberal-capitalism, socialism and communism. These will be viewed as alternative hypotheses, and then economics will compare their probable economic consequences in the concrete social situation. Economics will have to find an *optimum optimorum* under different or alternative systems of institutional and economic relations and values, and not the optimum of competitive equilibrium as the goal of economic policy. Such will be the impact of philosophical sociology upon the pre-suppositions and methods of economics in rival economic systems.[9]

In man's political relations the science of politics pictures the individual as the centre of power, wresting certain abstract, unconditional and costless "rights of man" from the state that becomes the focus of class struggles for dominance both in reality and in theory. The unfortunate experience is that neither freedom, nor happiness, nor social equality is hereby safeguarded, leading to resentment and creation of new rights. Philosophical sociology finds the association of duties with rights, and of power with service in man's political connections essential to his freedom, dignity, and security. This can be achieved only by the development of groups, institutions, and other cultural framework of avowed common meanings and values outside the system of rights provided in the political and legal setting. The method of freedom, security, and equality that philosophical sociology stresses is the formulation of good social habits, understandings and ideals that can implement the true meaning of political rights.

Thus the battle for liberty and security has to be won outside the realm of the state in the field of ethics and religion; while the development of autonomy and self-government in various local and functional bodies and associations may break down class divisions and foster a new ethic of service and solidarity as well as a corporate general purpose of the community, with the state no longer suppressing all other values and rights than its own, or becoming inept and futile as the result of the application of checks and balances.

Similarly jurisprudence has envisaged law as a necessary evil, an abridgement of natural liberties or certain mystic rights of the individual, or as a compromise or rational balancing of economic and social interests. Philosophical sociology, on the other hand, imports into law-making a theory of social ideals that not only reconcile and integrate conflicting or overlapping interests and values but assimilate the judgment of the right in law to the ultimate ideas and values above the clamant selfish demands of pressure groups, classes or individuals. It also aids the development of adequate legal norms in respect of distributive justice that underlies the increasing volume of modern social and economic legislation unhampered by the older naive faith in inalienable human liberties,

Thus does philosophical sociology supersede, in the various social sciences, the concept of the abstract individual by that of the social self or person, envisaged in terms of ordered and integrated structure of group and institutional relations and values, which indeed is the ground of all meanings and value experience. It also evolves a new system of ethical and legal principles and norms on the basis of existing social facts and emerging social values and norms. It will accordingly materially assist the redefinition of the presuppositions and methods of economics, politics, law and ethics that have now proved so utterly inadequate and futile in their practical applications. It will clarify, refine and restate the goals and motives of the social sciences according to a scale of values adequately analysed and validated with reference to the social situation, need and experience. Thus it will help these sciences towards attaining their various goals in the special fields for the supreme joint task of the total defence of modern society against the anarchy of values. Philosophical sociology vitally concerns itself with the scaling and ordering of instrumental and intrinsic values and the conscious pursuit and achievement of the latter in social and institutional life. Though the instrumental and intrinsic values are often fused and interwoven it postulates the autonomy and hegemony of the intrinsic values that can, however, be effective only through man's self-identification with these in the selection and pursuit of proper instrumental or intermediate goals and means. Philosophical sociology thus prepares the way for the exploration and emergence of the necessary social conditions and framework of social relations, goals and institutions that can bring about new value-orientations, new appraisals of social roles, new moral relations, eliciting human growth, wholeness and possibilities at ideal dimensions. It will free the social sciences from the grips of social Darwinism, psychologism and Marxism as well as from the current sociology of knowledge, derived from Weber and Mannheim, that all provide an extremely one-sided and fallacious evaluation of the nature and destiny of man. The stress of a unified value system for both the human person and society by philosophical sociology will also check the present tendency towards compartmentalization and segregation of the various social sciences and break down the barriers between the social sciences and ethics, religion and the humanities. Social thinking will then pass more freely from the bio-social to the ideal, metaphysical dimension and *vice-versa.* The schedule of ideal, intrinsic and ultimate values is much the same for entire mankind, rooted as it is in the commonness of human nature and strivings and the universal forward-oriented realization of the total personality of the human individual irrespective of society and civilization. Thus philosophical sociology will contribute towards welding together the oneness and solidarity of mankind as it will counter the regression of global industrial civilization into hedonism, immediacy and unwholesomeness.

References

1. The subject is treated in my forthcoming *The Social Dynamics of Morals.*
2. Compare Anshen : (Ed.) *Science and Man*; and Myrdal: *An American Dilemma*, Appendix (A Methodological Note on Facts and Valuations in Social Science).
3. See Dewey: *Theory of Valuation*, Chapter VIII; also *Problems of Man*, pp. 18, 233-235.
4. See particularly Bateson and Mead: *Balinese Character*; and Kardiner: *The Individual and His Society.*
5. *Reason and Unreason in Society*, pp. 202-203.
6. See the author's *The Dimensions of Values*, p. 116.
7. Compare G Murphy : *Personality*, and Lynd and Lynd : *Middletown.*
8. E.T. Mitchell : Dewey's Theory of Valuation, *International Journal of Ethics*, 1944-45.
9. See my *Institutional Theory of Economics*; compare also Parasons: *The Structure of Social Action.*

2

A SOCIOLOGICAL THEORY OF VALUES

The Separation Between Philosophy and the Social Sciences

The viewpoint is strongly held in contemporary philosophy that just as in previous ages philosophy has been primarily oriented to theology or to art or to history or to mathematics or to natural science, so in our day it should be primarily oriented to the social sciences. Even though it be admitted that social value is not the only value, it is the value that is most needed in our age.[1] In the present era of unprecedented social pressure and conflict, chaos and frustration of values as well as general decline of human qualities, philosophy should re-examine and correct, and at the same time explore new fields of values. In the task of working out a consistent and harmonious scale of values it would be greatly aided by advance in the social sciences. This implies that ethical problems should be framed in the vernacular of the social sciences, while the social sciences also should relate social activities and institutions to ethical norms and ideals. The social sciences themselves are not, however, fully alive to this most pressing obligation. Their analysis of human nature and values chronically suffers due to certain specious dichotomies. There is a hard and fast distinction between social and ethical theory, between the social order and the realm of moral strivings and aspirations. Morality is considered as identical with the discipline and purification of man's inner motives and enlightenment of his ends and values in the light of certain fixed, elusive and distant goals or divine decrees. Or, it is identified with external custom, social tradition and law that stifle and enslave the individual conscience. Man is treated either as a biological animal, ignoring the richness and significance of his inner life and his system of higher values or ideals, with society as a latter accretion improvised to deal with the troubles and maladjustments of such an animal. Or, in an age of technology and standardisation, society is considered as the sole fount of all values. Man's duty, then, is to adapt his desires and aspirations to the dictates of the Leviathan and other institutions, and ethics merges itself in politics. It is not adequately recognised that every human activity and relationship represent some striving and creative effort towards greater fullness of the good or satisfaction and clarity of the meaning in behaviour, toward certain immediate goals and values. In the social situation, goals and values are often derived from and defined by society that silently and powerfully regulates the conditions, occasions and objects of human preferences. Morality emerges out of man's active connections with fellowmen, out of intertwined human desires, values and activities in society. The social is the moral. But man is not merely social and gregarious. He builds up also an ideal morality, often in seclusion and detachment from fellowmen, and then gives his own definition of what is good and right in human relationships and interaction through an enhanced sense of consciousness of the whole or the totality. Thus the moral brings the social to an ever higher level of communion. The right, the good and the just are neither subjective whims nor rigid social controls, nor, again, timeless absolute categories, but constitute those goals that are continuous with the ends of social relations, behaviour and institutions, and what man's rational intelligence, conscience and faith find as the true meaning and destiny of the latter. The conscience, insight and idealism of the individual constantly express and embody themselves in the social structure and economic system, in rights, freedoms and laws, scrutinising and renovating the latter in the process. Institutions, rights and laws constantly aid the individual conscience and faith by safeguarding them from the vagaries of whims and caprices and the hazards of extraneous suggestions. In this way society progresses toward the better and the more righteous by establishing new loyalties, affections and reverences. Such is the interdependence of the quality of man's social and moral life. But the social sciences maintain a rigid, long-established gulf between social and moral action, the larger part of human relations, habits and behaviour being excluded from ethical attention and survey; while ethics as a division of philosophy concerns itself with categorical imperatives and fixed absolute goods, largely removed from the sweat, blood and tears of this world, neglecting the group organisation and the institutional background. The outcome is that in practical life moral values are regarded as entirely out of place, and dominant interests, and pursuits left to be regulated by opportunism and mass passion, often passing for a moral ideal, or by outworn custom and rigid tradition.

Effects of an Abstract Procedure in the Social Sciences

There is, indeed, a logic-tight separation in the social sciences between normative and positive theory. Although the problem of values is the core of all studies dealing with human relations and activities, yet there is a systematic tendency to eschew values and valuations from the structure of analysis in all social sciences and to rigidly demarcate between the 'world of facts' and the 'realm of values.' This has been due to the influence of positivism in philosophy that applied to life, mind and society the same methods of analysis applicable to the positive sciences, and entirely ignored that man, above everything else, seeks, creates and achieves values, and that it is his valuation that gives meaning to social facts, his actions or relations in society and his institutional set-up. There have been also other influences. The Cartesian outlook that dominates modern Western thought pattern not merely emphasizes the thinking of the isolated and insulated self as the one ground of certainty in respect of the existence of the cosmos but also derives all values from subjective feelings and desires. What are purely subjective become illusory, distrusted or discredited scienrism. The result is psychological and social atomism. To this must be added the impact of the Darwinian doctrine of individual competition and struggle. There have been also all-pervasive environmental influences. The scientific, industrial and technological revolutions through which Western Europe passed in the 19th century have demanded a tough, pugnacious, rationalistic selfhood, hindered spontaneous, creative communion of the self with fellowmen and cosmos and inhibited the development of values at the transcendent rather than the biological and social dimensions.[2] A recent writer observes: "The de-personalisation of modern life plus the glorification of the pragmatic approach and a conviction of the arid formalism of the schematic analysis, so usual a few decades since, has resulted in distrust of value schemes for measuring dynamic social institutions—a distrust exacerbated by the noble, but misguided blue-prints of a host of dogmatic reformers."[3] The older individualistic tradition has also died hard. This obtains support from the treatment in economics and stands in the way of an adequate analysis of the interaction between the values of the individual and the measures of institutions and behaviour patterns of society. Economics, which occupies the central place and was the earliest developed among the social sciences, has to deal with value and price. It has remained, however, a science of prices largely because of the abstractive procedure it has adopted, isolating the economic man and his activities and satisfactions from his social and institutional setting, and disregarding the issue of relating economic goods or values to life and society as a whole. Economics presents a half-baked psychological theory of value when it gives up the notion of the objectivity of the economic good or value, whether in use or in exchange, and treats value as the function of the relation of the good to utility or the satisfaction of desire. But the economic psychology is still largely hedonistic and associationist, and starts and ends with the desires and satisfactions of the isolated individual. Yet value, derived as it is from man's desires and interests, is shaped and moulded in its concrete content by the pattern of social and cultural conditions. The methodology adopted in economics on the whole divorces the treatment of values not merely from life but also from the social and cultural setting of the individual.[4]

Not only economics but also all the other social sciences that are concerned with human goals and ends of various grades and categories still suffer from what Dewey calls 'metaphysical individualism'. Yet there is no doubt that the system of natural liberty of classical economics or the utilitarian principle of the greatest happiness of the greatest number, that was accepted as the foundation of social analysis and policy, involves certain highly important moral norms or standards focussed round the ethical valuation of the individual personality. It is only recently that the Austrian school of economics, of which a vigorous representative is Lionel Robbins in England, have stressed an abstract procedure in pure economics, entirely independent, of any norms or schemes of ethics. Like a physical science, pure economics, according to Robbins, analyses man's "rational choice" between alternative ends, focusing attention on a particular aspect of man's behaviour, the form influenced by scarcity, assuming certain scales of relative valuation, and deducing their formal implications in different situations. Such an analytical procedure has also appeared in jurisprudence in the methodology followed by the Austrian jurist,

Kelsen. The Austrian school have had a blighting influence on the methodology of the social sciences, emphasising a purely logical structure without necessary relevance either to norms and values or to institutions, or regarding values as a rigid system rather than the flexible expression of the changing social and institutional process.

A fresh distinction, the dichotomy of means and ends, of instrumental and intrinsic values, usually forms the basis of differentiation of the scope of pure and applied social sciences. The latter deal with certain immediate values and goals of collective life, that are assumed from the existing social structure and ideology and from the state of development of the particular social science. Thus applied economics posits as its goals security and economic power; political science lays down peace or victory in war; applied sociology seeks social harmony and justice; and applied psychology such goals as mental health and happiness and efficient work and learning. But the relation between intrinsic and instrumental values constantly shifts. Thus ends or goals become themselves the means for achieving further goals that stand just above them in the hierarchy of goals and values. Further, the study of means as, for instance, wealth or economic power, peace or security, mental balance or the reduction of frustration and aggression modifies or appreciably transforms the ends or goals sought and consequently the entire attitudes of men or societies towards them- Both means and ends, instrumental and intrinsic values, are also found to be preferred according to the mental development of individuals and the integration of groups and the scale of values in society that exhibits various degrees of stability and consistency according to social cohesion.[5] To accept a particular means-and-ends chain is to imply acceptance of the existing order of society, and to disregard the ends and purposes in the living social context that usher in a different order of social relations. Both the relations between means and ends and the ends themselves are in constant flux. Without the recognition of this, social sciences lose all interest as well as the capacity for adequate comprehension and control of the social processes. The distinction, therefore, between means and ends breaks down unless a pure social science chooses to circumscribe its range of study and isolate the means from all ends, thereby making a caricature of the real social reality that is indeed shot through with ends in a long continuous chain rising to a *summum bonum* in respect of which all ends are means.

A False Subjectivism and Relativism of Values

Economics, politics, jurisprudence, anthropology or sociology in dealing with their particular fields of human desires and ends treat these in isolation, uninfluenced by the impact of man's social impulses, interests and values. Human motives are taken in the raw, as blind and organic isolated drives or impelling interests of food and hunger, or again, those of aggression and subordination. These are segregated from the entire cultural complex, traditions, norms and standards that are viewed as entering into the human mind from outside. Man's values and traditions, his personality and institutional life are considered as something merely added to a picture that is otherwise interpreted physically or biologically. For the sake of dialectical convenience a certain set of instincts and desires is postulated as uniform, stable and compelling and is rationalised and given apparent intellectual status and prestige as the ground of *a priori* social theories. The blending, integration and transformation of desires into values is overlooked; and as a matter of fact the higher social values are treated after the analogy of the lower instincts and desires. These being subjective and relative, a fresh error is introduced in treating all values, lower or higher, as biologically relative. The so-called relativity of human values and moral standards is largely due to different degrees of social and intellectual development and difference of man's interests, beliefs and faiths. Differences in environmental conditions, social and economic circumstances as well as 'accidental' variations and mutations in isolated human communities largely explain divergences of moral standards. But the moral standards are there regulating human relations and behaviour. Although there is no rigidity or absoluteness about them, social evolution does show the existence and survival of general moral standards, guiding and controlling man's evolutionary advance. Many ethical theorists now believe in the objective character of values, tested by experience either actually or in thought, and independent of the desires and emotions of man and claiming his allegiance in different situations. This movement is helped by the instrumentalism connected with the name of Dewey. But the older psychology of feelings and desires at the lower level still supports relativism and unstability of values and increases the gulf between the study of social facts and relations and the study of norms and values, that is maintained on the basis of a false subjectivism and relativism of values, on the one hand, and the older individualistic tradition on the other. Such cleavage all the more leads to the neglect or misinterpretation of norms and values and their opposition at different levels of life and in different sectors of society where different sets of values are considered to rule in their separate autonomous jurisdictions. The chronic conflict of desires and values of individuals as well as the struggle between values and ideals, met with in every society, are pushed aside as irrelevant due to the leaning on deductive reasoning. An important branch of analysis of social forces and institutions, viz., Marxist sociology, that has made social conflict and disorder the central theme of study, has considered human motivations and desires in the raw, organised into collective emotions and behaviour in the instinctive level, and untamed by the net-work of social institutions, traditions and cultural standards that encompass the individual. Marxist thought in its exclusive stress of economic motives and interests and its disregard of the potency of man's other goals and values regards even intellectual ideas and moral values as originating from and being clarified by economic facts and circumstances. The dialectical materialism of the Marxist system gave no room for moral motivation. Marxism concealed in its bosom a doctrine of the natural rights of man that however did not provide the basis of the gospel of human solidarity, left to be fashioned by the irresistible logic of economic forces, independent of the will and action even of the suffering working class which brings about the new social order.

The isolation of the individual for the purpose of valuation from his social milieu, the stress of a single set of desires and interests, wrenched from the living social tissue as the source of individual behaviour, and the notion of the ultimate or final values that exist apart from his trials and conflicts in the work-a-day world, all have gone together in disfiguring the picture of social man, and his constant endeavour to achieve a reconciliation "between the biological and the cultural in his modes of behaviour.

Two rival systems of social thought exist today : one the Liberal-classical, based on the ideal postulates of reason, self-interest and will of the individual, the other Marxist, with its doctrine of rationality and class interest. Both systems of thought give no clue to human values and the fundamental inter-twinings between economic, political and ideal values or to man's concrete value experience in his social culture, in the legacy of groups and institutions, traditions and laws, rights and freedoms through which values are actualised, sustained and transmitted.

Influence of Positivism on the Social Sciences

Even sociology that does not feel a similar dread as the other social sciences in dealing with valuation phenomena, nor draws any hard and fast line between the empirical social reality and process and the social goals and values is dominated by the notions of mechanistic causation and evolution in the naturalistic sense that Herbert Spencer imported, and that also have been buttressed by Marxist thought. Thus sociology leaves moral principles and values to ethics that on the other hand deals with the latter as independent of the empirical society and group life with their constraints, expectations and rewards, stressing the ideal morality of the conscience of the individual. Or else, sociology, as with Westermarck and Summer, regards morals as "relative", "historical" and "institutional" and denies objective validity to moral values and standards. "Morals", declares Sumner, "is an impossible and unreal category. It has no existence, and can have none.". Again we read: "Moral convictions are said to be no more than a by-product of historical circumstances, and to vary with these. Or such convictions are represented as mere factual consequences of given social structures which vary when these are changed".[6] Sociology thus invades the entire domain of ethics, leaving no subject-matter for the latter. So far as the present opposition between ethics and sociology is concerned, it is better to remind ourselves of the wise remark that "without moral philosophy sociology of morality is blind, and that without sociology of morality moral philosophy is empty". Unfortunately sociology takes its cues largely from biology and geography and from abnormal or Freudian psychology. The latter stressing man's organic drives, instinctive behaviour and unconscious life and paying inadequate attention to his reason and judgment and the effect of social and cultural factors has in some measure contributed to abolish the familiar ideas of right or wrong, and undermine the foundations of ethics and morality that in certain quarters are regarded as altogether exploded. False science condones blameworthy morals as the latter is attributed to endocrinal disorders, repressed complexes or hereditary defects in particular individuals.[7] Sociology all the more shuns valuation phenomena regarded as too subjective and elusive, though the methods and techniques of social control and planning have recently come in for a large share of attention.

The inheritance of sociology from German idealism seems now to be entirely dissipated in spite of the ethical stress in the writings of Lester Ward, Hobhouse, Giddings, Cooley, Ross, Ellwood and MacIver. Nor has the contrast drawn by Wilhelm Dilthey between explanatory (erklaerende) and interpretative (verstenhende) psychology or by Rickart (in his dictum 'Things we describe —the soul we understand') between positive science and history as Kulturwissenschaft been of any import to the methods of analysis in sociology. In Germany itself the concept of Geisteswissenschaften, calling for a new methodology in the historical and cultural group of sciences that is very different from the mechanical and naturalistic methods adopted in the West, has affected economics and political science in particular. Here Max Weber's doctrine of "ideal types" that take the place of mechanical laws and Sombart's principle of "understanding" as distinguished from "value-judging" and "law-finding" have altered the logic of obtaining knowledge in these important fields. Out of the discussion relating to differences of modes of arriving at knowledge that has proceeded in Germany, mechanical evolution in the naturalistic sense on the one hand, and a rigid system of values thought to be realised through the "progressive" unity of this evolution, on the other, are given up in the social sciences. This trend has been aided by the revolt against the rigid, classical and atomistic concept of causality in the physical sciences. Brinkmann observes, "The peculiar role of values in social reality is ceasing to be regarded in the light of a dualistic split between factual and non-positing statements and as a result of the writings of Edmund Husserl, Max Scheler and Nicolai Hartmann the ban on "value-judgments" in the social sciences has given way to careful and critical researches into their structure and systematic connection". The logic of Husserl, the phenomenological theory of ethics of the School of Cologne, the psychology of Brentano and the philosophy of John Dewey are now helping towards the ethical orientation in sociology, as discernible in the writings of Weber, Scheler, Bougle, Hobhouse and Mannheim, among others, although the general tendency is to look upon any attempt to introduce value analysis into the core of sociological theory as the survival of the theological or metaphysical outlook.

Values as Representing Uniformities in Social Behaviour

Sociology, occupying as it does the central place among the social sciences, is peculiarly concerned with the problem of values. For all social relations and activities are presented for man not as natural happenings that obey causal laws but as problems how to seek values, how to choose when values compete or conflict with one another in a given social situation, how to choose means of value fulfilment evaluated by society as desirable or undesirable, whether to conform to or deviate from social norms, how to augment, discard or modify some values according to the demands of the situation. The most important content of social facts, relations and situations is the values of other persons with which one's own come into conflict and co-operation. If men and their behaviour are regarded as a part of the system of nature with its laws and conformities, the system of ends and values represents such conformities that have their antecedent causes, and that in their turn serve as causes moulding and guiding human behaviour. Man's ends and values are modes of his adjustment to the rest of the universe that like his tools, language, traditions or other products are selected in the actual process of his living in society. Society exhibits an emotional solidarity that exercises constant, pervasive pressure or constraint upon individuals, preventing them from following their egoistic impulses and desires and establishing uniformities in their behaviour. McDougall observes: "The prevalence of a system of accepted values is the main ground of the unity of any social group, of such harmony and coherence and stability as it enjoys, and of the effectiveness of its collective activities. The community of values is the basic fact for all the social sciences, a fact which must be psychologically understood and explained before the social sciences can be firmly grounded."[8] The system of values is the outcome of uniform interests, beliefs and patterns of conduct of group members who all the time, as Vierkandt observes, "are occupied in forging chains which they have to wear themselves".

Values enchain individuals silently and invisibly. Values in conflict are also a common social happening, presenting an opportunity for accommodation, compromise and assimilation, out of which emerge a rational revision of values and restatement of an ideal. This keeps alive the social relationship. But values sometime meet values in combat, carried even unto death, which, and not reason and judgment, then decides what values shall prevail. In the major social conflicts of individuals and groups, social relationships out of which values emerge are altogether snapped. Thus the human struggle for ends and values becomes hardly distinguishable from animal struggle and survival. Society as a whole through the clash of ends and values tentatively works out like all living things, its adaptations to new environmental conditions and situations, the constant change in which calls for new social values and ideals to provide social guidance. Values inhere in, and are sustained by, ail social interaction, whether co-operation or conflict, and give their meaning to persons and social relationships, and to all the social phenomena and processes that constitute the subject-matter of the social sciences. The social values, though these do not show the rigid uniformity of the laws of causality in the natural sciences, are widely contormed to in society, and act as controlling or regulating forces of conduct. These, indeed, explain the continuity and uniformity of groups, institutions and culture systems, maintained by the various means of social control that society devises.

Influence of Faulty Methodology on the Chaos and Frustration of Values

Social relationships and processes are phenomena of conformity to values that are accordingly the focus of enquiry for the social sciences, just as the natural laws are for the positive sciences. Man's conduct and his ends or values are related to each other as part and whole. An investigation of values can alone enable one to organise a large group of social relations, and processes as data comprising a part of a larger system, and thus to understand and interpret these on the basis of a systematic classification. Thus man's behaviour, interpreted in positive terms of cause and effect and the objects of his desire or goals and values are inextricably mingled together in any social analysis. A social science that as science must be relevant to action in its particular field, *viz.* man's behaviour and relationship to fellowmen, finds such behaviour and relationship defensible or worthy in so far as a fellow human being is treated as an end in himself in the ideal sense. The goals or interests of different individuals and groups are often in disharmony or conflict, due to the development of man's individuality and the differentiation of interests by institutions. This requires reconciliation and accommodation. Again, the intrinsic and instrumental values of men, groups and institutions have to be graded, integrated or coordinated in order that social relationships and institutions may be enduring. Social relationship and behaviour involve techniques and concepts that must be relevant to the development of human personality on the one hand, and of social solidarity or commonalty on the other. For man, unlike any other social animal, is not instinct-ridden, while human society unlike the animal community is a communion of meanings and values. All such analysis comprises ethical facts and considerations: the description of values, first as facts or social uniformities that regulate the present relation between men, between groups and between institutions; and secondly as moral norms or ideals that envisage ideal individuals and ideal social relationships towards which society deliberately directs itself through education, law and social policy.

The social and the moral ideal remains the same, truth, beauty and goodness, man's supreme or highest values that tend towards an integral unity—"the triple chord, lightly broken". For the pursuit of each such spiritual value is the building up of a communal mind that permits individuals to live together cooperatively, justly and efficiently. In respect of truth-values and aesthetic values, it is only the participation of the entire community in fashioning the laws, relations and institutions in economics and politics, their identification with the system of industry and the state as a great co-operative enterprise that can lead to the achievement of such values by the people. Modern machine technology regiments man's desires and thoughts according to "the mechanism of conformity" that spreading from the industrial to the social order standardises man's satisfactions, enjoyments and "truths". It has become the greatest enemy of intellectual and aesthetic values that can be fulfilled only when not merely is there no external constraint from the system of life, but also when these can mould all personal and social relationships. The standardisation of human behaviour that is the inner counterpart of the precision, efficiency and security of the machine-process becomes deadly to the rhythm and spontaneity of human desires, values and aspirations. It engenders a matter of factness in human ends and attitudes. Ultimately this results in a complete distrust and repudiation of all higher values that transcend calculation, description and observation, and in the waste of the higher aptitudes and deterioration of man as he is encouraged by the system of life to produce achievement at a low level that standardisation always involves. Heterogeneity and freedom of interests and activities that yield satisfaction in themselves are the essence of discovery of new truth-values, aesthetic and moral values. It will be the task of sociology to check social value and norms against social consequences as well as check social consequences against values and norms. It will point out that traditional social norms and policies do not often have the consequences intended by the existing framework of institutions and laws, and thus help towards a higher measure of social morality by insisting upon an adjustment of social action to socially approved norms and values, freed from the pretensions of the power groups on the one hand, and the deceptions and rationalisations of the under-privileged groups on the other. It is true that social justice does not wholly depend on social intelligence. Man's vested interests and honest errors are stubborn social facts. But a rational analysis of social facts and values improves social relations and contributes towards the development of social justice. Under such a procedure the study of the institutional situation, the status-power system and the contents of rights and of law and the analysis of the system of values and norms help each other; and sociology and ethics show a continuity. A socio-economic structure in which the worker is a mere machine-hand, drawing a wage for routine task, and a state in which the citizen is not concerned with political goals except on the ballot day destory intellectual and aesthetic experience for the mass of the people. Goodness or moral value is a matter of right relations between individuals. It is reduced to a minimum in a regime of *laissez-faire* individualism and inequality in economic power. It is the institutional framework with associated laws, rights and economic and political power that is largely responsible for unfair or unrighteous relations between individuals and for the warping of human dispositions and character in modern society. The capitalistic industrial structure, even with progressive liberal economic legislation, militates against the establishment of the only socially defensible relationship between persons, *viz.*, as free and equal beings. Where a large field of social relations is intrinsically immoral, individuals and groups would be in chronic conflict; the lack of complete apprehension and sympathetic understanding of individuals, isolated from one another in their goals and values and also from the society, and the strong class feeling would break up the unity of the community life and consciousness. It is noteworthy that social science through its abstract neglective procedure and idealisation, detached from the concrete experience, has itself contributed towards a dehumanisation of industry and the state, that have been assumed to develop independently of human valuation and thinking. It has laid down certain laws like the Malthusian Law of Population and Subsistence and the Iron Law of Wages that have been posited as inexorable 'truths' like the laws of nature to which men have to submit in suffering, misery and despair. It is in this manner that a faulty methodology in social science, in which theorising and idealising have been dissociated from concrete human intelligence, effort and valuation, has proved to be a serious blight and an ideological obstacle to the development of normal and healthy human social life, relations and values. This ideological error of course goes back in Europe to the aesthetic attitude of Protestantism, to Cartesian philosophy and to the mechanical evolutionary outlook of the 19th century.

Method of Value-treatment in the Social Sciences

Certainly sociology should break down the barriers separating the logic-tight compartment within which it describes social facts and relations and discovers the regularities that are manifest in them from the compartment in which it hides its values and norms in safe custody. It is one of its prime tasks to examine the social relations and processes as valuation phenomena and establish a principle of unity in the world of human values that are now segregated in the various specialised social sciences. No longer should it remain satisfied with the present methodological position of keeping biological values, economic values, social values or ideal values like so many apples which one has to put in separate baskets. On the contrary, its concepts and theories should be such as may be essentially instrumental to the ordering, integration and achievement of the various social norms and values. It is not at all necessary in this connection for sociology to expound a philosophy of life or to champion a scale of values. On the other hand, the proper method would be to study the uniformity of social relations and behaviour and in the process to treat social values as hypotheses for purposes of scientific observation and description, or successively treat alternate or conflicting norms as data or hypotheses without considering their ethical implications and values. It is only an analysis of social experience that can tell us what social norms our social actions or institutions realise or violate, what norms are involved in an objective social situation, and which norms and values we want to follow and why.[9] To what extent the social norms of a particular culture actually meet the felt needs of the era or milieu and are thus validated involves a clear grasp of the institutional situation and possibilities and of the current ethic of a people in which the co-operation of sociology, ethics and all the other social sciences is essential. For systems, of values and propounded ethic are involved in all group relationships, economic, political or legal. Such sciences as economics, politics and jurisprudence deal with proximate and not remote social values, although the latter are implicit in the system of social stratification, in rights and duties, and in laws and decisions. Thus economics deals with the problem of the allocation of scarce resources between alternative uses in the light of the relative urgency of the different ends; politics deals with fellow-human subjects as means for the collective goals of the community within certain bounds designated as rights and freedoms of individuals; while law subjects to detached scrutiny and description man's actual conduct in a particular situation in the light of immediate and particular social goals implicit in the statutes. All such social sciences should define a coherent and common system of ultimate ends or norms that, indeed, defines the integrity and determines the continuity of culture. Otherwise the norms of efficiency in economics, of order and power in politics, and of justice in juriprudence cannot serve as safe guides for practical social control and direction, especially in an age marked by a chronic conflict between different types of institutions and goals in different fields and chaos of individual valuations. For such norms represent the intermediate empirical ends that break down at each time of crisis for individuals, classes and societies. Sociology will thus consider objectively the system of values reigning in a particular culture as the starting point, classify the various type-values in different social cultures, determine their genetic relationships, and also analyse the changes that the various type-values undergo with accompanying significant social and institutional consequences and vice versa. But the problem of *evaluation* of social values is far different, and sociology would leave this to ethics, metaphysics and religion.

Relations between Ethics and Sociology

The scope of these latter studies is different. Normative sociology, however, is nearest to these. It deals with the factual material represented by different types of moral values and aspirations that are functions of different groups and social cultures. It tests the adequacy or inadequacy of realisation of the values of life in the actual social or institutional situation. The possibilities, limitations and methods of fulfilment of ruling values and goods are the concern of normative sociology, whose analysis in this regard is grounded on the facts of social relations, processes and experience. On the factual evidences of the social situation and experience, it discovers a consistent basis of judgment of social and institutional forms in so far as these actually create, maintain or foster values attributed to them by society, or promote disvalues validated as such again by objective facts. Institutions are good or bad in so far as these shelter, maintain and enhance the values these are designed to promote or not. Similarly social and institutional norms and ideals are good or bad in so far as these meet the biological and social needs and situational demands of a social culture or not, as objectively studied and verified or reasoned from postulates containing statements of facts. Such validation of the system of social norms in terms of the experienced needs of the social and cultural milieu is of the nature of moral hypotheses and tentative generalisations rather than fixed and established moral values applicable everywhere. Normative sociology and ethics meet therefore on some common ground or borderland, and have a continuity of relationship.[10] The question then arises whether the social norm's and values are compelling moral obligations or imperatives. This is a psychological issue depending as it does on the dispositions, habits and sentiments of the individual or group that are in large measure socially conditioned. An imperfect or 'immoral' group or institution by education, pressure or mass propaganda conditions an experienced moral obligation towards values that all schools of ethics may regard as unworthy and unsatisfactory. Both social and educational factors are involved in most situations of 'reversion' and 'perversion' of the system of values, that can be remedied only by the combined efforts of both sociologists and moral philosophers. Normative sociology itself does not attempt any appreciation or valuation of value-judgments. Moral philosophy or ethics deals with norms and judgments for the regulation of man's behaviour, and enters into an examination of their validity. Yet the factual aspect of normative sociology and the normative aspect of ethics are bound up with each other. Orthodox ethics is essentially a study of the criteria of behaviour for individuals in their relations to others, "rather than as the more embracing study of the measures of the institutions and behaviour patterns of society as a whole." Thus Thomas I. Cook observes, "While the social nature of man is admitted, what it seeks is an objective basis for the valuation of the dictates of conscience, of the duty of the individual, given the existing environment".[11] The interchange between man's conscience and institutions, between individual and social morality is sadly missed. An ethical criterion of society to be applied to imperfect, and 'immoral' institutions, political, economic and social, is needed as a culmination of ethics in the traditional sense. This desideratum will be supplied by normative sociology.

Man's needs, aspirations and values are in dynamic interplay with the milieu, physical and institutional. Social and economic conditions and ethical attitudes constantly intermingle. All ethical norms and regulations in order to be successful fit into the present social attitudes and values, and have some relations with present laws and norms as expressed by social habits, group patterns and institutions. On the other hand, change of occupational balance or economic satisfaction, loss of wealth of the directive classes or their demographic decline, or, again, widespread revulsion of the population against the existing status-power system are objective social factors for new ethical norms and prescriptions. In a conservative stratified community the sharp division between the social classes or castes and lack of mobility of individuals and groups form the social background of various kinds of taboos and norms, especially with regard to food, marriage and social intercourse, the observance of which strengthens the social cleavage. In a revolutionary social situation, on the contrary, the change in the power system and abolition of class privilege and status accompany a disruption of marriage and family codes and conventions, and of religious attitudes that have played an important role in social integration. The rigidity or fluidity of the social structure and conformity or non-conformity to the moral code, faith and belief strengthen each other. The sociological whole situation cannot in fact be separated from ethical norms and value judgments. Further, the social relations and processes have to be measured by, and submit to, ethical norms and must be strengthened and directed by these in order that society can progress. While the prescience of ethics is aided by the positive material comprising the social structure of values and ideals as studied by sociology, the latter, having confirmed the value system in concrete social need and experience, reveals the social-psychological, cultural and educational factors and forces, conditioning that moral compulsion without which the higher values can neither be saved nor augmented in civilisation.

Society in the course of its evolution develops its forms of art, religion and education, and perfects its means and devices of propaganda and socialisation so as to integrate and carry forward the notions of morality, justice and harmony it cherishes, and develop its children and youth into individuals who might measure up to its standards of perfection. In society's work of controlling individuals and groups, emotional outbursts, threats and punishments are gradually eliminated. There is more of understanding, sympathy and appeal to fellowship and emulation and less of coercion by dogma and faith. In every field of human relations, persuasion and evocation are stressed as agencies of social integration and control. Modern social knowledge has altogether changed the old views of crime and its handling and treatment. The upbringing of children in the family and their education in schools bear everywhere the impress of continual improvement of the applications of science to the problems of hereditary defect, maladjustment and control. Religion now appeals to man less through its dogma and belief or the fear of punishment in hell, and more through social sympathy, goodwill and idealism. In society at large the techniques of propaganda and advertisement show a nice and subtle adjustment of means to ends unknown before. Society, moreover, takes cognizance of various kinds of small social deviation, unfamiliar in the past, and deals with them with the same skill and expertness as it shows towards crime and vice. Many social deviations are now found to be rooted in frustrations and inner conflicts, and the remedies adopted are not only proportionate to the causes, but the causes themselves are traced for cure and prevention to misfits in group life, tradition and culture. Means and mechanisms of social control are indeed subjected to a process of social selection in all human communities ; and the goal apparently is to make the struggle for normalcy in social living as rational as possible, divesting it of impulsiveness, inconsistency and amateurishness, and introducing into it skill, design and organisation. Psychiatry, social work, industrial management and education are all evolving a type of social control which though still forceful and dogmatic is far removed from the rod and shackle, and from emotional exhortation, admonition and invective, it responds to modern humanitarian ideals and provides full and appropriate opportunities to socially inadequate, diseased or abnormal individuals for adjustive realisational ways of life. In every field of social "therapy", instead of attacking symptoms, expert, dignostic survey of the type of handicap, and maladjustment in the total background of the family or primary group milieu and the societal ethos is stressed as part of long-run "social strategy". Progress, planned and directed by society, thus requires both clarification of values and rationalisation of symbol-devices employed for the control of men and groups achieved through improved knowledge, skill and techniques of the social sciences.

References

1. The Value Studies of the Ninth International Congress of Philosophy *Ethics*, Vol. XLVIII; McDougall: Philosophy and the Social Sciences in *Human Affairs; also Frontiers of Psychology*; and Barnes, Becker & Becker : *Contemporary Social Theory*, Chapters II and XV.
2. Mukerjee: *The Dimensions of Values*, p. 117.
3. Thomas I. Cook : Politics, Sociology and Values in *Journal of Social Philosophy*, October 3940.
4. See my *Institutional Theory of Economics*, Chapter III.
5. H. D. Jennings White : *Goals of Life*. See F. H. Knight : Fact and Value in Social Science in Anshen (Ed.) *Science and Man*, pp. 330-337.
6. Statement of an editor in a German magazine, quoted in Kohler: *The Place of Values in a World of Facts*, p. 32.
7. By way of contrast see Flugel: *Man, Morals and Society*, and Wad-dington (Ed.) : *Science and Ethics* fox recent, able discussions of the relations between psycho-analysis and ethics.
8. *Frontiers of Psychology*, p. 222.
9. Compare G. R. Geiger : *Philosophy and the Social Order*.
10. For a valuable discussion see Ronald L. Warren: Philosophy and Social Science, *Journal of Philosophy*, 1941, pp. 404—409; McDougall : Philosophy and the Social Sciences, in *Human Affairs* edited by Cattell, and Lynd : *Knowledge for What*?
11. Politics, Sociology and Values in *Journal of Social Philosophy*, October 1940.

3

THE SOCIAL ORIGIN AND EVOLUTION OF VALUES

The Beginnings of Valuation in Animal Life

Have animals any values? Many animals store provisions for the winter and decorate their nests with coloured objects. A few higher mammals make and employ objects as tools. A good many defend a bush, a mound or a foraging territory with great tenacity and pugnacity. In all such cases we have behaviouristic facts, displayed in attitude and conduct, of the preference and selection of certain things of the external world, for the satisfaction of the animals' organic dispositions although their lack of mental development may shut out value meaning on their part. Certain species of birds that have adopted a rigid territory system exhibit a peculiar fear of trespassing as part of their territorial instinct. A trespassing black-headed gull displays in an exaggerated manner those characteristics which in human behaviour might be termed the visible and outward signs of a thoroughly guilty conscience.[1] Here is an illustration of an inherited trend distinguishing between right and wrong in animal behaviour. One may refer to such examples as the beginning of an ethical code rooted in the genus of the animals. In the case of the social apes who represent a higher stage of mental evolution we see a good deal of group cooperation in food-getting, acquisition of territory for foraging and nesting and defence of a food object, a nest or a territory. Chimpanzees in captivity often collect all kinds of objects, especially attractive ones, which they carry about with them in their arm-pits. Thus these animals show evidences of recogntion and appropriation of "economic values" both by the individual and the troop. We also find a careful discrimination between kin and stranger in the family group, and the relationship of dominance and subservience is also well established in their harems or more extended societies. Since these are significant in introducing some order and organisation in a variety of activities of the troops connected with the food quest, migration, offence and defence, it is reasonable to presume that here we have rudiments of a conscious value experience with its multitude of variations and shadings. Chimpanzees and howler monkeys in particular exhibit along with dominance a system of serial subordination extending throughout the animal group. Thus these animals may be supposed to have risen to the level of conceiving the "value" of domination-subordination in groups of two, three or more in varied social situations, while accepting the leadership of a single individual for the entire troop. Male domination is markedly relaxed periodically at times of heat of the females, who then cajole and tease the leader in order to win temporary mastery. Most of the social anthropoids also exhibit in a most peculiar way signs of abasement, humiliation and "a sense of guilt" as they are caught by the leader of the troop in acts of encroaching upon his sexual "right". In this case, as Betz observes, "the animal has a guilty conscience but does not know that he has". Nor does the leader of the troop always force dominance behaviour. Defiance or disobedience is of course punished by assault or by expulsion of the subordinated individual from the troop, but the habits of behaviour crystallise to the extent that grooming that is the index of subordination is often solicited and begged for.

Scale of Animal Values

Nowlis has carried out an interesting experiment for ascertaining the relation of various degrees of hunger to competitive interaction in twenty pairs of chimpanzees. When the hunger of the dominant partners was decreased to satiation while that of the subordinate partners was increased by food deprivation for 25—54 hrs, the latter took precedence, that is, got more than half the test food. When both partners in a pair were highly motivated by long food deprivation, the relative dominance status remained the same as when both were fed in regular fashion. In an experiment of factorial design it was found that changes in the degree of hunger of the dominant partners have more effect on the food-taking of the subordinate ones than have great variations in the food-drive of the latter.[2] The experiment artificially introduces a conflict of the "values" of obedience and hunger, and offers an explanation of the critical effect of satiation of the dominant partner on the food-taking of the subordinate in terms of the relative punishment value of the partners for each other and the interaction between incompatible approach and avoidance tendencies. Another experiment by Crawford with female chimpanzees shows that in all pairs the dominant animal obtains food on the greater number of trials but the subordinate animal assumes response priority and receives more food during its oestrus phase. The value experience of obedience and disobedience, fellow service and defiance and of appreciation and punishment of "right" and "wrong", associated with these, are indelibly impressed upon these social animals by their heredity as well as by their social conditioning in infancy. The educability of the great apes has been scientifically demonstrated. The ape mother teaches her child many life habits both by punishing it with bite and slap and rewarding it with food and caress as the situation demands. Yerkes describes ourang and chimpanzee mothers systematically exercising and training their infants and restraining them from doing certain things until they have reached a definite stage of development and then encouraged and aided to do them. Carpenter also observes that howling monkeys seem to make use of certain noises as meaningful cues in certain situations. Adult males interfere by a kind of growl when they notice that the young monkeys become too wild in their fighting play, whereupon they immediately stop it.[3]

The "Morals" of Social Animals and Insects

Among anthropoids, birds and other social animals which exhibit a striving for self-assertion and dominance and develop a marked status system, the biological and social significance of stratification is that the dominant animals obtain for themselves special privileges with regard to foraging and possession of females. Thus such behaviour is a means to the satisfaction of the major biological values. On the other hand, the social hierarchy or serial subordination that is met with is of advantage for the whole animal group for defence, migration, food quest and even offence. As a matter of fact the troop gains in stability, coherence of organisation and tradition of mutual aid and cooperation. With the values of leadership and dominance, "guilt" and punishment those of mutual aid and "altruism" are also recognised.[4] Many higher mammals are found to aid sick or wounded comrades, and nurse young animals, who have lost their mothers. Chimpanzees provide first aid to the wounded by licking and caressing. Mutual assistance is shown in the case of many animals who rush to the aid of others on hearing cries of warning or distress. It is also noteworthy that sometimes sick or wounded members of a colony of beavers and marmots that endanger the life of the colony as a whole are expelled or even exterminated. Alverdes observes that "the biological significance of such a phenomenon is clear, for when an individual dies during hibernation the whole troop is endangered by its dead body".[5] All this indicates that there is no absolute gap between value experience and "morals" of animals and of men. Similar value experience does not hold good of the insect societies that exhibit an elaborate social stratification and specialisation of physiological castes. Here the mechanisms of maternal care and nursing of the larvae, various kinds of co-operative activity for securing and conserving food and for defence of the entire colony and general subordination of individuals to the welfare of the species are wholly instinctive. The ant-hill, the beehive and the termitary are external repositories of the "values" of matriarchy that govern their differential behaviours and that have helped towards the selection and survival of these social insects for millenniums. But these are in the realm of tropisms, reflexes and instinctive activities and do not rise to the level of a value experience and a value meaning. Yet there are marked differences between the rigid and repetitive tropisms and reflex activities in the ant-hill, beehive or termitary and the specific, flexible and forward-oriented activities of mutual aid and cooperation in the colonies of beaves, praire dogs and monkeys. These gregarious mammals often bequeath their rest and habitation—external registrations of their social gains and experiences for the next generation. The higher social animals can be considered as possessing a rudimentary, inchoate and inarticulate value system. The creation, conservation and transmission of values proper obviously rest on a level of memory, imagination, social learning and communication that animals with rudimentary mental growth do not possess. Only the great apes through social conditioning and canalization of their activities and their educability can show a near approach towards awareness of meaning and even the association of sounds and gestures with meaningful cues characteristic of human value situations and experiences.

Human and Animal Speech and Valuation

It is because animals lack language that they cannot express judgments nor embody in words the memories or promises of satisfactions from objects that fill them with emotions, nor, again, formulate principles of behaviour and selective attitudes. Man's inheritance of the 'tool' of language prepares him for events and experiences he has not encountered before and facilitates his adaptation. Knowledge and experience of the past are transmitted to man through language. But language also aids him to add to this legacy his own judgment and emotions in different situations. Language accordingly provides the mechanism for reflection and selection of experience of both himself and others that represents the essence of the process of valuation. Valuation in the case of the human species is, indeed, powerfully aided by language and the expression of emotions. Language operates in a universe of common meanings, ends and values that it focusses both by expression and introspection. In the case of the apes value experience is possible in some measure due to their possession of a much larger repertory of sounds and gestures than other animals. Their cries and gestures can, indeed, express collective feelings of subservience to their leader who reciprocates by particular cries and gestures of his own, and induces appropriate deference or co-operative activity on the part of the whole troop, but cannot formulate principles of conduct. Thus the ape world remains incapable of being moved by abstractions. Man has words for both emotions and objects. Since a concrete object or a particular person is related to a class or category, to an abstract principle, man through conceptual thought can epitomise individual judgment, meaning and experience for collective behaviour. His imagination and memory can also revive the judgment, meaning and experience both for himself and for the society through words, signs or symbols without even the presence of the concrete object or particular person. This intensifies the dynamic emotional backing of the valuation. Man's capacity for abstraction is the fount of a complex of practical ideas arising within social situations with their opportunities, suggestions and traditions that comprise his system of valuations.[6]

Language, the Vehicle of Social Values

Both the abstraction as well as the developed differential sentiment and attitude correlated with valuation alike rest upon a social background that moulds man's psychic life and are a part and parcel of the creative adjustment inseparable from his social evolution and survival. Such 'conditioning' of man's psychic life begins in childhood and is carried on largely through the instrumentality of language, gesture and symbolism. The parents' words or gestures, saturated with emotions and fantasies, constantly define particular situations for the child who thus becomes early habituated to certain actions that are right or proper, and learns quick adaptation without giving thought to these. In fact it is the growing child's repertory of words full of ethical meaning that from the very first year of his life equips him in advance for his definition of social situation and moral judgment. The emotions associated with such words as right and wrong, good and bad, proper and improper, mean and brave which he imbibes in early childhood and to which he learns to reciprocate impel moral behaviour. The moral habit is inculcated also through myths, legends, anecdotes and proverbs that suggest and define the situation and govern the moral response. "Fables and stories", observe Smith and Guthrie, "become the common heritage of society and usually involve the ambivalence of hero and villain". Praise or blame reiterated in adjectival epithets or nicknames in the home also conveys to the child in his formative years the kind of social expectancy in respect of his role as the "good" or "bad" boy and organises his attitudes to self and fellow men in the roles that he may take up in the future as the "patriotic citizen", the "devout Christian" or the "shrewd business man". Dewey observes: "In language and imagination we rehearse the responses of others just as we dramatically enact other consequences. We foreknow how others will act, and the foreknowledge is the beginning of judgment passed on action. We know with them; there is conscience". A recent analysis of linguistic expressions of children in Hamburg has shown that the child expresses his entire social attitude each time he addresses another person. This attitude is subject to continuous modification and contains the roots of his later social consciousness and position in the social order. The experience gained from verbal contacts with an actual partner leads to his concept of social relations with his family, friends, youth groups and ultimately to his identification with his national group.

It is the maxims, slogans, concepts and stereotyped terms of approbation and disapprobation of all shades, with the trail of ideas, emotions and fantasies instilled into the mind of a child at home, that are largely responsible for uniformity in his valuation and manners and patterns of behaviour and determine his social consciousness and his role and station in life. The supremacy of words and gestures that do not denote a bare state of consciousness in man but are foci of emotions, values and meanings of social situations and experience, and pervade and direct all co-operative activity is equally marked in the primitive community. Language thus becomes the vehicle of social values carrying the significant conversation of the cries and gestures of animals, through conceptual thought, memory and imagination, to its highest range and development. Boas who is an authority of primitive language points out that language of the savage peoples is an accurate, authentic reflection of the state of culture and follows in its development the demands of culture. Words and phrases are symbols of moral and cultural attitudes and with the strong emotional appeal that is characteristic of all symbols mould man's morals and manners according to the tribal pattern. In advanced civilisation, battle cries, war songs and national anthems excite masses of men to battle; while many terms, titles, phrases and symbols that give a succinct expression to social attitudes and norms bring about conformity in man's behaviour and stabilise existing groups and institutions. It is not, however, articulate language alone that serves as the vehicle of meanings and values in social culture. There is also the language of the emotions of a people, its heritage of art, myth and literature recording its moral and cultural norms and attitudes. These are interiorised in the individual and give an order to the organisation of his impulses and interests. Not less meaningful is the economic tradition, the heritage of practical tools, contrivances and procedures. This contributes towards giving the physical environment an orderly shape and pattern, and the manipulative impulses and efforts a coherent direction in co-operation with those of fellowmen, producing socially useful results prized and enforced by the community. Language, aesthetics, religion, science and economics become integrated into a unified pattern or culture-system which gives opportunities for the fulfilment of man's major interests and values, supplies norms of his behaviour in the different fields, and serves as a selective agency for individual habits, attitudes and values. The culture-system by virtue of its definite organisation acts, indeed, as a frame of reference, defining, approving, eliciting and rejecting attitudes and values with such consistency as to evolve as definite personality type. Yet, no doubt, the individual due to his mental variability reacts to the social situation differently, giving rise to different degrees and scales of values of objects, men, groups and ideas. The French psychologist Blondel observes; "The individual does not invent his religion, his morals, his laws, his aesthetics, his science. his language, the patterns of his everyday behaviour with his equals, superiors or inferiors, with the strong and the weak, with the aged, women and children, his manner of eating and conducting himself at table, the infinite detail, finally, of his thought or his conduct. All these he receives ready-made, thanks to education, to instruction and to language from the society of which he is part. These include, to be sure, conscious activities; but they are mental states whose most essential characteristics are distinguishable from the purely individual states. If they are common to all, not only are they not peculiar to any person, but further they are not entirely realised in any of their individual incarnations. The ideas of the moral men are not morality; those of the savant are not science; our tastes are not aesthetics; the words which we exchange are not language".

Objectivity and Compulsive Character of Values

Man's world of norms and standards, his economic or moral, aesthetic or religious values are given things for the individual. These are fairly constant for an age or people and have an objectivity for they mould his desires, interests and outlooks. Values may be rooted in man's organic dispositions, instincts and desires, but their real nature can be understood only when these are seen as products of man's social nature and selection. Expressed in forms of common language and of common thought, these are the chief instruments of society for ordering and regulating man's instincts and desires, and for lifting him up to an ideal that he alone can conceive and adore. Without the creation and recreation of values, virtues and ideals, societies cannot exist. With the evolution of societies to higher levels of integration and solidarity, values, virtues and ideals beckon man to yet higher vistas of imagination and achievement. The scintillating flame of values, fanned by the breath of the gods among men, shows the myriad possibilities of society. The wick and the oil of society's daily routine of work, love and worship eternally keep alive the radiation of that skyward, sacred flame, the maintenance of which is vital for every society. Between society and its shining idols that dwell apart—values—there is a give-and-take which has no end.

With man's capacity for abstraction, generalisation and formulation of principles, with his language to clothe these in words and symbols, with his memory that governs the experiences of the past, and his imagination that foresees undreamt-of possibilities of satisfactions and, above all, with the intensification of feelings and sentiments that springs from imitation, sympathy and competition in the social atmosphere, man constructs his sets of values and ceaselessly struggles for them. The system of values comprises the golden chain woven through successive generations that binds mind and mind, and transforms society from a biological aggregation of population and an economic scheme of division of labour into a communion of ideas, feelings and sentiments. In short valuation that is a distinct trait of man's nature or rather of his social nature which he carries within himself converts society into a civilisation.

Because of man's social nature and of his dependence on society in whatever he achieves or obtains, and of the society conditioning and moulding his behaviours in ail their aspects from nutrition and reproduction to toil, play and recreation, social values are powers in his life. He is surrounded by them and must reckon with them in all his adjustments since these latter take place not in his primary environment, but in a derivative environment refashioned for him by culture. In the satisfaction of all his requirements in the social milieu, man encounters a vast controlling apparatus of values of all kinds, from simple to highly complex, from plastic to highly rigid, that are indispensable aids to his adjustments and fulfilments. Durkheim observes that we all recognise a socially objective scale of values which is seldom identical with the scale of the individual. Besides, there is a "constraint" in values which can be explained neither by the object nor by the individual.

The pressure and the compulsive character of values arise from the fact that it is society and man's social nature that create values. Because values are social products embodying intellectual judgments that are collective judgments, these compel individuals through helping them with appropriate mental sets and habits for action. Individuals discover in these judgments of value a ready-made ensemble of rules, habits and ideal forms that over-reach their personal achievement, and that offer an easy and effective guidance to their complex judgments in society. Revealing the enduring lessons of the past through selection, competition and co-ordination of the various alternatives that have appealed to men from age to age, these obtain universal allegiance and as the result of the interstimulation of minds also kindle universal enthusiasm through generations. Because these express man's social nature, these do not appear as drags and burdens for the human mind but rather awaken, stimulate and uplift it, raising it above the temporary sansations and desires and the passing moods and attitudes of the individual. The individual is not a mere passive entity reacting to his milieu, but there operate in his mind impulses that make him consciously seek and struggle for values that aid him in adapting himself to and reshaping his milieu. The effect of culture conditioning and moulding of individual behaviour has also to be considered. Social suggestion, language, training, custom, law and propaganda overcome individual resistances, and man's behaviours become limited and oriented and his outlook moulded without his perceiving it. Thus values employ various means to make themselves universally heard and respected from the fear of the Lord, the inexorable fiat of the priesthood, and the dread of social ostracism or punishment by law to the subtle propaganda of art and the affectionate counsel or admonition of the elders of the family. The supremacy of higher values is, to be sure, the *sine qua non* of culture, of civilisation, of the evolution of man from animality to humanity.

Juxtaposition of Values in Primitive Society

Man is actuated by manifold instincts, desires and interests, and participates in many social activities, groups and institutions. Different types of values emerge in each social context and regulate individual desires, interests and activities. There are also competition and selection of values in each sphere of human interests and activities. And yet some values are more pervasive, clamorous and enduring, maintaining themselves in the movement of happenings and cross-current of individual preferences and social ends. These tend to over-step their own sphere, dominate over other values and tend to regulate the whole of life's interests and activities by establishing the hierarchy of values under their monitorship.

How did different categories of values emerge and function in the early stages of social evolution? In the dawn of civilisation and in savage communities of the modern age, man's values and activities are not divisible into watertight compartments. In primitive societies the social force that establishes the inner unity of the horde, the tribe and the community is represented by the all-pervasive and mysterious supernatural powers, totems, animal guardian spirits, ancestors and gods that participate in all tribal activities. The pattern of tribal behaviour is woven out of the subtly combined threads of magic, art and economics, and it is difficult to separate a particular strand from the total value meaning and experience. Religious or magical, aesthetic and economic values are all jumbled together. As the primitive community undertakes its ritual observance, and represents or dramatises on such an occasion the expected hunt or war expedition, the movement of its food or guardian animals or, again, the resurrection of vegetation in spring, all interests and values have their full say under the influence of strong collective emotions discernible in the elaboration or repetition of the actions, gestures or spoken words. Totem, spirit, ancestor, god or the *mana* embodying the values primitively unified by magic and religion, enliven by their presence hunting and fishing expedition, agricultural toil, war and chase. The inner rapport established by magic, myth and religion is thus mobilised for the practical tasks of food collection, fishing, hunting and military expedition. Aesthetic and economic values blend easily with the magical, the moral and the religious. Art completes an economic task by representing it in the mimetic gestures of the rite in all its entirety without slips, errors and disturbances, adding to the sense of collective competence a profound joy arising from the rhythm of the chant and dance in which the entire tribal group participates. Clapping, swaying, dance and chorus, all subserve the function of strengthening and defining the solidarity of the group for success in economic activities by the unity and sureness of the rhythm. Primitive agriculturists have not much faith in their economic toil in the fields. Their agricultural routine is preceded by a dance-ritual in which some men imitate the copulation of various birds and beasts, while naked women also dance around, and scatter imagined seeds in the ground. Without the invoking of the mysterious fecundity of the soil by the dance of copulation, the spilling of blood of sacrificed human or animal victims or the worship of the Great Mother, agriculture cannot succeed with many peoples. Man's ideas of the right conduct are first systematised and regulated by the common set of attitudes and feelings in which magic, religion, art and economics blended together, with magical values dominating everything. In the social myths of primitive peoples, it is not moral sentiments but a strict observance of magical taboos and superstitions that safeguards good conduct. As Briffault observes: "In the same manner as savage humanity substitutes supernatural agencies for intelligent provisions and devices, irrational means for rational ones, so the rules of conduct to which it attaches the greatest importance are founded upon categorical imperatives and not on justice or consideration of human welfare."[7] The man who is most endowed with magical power is the most moral, and at the same time, the most successful person enjoying the good things of life. Not to follow the dictates of magic is to court disaster for crops and cattle, defeat in military adventures and failure in love intrigues; while magic is also the means by which evil action can be atoned for and the famine, blight, disease, murder or accident, associated with it, avoided. Primitive myth, accordingly, is empty of ethical content. It prescribes taboos and injunctions for ensuring morality, good behaviour and manners, but hardly refers to any primordial cause nor establishes any connection whatsoever between human conduct and supernatural favour or disfavour.[8] On the advanced level as magical myth develops into religious myth, the system of values that the myth postulates and prescribes becomes more specific and explicit, and is buttressed by divine sanction and retribution ; while some kind of simple logic supersedes magic in establishing rationalised linkages between various natural and social happenings. In most cultures the moral code is grounded on the rationalised connection between divine reward and human piety, between divine punishment and sin or crime. It is the religious myths which maintain this connection. But religious myths presuppose a definite advance in primitive mentality in which there are provided in thought intermediate links between systems of human and natural and supernatural phenomena that are no longer blurred nor merge in one another; while in social action too there is intelligent adaptation of technic means and devices to ends and goals, associated of course with prayer and worship that ardently invoke the beneficent intercession of the supernatural, especially in hazardous and critical social situations. As a matter of fact even in modern society there are sectors of life, full of hazards and uncertainties, where the civilised mind still believes itself under the influence of magical values. Love, marriage, gambling and war throw to the winds the values systematised by religion and science through the centuries and encumber modern youths with the obscure superstitious scruples and regulations of magical lore.

Supremacy of A-moral Magical Values

The large mass of populations all over the world is still dominated by magical values. Their exponents and guardians are rain-makers, medicine-men, diviners, priests and prophets of all sorts who seek to influence the course of nature or the behaviour of man by sympathetic magic. Primitive society is concerned not with motivations but with the concrete qualities and consequences of behaviour. Differences in human traits and personality are not taken into account, nor their influence upon behaviour. More than any notions of social justice or human good will or dignity, it is the adherence to taboo injunctions and superstitious rules, sometimes enforced with fierce zeal and punctiliousness, that form the basis of morality of the primitive peoples. In the Samoan code of morality, according to Margaret Mead, the whole preoccupation is with the individual as an actor, and the motivations peculiar to his personality are left an unplumbed mystery. A good child will be said to listen 'easily' or to act well. 'Easily' and 'with difficulty are judgments of character. The Lipan Apache Indians of the American Southwest follow the norms of conduct set by the supernaturals and animals of early times. The well-esteemed follow the ways of the culture hero, Enemy Slayer (the sun); while the inept follow Coyote's way. "To be foolish and fickle as Coyote is forgivable; to be aberrant in unfamiliar or unsanctioned ways is the real offence", records M. E. Opler. The objects, forces and beings of the Lipan world become animate or personified in order to aid the deserving or to punish the erring. The aid offered a human being may be for the occasion only or it may consist in the granting of a magic which insures supernatural help in recurring crises. Magic provides the sure clue to ease or difficulty of action in the savage world as well as to a great extent in the agricultural world. Frazer attributes the widespread vogue of magic to the fact that magic is nothing but the mistaken application of the very simplest and most elementary processes of the mind, viz., the association of ideas by virtue of resemblance or contiguity. Small minds under emotional stress, suspense or bewilderment easily fall into this error, and cling to the belief that things succeed each other in life and nature simply because these are like each other or have been found together in their experience. Such thinking is, to be sure, of the most primitive kind and is a measure of the continuance of savagery in civilisation. In judgments of value based on sympathetic magic the modern man continues as a savage or barbarian. The primitive man's notion of his own personality is inchoate, diffuse and blurred. The self is inextricably mingled with the surrounding personalised world. There is no dissociation of self from an affective relationship to the environment. Like the animal he cannot free himself from his emotions, from his personal and impersonal world. Thus one Brazilian tribe attributes the cannibalism of a neighbouring tribe to the fact that the latter have descended from jaguars.[9] For the same reason, the primitive man's morality is conceived in terms of behaviour, pleasure or displeasure. "The Winnebago moralist would insist that we have no right to preach an ideal of love, or claim that we love, unless we have lived up to the practical implications of this sentiment".[10] The primitive man's crime or misdemeanour has nothing to do with his inner motives, but is judged in terms of overt conduct. Speaking of the primitive Brazilian Indians, Kari von den Steiner observes, "goodness and badness exist only in the crude sense that one can give another pleasure or displeasure, but a true moral perception and an ideal beyond the notion of reward or the fear of punishment are completely absent". Werner considers that the primitive man's personality has every resemblance with the child's in his relatively diffused and syneretic structure. With reference to morals, he refers to Piaget's experiments with the child's concept of responsibility that plainly demonstrate that the younger child's evolution of misdeeds is a matter of objective rather than of subjective import, and that the idea of moral default and responsibility as something to be judged in terms of overt behaviour appears in children only after the age of ten.[11] After this age the child ceases to consider rules to be external but within the range of his own decision and develops the notion of justice or fairness based on a progressive sense of equalitarianism. This is intimately concerned with the growth and differentiation of the individuality. In child as well as in primitive psychology the personality is concerned in terms of concrete behaviour while behaviour is dominated by belief in magical influence that spreads from person to person and from person to the environment. The "blurred" personality of both primitive man and child does not show the sense of moral responsibility.

Predominance of Religious Values in Later Culture

The development of the human mind and increasing individuation between person and world eschew the faulty logic of man's influence over the happenings of nature and fellowmen through his spells and enchantments and the consequent emotional excitement and release. Step by step magical values are driven back from their hegemony. Religion banishes her stepsister from the throne, and for long centuries all values are focused round the worship of the gods. So pervasive becomes the influence of the collective attitudes and sentiments of man's entire dependence on the divine that the gods become the supreme, universal and ubiquitous values participating in all human interests and functions and dominating them. Men who wanted to succeed in life whether in ancient Egypt or India would seek the favour of the gods through a set of rites, sacrifices, prayers and chants which the gods had revealed, and which only the priests connected with the temples knew. "It was science, art and industry united, this temple and this priesthood," was observed in respect of the Egyptian priests. All human interests and activities, learning, arts and crafts, government, justice and economic life come under the grip of religion whose mandates ruled all the affairs of men through the divine rulers or the God's elect—the priesthood. The fine arts served faithfully the cause of religion. Massive temple architecture and sculpture and the composition of epics, hymns and legends ministered to the needs of the prevailing cults. Art constructed the temple or remade the mountain, imaged the deity in the form of the idol, decorated the altar, dramatised the lives of the gods and goddesses in myths and legends and fashioned rituals, symbols and gestures— the means by which men entered into communion with the deity. The subordination of aesthetic to religious values is further illustrated by the rendering of worship in music and dance, mimetic offering and petition and in an elaborate set of liturgic gestures and movements, —not to speak of the appeal of beautiful images and paintings of the deity, all of which intensified and consolidated the religious sentiments and values. Hindu and Buddhist art invested the human figure with the highest moral and spiritual values under the leadership of Brahman literati and Buddhist monks. Monks who used to take shelter in the many caves during the rainy season decorated the cave walls with gorgeous and enchanting frescoes. Mystical contemplation and painting went hand in hand, producing some of the world's most magnificent painting that cannot be called religious, since the immanence of the deity invested every form of life, from plant and animal to king, woman and child, with profound charm, dignity and serenity. In caves and temples filled with forms of life from the lowest tier to the ceiling the stones were elevated to the highest spiritual and moral truths and values. Similarly the major value of Western medieval culture was God, as Sorokin aptly observes: "Its architecture and sculpture were the "Bible on stone". Its literature, again, was religious and Christian through and through. Its painting articulated the same Bible in line and colour. Its ethics and law were but an elaboration of the absolute Commandments of Christian ethics. Its political organisation, its spiritual and secular powers were predominantly theocratic and based upon God and religion. Even its economic organisation was controlled by a religion prohibiting many forms of economic relationships, otherwise expedient and profitable, and stimulating many forms of activity, otherwise inexpedient from a purely utilitarian standpoint."[12] Not merely is the history of Buddhism and Hinduism and of Christianity in the West associated with some of the noblest achievements in architecture, sculpture and painting, but even now in certain countries religion and art are inextricably blended in the expression and consolidation of the moral, aesthetic and spiritual values and in social manners and etiquette in a manner unknown in modern industrial civilisation. Such integration of moral, aesthetic and spiritual meanings and values is true only of certain rare moments in the history of civilisation. Man's heart is then broadened with a mighty understanding and an all-encompassing good-will. The concrete and the abstract, the mundane and transcendental values then easily slip into each other, which is, indeed, the summit of man's valuation and experience.

This all-pervasiveness of the divine is in some measure a legacy of the early magical notion of the all-comprehensive mysterious spirit, *mana* or supernatural power. The connection is now hardly recognisable due to the reorientation of theology by which the religious myths and faiths of a people are oriented to religious needs with their intellectual advance. Intellectual rationalism has superseded the primitive cults of magic and animism by pantheism, or the immanent conception of the deity especially in the religions of the East. As the result of the supercession of primitive magical beliefs by new metaphysical notions, the conception of the soul and of the supernatural powers becomes also adapted to the requirements of morality and the social order. Such organised religions as Hinduism, Buddhism and Confucianism postulate the doctrine of the transmigration of the soul according to which people can endure misery and suffering in present lives due to misdeeds in the past and look for happier lives in the future by good actions in the present. Such a belief, born of religious and ethical reflection, is as significant for inculcating morality among the masses of peoples as their worship of special gods and goddesses that protect the social order by punishing the evil-doer and rewarding the man of good deeds. The gods of clans and tribes, the local gods of villages, cities and kingdoms protect the spoils of the hunt and the harvests and fruits of the fields and gardens by assuring strength and cunning to the people and timely rainfall and sunshine for agriculture and gardening. These also secure victory over enemies in both defensive and offensive operations. At the same time such gods are guardians of morals as they avenge serious lapse from immorality of individuals as well as general wickedness of men by bringing upon them pestilence, famine or subjugation by enemies. Certain religions like Hinduism and Christianity also put forward Messianic hopes and moral prophecies that contribute not a little in periods of social disintegration and misery of the masses toward reconciling them to their present hard lot. The dualism of good and evil in Zoroastrianism is another solution of finding a value of the good and bad things of the world with a growing rationality of the conception of the universe. All through the centuries it is the strata of mystics and intellectuals who have been the carriers of genuine religious values that gradually spread from them through the elaboration of metaphysical doctrine, rituals and methods of worship and communion to the masses. Especially among the people of Asia, as a result of diffusion of religious values through the development of a large number of religious sects with their myriad divinities and methods of contemplation and achievement of mystical insight and ecstasy, the belief has become well-nigh universal that the universe has its divine meaning and purpose, that the social order is the reflection of the meaningful, purposeful cosmic order.

This universally diffused attitude according to which religious contemplation throws open to man the highest spiritual values accessible to him has profound social and moral consequences. These may be briefly indicated. First the emphasis of the Beyond and a general tone of 'other-worldliness' check the development of the appropriative, possessive and exploitative impluses of men and set ascetics, saints and men of character above the wealthy, trading and merchant classes in social ranking. "It is a positive social and moral advantage to the community", observes Coomaraswamy referring to the Buddhist church in Asia, "that a certain number of its finest minds, leading a life that may be called sheltered, should remain unattached to social activities and unbound by social ties". In Burma it is customary, nor merely for all life ascetics, for all men of whatever calling who profess the Buddhist faith to spend a shorter or longer time within the fold of the order. Both the Indian Brahmanical ideal of plain living and social discipline and Buddhist monachism have contributed not a little towards the inculcation of habits of righteousness, compassion, non-violence and freedom from passion and selfishness among the masses of Asians. In Buddhist countries the monks took charge not only of moral and religious instruction of the masses but also considerably and more so in later times of general education and learning. This has largely accounted for a larger diffusion of literacy and learning in many Buddhist countries in Asia prior to the advent of the Europeans. It is the men of religion and character who form both the highest stratum of ritualist and spiritual advisers for individuals and groups and the stable focus for social stratification in Asia and leave their stamp not only upon the social hierarchy but also upon the customs, manners and ways of living and social education and discipline for other castes or social groups. Secondly, man's rank, occupation, and caste, however low in the social scale, obtain a new esteem. The indignity, dishonourableness or unattractiveness of a craft or occupation are removed by the notion that each person in the social order is the agent or tool of God in a long scheme of things, and that honest, righteous and pious livelihood without desire, resentment and glamour is the supreme value. Thirdly, the ideal is inculcated for every person, whatever his rank, status and position, that there is for everybody in old age the call of the contemplative life that must be answered. In Brahmanical doctrine, a man should retire from the world late in life, after his social debts or obligations are duly redeemed. Contemplation abolishes all statuses, roles and positions in advanced age when religious values compeletly replace all other interests and values in life. With the maturation of the personality, there is wide scope for the cultivation of a variety of interests and values as men undertake their duties in their own professions, occupations and niches in life, until old age silences the stir and bustle of life and prepares itself for merging into the serenity and bliss of the Alone.

Yet it is impossible that the entire structure of social life can be permeated by the value and achievement of contemplation. The agricultural orders, for instance, whose hunger or well-being is so much bound up with the forces of nature, soil, climate, rainfall, animal and insect have not yet moved far in most parts of the world from concrete agricultural magic. Along with the worship of beneficent deities of the field, the forest, the hearth and the village, they still continue to appease by magic the spirits who rule over or through the forces of nature. Magical rites of voluntary suffering and mortification are transformed by organised religion into a system of ritualised penances, fasts and abstinences from food, sleep and sexual intercourse, especially in those critical periods of sowing and harvesting when the good-will of the supernatural powers is so important, in India in spite of centuries of practice of rational religion and worship inculcated by the cultural literati, the earlier primeval magic and observance, including even fertility ritual and magical dance or orgy are still found to survive side by side with Hinduism that has been compelled to legitimise these as recognised cults. Similarly among the peasant folks, possession by gods, demons or spirits or mystical ecstasy brought about by means of intoxicants and drugs or by the collective dance, though looked upon as *infra* dig, is tolerated by the higher religion. At the bottom of Hinduism there is a vast rank jungle of archaic magic which has not yet yielded to the religious movement of a rational and ethical character. An interesting bridge between agricultural magic and ethical religion is represented by the popular cult of Krishna in Northern India. Krishna in Indian myth is *par excellence* the god of the shepherd and peasant folks. His childhood exploits, loves and struggles with the monsters of the marsh and the mountain are all intended for the good of the crops and cattle, fields and pastures. In his youth Krishna as the Eternal lover of the shepherd women of Brajabhumi, becomes the focus of many tender legends and songs that speak in mystical imagery of the nuances of the love-sick soul pining for the deity, in which human and spiritual love patterns slip into each other. Above all Krishna embodies the spirit of resurrection of the fields, pastures and forests in spring for which agriculture in India waits in such pious hope and suspense in the cycle of the seasons.

The sacred values of a religion are largely those that fit harmoniously into the economic and social values prized by the particular social strata, in spite of the teachings of scriptures and prophets. In other words, it is the interests, values and ideology of the social strata which mainly govern the practical ethics of their respective religions. While the cultured stratum in Hinduism—the Brahmans who were the creators and the transmitters of the religious tradition—favoured other-worldliness and the individual quest for salvation, the masses represented by the warrior class, traders, peasants and artisans looked to religion for the essential values of health, longevity and wealth. The entire body of polytheistic cults in Hinduism promoted the pursuit of the good things of the world—not transcendental joys. Even such an other-worldly religion like Buddhism that completely abjured the world and the flesh emphasised for the religious laity (though not for the monks who had no homes and wandered about) the pursuit of natural and righteous family goals, the training in the arts and sciences, guarding of property and inheritance and the practice of good works, including the ministration of the sick and charity to the monks. Buddha addressing the laity observed that if a righteous house-father lives virtuously, he comes by a great mass of wealth due to his own exertions, a good reputation, boldness and self-confidence in society and an untroubled mind.[13] Such are the social values posited for the householders by Buddhism that was in the beginning a religion essentially for the wise who felt the call of release from the bondage of the world. ("To the wise belongeth this Law and not to the foolish".) Different social strata naturally pursue different religious objectives that fit harmoniously into their general economic ethics, occupations and routines of life. It is impossible to expect that the social and economic classes below the highly cultural Brahmanical group could aspire after the transcendental bliss and insight that came easily to them due to their long tradition of remoteness from positions of power and enjoyment of wealth and pleasure. Islam imposed rigid and austere discipline upon its favoured stratum of the warrior class that went out to conquer the world in exchange of wine, fairies and luxuries in heaven. But for the religious laymen of inferior value, the solid goods of health, longevity, polygamy and wealth were safeguarded by regular congregational prayers, purity rituals, sacrifices, fasts and abstinences. Christianity was first preached in the world as a doctiine of the have-nots—the slaves, the artisans, the journeymen and the labourers. But the dogma of primitive Christian communism was completely transformed when Christianity became a state religion and was patronised by kings and nobles, popes and monks with their vast wealth and land endowments. Popular mystical religious movements such as the Bhakti cults in Hinduism, Sufism and Dervish cults in Islam and various religious revivals and ethical movements of Calvinism, Puritanism and Methodism in Christianity have now and then swayed the masses and torn them away from their moorings in life. Thus sometimes in religious history, the highest sacred values are borne by the lower strata with their various popular forms of ardent mystical communion. The picture of religion is therefore split up into different ideologies, sentiments and experiences of different social strata. No particular social stratum, however long and creative its religious heritage may be, can exercise an exclusive or even dominant influence throughout the course of development of a particular religion. It is true that the strata of intellectuals amplify, expound and reinterpret the metaphysical doctrines and on the whole bear and transmit to posterity the essence of genuine religious rationalism. But what is socially leveling is not religious rationalism but religious mysticism, and it often happens that metaphysical doctrines and dogmas inhibit the mystical predispositions. Secondly, religion which deals with the most intimate, personal and unique in experience is naturally governed by the life situation and conduct as a whole of the groups and strata that acknowledge it. Students of comparative religion have dwelt on the metaphysical conceptions of the deity and universe, and largely ignored the moral implications of concrete religious faiths and practices of different social strata of groups which have acknowledged them. The influence of different social groups upon the practical ethics of their respective faiths has remarkably varied according to social history in different countries, and is often even more important than the accepted tenets and dogmas of the religions.[14]

Religion is not only the supreme value in society but it is also the value of the scaling, ordering, integration and regulation of all other values of life. But this is the acme of value experience; it can be reached only by such individuals as great mystics and prophets. For the community as a whole religious values proceed from churches, temples, sects and religious brotherhoods, under the leadership, of course, of the stratum of priests and intellectuals, well-trained in theology and ritual. But outside this fully recognised religious social stratum, with whose ideology religion becomes more or less completely identified, religious values have to compete with other important values, prized by groups and individuals as distinguished from personal religion or mysticism. For the latter, "institutional religion" posits attitudes and values that can integrate easily with other value-determinants of life-conduct. The spread and success of world-religions are largely governed by the way in which the dominant religious social stratum can so mould religious myths, imagery and rituals as to harmoniously fit in with the economic and practical ethic of other social strata and communities.

Differentiation of Values in Groups and Institutions

Mental evolution shows a dual trend. The primitive man's image of the world is one integral, unified whole in which every happening is concrete magic. Man's rational cognition and control of the environment split up this blurred apperception mass into myriad specific images, interests and values. This keeps pace with the evolution of man's technology and arts of utilisation and development of his occupations and professions. At the same time he wants to comprehend and appreciate the world and its meaning and value as whole. This is the sphere of art and religion that are the sources of integrative, ineffable, mystic experiences in which all meanings and values merge. Thus there is a recurrent alteration in the human mind between differentiation and integration of values, world activity and world-flight, to use Hocking's apt words. Bougle considers the differentiation of values as the spiritual side of division of labour. The history of society, according to him, is a history of the differentiation of values contributing its share towards the differentiation of human souls. The human mind gradually develops flexibility and capacity for abstraction that enables it to distinguish between different kinds of meanings, values and experiences. To adopt different criteria for judging ideas, institutions and cultural experiences is to be able to understand and appreciate the better. As a matter of fact an individual can obtain the maximum of meaning and satisfaction from them if he can appreciate different points of view and categories of judgment. To appreciate such distinctions is, to be sure, a measure of the mind's plasticity and freedom.

Man is aided in acquiring his mind's flexibility and capacity of inhibition and of specification of attitudes and sentiments by group orientation. He develops various "social selves", each part of the self obtains its satisfaction from a particular group or association—religious brotherhood, a trade union, a political party, an art club, a society for the cultivation of science and so on. Man develops myriad group loyalties in order to enrich his life with a variety of interests, meanings and values. The history of social development shows the differentiation of interests and values in groups and institutions that have embodied these and indicates the trend which man's interests and values are taking. Many of these operated in function though were not present in structure in older customs, institutions and ways of living. But gradually these find embodiment in particular social structures and processes with specification of interests and values that accompanies the evolution of civilisation. Thus G. H. Mead observes: "As it is possible to find all the essential physiological processes of the most complex animal form in the life-process of an amoeba, so we can discover in a primitive community all the functions that answer to the structures of highly elaborated institutions in complex societies and these functions must persist even if the values which the institutions mediate find themselves in conflict."[15]

Mutual Support or Conflict of Values

No set of values and institutions can live and thrive in isolation. Values and institutions aid one another. Man's increase of wealth, economic security and freedom foster a zeal for knowledge, art and other leisure-time interests. The pursuit of intellectual interests and values is a prelude to freedom of religious worship and release from the authority of obsolete customs and traditions and effete institutions whose social values are outgrown. It is only in a regime of political stability where there is a profound regard for the values of law and order that wealth, learning and recreational and aesthetic interests can thrive. Thus does the evolution of each single value depend upon the process of valuation in the entire group or institutional life. A society that is adequately integrated nurtures a set of common values that all involve one another and in some respects belong to each single group or institution that is inextricably interlocked with other groups or institutions. This is not true, however, of all communities or stages of social development. Human interests and values often compete with and oppose one another, and sometimes a social situation so develops that some values that are not too dear are sacrificed or, what is more probable, all values are transformed in one way or other for the resolution of conflicts. Thus in the on-going processes of social living values exhibit a viable equilibrium.

In the daily routine of life of modern industrial communities specific interests and values are kept in water-tight compartments. Each group normatively systematises and standardises the fractional behaviour of each individual and assures him status and position. The group itself is regarded by outsiders as a conscious, moral personality and enters into transactions collectively with other groups and outsiders, while for its own members it strictly and rigidly imposes its restricted pattern of valuation and the standards of how their personal roles should be played for the appropriation of the limited goals of life. Such specific roles that differ from individual to individual in the same group invest him with a certain status or quota of "rights" that the group assigns to him and which he also expects of them. Conscious of a similarity of scale of valuation and attitude, members develop a *rapport* in their pattern of ideas, sentiments and outlooks and an ardent solidarity that is strengthened by the development of special traditions and manners, legends and cults. All this makes social adaptation in a complex civilisation easier. Thus the mottoes, Business is business, Each man for his profession, Politics is politics, Art for art's sake, The Church knows the truth, illustrate the compartmentalisation of modern life, each compartment claiming only a fragment of man's social self and fulfilling certain specific and specialised values to the disregard of the other interests and values of life. The business man and the aesthete discard morality, the ecclesiastic refuses to learn from science, and the statesman denies both science and morality. Social development accordingly shows a progressive realisation and participation of certain specific values, accompanying a rapid decline of others. Thus health, security and wealth may have grown, and disvalues like disease, insecurity and poverty have been removed for a considerable and increasing section of the population. At the same time there may be progressively less participation in the values of personal association in family life, of freedom, justice, art and religion, It is not easy to estimate the trend of such value changes and transformations. For many values that were appropriate and life-maintaining for one social situation cease to be so in another. Some change their forms of expression and fulfilment and it may be difficult to recognize them in new practices and institutions. The manner in which the architecture of values grows is a matter of culture. No culture can be considered dynamic if it sustains, repeats and reinforces one set of values, say, economic or religious, excluding novelty and conjunction in value experience. A long-time, exclusive pursuit of fixed ends and values, of changeless patterns of ideology is a handicap to social adaptation, in the fullest sense of the term, to full understanding and control of the universe. Some principle of ethical balance, indeed, underlies the preferences of every culture.

Unless culture has altogether gone off its feet, the competing or conflicting values have their proper place in its scheme of life as ends and aspirations. The member of a particular group or institution cannot accordingly deny the values that any other group or institution represents, but only gives it a more adequate definition from his own viewpoint. A human community rests in fact on the conjunction or interpenetration of values. At the same time in no society can the individual be a full participant of the totality of values and interests. The efficiency of the social organisation demands the differentiation of roles, occupations and jobs of individuals according to age, sex, status and personal talent and capacity. That society succeeds which throws open to the elite those specific values and interests that need the greatest stress as the cultural objectives of the community as a whole in its particular situation or stage of development and at the same time permits the sharing of such values and interests among as many social groups as possible either through an upward social movement of individuals and groups (social mobility) or through the system of rights-and-duties.[16]

Restriction or Participation of the Values of Life

In savage or backward communities the restriction of social roles, goals or values is drastic. Thus speaking of Comanche culture in America, Ralph Linton points out that its highest values that were attached to individual initiative, aggression and competition for war honours were restricted to men between approximately 25 to 45 years of age. Old men or boys must refrain from aggressive and competitive behaviour, and in fact great warriors were rarely successful or happy old men who must work at the cause of peace even at the cost of their own dignity. "Direct socially approved expression of culture's dominant values was thus limited to a small, clearly defined segment of the total society". Social progress implies, on the one hand, that the community seizes upon its dominant values and interests for expression and record in all its major institutions or on critical occasions such as marriage, death, or puberty in familistic life, and hunting, war, pastoral expedition or agricultural enterprise in collective life. On the other hand, many cherished values and interests that are not accessible to all due to economic or social disabilities are made available for the average individual through customs, mores, laws, rights and liberties enabling his fuller participation in the culture of the community. Linton's conception of the division of a total culture into constellations of elements within which individuals and groups in their well-defined positions in the social system are circumscribed is true only of primitive and caste-ridden societies. Social progress normally implies the participation of all groups and individuals in the totality of culture, and the struggle between the social groups or classes and change in the status-power system have for their objective the appropriation of values restricted to a small elite or privileged group. As such values become a common possession through the fundamental processes of status and mobility, these come to be regarded as a part of human nature and acquire a blind, compulsive character, sometimes adding to the pattern undesirable cultural accretions so that these are obscured or get out of control.

Gradual Diffusion and Interpenetration of the Essential Values

There are therefore two antithetical trends of valuation. Each group or institution asserts and cherishes its own values that may compete or come in conflict with the values of other groups or institutions. On the other hand, the progress of society towards solidarity means not only that each group or institution must not deny or postpone other values but also define their goals and behaviour in such manner as to recognise all the values involved and share these as far as possible with other groups and institutions. Thus social progress brings with it both gradual diffusion and interpenetration of all essential values and re-orientation of groups and institutions so as to marshal all new values that are rejected by the existing institutions and social procedures. The individual mind constantly seeks new definitions of social situations, challenges and modifies old values and formulates new ones which at each social transition determine the proper relationship of man to society. At the same time in the new social orientation old values are enriched and resurrected and become new goals. In fact the individual by his very process of social living and experience in some measure reconstructs values.

Ordinarily, however, much of human relationship and behaviour is mere conformity to unquestioned ends and set attitudes and values. Fixed custom and immemorial social habit do enshrine certain values the adherence to which is the outcome of personal dispositions and attitudes of the individual. Recently individuals have been classified and portrayed on the basis of highly generalised attitudes or "dominant value directions" by Spranger who describes six basic types of values. There are (1) the theoretical or intellectualist, (2) the economic or practical, (3) the aesthetic, (4) the social or altruistic, (5) the political or power-seeking and (6) the religious or mystical. The above six sets of values representing "eternal" or ideal types of personality in Spranger's conceptual scheme have been tested and verified by G. W. Allport and Vernon who have devised a 'Study of values' scale for measuring the interests and values of individuals. Except for the social or altruistic type of values and personality, Spranger's classification has on the whole proved reliable and useful although he has neglected hedonistic, sensual and vital values that, as G. Allport points out, are the foci of development in many individuals. It must be understood that Spranger endeavoured to work out "the few most general forms of personality", and that in actual life values and personalities are woven into complex patterns out of the various categories and cannot altogether be schematised. Yet Spranger's basic sets of values are, broadly speaking, sought in varying degrees by different individuals and largely determine their occupational choice. It is also interesting that such values integrate themselves in certain combinations and that individuals who are relatively high in certain values show definite opposition towards other values and interests. This is shown by Pintner who examined the attitudes of 187 students toward the church, toward prohibition, toward war and toward the Negro and compared these with their value scores. The theoretically or scientifically-minded students were relatively favourable toward the Negro, were opposed to war, prohibition and the church. The economically or practically-minded students were unfavourable toward the Negro and prohibition and favourable toward war.

The *Table* 3.1 summarises the results : Women show higher scores on aesthetic, social and religious values and lower scores on intellectual, economic and political values.

Right Ordering of Values

Men's attitudes and values are differentiated as a result of differences in their make-up, in their social teaching and environment

TABLE 3.1

Correlation between Values and other Attitudes[17]

Value	Attitudes Measured			
	Church (low-score favourable)	Prohibition	War (low score favourable)	Negro (high score favourable)
Theoretical	0.41	.27	0.208	0.35
Economic	.02	.14	.43	.28
Aesthetic	.28	.06	.33	.23
Social	.01	.28	.16	.08
Political	.28	.36	.36	.31
Religious	.8	.36	.10	.19

and in their personal history. Conflicts of values are often glossed over due to habit and inertia. But some individuals faced with the situation of value conflict do not follow habits or routine behaviour patterns nor repeat stereotypes without adequate understanding, but endeavour to rearrange their behaviour through deliberation. In such reflection the higher levels of the self are involved and a reorientation of values and reconstruction of the social world may be brought about. At the highest level of personality experience the individual obtains a most profound insight into the social character of the universality of values. Mystical insight and excitement serve as the ground of an ideal social order that often has moulded the history of peoples. A social crisis or an awakening in individual lives makes it impossible to separate values from each other like eggs in separate baskets. The ultimate values, truth, beauty and goodness, are determined to regulate all transactions of life and refuse to concede their claims to other values. This is Spranger's basic religious type of values. "A religious man is he whose whole mental structure is permanently directed to the creation of the highest and absolutely satisfying value experience." This is a prelude to revaluation and the restoration of the supremacy of the higher value in the life of the spirit.

No doubt the individual becomes almost unadaptable to social life in both ways: on the one hand, if he is unable to specify values and separate them from one another with certain reserves safeguarded for each, and, on the other, if his divided allegiance leads to the confusion of values in his inner life, i.e., lapse from his due reverence for the ultimate values that must have their say as to the whole of his conduct. The differentiation of values thus keeps pace in every society with the right ordering of values.

Man controls and directs the process of organic evolution of which he is a product. Out of the process of adaptation and control that rises from level to level emerges his hierarchy of values that he reshapes and reinterprets as social evolution proceeds. He defines progress through his increased control of his environment, and this implies his improvement of ability and inclination to take into account all the values and all the interests that he considers worthwhile and orders them according to a system. Now, ordering in the face of a conflicting value situation is a value in itself. It is a value that is essential to right behaviour, bringing all the ends, loyalties and virtues involved into thinking and action. Man's mind has some sort of scale, a kind of hierarchy of values to which loyalties can be related. It is suggested that evidence for this assumption can be found in the "field" theory of modern psychology or Jung's theory of the collective unconscious containing the archetypal symbols derived from the intellectual and moral heritage of the race.[18] Dr. K. J. Neumann aptly observes: "It is important to realise that the elements of the hierarchy of values do not form water-tight compartments, being integral parts of the human mind. It is quite safe to assume that all or most of the hierarchy belongs to a particular part of the mind, that is, the part with which the individual helps to form social groups. According to Simmel, these are the parts with which the individual helps to contribute to the "reveilement" (leveling) which is the condition of group or mass attitudes." In man's reflective thinking what are most worthwhile and imperative for him are the spiritual or ultimate values that can achieve the highest mutuality. Thus the conduct of the individual, his control over the environment that is implicit in his social living come to be motivated by such ends and goals that are in the largest commonalty spread. The law of value thus is that the human mind in rationally dealing with the values involved in a given situation chooses those that can be most widely shared by others, such choice being inevitable due to the structure of the human mind itself. The fullest realisation of the values of life proceeds from the trans-human stratum of the human mind that is the repository of love and goodwill poured out to the universe without seeking any returns.

Each Culture, an Experiment in Value Hierarchy

The principle of classification, of order, of hierarchy is, to be sure, a fundamental law of value ingrained in the experience of the race, and inherent in the valuing consciousness of each single individual. There is a struggle going on between cultures with their distinct type-values and deep-rooted preferences of "the paths of life", such as Buddhist, Maitreyan, Dionysian, Promethean, Apollonian, Christian and so on. Each culture nourishes and champions personal qualities and virtues of a certain type, and it is not easy, though not impossible, for an individual to rise to a synthesis of values and virtues that may represent a wise combination of the values of different historical cultures. The average individual chooses his path of life from the table of human values inherent in the stratification of the society in which he is born. Every society's scaling of values is recorded in its scheme of stratificatory status, social mobility and distance. In India and China mystics, saints and learned men, in Europe and America the politicians and big businessmen, in Soviet Russia the engineers, teachers and nurses, command the highest prestige and deference. A study of the occupational preferences of American children shows that in prestige the banker ranks first, followed by the college professor, doctor, clergyman, lawyer; last come the coal-miner, ditch-digger, street-cleaner, etc. But in Russia first places go to the peasant, aviator, doctor, and coal-miner and last places to the businessman and banker, then the street-cleaner.[19] Different cultures and economic systems order their values and goals of life differently: each has its appropriate scheme of status assignment and of social distance which is a symbol of ranking. For each the social gradation, to be sure, gives the highest prestige and power to those who can most successfully achieve the values, whether religious, aesthetic, intellectual or economic, that it prizes most. The rivalry of the various values and ideals for control and hegemony may engender multiplicity of attachments and develop tolerant, humane personalities; or it may result in moral confinement within a limited set of values, the production of highly efficient, but cramped souls. Such alternatives are a matter of the ethos and social history of different peoples.

In Oriental civilisation the tendency towards integration of values and multiplicity of attachments is secured or encouraged in more ways than one. In the East group organisation does not favour the tendency of values, economic or aesthetic, religious or moral, to constitute their autonomous realms. Groups are so constituted on a neighbourhood, kinship or functional basis as to enable individuals to serve as many interests and values as possible. Religion and occupation, hygiene and family life, morality and civic life equally resist in the small, autonomous groups the forces of dispersion, and encourage the forces of the conjunction of values. Families, castes, village communities, clans and folks realise a variety of values integrally and thus build up social continuity and solidarity. This has been possible largely because both India and China have preferred values of life that may be shared rather than exclusively appropriated and possessed. The hierarchy of values in Oriental ethics are religion, learning, family and wealth. In the Orient men of the highest learning and spirituality have always obtained the highest status and deference. Besides India and China have worked on the social assumption that where there are many values presented to every individual in a complex civilisation, selection of the goals of life is the sure road to greater fulfilment and happiness. Their ethos and culture have succeeded better than those of Western communities where in the search of everybody for *all* human values,—wealth, status and power—the considerable majority of the people lose status, self-esteem and happiness. In the Orient the majority, though circumscribed within restricted social roles with limited goals of life, enjoy contentment and do not exhibit personal stresses and maladjustments. Within a limited social space the social group in the Orient, indeed, aims at fulfilling a variety of values and interests integrally; it is not "unilateral" but all-embracing, and gives full scope for man's attachments and satisfactions within a narrowed range. Even a closed group like the caste in India seeks a multiplicity of values, limited as these are to certain families by heredity and vocation. A caste is not merely an economic organisation, It has its code of morals, social etiquette and manners, its gods, temples and religious processions as well as its recreations and amusements. Castes no doubt restrict the goals of life for the individual. But within the limited social space castes give opportunities to the individual for variegated satisfactions at the same time. The caste where the corporation is at the same time a kindred, a religious brotherhood, a civic unit and trade-guild, places at the disposal of the individual a whole world of values. The Indian village or the Chinese clan with its castes, sects, temples, guilds, co-operatives and schools appeals to a wide variety of human interests and values, and is thus an enduring institution. Groups split up and subdivide more quickly and institutions stagnate or outlive their usefulness if these comprise only segments of man's interests and satisfactions, however imperative their claims may be, and do not afford opportunities of full play for man's behaviour. The rivalry of sovereign values in their autonomous sphere co-exists with the confusion of values and disruption of the unity of the self.

Each culture experiments with values, with groups formed to nourish these and with institutions established to serve these. As a person participates in the activities, traditions and power of each group or institution he serves certain "values" and a certain "status" accrues for him as indicated by the "rights" which the group and the person himself recognise as due to him in his role. Each culture is a creative synthesis of group norms, a framework of rights-and-duties for each status or role of individuals, whose social selves are moulded and conditioned to use various categories that have been discriminated in the world of values in the course of social evolution. That culture succeeds best which orders the values of life, the higher and the lower, the greater and the lesser, the intrinsic and instrumental ends with wisdom, and orients its groups and institutions in such a manner as to give the most effective guidance to the individual to construct for himself, by reflecting on his own specialised appreciations and experiences, that hierarchy of values that the society holds most dear to itself. The society's scale of values is consolidated and renewed ceaselessly in its group organisation and institutional framework.

References

1. Miriam Rothschild : Lecture, Institute for the Study of Animal Behaviour.
2. *Journal of Comparative Psychology,* 1941, vol. 32.
3. *Comparative Psychology Monograph,* vol. x, 1934.
4. See my *Social Ecology.*
5. *Handbook of Social Psychology,* p. 197.
6. See M. Sherif : *Psychology of Social Norms*, pp. 58-60; also C W. Mills: Language, Logic and Culture in the *American Sociological Review*, 1939, pp. 670-680.
7. *Sin and Sex,* p. 26.
8. See Radin : *Primitive Religion*; also Malinowski : *Coral Gardens and their Magic.*

9. Werner : *Comparative Psychology of Menial Development* p. 490.
10. Radin : *Primitive Man as Philosopher,* p. 72.
11. See Werner, pp. 444-445; also Piaget: *Moral Development of the Child.*
12. *The Crisis of Our Age,* pp. 17-18.
13. The duties of laymen are set forth in the Singalavada Sutra and the Digha Nikaya.
14. See J. Wach : *The Sociology of Religion;* also his chapter in *Twentieth Century Sociology,* pp. 435-436
15. *The Philosophy of the Act,* p. 498.
16. See my *Social Ecology,* pp. 60, 199-200.
17. A Comparison of Interests, Abilities and Attitudes. *Journal of Abnormal and Social Psychology,* 1933, pp. 351-357.
18. K. J. Neumann: Tyranny and Group Loyalties, *Philosophy,* July 1943; see also Bleuler : *Autistic Thought.*
19. Davis : Testing the Social Attitudes of Children in the Government Schools in Russia, *American Journal of Sociology,* 1929.

4

THE PSYCHOLOGICAL LAWS OF VALUE—FROM INSTINCT TO SOCIAL NORM, FROM CROWD TO COMMONALTY

The Social Discipline and Integration of Instincts

Man is a social creature grafted on to a biological one, observed Tarde. From his animal ancestry man derives the fundamental instinct of self-preservation that is amplified and extended in human evolution into the supreme values of individuality and personality. In the lower levels of organic evolution the individual is often sacrificed for the community or the species, as among the social insects. In vertebrate evolution we mark however the trend of preservation of individual life that has reached its culmination in man. In his animal origins, again, are rooted the equally insistent instincts for the maintenance of the brood, the group or the community that are fashioned in man's evolution into the great values of sympathy, sociability and solidarity. There is a permanent tendency in man toward the intermingling of instincts, satisfactions and values of egoism and altruism, of self-preservation and group-preservation. All values, actual or potential, are related to the instincts and desires of man both as the biological and as the social animal, values being defined as objective sources of satisfactions, actual or potential.

The fundamental feature of values expresses a tension and the satisfaction or mitigation of this tension. For a full consciousness of value, the instincts and desires which strive to be realised for the removal of tension should be stable and the object sought should also be relatively constant. It is the congruence of the two and the consciousness of this congruence with memory of the past enjoyment and imagined enjoyment, associated with the future consummation, that establish the experience of value enjoyment or fulfilment of integrated instincts and desires in terms of their object. What is even more significant in the value situation is that the organisation of desires and the mode of fulfilment of these are defined and regulated by society working upon the hereditary instinctive equipments of individuals; while the objects of the environment striven for are also transformed and re-shaped by it. In the value experience of adult individuals both the primitive desires and satisfactions and the object sought to be attained or the environmental situation controlled are recreated into new patterns and integrated into the larger adaptation and development of life.

Man's desires, interests and satisfactions are found to blend and interfuse with one another. Instincts and desires do not run their own separate courses in the normal individual, for the human mind seeks an orientation or unity of direction in which as many of the major impulses or desires are fulfilled as possible, even if unconsciously. This is the transformation of instincts and interests into values. The inhibition, integration and unity of direction of instincts and satisfactions come less from man's reason and choice, and more from society. For as a social being his desires and satisfactions are expressed and fulfilled not in terms of ego-centric isolation but in those of social intercourse and cooperative action between and among individuals. Like his tools, language and gestures, man's values are a means of directing social interaction.

The Blending of Biological and Cultural Values

Values thus emerge as a result of fulfilment of urges of individuals in contact with other individuals in society. These are essentially social products, realities for the social sciences. Hunger, sex, territory, self-preservation and the normal rhythm of play and repose for the human organism have all to be satisfied permanently in man's social milieu. Their non-satisfaction implies disvalue—malnutrition, bodily discomfort and decay—and makes it impossible for man to strive after the higher desires, satisfactions and values. The organic satisfactions comprise the 'biological values' that serve as the foundation of all other progressive values. But even the biological urges and satisfactions are shaped and moulded by culture and directed into socially approved channels. Man is guided in his satisfaction of hunger and sex by the social group and its norms. He eats things that are socially sanctioned and at times that are prescribed for him. Food which is prohibited or regarded as 'unclean or repulsive given to a famished person instead of giving him satisfaction often produces sickness. Man finds his full sex fulfilment not by giving vent to his natural appetite but within the socially regulated limits of courtship and marriage, pre-marital and ex-marital intercourse. Illegitimate or illicit sex satisfaction brings about neurosis and functional derangement. Thus even in the case of such primeval impulses as hunger and sex both need and satisfaction are profoundly modified by social norms.[1] The value of the human mate does not depend only upon physical attractiveness which is again determined by social conventions, but also on factors of economic efficiency, wealth and status; while procreation is profoundly affected by custom, standard of living and the personal scale of ideal values. Thus food, marriage, family-raising, all become cultural values for man refashioning the raw materials of human biology, *i.e.*, the biological and the social or cultural values blend and are integrated with one another. It is on the basis of integration, for instance, of sex, food and play with other social or cultural interests and values that man can derive permanent satisfactions from them in society. The pursuit of biological values *per se* leads to personal and social disorganisation. Thus biological values are a misnomer shut out by man's social nature. Yet man is so constituted that his bodily appetites and pleasures may be in some measure dissociated from instinctual need and fulfilment, and may become ends in themselves. Animals exhibit a complete balance between the fufilment of biological needs and enjoyment serving the purposes of self-preservation and reproduction; therefore excesses are unusual. Man's excesses in the indulgence of sex, food, drink and drugs by which he brings about his physical and mental ruin are unnatural; and yet certain civilisations and epochs have cultivated such biological disvalues. This is pathological.[2] Animals, again, have a definite scale of organic drives, hunger, sex and play being the most powerful with one or the other dominant according to the immediate situation. They have to contend with a natural, and not a derivative, artificial environment. In man the social milieu creates many desires and values that compete with and even supersede biological values and thus endanger the individual and the race. In both these respects man shows a disbalance between the conditions of his survival and the sophisticated norms of his culture. But, normally speaking, the entire social and institutional framework not only gives opportunities for the satisfaction of man's organic needs but also regulates the biological values in such manner as to safeguard the stability of society and the health and vital well-being of the individual. This is the essence of social adaptation the failure of which spells both personal disorganisation and disintegration of society.

Human Values are all Derived Social Values

In the realm of economic life the primary instincts of appropriation, possession, curiosity, constructiveness, maturation and movement are even more profoundly determined and directed by the derivative economic environment. Man seeks the satisfaction of his economic needs not by directly manipulating the environment, but through the mediation of his fellowmen and group who co-operate and compete with him, and through technology—the system of production, distribution and transport that he has inherited as social legacy. Man seeks all his economic values in a socially derived economic environment. It is the economic organisation of the community through its pattern of class or caste, its laws of property, competition and contract and its opportunities and provisions for employment, industrial training, economic security or housing that dictates economic values and the modes of their fulfilment. These are summed up in security and the maintenance of the standard of living by the individual and the group. For man's social life, society's scheme of status assignment and maintenance for the individual and the group, with its legal rules and moral conventions and institutional distribution of power and such concepts as honour, freedom and justice, represents the framework within which man finds all his social goals and values. Finally, man's ideal values are also sought in his social milieu in the network of human relationships and intercourse that become the bases of his search and fulfilment of his notions of truth, beauty and goodness. This is facilitated by various culture products—creations of the fine art, objects of worship, moral and legal codes.

The Transformation of Wants into Values in Economics

The above represents the progressive levels of values met with in society. The science of economics dealing with wants, satisfactions and activities has developed a wrong psychology of values. It postulates a homogeneity, simplicity and atomic character of wants and uniformity of their satisfactions that are not true even at the biological level. The picture of the economic man calculating the urgency of his varied homogeneous items of wants at their margin is a scientific absurdity. Even the bare physical wants of food, clothing and shelter show a wide variety according to social groups and classes, and their urgency as well as manner of their fulfilment are governed by a variety of personal and social factors that do not yield to an arithmetical treatment. Man is hardly motivated by a single want. Even in the satisfaction of hunger or eating several impulses, some being social, are integrated. Wants are complex tendencies to modes of action that cannot be attributed to the primordial physical nature of man nor do these multiply geometrically as a uniform series like single-tracked, simple, mechanical items of experience. Modern psychology shows us that wants from their very nature are unstable, ever-varying in response to various kinds of influences, while the objects which are rationally formulated in economics are themselves provisional and instrumental. Man's wants become ever more new, socialised and intellectualised, and his activities which are directed forward and upward indefinitely involve criticism, evaluation, judgment. In these, society or culture plays an important role. A rational consideration of alternative wants or anticipation of their respective satisfactions does not determine economic effort. For both wants and the modes of their fulfilment are largely governed by group or social pressure and scale of values of the social stratum that determine the relatively fixed possibilities of wants, satisfactions and activities of individuals. The improvement of individual income, however, throws open opportunities of satisfaction of new wants, aesthetic and intellectual, that the scheme of social mobility encourages, and thus the curve of utilities and activities is raised to a new level. A new social status and personal worth and achievement change quantity to quality, aided by man's own judgment and self-esteem—the curve of wants and satisfactions thus rising from level to level.

Economic psychology also does not distinguish between legitimate and illegitimate wants and satisfactions that go into the roots of moral and social patterns. It is culture that is the guardian of judicious consumption and of the right and legitimate manner of fulfilment of wants that become prime movers in economics only after social approval. Society through its customs, traditions and institutions disciplines, coordinates and integrates the desires and wants of men in a manner that will serve it. This is the transformation of wants into values. Thus the creation of interests, values and habits is more significant than the satisfaction of wants, and neither economics, nor ethics, nor sociology can afford logical separation from each other.

Values are rooted in instincts and desires. The instinct hypothesis as applied to human behaviour has fallen into disfavour because of the loose manner in which catalogues of instincts were framed and also because human motivation is often compounded of a number of instincts. Many of the modern psychologists accordingly list fundamental drives of motivation. A sound listing of such drives is that given by Prescott who divides these into three classes: physiological, social, egoistic. The first has to do with physical demands of the bodily survival: air, food, elimination, shelter, avoidance of disease and danger, activity and its counterpart rest, and sexuality. All these may be more or less influenced by learning. The group of social needs are chiefly those of affection, "belongingness" or participation and "likeness to others". Finally, the ego needs are concerned with the organisation of selfhood and have to do with such matters as adequate contact with material and social-cultural reality and a satisfactory degree of harmony therewith, including adequate realisation of the "authority" of things and persons.. Furthermore, selfhood involves the increased "symbolization" or meaningfulness of experience, "self-direction" of one's activity, a capacity to effectuate "a fair balance between success and failure" and an attainment of adult individuality or that unique integration of self which operates to make adaptation particularly one's own yet efficient with reference to the obligations to others.[3] According to Woodward, the three fundamental "wishes" that inescapably emerge in the social situation for the group-living human animal are for security, for response and for recognition (status). Thomas and Znaniecki list the following four "wishes" or "tendencies" (re-stated by the latter) of human nature in the social milieu viz., response, recognition, security and new experience. All these motives, biological and social, are often found in combination. Thus the social motives blend with sex, aggression and the demands for subsistence. This has been stressed by Freud with whom the basic drives are the life instinct associated with the emotions of love, sympathy and sex, and the death instinct linked up with man's aggressiveness, selfishness and development. Even in man's physical satisfactions of food, sex, clothing and shelter the influence of group standards is discernible. Society not merely converts ego-centric desires into uniform and stable wants, values and habits that motivate activity over a wide range of situations, but also transforms lower wants into higher, e.g., sensuous into imaginative and aesthetic, or egoistic into altruistic wants, by transfer of interest and imaginative or symbolic transfiguration so that these are multiplied and renewed, and ramify into manifold new series without being accompanied by satiety and disgust. The so-called progression of wants into geometrical series with the phenomenon of diminishing utilities does not apply even to bare physical satisfactions, integrated as these always are with social and cultural values. The true law of wants is that of the enlightenment and transformation of values and satisfactions from individual to collective, from momentary to enduring, from immediate to deferred and from biological to social and ideal.

The Laws of Desires and Values

Neither sociology nor ethics has paid much attention to the manner in which man's desires, values and satisfactions are built up. Ethics, in spite of its modern emphasis of the principle of personality realisation, has not grounded itself on an adequate psychology of desires and values, ideal and moral, furnished by recent advances in instinct and social psychology. A few general principles are here briefly set forth:

(*i*) All human motivations are transformed into values through the regulation or approval of society. Society not only moulds or shapes all urges, including the basic ones, but also determines the modes of their expression or fulfilment. Man's basic urges or desires that have to do with the physical demands of bodily survival are universal and imperative. Though social and cultural factors play a role in their forms of fulfilment, their existence is independent of society. As these urges or desires are repressed or baffled, the deep unconscious tendencies may find expression in forms of fulfilment that are not socially approved or in disguised substitutes, symbolic activities or phantasies through the operation of certain mental dynamisms with which psycho-analysis has made us familiar. In the formation of such substitute or sublimated satisfactions, social norms, taboos and prohibitions, play the leading role. Man is both the carrier and creature of values. It is social culture that provides everywhere the frame within which the individual can satisfy adequately or is baulked in his basic needs and urges and develop his personality. This frame is called the "basic personality structure" by Abram Kardiner.[4] It is by analysing the basic personality structure that we can really understand individual behaviour and know in what manner social culture fulfils, regulates or frustrates basic needs or values and engenders happiness, gives rise to substitute satisfactions and sublimations, or to aggression, fear and anxiety. The whole cluster of biological or basic values must be recognised and satisfied for the erection of any value system. The higher values rest on the conditions of bodily health and growth including sexual expression that are specific for each individual with reference to his maturation and also his habits of living and environment. On the other hand, the persistent frustration of such elemental needs as hunger and sex leads to the disintegration of personality and free expression of the unconscious urges that end with withdrawal from society or violence towards fellowmen according to individual peculiarities. It is thus a fundamental law that as no human urges can be adequately fulfilled in social isolation, the deprivation of imperative urges increases their strength to such intensity that these must be satisfied vicariously or there is serious depression leading to isolation (schizophrenia) or active anti-social behaviour, both being mentally pathological. There is, accordingly, a three-fold origin of negative values or disvalues. First, disvalues arise due to denial or deprivation of basic physical or biological needs and conditions of homeostasis and growth, inhibiting or preventing normal human maturation and development. Physical pain and discomfort, malnutrition, lack of protection against excessive cold or heat due to insufficiency of clothing and shelter, illness and retardation of physical and mental growth and maturation are all dis-values arising out of physical or biological causes. Secondly, disvalues arise due to man being a prey to severe psychic tensions and conflicts. These may spring from the chronic inhibition and frustration of the basic needs of food, love, recognition, status and security, the fulfilment of which is necessary for psychological health and self-actualization. He then develops a set of artificial, counterfeit and twisted values, either self-defeating or deviant ways of gratification and fulfilment of impulses and desires that become disvalues. Thirdly, the complexity and plasticity of human mind are such that man in the face of conflict situations turns to compulsive sexual hyper-activity and hyper-gratification of food, drink and drug that run counter to his physiological needs. These are equally complex distortions of values or disvalues involving symbolic, compulsive and phobic mechanisms forming around warped bio-genetic functions.

(*ii*) Satiation of these basic values produces ennui or indifference or a shift from preference to avoidance or aversion. There is an original organic and later an acquired limit to the satisfaction of many primary as well as cultural values. This may be called the law of the cycle of values, efforts and satisfactions that society and culture, however, constantly modify and qualify through offering the individual new desires, new goals and new models of their fulfilment.

(*iii*) Desires or values are found fused with one another and constantly shift in their combination. Man's behaviour patterns express the combination of several desires or values, sometimes harmoniously sometimes disharmoniously blended. Man's behaviour in the satisfaction of values often becomes erratic or eccentric due to lack of integration of impulses and desires that leads to mental instability, duality of purpose and 'reclusiveness'. Persons are characterised by the opposing psychological traits of 'expansiveness and 'reclusiveness.'[5] A person who cannot adequately blend his ego-centric desires with the social impulses keeps his own ideas and values to himself and segregates himself more or less from the social group. Idiosyncrasies of value-satisfactions are, however, restricted by modes, codes and manners.

(*iv*) Desires and values are found in competition with one another. Out of the ceaseless conflict of desires and values man and society evolve and select a "natural" or organic hierarchy of values—the supremacy of intrinsic and ultimate values prized for their own sake over instrumental and proximate values regarded as means to serve and promote the former. It is the notion of intrinsic value which provides each individual and society the criterion in the light of which alone they can decide whether the instrumentalities are instruments of values. The divorce of instrumentalities and immediates from the intrinsicalities and ultimates of life is a basic symptom of the sickness of men and societies. A sane individual, society or culture reconciles or fuses the intrinsic and the instrumental values, and safeguards that every goal, act or relationship becomes meaningful and *symbolic* of the intrinsic and ultimate values of life. When certain fundamental values cannot be fulfilled together, man obtains satisfaction through a symbolic process, the essence of which is transfer of interest and emotional values. Certain objects stand for (symbolise) or represent another object and thus a particular desire obtains disguised satisfaction.

Again, many ends that are remote and final, as contrasted with immediate or instrumental ends, are sought by symbolic means. Money is desired for the satisfaction of wants as well as for economic status and power. The standard of living stands as a symbol of class distinction and prestige. The display of the standard of living is even more important than the standard of living itself. The attainment of man's absolute and infinite values that cannot be reached by rational methods and techniques is always sought through symbolical means, such as magic, ritual and religious observance. All these play a peculiarly important role in the integration and fulfilment of the ideal values, and hence in the social routine of a people. On the other hand, the fundamental interests of life, as these become permeated by absolute and infinite values, give rise to symbolical action and relationship. Thus symbolic ritual actions are found to interpolate with the technical operations or rational procedures in the satisfaction of many major values of life, engendering a sense of self-competence and wholeness and joy, not otherwise obtainable.

(*v*) Many desires and values are in conflict with one another. The individual depends for the avoidance or resolution of value conflicts not merely upon the inner mechanism of repression, sublimation and phantasy-making but also on the entire educational process and the guidance of groups, institutions and social codes that present before the individual channels of behaviour or social habits in which the conflict of impulses is brought down to the unconscious level. Values in conflict also present the occasion for the individual mind to rehearse the consequences of alternative modes of action. From this arise both the consciousness and rational formulation of values. As values are opposed to one another man is able to conceive ideals and systems of norms taking into account larger and larger patterns of interests and values which do justice to his total developed natures.

(*vi*) Society or culture provides man with the basic pattern of desires or values. It stimulates or inhibits man's desires and satisfactions and also lays down the modes of satisfaction. All human desires are fused with the social impulses. Human values are symbolic of man's social relations. It is culture, tradition and training which create the basic value systems and weave these into social ends and goals that regulate the nature and mode of fulfilment of desires and values. Such culture and learning depend usually upon the stratum or group to which man belongs in society. Every society is a system of inter-related strata and statuses, and the social stratification largely determines whether man's satisfaction is to be derived from increase of the quantity of goods and services or from increase of new satisfactions and values. Each social stratum or group requires that a minimum standard of satisfactions of desires and values it approves and expects should be adhered to by all individuals. Poverty becomes intolerable not merely because of the deprivation of man's biological desires and values but also because it leads to loss or attenuation of group contact, status or caste. Man's desires and values are organised and integrated into living and cultural standards for groups or classes that maintain social distance between them and that serve to regulate the distribution of efforts for reaching the group scale of consumption as the criterion of wealth, status and power. The scale of value satisfactions differs from class to class and alters with social progress and with this the criteria of wealth, status and use of leisure. It is upon the total cultural configuration and not upon economic conditions or pressure or biological needs that the ways of competitive or cooperative living and behaviour depend among various primitive communities. This general conclusion is the result of Margaret Mead's analysis of the culture of thirteen primitive tribes carefully surveyed.[6] In competitive societies we find along with the stress of the values of personal initiative, power and property, a single scale of success, inequality of value-fulfilments from stratum to stratum, with symbols of rank and prestige, and a belief in arbitrary supernatural powers. In cooperative societies we have a high degree of individual security, a weak emphasis upon rising in status, a general participation of the community in the major interests and values and a faith in an ordered universe. "Social life goes on in response to a structural form expressed in a calendar, a court-ritual or a seasonal rhythm." A single or differential scale of values and of value-fulfilment largely depends upon the social framework of a culture with its characteristic symbols of stratum distance or proximity and modes of display of these. Comparative social psychology, working on the concepts of the basal personality structure (Kardiner) and the dominant theme or value system (Opler and Spicer) of the community can lay bare significant differences in respect of certain fundamental matters such as sources of ego-development or repression, emotional security or unhappiness of the individual and of competition and aggression or cooperation and amity in social relations.

(*vii*) Man's reason and judgment and society's experience build up the scale of values or preferences for every society which acts as a sieve of selection of values and efforts and distinguishes between the higher and the lower, the instrumental and the ultimate values. Without a fixed pervading gradation of values, society lacks an essential principle of organisation and the individual the principle of personality integration. This hierarchy of values is transmitted to successive generations as a social heritage. It embraces and organises every field of human relations and activities, and is reflected in the status-power system, in law and in the system of rights-and-duties. No intuition or revelation of an absolute and right hierarchy of values need be posited. The hierarchy of values is contextual, part of the social process, of the cultural and 'technological' experience.[7] Outside the culture, the structure of values becomes meaningless or arbitrary. The structure of values is itself dynamic and evolutionary, developing harmoniously within a set of functional social institutions. Yet it comprises honest choice, initiative and creativeness of the individual.

(*viii*) Another law of desires and values is that of the individuation, differentiation and unique satisfaction of man's desires and values due to difference of aptitudes, habits and capacities. There is no end to the subtlety, variegation and ascent of values. The more significant law of the progression of values is not quantitative increase but qualitative improvement, from the biological to the ideal, from the egoistic to the altruistic, from the fluctuating to the enduring, from the partial to the integral and so on.

(*ix*) The qualitative improvement of desires and values takes place in the social milieu, in the social setting of man's group and institutional relationship and experience. As the group improves in cohesion and solidarity from Interest-association to Society and from Society to Commonalty, values become more integral, self-sufficient and permanent, and engender striving for further value potentialities in both the individual and society.

(x) Every group, every institution represents a stable organisation of impulses and interests of the individual and thus acquires a secondary value that is consciously striven after. Man thus comes to find the *purpose* of the group and institution, and also rises to an *ideal*, especially where the relation between group and group and institution and institution comes uppermost to the mind in a conflict situation. The ideal integrates into a larger mental system many competing impulses, interests and values; it represents a decisive progress in the organisation of impulses and interests or the different planes of value. Man's experience, imagination, criticism, reflection and judgment are all implied in the formation of the ideal that integrates all the competing or coflicting interests and values into a harmonious whole and stimulates and directs the will to a definite channel of activities or series of activities. A vivid perception of the goals, strong sentiment and conscious pursuit of a pre-determined plan of action are linked together in the realisation of the ideal that looks both forward and backward.[8] Transforming as it does the naive erratic impulses into stable, rational goals and purposes, it accounts for the integrity, solidarity and permanence of groups, relations and institutions that shelter it. It builds up that enduring fusion and harmony of mental patterns which is called *character*. By organising and coordinating various conflicting interests, values and loyalties it gives a definite and unique shape and direction to man's conduct associated with what is called *personality*. The ideals sometimes widen their range and become comprehensive in their contents and scope, forming a coherent and harmonious structure among themselves. These thus rise to *norms* or normative ideals. The system of norms can resolve conflicts of values and ideals in all possible individual and social relations and situations. It embodies all the desires and aspirations of individuals and groups, and increasingly indicates the lapse from truth and harmony of any specific values and ideals. It acts as the supreme arbiter of value-claims of different planes and of different groups and institutions as these range themselves in perpetual discord in individual and group relations. The system of norms emerging as it does from man's systematisation, classification, and ethical contemplation and development of ideals shows a rationality, impersonality and universality that ideals cannot possess. The system of norms such as those of Truth, Beauty and Goodness are related by man to the order of the universe and the purpose of the Divine Mind. The norms represent the final stage in the evolution of values as these embody the highest "requiredness" or ""ought".

(*xi*) Man's ideal values, intellectual, artistic and religious, are rooted in his intuition and empathy and social co-operation and intercourse. All great men in art, music, literature and religion are especially gifted with high degrees of both intuition and empathy or imaginative sympathy that enable them to discern the fundamental laws and values of life and reach these to the people in a most effective manner. Great mystics and poets have an undoubted ability to delve deep into universal consciousness that enables them to create and renovate values and sway the imagination and behaviour of men in distant countries and epochs. Intuition and empathy are very real gifts as the lives and achievements of great founders of religion and of leaders in music, art and literature amply testify. Mankind owes its spiritual oneness to them. As ideal values deepen the communion between man and fellowman, brooking no boundaries, their cultivation is associated also with the unfoldment and expansion of the human spirit. Man's intellectual curiosity and creative impulses, his phantasy-making and co-operative imagination are aided and stimulated by the literary and artistic heritage and traditions, by the accumulation of tools, implements and procedures that he already finds operative in society and that direct his intelligence and imagination to social objects and uses. His intellectual, aesthetic and moral values are all social and communicative, springing as they do from the background of collective culture products and traditions. The association of many minds in the past builds up language and literature, aesthetic and moral standards in and through the media of which new appreciation and evaluation take place. A close and emotional rapport and sympathy with fellowman underlie every new creation of art, scientific and technological discovery or great aspiration of social good-will. Thus social intelligence, emotion and action contributing towards more intense social participation or communion become themselves supreme values.

(*xii*) Man's ideal values, his insight into truth, aesthetic and religious apprehension, his practical invention and experimentalist control and zeal for goodness and service owe, to be sure, their strength and persistence to social culture that encompasses individual lives. These enter into the social relations and the processes of the world and adding to their content of meanings and values become constant operative forces in the environment. Social culture thus maintains itself and understands, utilises and controls the total environment of man. This it does through the use of a vast variety of symbols, verbal, pictorial or material, that embody and communicate meanings and values of objects, situations and relations of man's physical and social environment. Symbolisation or realisation of the value or meaningfulness of experience is one of the basic needs of the ego; as these are defined by Prescott. Social culture may be regarded as a unified system of symbolic devices that enable man to define, appraise and control the world of situations around him.[9] Many of the 'Thou shalts' and 'Thou shalt nots' of early childhood, the Golden Rule or the code of honour are mnemonic symbol-devices and dramatisations, guiding the conduct of individuals. The mechanism here is an automatic or quick arousal of anticipatory images and concepts in their minds safeguarding them against temptations. From the precepts, shibboleths and slogans of the home, the police-man's arm signals and the notices of the law-courts that are admonitory to the ideal characters or models of myth, fable and literature, the motifs in painting, sculpture and architecture, the modes of music and dance and the images of religious worship that are inspiring and evocative, man obtains meanings and values differently from his world of sensory-verbal symbols. These enormously expand and become complex with the development of civilisation as communication becomes more and more mechanically mediated. At the same time the symbolical devices and techniques vary greatly in their efficacy for social control and also sometimes lead to the formation of antisocial habits and attitudes. Social culture largely rests on the efficiency of the symbol-devices, objects, persons and situations in the personification and projection of values for the purposes of quick, automatic adjustment of the individual to physical nature and to fellowman. Symbols take him beyond objects and situations to a universal world order with which he finds a kinship in thought and imagination. The unity and orderly relations of the universe envisaged by art, religion, law and morality—man's social control devices—spread their meanings and values to and regulate all human behaviour. Man's universe is both material and immaterial. It is the immaterial environment of his language, art and religion that organises his inner life, takes hold of his material environment and directs his adaptation to it as well as to the inner universe of his own making in which he lives and moves, dreams and aspires. This immaterial world of values is always augmenting. On the one hand, the creation of values depends on extensive and long-continued co-operation and communication between members of the social group on the plane of deliberate interchange and integration of ideals, humane sympathy and practical social cooperation. On the other hand, as these values are created they endure in man's social relationship and experience, proving their authenticity by inspiring new insights into truth and new visions of beauty, holiness and goodness. Thus are values conserved, augmented and transmitted. Knowledge, art and religion, adding to the value content of society through the heritage of its cultural, religious and aesthetic symbols and experiences, continuously aid the creation and realisation of new ideal values by individuals that again enter, enrich and transform the world. This process of fruitful interchange between individual creativeness and social inspiration goes on without end, progressively augmenting the value configuration of the cosmos. There is a dynamic interchange or interpenetration between the Human Person-Values and Cosmos that introduces a prophetic element in the assumptions and goals of sociology: the human person always progresses towards universalism or cosmism; values are ever universalized, refined and deepened through participation and sharing; society ever passes towards the unlimited commonalty which is the cosmos.

(*xii*) The psychological laws of value became philosophical when these acknowledge and follow the logic of dialectic. Man, values and society are loci of dimensions and polarities. The world of values is founded on the reconciliation, fusion and coordination of antinomic or alternative modes of fulfilment, both of which demand full discovery, expression and protection within a wider organization of values. These are the polarities of individuality and order and fitness and continuity at the biological dimension ; of inhibition and discipline, and self-actualization and self-transcendence at the psychological dimension of desire and conscience, egoism and altruism and intrinsic and instrumental values at the moral dimension; of *Gemeinschaft* and *Gesselschaft*; freedom and organization and status and mobility at the sociological dimension ; and of self-valuation and self-transcendence at the metaphysical dimension.[10] According to White-head the World of Value is the coordination of the infinitude of possibilities for realization. This "involves harmony and frustration, beauty and ugliness. Also there is a measure of fusion in respect of each pair of antithesis—for example, same definite possibility for realization will involve same degree of harmony and same degree of frustration, and so on for every other pair of antithesis."

Man, as he grows, matures and fulfils himself, abolishes these and many other polarities and contradictions of values that belong to the various dimensions or orders of human living. Multidimensionality and dialectic comprise the primary foundation of the world of values.

What is the supreme dialectic that guides and directs man's social progress? This has emerged in human civilization in the pattern of the dialectic of man's self-actualization and self-transcendence and the beauty and harmony of the unlimited cosmos. Whitehead has phrased the two as the uniqueness of the. individual and the generality of harmony. The first means, according to him, love and the second order. Truth, love and goodness speak everywhere the accents of the unfolding dialectic of the uniqueness of human personality development expression and social order and coherence. The dialectic of love and harmony, reality and appearance, being and becoming in the human world echoes the primordial rhythm or polarity in the cosmos of silence and manifestation, stability and change, unity and individuation, tension and possibility. The human mind in its nisus towards development and completion shows a dialectic. As long as it is healthy, wholesome and maturing, the polarities or complementaries are reconciled fused and harmonized with one another in a dynamic total pattern.

The Stages of Value Experience

We may now from a different angle briefly examine the stages and levels of value experience that are related to the whole organisation of the self in its physical and social milieu. In this process both the development of individual character and personality and social integration are involved— complementary aspects of the same organisation. The organised achievement of values means not only complete self-realisation and happiness of the individual but also communion and solidarity of the social group. From the simple to the most complex value situation we have to take into account both the orientation of human nature as a whole as well as of social relations. *Table* 4.1 illustrates this.

Goals, Ideals and Norms

A value is a complex *Gestalt*, a conscious vital-social-ideal situation. Value is experienced in the total situation; and is neither purely or primarily biological, social or mental. There are *levels* of all value experience; and at each level the primary values are associated with major urges, *goals* and ideals as well as ethical norms. The first step in value experience is the specification or preference of

TABLE 4.1
Stages of Value Experience

A Stages of Valuation	B Organisation of Values	C Nature of Values	D Nature of Social Relations
I. Choice of goals	1. Determination of specific urges and interests. 2. Competition and conflict of urges and interests. 3. Instinctive and casual behaviour. 4. Development of individuality.	Subjective; instrumental ; fleeting and potential.	Constant opposition between personal goals and social requirements. Casual social relationships; rigid control and conformity.
II. Construction and cultivation of ideals.	1. Criticism, appreciation and ranking of urges and interests. 2. Integration of urges and interests into a common 'purpose.' 3. Transformation of 'behaviour' into 'conduct'. 4. Stimulation of will. 5. Organisation of urges, sentiments and achivements into character and personality.	Subjective; instrumental; stable; and potential.	Validation of personal goals by society; establishment of stable social relationships; criticism and improvement of social relationships in terms of ideals.
III. Systematisation and prescription of norms	1. Intellectual reconstruction and development of the ideals into a coherent harmonious organic structure. 2. Identification with the spiritual order of the universe. 3. Complete resolution of conflicts of goals and ideals of every individual and of every group. 4. Highest order of truth, universality and requiredness. 5. Highest development of character and personality within the social community.	Objective; instrinsic; actual; and imperative.	Validation of goals and ideals by the transocial reality or deity; establishment of the deepest self and the widest communion or commonalty; recreation of human reltionships and the social order by standards that transcend current social codes and moral practices.

goals rooted in the primary urges and interests of man. The second step is the determination or formulation of the ideal or idea. All goals are instrumental values, *i.e.*, means for the fulfilment of intrinsic personal values. Without the control and experience of goals from level to level of social adaptation, the experience of the intrinsic values of life becomes haphazard and accidental. All ideals are also instrumental values. Man's knowledge of the ideal is a means to the production and experience of values. In the value-situation experienced there should be not merely a feeling of fulfilled urges, preference of enjoyment but also a clear definition or classification. The value-situation is clarified, criticised and classified in the knowledge of the *ideal*, Man's value experience thus includes both the feeling of satisfaction of specific urges, interests or goals and the knowledge that he *ought* to prefer the goals shared or divided with fellowmen in society and in preference to or association with other goals of life. A goal and an ideal are different from a norm. Amidst the conflict and tension of empirical goals and incomplete ideals, stability, harmony and coherence are provided by *norms* that are characterised by imperativeness. Neither human goals and interests conceived biologically or economically grovel on the earth; nor ideals or norms live in paradise. All cooperate and interpenetrate in real life, in concrete human relations, achieving the eternal, the rational and the universal on the earth here and now.

The primary experience of value cannot be analysed except from the integration of the biological, sociological and philosophical viewpoints. Society guides man in the differentiation, gradation and preference of his various urges, interests or goals in the biological, economic, social and spiritual spheres. Social intelligence, belief and communication help not only in the organisation of man's goals and values with reference to one another and in the definition of the properties and quantity of the objects of values, but also in the criticism, appreciation and validation of goals and values, i.e., in the formulation of ideals. The individual rises above private, evanescent goals and values in his choice and appreciation of ideals that imply criticism, reflection and intellectual reconstruction of values. Memory and imagination help him to stabilise and enhance values as ideals amidst the frustrations of actual life; while the abstraction and generalisation of ideals give values a new tone, dimension and context. Along with intellectual systematisation, there is also the organisation of the will in the realisation of the ideal. The ideal stimulates the will to a particular goal and course of action; it changes instinctive and casual behaviour into *conduct* and competing or conflicting *goals* into conscious aims or *purposes*. It also reshapes the psychological individual into a social person whose value-seeking not only secures self-realisation and happiness but also welds him to the community in a variety of stable social relations and institutions. The value situation involves not only a unique enjoyment of certain specific instincts and interests and a certain specific consciousness of goals and their consummation, but also the deliberate pursuit of these as *purposes* for complete living in a socially organised world.

Man is concious of both the search and achievement of the ideal and of its relations to each other in the total movement of a life's plan set harmoniously within the historical social world of common purposes and ideals. This implies twin series of movements, inward or mental, outward or social: (*a*) the conscious striving after certain values in preference of others amidst a multiplicity of human values of different grade and urgency. Persistence, harmony and ranking in value-seeking and achievement are associated with happiness, self-realisation and completeness. The organisation of the various types of values, biological, social and spiritual, and the corresponding systematisation of attitudes, sentiments and achievements measure the development of personality and character; (*b*) the conscious control or transformation of social situations by their translation into terms of particular values and ideals. This is associated at once with man's self-status, and social status, and with the improvement and enrichment of human relations within the process of realisation of values. Man's real sense of values includes both status-seeking and an ideal, prophetic criticism of social relationships that bear the seeds of the transformation of social groups. These movements are complementary to each other in the individual's mental development in a social milieu within which he appreciates, judges, and achieves values. The ideal indicates both the conscious realisation of the total self of the individual as well as the parallel of the social community. In the ideals, values are rationalised and impersonated, integrated with the ever larger organisations of experience, past, present and future as well as individual and collective.

Over and above the ideals are the *norms* that are universal definitions of perfection—the imperative ideals of the evolutionary struggle of life, mind and society. Norms have a detachment, impersonality, universality and requiredness that ideals, not to speak of goals, never possess.[11] Norms are related to the heart of the self and of the world process, to Being and Becoming. Man by the untrammelled play of his intellect and sentiments, his profound insight and ecstasy finds norms as constituting both his deepest self and the essence of existence. Man and society in a regime of chaos and confusion of values choose special kinds of ideals that must be realised by everybody everywhere and that form a coherent, harmonious structure among themselves, *i.e.*, they prescribe norms. The norms define objectively the true teleological structure of the cosmos, Forms and Ideas of the just, the good and the beautiful. These are purposes of the cosmic Group mind or deity, but their home is in man's reason, honour and conscience and their work is in his social and legal order, in his freedoms, laws, rights-and duties and institutions. Value experience is always experience within the social community, a Crowd, Interest-group, Society or Commonalty, indicating different levels of social integration and depths of the individual self as well as the status of values. The organised realisation of the highest values implies at once the profoundest depth of the personality and the most intense temporal equality and solidarity of mankind. The normative order that is grounded in the teleological nature of the universe beckons both individual and society to reach out to goodness, justice and wisdom greater than are yet realised. In its creativeness, self-criticism and self-transcendence, it ever draws man and society onward in their strivings to fulfil themselves as parts of an unrealised future, of the eternal movement of history. No doubt religion supplies the inspiration for the sense of the universal validity and imperativeness of norms as defining the order of the universe and the purpose of the cosmic mind or deity. Norms can in fact never emerge unless the world process and existence or some aspects of this are conceived in some manner as eternal, spiritual or teleological.

Religion as the Supreme Trans-personal Value of the Ordering and Sharing of Values

The most supreme and integrated among the ideal values is that represented by religion. Religion comprises man's art of inner adjustment by which he apprehends the universe as a whole instead of its particular parts that in its divisiveness and multiplicity are of significance in his practical adaptation to the material world out of which science arises. The 'holistic' approach of art and religion is to be contrasted with the analytical method of science. Man's feelings of awe, wonder, holiness, unity or harmony are imposed by the experience of totality and wholeness, and are universal and constant, although these are developed most among the mystics whose elevated ecstasy, competence and mastery over the environment have stimulated man's hope and courage in the bafflement, perplexity and unhappiness of his lot through the ages. Religion is thus grounded in the universal nature of human consciousness itself. "The universe takes man all of a heap" and this accounts for the sense of mystery, wonder or abasement characteristic of the religious sentiment. The stirring of the deeper levels of consciousness and apprehension of identity of self, its values and the universe produce the quality of ensemble associated with the insight and emotional ecstasy of the noumenon. At the same time man finds the religious object or the noumenon akin to him, deeply satisfying and enhancing his own impulses, emotions and strivings and so personal. Man's strange fetishes, heroes and gods of worship are always personal or superpersonal embodying human life goals, perfections and aspirations. It is out of the thrill, expansion and depth of his emotions and desires that he usually experiences the universe as a continuum and whole, and thus the universal is revealed in religious contemplation as the universal self or his own self or as the deity with the reconciliation to whom his whole life is bound up. The intimate human relationships in which man experiences a pervasive joy, serenity and poise become the creators and carriers of religious sentiment and experience. Religion accordingly develops the all-important social function of creating and maintaining the conditions of enduring and satisfactory human relationships. Out of the joys and intimacies of stable personal relations emerges man's valuation of himself and others. He finds that the stability and perfection of human relations lie not in domination and subordination, but in equality and fraternity, not in the use of a fellow-human for his own end or interest but in reciprocal love and tenderness. Such equality and fraternity, love and tenderness carry the self beyond the limits of finite experience. An ecstasic contemplation of the relation of self to another self reveals the infinite and the universal in the finite and the particular other person. The infinite and the universal that is thus revealed through the emotional rapport and elevated contemplation of mutuality between one person and another is the Person of Persons or the Universal Personality, who becomes the source, the norm, the model and the symbol of all finite human relationships. The idea of God as the Supreme Person whether as the Eternal Lover or the Beloved, the Universal Father, Madonna, Friend or Master is the outcome of the universalising of man's actual intimate loves, tenderness and loyalties in the family and kindred. The true meaning and significance of concrete personal relationship are disclosed to elevated contemplation as the self stands in universal relation to the Universal Personality, and this completely transforms and transfigures the concrete human and social world. The core of the religious sentiment is the valuation of personal relations and experience, the quality of which depends upon sharing, communion or rapport. Religion, above everything else, stands for the equality of the human person and the sharing of the values of life in a spiritual family, brotherhood or commonalty that it imposes upon the human community. Like human loves, affections and loyalties through which man transcends himself in a concrete empirical experience, religion imports the absolute and transcendental values into finite human relations and experience. Religion bridges the gulf between absolute and empirical values, between transcendence and desire. Religion impelled by such instinctive patterns as calm resignation, consecrated service and the love of parents, of child, of friend, and man-woman love, or rather expressing herein the fundamental needs of man's own nature, ensures stability and balance in emotional life and gives him not only a supreme competence in ways of living and adaptation but also a transcendental vision of personal relationship that infinitely enhances his capacity for effective and harmonious co-operation in society.[12]

Borrowing its symbols from the varied loves and loyalties of human relationship, religion gives to the world the social ideal of an infinite charity, compassion or love that bind together all men in one simultaneous and eternal relationship with God. It is thus that from man's relation to God all finite human relationships are derived and measured. Religion as the sense of the universal includes the social. The formulation of social and of religious ideals often corresponds. Where religion is not prevented nor obscured by dogma and superstition, the bonds between man and fellowman are transformed into religious symbols and *vice versa*. The potentialities of religion for society are best discerned in the revelation of human acts of fellowship, love and service as religious rites and observances. Religion places human relationships on a satisfactory footing beyond the recurrent menace of injury, warping or exploitation and proclaims the infinite value of personality-in-the Divine, the majesty and dignity of the common man. It converts the Crowd, Interest-association and Society into Commonalty. All its rites, ceremonials and observances become symbols of man's amity and brotherhood that in some world religions have embraced a world community, a brotherhood of all humanity and even of all sentient existence. Since religion offers man the highest both in the order of Nature and in the destiny of Humanity, it comes to assume the function of guarding, integrating and ordering the varied values of life. Eliciting as it does the highest adoration or reverence, it unifies man's desires and values by a proper and orderly hierarchy, and gives a wholeness, unity and superhuman direction to his personal life. Religion in the full universal scope of its function is the supreme creator, protector, arbiter and guide of values. Many ideal values, again, cannot be achieved or established in society. It is religion that makes man cherish and aspire after them in the midst of his defeat and despair. Religion in the last resort is the ultimate sustainer of values, projected as these are to the Divine personality in which man's finite values have their ground and being. It therefore sustains his imagination, love and social sympathy in his manifold crises and defeats. Without the transcendental hopes and passions of religion no society can maintain the courage, determination and faith in the visions of social equality, justice and love that are recurrently shattered by the social processes.

The Social Nature of Ideal Values

Society and nature constantly impinge upon and qualify man's ego-centric instincts and desires and at the same time provide the individual with new goals, values or ideals in which such instincts and desires could be redirected or fulfilled through sublimation or disguise in keeping with social harmony and efficiency. Therein lie the unique and dominating roles of imagination and symbolisation in the satisfaction of the ordinary desires and values of life. In this hard and cruel world, it is the symbols that society creates and easily communicates to the individual, and the latter's capacity to respond to them that underlie the adequate fulfilment of a great many values in life. T. V. Smith aptly remarks: "Historically man's life has been a dreary story of lacks, of pressing wants and unsatisfied desires. Now, the basic trait of the human animal is that given a lack he supplies it with a fancy. If emotional satisfaction is denied, the object or experience which would satisfy arises as an idea: the hungry one dreams of food; socially isolated under the pressure of glandular growth, one conjures up in imagination Ideal Maidens and Prime Charmings; pinched by penury, one fabricates scenes of golden grandeur. That man acts thus is a commonplace; but it is perhaps not quite such a commonplace to say that all our sciences and logics are but the several deposits made at successive levels by the human imagination in its restless flight from nagging want."[13] Society and culture also select and grade instincts and desires and their modes of fulfilment, fashioning and consolidating both the principles of personality development and expression and of social integration and solidarity. From the point of view of human motivations those are worthy that integrate themselves with the largest number of impulses and attitudes in man's social living; and this is possible only through some degree of intellectual or ideal satisfaction that permits the amplest scope for the expansion of certain specific impulses and the expression of other impulses. From the standpoint of human goals and values those are worthy that lead to the integration and expression of the individual as a social being. Society and culture ceaselessly promote the qualitative improvement of human impulses and attitudes so that these multiply and reinforce themselves and expand and awaken other impulses and attitudes as well. Such is the elevation of impulses into ideal values about which law, morality, art and religion gather. On the one hand, ideal values make the full integration and expression of the self possible. On the other hand, the solidarity of society or the development of moral consciousness of the community rests on the awakening of ideal values. Because of the social nature of human nature, ideal values must be also social in their nature and reference. Ideal values depend for their strength, variety and richness on the spiritual legacy of the society, and serve as constant spurs to fresh intellectual insights and understandings and moral visions of beauty and goodness, that progressively bind man and man by ever new affective and intellectual ties, in ever new shared feelings and experiences. Society and culture thus harness, educate and transform the basic human motives for building up emotional patterns that down the ages and in all societies bring about poise, competence and mastery of the individual over the environment, and also a richer and more harmonious communion between the individual and society. The acme of ethical culture is rooted in the processes of learning and social conditioning, of the facilitation, inhibition and organisation of primordial instincts and desires that become the seats of man's supreme understanding and valuation of himself and his fellowmen.

The Divergence of Morality in Typical Social Relations

The above analysis of the transformation of impulses, desires and attitudes into ideal values enables us to arrive at an adequate classification of man's basic social relations and degrees of group cohesion or solidarity. The stability and solidarity of the group depend upon the range and variety of impulses, attitudes and values it can integrate and include. Raw emotions acting blindly and isolatedly and primitive behaviour sunder man from fellowman and split up groups. Social evolution implies the discipline of egocentric impulses, desires and satisfactions in the milieu of groups and associations. These latter blend and co-ordinate the ensemble of impulses and desires in a manner that will serve society. Thus the complex and intricate pattern of Interest-group and other stable groups of various kinds—replacing the Crowd and the Mass elevates naive impulses and desires into ideal values and rational goals that society deliberately creates and nourishes for its own welfare and permanence. Such ideal values and enduring purposes permit the largest number of desires and impulses to multiply and reinforce one another. This contributes towards the highest solidarity and universality of the group. Man's pattern of group life and connections, acting for several generations, determines the organisation of desires and interests and hence the components of personality. The various types of groups determine what impulses and values compose the foreground, how the mass of impulses, interests and values is blended and harmonised and what combinations produce that enduring harmony which we call character in the life of the individual and morality in the life of society.

Table 4.2 gives the basic categories of groups that may be regarded as ideal "types", using Weber's methods, abstracted from the social reality, but characterised by psychological trends significant for sociological and ethical classification.

The four contrasted basic types of social integration viz., Crowd, Interest-association, Society and Commonalty are met with in ail human communities. The Crowd is the most unstable group exhibiting primitive types of relation and behaviour and is not constructive at all. On the contrary its action, dominated by primal instincts and emotions, is often destructive. In the history of social development the Crowd is the mechanism by which individuals seek by direct action immediately and spontaneously to remove lapses, offences or evils that law, custom, folkway or tradition would do slowly. Thus crowd behaviour is lawless behaviour. In modern communities the crowd is the device universally used to develop a revolutionary situation for asserting, attacking or wresting economic or political power. The Crowd operating violently on primal motives is an enemy not only of law and order, but also of private interest and judgment of the individual. For the crowd or mass-man, ego-consciousness and hence the sense of individual responsibility completely disappear. The rapport with the crowd is the result of the attenuation or negation of individual consciousness. In Commonalty there is a maximum interpenetration of consciousness and behaviour, as in the crowd, but here it is the result of conscious discipline, intellection and deepening of consciousness rising into mystical ecstasy and insight. Sometimes as a result of war, revolution, persecution and threat of disaster, society in which unity or cohesion is inherent suddenly develops into a complete fusion, i.e., into Commonalty. On the other hand a state of cohesion under intense social pressure often takes the character of crowd or mass. The difference of cohesion in crowd or mass and in commonalty rests on the stress of primal emotions and instinctive reactions in the case of the former and of intellectual or ideal values and rational purposes in the case of the latter.[14]

Commonalty may be and often is achieved by meditation in isolation from the community when the individual can experience a most intense "self-consciousness that at the same time becomes the most profound consciousness of solidarity. Crowd rapport must always presuppose not only physical contiguity of individuals but also similarity of their psycho-physical constitution, interest and experience that helps towards an easy banishment of self-consciousness and feeling.

In the deepest recesses of the self dwells the sense of the whole and the eternal that elicits cooperative and infinite love and frees it from the shackles of eager desires, trivial thoughts and little deeds. A new understanding of the universal and the infinite, a new feeling of membership of the whole lead to communion and sharing

TABLE 4.2

Classification of Groups, Values and Morals

A Type of Group	B Nature of Group Participation	C Nature of Self-consciousness
I. Crowd	Instinctivemotor, non-moral.	Primal gregarious self, imitative, suggestible, emotional, with complete inhibition of thoughts and ideas.
II. Interest-Association	Emotional-rational, a-moral.	Fractionalised occupational self, egoistic and aggressive with strong class consciousness and feeling.
III. Society	Emotional-rational, moral	Fractionalised self of status, rank and power with less exclusive ideas and feelings.
IV. Cmmonalty	Ideological-mystical, trans-moral	Most profound integrated self of contemplation and ecstasy, corresponding to the most intense collective consciousness and feeling.

TABLE 4.2

Classification of Groups, Values and Morals

D Nature of Group Reactions		E	F
Positive	Negative	Ethical Norms	Nature of Morality
Group solidarity based on primitive emotions; irrational group behaviour based on suggestion.	Group exclusion based on blind mass anger, hate. aggression and destruction.	Nil	Heteronomous : Strongest external pressure of the community; punishment by law.
Individual assertion and reciprocal impersonal service; individual conduct based on accommodation of interest to interest.	Impersonal conflict and retaliation without abrogating economic reciprocity.	Reciprocity or "Rules of the game" fairplay and consideration	Heteronomous : Moderate pressure of mores customs and folkways. Realisation largely of instrumental values by the individual.
Group solidarity based on integration of desires, emotions and interests ; group and individual conduct based on the adjustment of personality to personality as well as of interest to interest.	Group and personal egoism and conflict without abrogating rights of individuals *qua* individuals.	Equity and justice.	Autonomous : Realisation largely of intrinsic values by the individual.
Impersonal and universal goodwill, altruism and devotion to one's role and duties in complete detachment.	Nil	Love, equality and solidarity.	Autonomous : Creative moral initiative and freedom both of individual and society. Least pressure of external restraints.

that extend from the Interest-group and Society to Commonalty. In Commonalty the distinction between altruism and egoism: between social consciousness and self-consciousness vanishes. Man loves and serves his neighbour because he strives and suffers in his own impulses and aspirations; the neighbour is a part of himself as really as he himself exists. The neighbour is a symbol and a value that is infinite and universal, and it is this symbol or value that claims and dignifies all the evanescent, inconsequential thoughts, emotions and acts of the self. One who does not love his neighbour does not understand the potentialities of his own nature, nor the conditions under which shared values can transform him and society. The love, the compassion, the sympathy that the neighbour arouses are no more his than the self's, and thus these brook no boundaries. Self and neighbour merge together in Commonalty whose range is measured by the highest possible social consciousness, i.e., the deepest possible self-consciousness. Knowledge and love, understanding and sharing, one and indivisible, are the inherent laws of mind and society. The most intense and deepest self is the largest social community—Commonalty. It is noteworthy that in Hinduism and Buddhism there are mnemonic metaphysical symbols and symbolic formulae of meditation that help to break down the barriers between self and not-self, and establish the widest communion and solidarity. Such symbols may be contrasted with the slogans and catch-phrases that seek to create and maintain crowd hysteria or perpetuate the ideological differences between economic-classes and political parties.

While Crowd and Commonalty represent maximum social fusion, the special Interest-group and the Culture group in which individuals participate with fractions of their social selves are instances of partial fusion. Every society through social communication, discussion and judgment seeks to eliminate impulsive mobs, crowds, masses, gangs or magical sects. Real sociality rests on the differentiation of Interest-groups such as professions, classes, trade-unions, and political parties that lead individuals towards specifications of their habits, interests and values and of Cultural associations, churches and religious brotherhoods that lead them towards universality. Interest-groups are for the most part concerned with fractional, divisible, instrumental values, in which all individuals in a community cannot share. Society and Commonalty rest on the basis of realisation of indivisible, integral, intrinsic values that are enduring and also unite men in a common possession. Scheler observes: "That the social conflict of interests depends upon material goods and not on spiritual, rests not on the nature of the interest directed towards them (not, as it were, in the greater intensity of this), but on the nature of the values." Most instrumental values such as wealth, property, standard of living, social status and interest of the class are competitive in character. The success of an individual or group to acquire these implies a corresponding failure of others. instrumental values separate the persons who share them; intrinsic values, including health, appreciation of beauty, development of understanding and the great moral values are all unifying, defined as these are in terms of individual need and worth and social well-being. The realisation and enhancement of the intrinsic values of living indirectly promote full and rich mutuality, offering opportunity for the transition from the level of Interest-association to that of Commonalty. Every step taken by an individual in the common life with fellowmen is a sacrifice or sharing of goods or instrumental values with others even though the latter may not be aware of this. Interest-association, Society and Commonalty are the three major types of rational social participation. These are all absolutely indispensable; none can be eliminated without detriment to the whole culture.

Man's social selves are indeed distributed between the Interest-association, Society and Commonalty fulfilling the fundamental interests and values. Each type of association, each level of social cohesion is based on different valuations and develops divergent attitudes, loyalties and virtues as well as distinctive norms or standards of conduct that are obligatory for the individual, of course with variations of order and stress. Through the functions each group pattern fulfils in society, a different type of behaviour and loyalty is elicited as well as the most relevant norm and code for regulating conduct. At the same time every culture, every community promulgates with justification its own scale of values, norms and virtues. For neither the major values of life cart be pursued nor harmonious social co-operation maintained without ethical demands or personal qualities that are more or less restricted to each level of social participation such as Economic Reciprocity within the Interest-association, Equity and Justice in Society, and Equality and Solidarity in Commonalty.

Yet the different norms and standards often intermingle and mutually support one another. Each single human association, indeed, combines elements of Crowd, Interest-group, Society and Commonalty in fluctuating proportions; and the group behaviour is a synthesis of the norms or standards relevant to each level of a "social integration". Men also think, feel and act in logic-tight compartments. Thus individuals may "commune" in the family group and with other individuals, as a religious sect, form a crowd with different individuals in regard to war, strike, election and other matters of social emergency, and compose a public with yet other individuals in respect of law and order and moral duties. The many mutually exclusive groups claim man's loyalties in the pursuit of the major values of life; and he gravitates to one or other of the stereotyped social interactions according to the level of his personality and the concrete social situation and experience. Thus his personality and intensity of social participation are in a state of viable equilibrium with a fluctuating scheme of values, duties and virtues.

The quality of the social group and of the values it stands for declines or improves with the stress of specific social relations belonging to the next lower or higher phase of social cohesion. Normal individuals regress to their primal psyche when they are members of a crowd or mass demonstration. Mass meetings, revivals and processions are mechanisms for transforming a sedate population into a Crowd. Catch phrases, set formulae, stereotyped greetings or slogans, flag-waving and brass-band maintain the crowd mentality and perpetuate the crowd mind in the personality of normal people. Propaganda is a most common instrument by which the mind of normal persons is transformed into the crowd mind. Not until the idea, beliefs and emotions—the subject matter of propaganda—are brought within the ambit of critical reasoning and discussion can the normal self replace the primal mass-self. Again, due to circumstances within the group and external pressures or the spell of the leader, an Interest-group of discontented or unemployed workers easily lowers itself to the level of a Crowd or mass at least for the time being. Or the mob, Crowd and strike demonstration may be pacified as the result of collective discussion and satisfaction of their legitimate demands and transformed into a stable Interest-group. Such transformation accompanies the supercession of methods of violence, sabotage or direct action, that are "immoral", by the acceptance of the norms of reciprocity and fair play and consideration that underlie the stability and recognition of a legitimate economic class in society. With the expulsion of fiery malcontent elements advocating class war, the Interest-group also attains greater solidarity than is met with in a rowdy demonstration of strikers or an assemblage of fire-eaters. It is also found that while the mass or crowd tends to spread out and grow in size like a tumultuous, enlarging avalanche, the trade-union organisation, where the solidarity is swayed less by primal passions and more by deliberate judgment and experience, falls off in numbers. In modern industrial communities the greater vogue of parliamentary, judicial and expertized enquiries and discussions tends to smooth out disagreements in the industrial field and leads to a reciprocal understanding and integration of antagonistic economic interests on the basis of fair play and justice. As the demands of groups and classes become less exaggerated and rebellious, there is more of toleration, forbearance and security in society. Methods of social control become less arbitrary, forceful and repressive; propaganda on both sides is carried on with less zest and hood-winking; and all elements and factors in conflict situations are brought into the open for public criticism, discussion and judgment, aided by the specialised knowledge and experience of experts and technicians. Out of a free, full and undistorted debate of the issues in which not separate publics but the total society takes a keen and intelligent part are hammered out social consensus and solidarity and consistent social policy. The Interest-group achieves even greater solidarity if its rules of the game of reciprocity and fair competition are supported by a mutual recognition of the personality of the partners in an industrial enterprise. It is in this way that equity and justice can strengthen the impersonal, objective economic bond based on reciprocal interest or service and establish a new industrial partnership and morale. Similarly as Society advances through the cultivation of the spirit of mutuality to Commonalty, equity and justice based on a prudential consideration of competing interests and rights of individuals are given up. In the intimate and personal relations of Commonalty, love, equality, and solidarity replace justice. As a matter of fact perfect justice that seeks the equalization of opportunities for all cannot be established in society without the spirit of mutuality being raised to white heat by some kind of a religious morality with its trans-social ideal that can temper equity and justice by the equality of love and affection. As Niebuhr puts it, "Any non-rational instrument of justice cannot be used without great peril to society, if it is not brought under the control of moral goodwill. Any justice which is only justice soon degenerates into something less than justice. It must be saved by something which is more than justice".[15]

Nor is the spirit of mutuality or communion always integrative and expansive. Commonalty in the family, caste, gang, artists' brotherhood, political party or nation often confines love, devotion and sacrifice within the boundaries of the closed group. Thus familism, parochialism, gangsterism, nationalism and other forms of "in-group" exclusiveness become great enemies of the moral life. The solution lies of course in the development of "open-group" equality and solidarity, based on clarified, sublimated and idealised loves and sacrifices that may be extended to all humanity—the brotherhood of man, of all life. This is achieved mainly in religious contemplation and morality that canalise human devotion and solidarity to universal and trans-human channels. It is clear that in cases where Commonalty, as a real solidarity, instead of leading towards universalism, tends towards the particularisation of groups such as castes, religious sects, gangs, trade-unions or political parties, the bond is an intense emotional interpenetration that is to be clearly distinguished from rational social insight, clarification and communication that never recede in the background. A closed union like the political party, gang or secret revolutionary society shows an almost ecstatic fervour of cohesion, especially under cruel persecution or mortal danger, and develops symbolic rites of initiation and participation like the church or a religious brotherhood. Such groups indeed maintain often their social cohesion by splitting up into smaller groups acting with great solidarity under different leaders.[16] The psychological mechanisms of their unity and stability as well as their ethical norms are also far different. Devotion and solidarity in their case never go beyond their very restricted membership, while these extend in expanding circles in the case of the communions of spiritual contemplation.

Each individual in any particular social relation or group encounters a specific ethical problem, how to construct his life-organisation and orient his order of moral values binding himself, for example, to fair competition and consideration or to equity and justice, or again, to love and solidarity in the successive levels of life as represented by the three basic, stable social connections. The norms of conduct derived from the three fundamental categories of social groups and relationships constitute, indeed, a comprehensive ethical system for man in any society. No formal, absolute, super-personal or trans-social norms and imperatives are here postulated. Norms and ideals here emerge out of different categories of social interaction that become the seats of evaluations themselves. These are inherent in the different types of social relations that are the framework of value meaning, experience and fulfilment, it is the state of social participation of the individual or his group consciousness and feeling that determine both the category of social relations as well as his moral attitudes in ideal and in reality. Sociology furnishes norms and rules of conduct that are obligatory in that the obligation is operative or derived from certain existing and postulated social connections that cannot be abrogated without detriment to both society and the personality of the individual. In other words ethical principles and norms are not remote nor disinfected but are the data of sociology. These exist not in the abstract but only within a set of functional groups and institutions, only as ethical principles and norms relevant to and promulgated by the different group patterns.

Each of these ethical principles can build up whole social systems and cultures. Ordinarily for social adaptation what every individual does is to confine the different ethical demands to the different types of social groups and relations among which his social selves are distributed. Thus in the familistic group love, devotion and solidarity rule. These subordinate egoism and self-assertion of business, profession and politics and stress a complete sharing of life and its values that rises above the shrewd calculation of claims and counter-claims by justice. In the secondary Interest-groups fair play and consideration are fundamental, eliminating dishonesty, unreliability and an inadequate, inefficient or unsatisfactory fulfilment of the job, service or accepted obligation. In other types of social relations, outside the economic and the familistic, equity and justice are the accepted norms. Man's total conduct exhibits conflicts and contradictions that sometimes through the loss of self-status leads to personal disorganisation. But often he can also harmonize the divergent ethical claims satisfactorily. All this depends as much upon his family tradition, social and religious milieu as upon his moral creativeness and experience.

The Three Successively Higher Ethical Principles

The divergent ethical demands of the individual are applicable to groups and collectives. As a result of social communication, experience, discussion and judgment the ethical norm derived from each particular type of social grouping is intellectualized and idealized and extended to all inter-group relations. Each ethical norm, Reciprocity in the Interest-group, Equity and Justice in Society, and Love, Equality and Solidarity in Commonalty, is sought to be elevated by every culture into an ideal, universal ethical system. Reciprocity is extended to economic relations between different nations that are sought to be welded together into a world economic community by international codes of labour, inter-regional and international agreements in respect of trade, employment, monetary policy, supply of food and capital needs, labour conditions, standards of living or migration and cooperation in positive international tasks such as rehabilitation, reclamation and colonisation. The UNO, the ILO and the FAO have now set before themselves these programmes. A world community and world citizenship are also now envisaged based on the recognition of the rights of colonial and less advanced peoples. The aggressive and exploitative colonial policy and imperialism of the past decades are sought to be counteracted by international collaboration for the general improvement of mankind through an extension of the principles of justice and equity to all backward peoples. Finally, love, devotion and brotherhood in the family circle are extended to the tender care for the handicapped, the diseased and the unfortunate in society and *ahimsa* or non-violence towards the animal world. The equality and solidarity of all life that Commonalty claims indeed characterise the morality of Hinduism, Buddhism and Christianity. Such world religions have contributed in no small measure to educate mankind in charity, compassion and love, eliciting individual and group sacrifices through the centuries. It is noteworthy that in the Kantian system of ethics the qualities, compassion, charity and solidarity, have no place although the major religious systems have established solidarity as a universal ethical principle.

Even as a universal ethical principle, reciprocity or justice shows its limitations and is incompatible with world ethics and citizenship. The dissipation of scarce resources by a particular people and the bolstering up of its standard of living through economic imperialism or rigorous immigration policy lower the standard of living of other peoples and regions. The world economic community can be achieved here by something which is more than economic reciprocity. Economic conflict and struggle of peoples cannot indeed be eliminated except with the recognition of the equal rights and status of backward and coloured peoples. Without a new hierarchy of values economic internationalism, based on the principles of reciprocity, cannot, therefore, succeed. Similarly within the boundaries of the same political community, the policy of the conservation of resources involves the reduction to some extent of the standard of living of the present generation in the interest of the future inhabitants. This is possible only as a result of sacrifice for the brother of tomorrow that is excluded from the economic ideal even of a socialistic community as represented by maximum aggregate satisfaction. It is also coming to be more and more recognised that the unity of mankind cannot be achieved only by the instruments of justice and equity. For the precise definition of equity and justice leads to assertion and counter-assertion of interests and rights and to coercion against those who encroach upon the rights of others leading to fresh conflict, and this develops into a vicious circle. Without the extension and elevations of the spirit of mutuality in international relations the attainment of justice in world affairs is impossible. It need not be stressed that many of the unavoidable oppositions between the different universal ethical principles have yet to be grappled, and as a matter of fact the extension of these to humanity has sometimes been emphatically denied. For instance, it is declared by Hugh Cecil that "all that department of morality which requires an individual to sacrifice his interests to others, everydoing which falls under the heading of unselfishness, is inappropriate to the action of a state. No one has a right to be unselfish with other people's interests."[17] Modern civilised man is indeed morally distraught when what he adores in his conscience and strives for in his inter-personal relations is altogether eschewed in his complex, indirect and collective human relations. In so far as he cannot translate equity, justice and goodwill into actual collective relations and organised community goals these qualities become ambiguous, futile sentiments—called universal love, humanism or the brotherhood of the race—which have no meaning and with which contemporary politics and sociology are so replete. Yet no doubt that in the social and cultural situation of today the individual is morally much more creative and powerful than his group, class or nation. The selfishness and egoism of his class are an insult to his reason and sense of fair play as his nation's aggressiveness and economic injustice to other countries and peoples frustrate his ideal of equity and justice. The brotherhood which his community achieves also falls short of what his passions of love, equality and goodwill would establish. It is thus that the conscience and faith of the individual will moralize the community and add to the majesty of its power, the depth of love and goodwill of the individual.

References

1. See Malinowski : The Scientific Approach to the Study of Man in Anshen: *Science and Man*, pp. 213-235, and *Freedom and Civilization*, pp. 134-137; also Klineburg : *Social Psychology*, pp. 150-153.
2. Katz mentions that the only example of animal use of intoxicants is that of ants drinking the exudations of beetles that they tend in their nests and in their intoxication even giving their brood to the former as food. (See his *Animals and Men*, p. 175.)
3. Prescott : *Emotion and the Educative Process.*
4. *The Individual and His Society.*
5. G. W. Allport : *Personality*, p. 150.
6. *Cooperation and Competition among Primitive Peoples.*
7. This technological theory of value is recently stressed by G.R. Geiger and C E. Ayres.
8. See Boodin : *The Social Mind*, pp. 307-313.
9. See Langer : *Philosophy in a New Key;* and Morris : *Signs, Language and Behaviour*, ch. VII.
10. See my *The Philosophy of Social Science*, pp. 5-8, 111-112.
11. E. S. Brightman : Value and Existence, *Philosophy and Phenomenological Research*, December, 1943.
12. See my *Theory and Art of Mysticism*, Macmurray : *Structure of Religious Experience* ; also Gibson : *The Structure of Community*, pp. 98-107.
13. Philosophical Ethics and the Social Sciences, *Social Forces*. September, 1928.
14. The distinction has been ignored by Gurvitch. See his article, Mass, Community, Communion in the *Journal of Philosophy*, 1941, pp. 492-495; also his chapter on Social Control in *Twentieth Century Sociology*, pp. 287-291.
15. Moral Man and Immoral Society, p. 258.
16. See Spykmann : *The Social Theory of Georg Simmel*, p. 117.
17. Hugh Cecil : *Conservatism*, p. 182.

5

THE ORDER OF MORAL VALUES AND SANCTIONS: CONSCIENCE, HONOUR AND LAW

Human Culture and the Biological Drives

Man satisfies all his basic instincts and desires in a derivative environment. His secondary milieu, for the sake of convenience, may be classified info four orders, biological, economic, social and ideal. For each order, his divergent instincts and needs are satisfied in an indirect manner through a complicated system of culturally derived, instrumentally adjusted responses. All values of the different orders are achieved through the complex, all-pervasive instrumentalism of human culture that guides him in finding a much more effective and readier adaptation to the environment than in the case of animals. Such adaptation is also conscious. Man unlike any animal is aware of his round-about, complicated adjustments, and changes deliberately the conditions of his adjustment through remoulding his cultural heritage or the set-up of normative rules, traditions and beliefs to suit his less malleable instincts and desires.

From the very beginning of human social development cultural interests are superimposed upon and modify the organic and imperative drives. The view of some social psychologists that hunger and sex remain the fundamental autonomic drives or that the goals of culture comprise the satisfaction of the wishes for security, response, recognition and new experience is inadequate and unacceptable. No stage of man's corporate existence is conceivable without the interplay between man's organic and utilitarian needs and culturally derived, ideal values and symbols expressed in social custom, usage and institution. Primitive men's use of economic tools and procedures was enlivened by the artistry of religious dance and ritual. Their love and courtship were elaborated and refined by social etiquette, dance and music in an atmosphere of collective romance and hilarity that made sex shed its grosser features. Men talked or sang or danced or discussed one another's experiences as they performed their exacting economic routine or undertook new adventure. The invention of tools and weapons was the result of co-operative discussion. The hunting and fishing expedition or the arduous labour in the fields and orchards was preceded by magic and ritual observance, and relieved by choral song and rhythmical bodily movement. Magic and religion performed the psychological function of instilling confidence and power against animals or human enemies, dissipating fear among a primitive people stricken by forest fire, hurricane, earthquake or epidemic, and engendering optimism in their chase, fishing or agricultural operation. Taboo, etiquette and ritual were all inextricably interwoven with the daily routine of life or the crises of birth, puberty, marriage and death. These represent the beginnings of morality rooted in the community's approval or disapproval, praise or blame of certain behaviour patterns. There is hardly any level of man's adjustment, biological, economic or social, in which evocative and stimulative symbol devices, enhancing the satisfaction derived from the discharge of routine duties, and repressive symbols such as taboos and regulations, preventing or punishing failures or lapses therefrom, cannot be discovered. In hunting, in the domestication of animals, in agriculture, in the construction of houses, in love, in warfare and in trade, man's ideal values and symbolic and cultural activities proper, as represented by his search for practical knowledge, justice, beauty and religion, interpolated. These yielded profound group satisfaction and cemented the unity of the tribe or horde needed for co-operative effort. Gradually as culture progressed, knowledge, art and religion came to be sought as specific values or intrinsic values. But from the very start of civilization man's cultural products and symbolic devices took hold of and became continuous with the fulfilment of his organic urges and interests.

The Genesis of Morality

Human culture that constitutes man's derivative environment is an ever-changing, dynamic legacy of tools of adaptation, objective and symbolical. It comprises both the fluctuating pattern of groups that focus and create values and symbols, and the more enduring institutional framework that integrates and conserves values and symbols. Man seeks and finds values, to be sure, not in isolation but through the mediation of groups and institutions. These are indispensable for his adaptation in an environment, refashioned and readjusted. At the same time these condition and mould his impulses and behaviour, modifying and extending both values and the manner of their satisfaction. At different levels of adaptation, this derivative environment imposes restrictions at the same time as it presents opportunities for the fulfilment of urges and values of the different orders or planes. The derivative or secondary restrictions are defined into imperatives—man's rules of conduct in the biological, economic and social planes. For each order or plane values are sought and achieved within a set of laws, regulations and conventions in respect of the use of tools, labour and property, in respect of mobility, freedom and power, or as regards sex, marriage and parenthood; and his code of honour and ethical and religious norms and principles and such concepts as equality, justice, solidarity, truth, beauty and goodness also impose imperatives upon his conduct in society.

All these make up the individual's code of duties, moral, jural and religious, besides the *mores* or technical code of duties that are concerned with the daily routine of economic toil and social etiquette and intercourse. Mores and other folk-ways are to be contrasted with morals. The former are "practical, expedient and compulsive" and represent horse-sense. Repetitive routine, habit and practical convenience underlie their ascendancy in every society. These are so pervasive that a mature person obtains automatic guidance in most social situations in their terms rather than with reference to more rational procedures. Morals, Lee has aptly stressed, have no necessary congruity with a group's mores or with an individual's conscious habit patterns, and in fact the process of becoming mature in the group consists largely in a person accommodating his moral super-ego to the needs of a moretic person. On the other hand, much of theology is concerned with working out rationalisations between morals and group mores.[1] The conventionalities of social intercourse, though these skim over the surface of human nature and do not touch the deeper levels of self, yet have an ethical significance of their own. 'Good form', tact, propriety, politeness and considerateness, whatever be the name adopted for the delicate and minute forms prescribed for day to day social dealing, are all based on certain genuine values of human disposition without which social bonds snap. It is only a person who lacks the irreducible minimum of self-control, simplicity, trust, dignity, sincerity, modesty and kindliness that violates the conventions of social converse, representing the necessary pre-conditions of the maintenance of social life. Even the superficial and external usages, manners and graces of everyday life accordingly rest on moral values, and obtain refinement and urbanity in some measure according to the sensitiveness and depth of the individual's moral feeling. In mores, manners and usages, then, ideal values are in some measure implicated. Aristotle also refers to certain virtues connected with man's converse and demeanour in word and act. It is not law but social etiquette and manners that comprise the ethical minimum. While a criminal is punished by law, a person who transgresses the ordinary conventional forms of social intercourse is punished by less formal and unconscious social mechanisms—laughter, derision, boycott and ostracism. Manners and conventional decorum are significant because these supply the inescapable, universal framework of human interaction within which individual emotion and valuation are compelled to work. Giddings wrongly excludes them from any reference to ideal values, He calls mores, social manners and conventionalities "non-appreciative" patterns or standards as contrasted with the appreciative ones, viz., moral, jural, aesthetic and religious. These latter may also be described as "symbolical patterns", (Gurvitch), symbols being related at once to ideals and to reality and mediating between both.

The distinction between appreciation and non-appreciation goes into the roots of the genesis of social morality. With Sumner mores have only a utilitarian basis. Mores are mores, and can make anything right or condemn anything as wrong, provided that these are backed by some customary routine or sanction. Similarly Westermarck stresses the emotional rather than the utilitarian basis of morality. With him the emotional expression of collective approval or disapproval is enough to distinguish between right and wrong. A French writer, Hopmann, has recently revived the sociological theory of morality of Sumner and Westermarck. According to him moral acts are judged on the basis of pleasure and pain derived from them; so that the criterion of good and bad depends on the social consequences of the act rather than upon the individual performing it. The approbation of society provides the pleasure derived from a moral unselfish act and promotes psychic equilibrium of the person performing it. On the other hand, disapprobation by society eschews socially disapproved behaviour through the effect of the painful feeling associated with it. Thus moral obligation is grounded in the utilitarian motive of pleasvire and pain derived from approving or disapproving reactions of society. In every community moral life, however, presupposes something more than mere rigid adherence to socially approved patterns or standards, whether these may be traced to utilitarian advantage or to the regulative and stimulating pressure of society in its role of the "headmaster". This is represented by the element of what Giddings calls "appreciation" that involves conflict, revolt and creativeness in the sphere of individual conscience, reason and faith. To miss this element of individual appreciation or spontaneous creation and transformation of patterns of conduct on the basis of the personal vision of ideal values is to ignore altogether the enrichment of group morality and culture by the contributions of individuals.

Morals owe as much to collective habit, experience and judgment as to the creative ethical genius of the individual that transcends the established patterns or standards of the group. "At different times," observes Bergson, "exceptional men appear in whom absolute morality seems to be embodied." Timasheff mentions that even in less highly developed societies (where higher types of religion are still impossible) a similar means of "moralising" the people has been tried. The Maoris instituted a "selection of girls to be trained as examples of conduct."[2] Such individual spontaneity, revolt and creation are discernible in all types of societies in the various fields of appreciative patterns of conduct, viz., moral, aesthetic and religious. Not merely morality but also art and religion are constantly renovated by the apprehension and creation of new values and ideas by individuals. Georges Gurvitch considers, however, that moral values should be distinguished from other ideal values in view of the greater role played therein by individual aspiration and creativness. "The moral life in all its manifestations is distinguished from jural, religious and aesthetic attitudes by its propulsion tendency towards the future, by a perpetual anticipation, by a constant revolt against all crystallizations and achievements of the past, which are regarded as obstacles to be transcended. Hence in both collective and individual life, usages, standards, symbols, in so far as they are related to moral values, are only the solidified results of past creativeness, which must ever be transcended in new efforts. This does not exclude the possibility of variation in the effective role of static and dynamic elements in moral life within different types of societies and at different historical epochs. Thus, for instance, one can explain the relative rigidity of moral standards and usages in primitive society by reference to their connection with religious taboos."[3]

Difference between Conscience, Honour and Law as Sanctions of Values

Morality and law express the conscience of the individual and the objective norm and standard of the community for the fulfilment and expression of human values and ideals. Sometimes the freedom and creativeness of individual genius, sometimes the collective habits, institutions and pressures of the community play the more effective role in the creation and transformation of the value system. Psychologists and sociologists have, however, ignored the social function of human honour. 'The sense of honour' is rooted in what McDougall calls 'the self-regarding sentiment,' and in the ego-drive of Freudian theory. From fellowmen's responses of praise or blame arises the feeling of honour or self-esteem. It is an integrated experience pieced together out of man's many statuses with his fellows in various groups—the family, the class, the profession, the church and so on. The approbation or disapprobation of fellowmen in a person's diverse roles and statuses in social life brings about a corresponding reaction in his inner life to his own attitude or conduct, and thus regulates his inner drives. And yet man's ego-esteem or honour, derived as it is largely from social interaction, is something different from conscience. Honour belongs to the superficial group and institutional selves of the individual. Conscience belongs to the most profound self. According to the psycho-analysts, conscience is derived from the unconscious and is equivalent to the super-ego. A part of the structure of conscience is no doubt inherited and primitive as the Psychoanalysts demonstrate although it differs from individual to individual. This is the Freudian super-ego but the Psychoanalysts miss the educability, maturation and transformation of the superego through social conditioning, training and guidance in value-fulfilment. The super-ego is not the whole of conscience.[4] Conscience has a significant, creative, rational part, which is entrusted with the role of total self-functioning, self-fulfilment and self-perfection, and to which the Psychoanalysts have not given sufficient attention. The super-ego, honour and creative conscience comprise a spectrum of internal standards and sanctions. Both the super-ego and honour are concerned with social adjustment, expectancy and approval and are coercive. More than the super-ego honour touches man's own ideal of self-functioning and self-status in the group or community. But it is conscience which best embodies the proper total functioning or disfunctioning of the self as it grows and matures, and elicits man's supreme moral adventure with associated inner joy, self-competence and pride. The calm triumph and exaltation of man's genuine creative conscience over the limitations of his weak body are far different from the negative sense of guilt and self-torture due to response to the super-ego and from the negative feeling of humiliation and loss of self-status due to response to honour, standing and prestige. Man's sense of honour, standing or prestige is to be distinguished from both his conscience and from law as a guardian of right conduct. Conscience is the ultimate sanction of the values of life, the final and supreme judge or arbiter of all norms and behaviours. The sphere of conscience is the most extensive, just as there is no higher authority than its particular judgment of specific values and social situations. This is well brought out during the famous trial of Socrates. The ambit of law is the least extensive. Law does not go beyond the minimum of social control of individual behaviour and therefore depends upon physical force or constraint for its sanction. Man's honour depends partly upon his own character and self-respect, and partly upon the behaviour pattern of the family, the caste, the class, the profession or the gang to which the individual belongs. Right or 'honourable' conduct in this case rests on both what the norm of the group and the self-esteem of the individual demand. The sanctions of honour are accordingly both the subjective feeling of total self-status and social expectancy, approbation or ostracism by the group. Honour, unlike conscience, is not concerned with the deeper levels of the personality, but with the social or institutional selves that are distributed between the various groups in society building up the total self-status or honour of the individual. Just as conscience is the custodian of the autonomy of the individual, so honour safeguards the norm of value of the group more silently, pervasively and effectively than law or convention can do. Georg Simmel observes, "Conformity to the moral standard has no stronger sanction than that of good or bad conscience. Honour takes an intermediate position. Non-conformity is punished by means which are neither of a purely subjective character, like moral discomfort, nor of a purely external character, like the physical restraint in the legal sphere. With the formation of an honour standard protected partially by subjective moral consequences, society creates a guarantee for an adequate individual behaviour in spheres which lie outside the field of legal provisions and which cannot be left to individual morality."

Degrees of Sociality and Means of Social Control

Out of the interchange between the individual and the community, conscience, morality, honour and law have all emerged, guiding and regulating the individual's search for and achievement of values, and also man's behaviour and relations in this connection. Conscience regulates solely subjectively through the sense of guilt and inner harmony and joy. Honour regulates both subjectively and objectively through subjective feelings and pressures of the group. Law regulates solely objectively by physical methods. Conscience, honour, positive morality or law, springing as they do from the same human spirit, however, depend for their respective development on reciprocal aid and interpenetration, *i.e.*, the degree of social integration, stability and universality. We indicate in *Table* 5.1 the respective spheres of these means of social control and their sanctions that establish a scale of the degrees of sociality, *viz* Crowd, Interest-association, Society and Commonalty from both moral and sociological points of view.

Crowd represents the lowest and Commonalty the highest depth of sociality. Crowd or mob action is "immoral", dominated as it is by the primary impulses and the inhibition of the intellectual processes due to the exaggerated roles of unconscious imitation and impulsive suggestion. Social solidarity rises from instinctive-motor through emotional-moral to ideological-mystical unity. The Interest-group stands in between in respect of integration or stability. In Interest-group cohesion or stability depends upon rational calculation of the reciprocal interests of the individuals and is achieved or lost if the interests of either party are nullified or thought to be nullified. "The rules of the game" are here the rules of conduct that do not involve sacrifice, but on the other hand leave adequate room for self-assertion and aggression. Conflicts are here settled by law, appeal to the code of honour of the group, compromise, agreement or arbitration. The Interest-group is as removed from the ephemeral Crowd as from Society. The latter is characterised by common understandings and feelings, a genuine "we" sentiment with which are associated mutual respect of one's personality and rights. Hence

TABLE 5.1

The Order of Social Participation and Sanctions of Law and Morality

Degree of Sociality		htnical Norm	Means of Social Control	Sanction	Medium of Value Experience
I.	Crowd	Doindividualisation and Imitation.	Law.	Physical Restraint.	Primitive, Irrational Behaviour.
II.	Interest-association	Reciprocity or "rules of the game." Fair Play and Consideration.	Law and honour.	Physical Restraint and Social Expectancy.	Rational Fractional Behaviour. subject to customs, folk-ways and *mores*.
III.	Society	Justice and Equity.	Honour, Positive Morality and Law.	Physical Restraint, Social Expectancy and Self-status.	Rights-and- Duties in groups and institutions with their own moral standards, values and ideals.
IV.	Commonalty	Love, Equality and Solidarity.	Honour, Positive and Personal Morality, Conscience and Law.	Conscience (sense of self-hood, sei-censure and self-praise) and Creative Moral Freedom of the Individual.	Personal Creeds, Values and Ideais that transcend general social norms and prescriptions.

in Society, justice and equity emerge as rules of conduct added to fairness and consideration that are the virtues of reciprocity relations. In Commonalty we reach the most profound unition, the most intense "we", bound together by common understandings, meanings and values. The rules of conduct here are based on love, equality and sacrifice for the whole whose range knows no limits. Commonalty can embrace all mankind, even all sentient life. It demands universal love, devotion and brotherhood. The ethics of Commonalty is religious, trans-social. Thus religion is the guide and the best education for Commonalty. The equality and solidarity of all life are mystical concepts, representing at once the highest moral principle of conduct and the profoundest knowledge. It is a paradox that the most intense state of collective insight and ecstasy comes to man in his isolation and detachment from society that provides the condition of the greatest autonomy and creative freedom of the individual. Conscience is the supreme judge of all means of social control that are, indeed, transformed into blind despotic forces without its support. Man's sense of honour, positive morality as represented by mores, traditions and conventions, institutions as well as laws can remain living and become capable of progress only when these are in constant contact with the creativeness and venturesomeness of the individual conscience. On the other hand, his conscience can unfold itself only by working through and upon law, positive morality and honour. It is only through conformity to them that it can appraise their real signification and then criticise and revise them. As Socrates acquiesced in the death sentence meted out to him by law, the truth and goodness in the latter were realised. Law says to Socrates, "To act as though thou wert on due equality with thy country and with the laws, to return them wrong for wrong, blow for below, to attempt to defeat and destroy them, whereas, but for them, thou wouldst be neither a citizen nor a man, wouldst thou call that justice, thou who claimest to be enamoured of virtue ?" Yet Socrates had the supreme satisfaction as he embraced death of a good conscience, which is indeed the final judge of conduct.

Integration of Law, Morality, Honour and Conscience

The sanction of good behaviour is physical force exercised by law where man is dominated by primitive passions and desires and in his lowest stage of social integration as represented by the crowd, herd or mass. The latter are unstable social units, where he is swayed by temporary gusts of collective emotion. In integrated society with its variety of groups and institutions, real and stable collective units, his right and 'honourable' conduct is secured by his family honour, caste honour, professional standard or 'honour' among thieves and by the entire schedule of mores, manners, traditions, rights and duties and laws. In the highest stage of social integration or Commonalty when he experiences through insight and ecstasy the most profound rapport with the cosmic group mind that it identifies with Over-self, logos or God, it is his own reason and faith that determine the right or wrong of conduct. Law, positive morality, honour and conscience represent diminishing ambits of jurisdiction in respect of the regulation of human relations and behaviour. Conscience eludes both law and positive morality as it dictates what honour and law would demand from the individual. The sense of honour secures good conduct in spheres of human relations that can be reached neither by law nor even by social traditions and conventions. Finally, law can secure the right and just conduct only within the minimum spheres of human relations amenable to regulation by physical force. The good society uses the physical restraint of law to the minimum, and at the same time selects those types of restraints that are in consonance with the freedom, reason and moral initiative of the individual and with ethical social norms. A society using coercion not in the end of social justice and equality but for class interest and privilege on the one hand and temporary gusts of social passion and resentment on the other defeats its own ends. The doctrine that coercion is inevitable and must extend its range because man's selfishness and aggression cannot be completely subjugated creates more social inequality and injustice and disbalance of individual and social interests, leading to fresh laws and formulation of fresh rights that extend their range in a vicious circle. With education and extension of social intelligence and good-will, his conscience and honour will bring about a voluntary adjustment of interest to interest and right to right. The sharing of life, the exclusion of aggression and exploitation in every field of human relations will accompany the minimum of constraint and limitation of freedom and 'justness' of such relations based on the principle of communion or equality. It is through a communion of understandings and values rather than through laws, rights and institutions that social peace, justice and solidarity can be more easily reached.

All societies guide and regulate human relationships and behaviours and orient and integrate the values of life through law, honour, positive morality and conscience that assist, blend with and are determined by one another, and that have their respective expanding spheres of control from overt action to the imponderable values and attitudes according to the successive depth-levels of the self and of moral action. In the creation and transformation of man's moral values and ideals, not merely are the various depths of the personality involved but also various group and institutional selves that find themselves often in conflict with one another. Man lives constantly in the midst of a great battle of values and ideals. He has thus a viable scheme of values and patterns of behaviour—the outcome of a variety of subjective and external factors and norms as represented by law, habit, custom, tradition and group honour on the one hand, and the conscience of the individual on the other. The struggle for the higher values within the self seeking to achieve deeper and more integrated levels of experience, and the struggle for a better, juster society with more righteous social habits, customs and laws, act and interact. The social process reflects the faith, reason and moral freedom of the individual. The conscience of the individual is fortified and awakened by the habits, traditions and laws of society. The moral initiative and creativeness of the individual, whose conscience unfolds itself neither in isolation nor in independence, as it is often assumed, and the norms and laws of society are inseparable from one another.

The Ascent of Values and Norms—the Principle and Impulsion of Social Progress

Society directs the value-seeking of the individual. It instils into him conscience and the sense of honour, fashions moral code and law, and provides repressive and stimulative mores, standards and patterns regulating the fulfilment of his values. It also ensures and provides opportunities or conditions of such fulfilment; it creates claims of individuals and groups, *i.e.*, *rights*. The right of the common man to a decent standard of living is comprised of rights to food, work, marriage, family raising, property, education, protection, social security, leisure and wholesome recreation,—all the goals mentioned in *Table* 5.2, Column B. Such rights have increasingly asserted themselves in the laws of civilised communities. The right to, and duty of, maintenance of the standard of living coexist. The right to, and duty of, maintenance of status pertaining to one's occupation, profession or role also exist together implying the development of his occupation or status personality. A society's scheme of social stratification, mobility and distance recognises and supports the assignment and maintenance of individual's role, position and power. Law also comes in for the protection and support of these social values through the guarantee of several freedoms, of association, speech, assembly, movement and contract. The finer

TABLE 5.2

The Hierarchry of Goals, Ideals and Norms

A *Basic Desires, Tendencies and values*	B *Goals*	C *Ideals*	D *Ethical Norms* *Individual*	 *Social*
I. Biological: Hunger, Sex, Territory. Self-preservation, Rhythm of Play and Repose.	Food, Marriage and Family, Territory, Work, Use and Ownership of Tools, Education, Protection, Leisure, Recreation.	Human Individuality	Improvement and Survival of the Psychogenetic Personality.	Bio-ecological Co-operation for Continuity of Race and Habitat.
II. Economic : Appropriation, Possession, Curiosity, Constructiveness. Maturation, Movement.	Wealth, Domicile and Dress, Property, Competition, Co-operation Contract, Technology, Efficiency of Labour, Employment, Training and Apprenticeship, Security.	Security and Standard of Living.	Development of Occupation Personality.	Maximum Satisfaction and Minimum Sacrifice.
III. Social, Aggression and Sympathy, Response, Recognition {Slatus); Security, Dominance and Submission, Imitation. Suggestion.	Mobility, Freedom of Association, and Movement, Privilege, Power, Honour, Prestige.	Status.	Development of Status Personality.	Justice.
IV. SPIRITUAL : The Creative Impulses. Curiosity, Anxiety, Phantasy, Compensation. Reparation.	Knowledge, Art, Religion.	Character.	Development of Spiritual Personality.	Universal Personalism, Personal Equality, Freedom and Solidarity.

differentiation of the human soul (character) is also man's supreme duty and privilege (*Table* 5.2, Col. D). His pursuit of the spiritual values with which are associated the values of personality are protected and furthered by law through the implementing of the rights of free education, and freedom of worship and protection against exhibition of ugliness, vice and obscenity.

Values at each level are embodied in laws, especially the lower and more basic values that serve as conditions for the fulfilment of the superior values; and, what is more significant, law not only regulates by physical methods the field particularly of the lower values, but also embodies, roughly at least, the hierarchy of values. The distinguished jurist, Cardozo, points out, first of all, the dependence of law on ethics, showing that legal concepts, when divorced from ethics, tend to become tyrants and fruitful parents of injustice. But he makes it clear also that when conflicts in the law take place the resolution of these conflicts always indicates that a certain scale of values is presupposed, and certain principles of precedence acknowledged. Thus on the whole modern legislation and court decision put moral ends over economic, and aesthetic over economic. "Progressively more and more personal values are put above the values of property, and more and more the spiritual values are furthered and conserved," observes Urban. The orientation of groups fulfilling values of different levels; stratificatory status giving the highest privilege and prestige to individuals and groups seeking values most prized by society; law, honour and conscience formulating the individual's claims and obligations— rights-and-duties—in the fulfilment of values; and the society's notions of goodness and evil, virtue and vice,—all contribute to defend and further a certain hierarchy of values and certain principles of precedence. The moral order creates and recreates the economic, social and legal order. Man's social order is the bridge between the system of ultimate values and his actual experience and transformation of the universe. The ultimate values are the "not yet" in social life. The moral law that is the universal rule of the cosmic process finds fulfilment as much through man's ideals as through his frustrations- The absolute hierarchy of values that is inherent in the cosmic process is inseparable from his routine of conduct and experience, his aspirations, his successes and defeats. It is the supreme judge of his conduct, institutions and experience, the principle and impulsion of progress.

The above presentation of desires, values and ethical norms in groups suggests, indeed, a kind of order or hierarchy that receives universal assent. Man's values fall into this hierarchy in every age and civilisation. Biological individuality and the maintenance of the standard of living would be considered basal or fundamental to life, but culture is judged from the standpoint of what is more significant for the spiritual life—the unfoldment of character. From level to level, there is the ascent of ethical norms for the individual—development of the psycho-genetic personality, of the "occupation personality", of the status personality and of the spiritual personality defining both his duty and privilege. The notion of *degrees* of personality development offers the clue to the interpretation of the scale of human values. In order that the integration of the human community may expand and deepen, there is also the ascent of ethical norms for the collectivity, imposing new imperatives for organised society from level to level of social adaptation—bio-ecologic co-operation, maximum satisfaction of wants, justice, equality and the spirit of mutuality.

From the internal perspective the moral ideal ascends from the greater symbiosis or continuity and happiness of society in the ecological and economic levels to justice in the social, and to equality and solidarity in the spiritual level. Happiness is an economic concept, as justice is a political one, involving equalisation of satisfactions and opportunities for individuals and groups. Equality and solidarity are sociological concepts involving communion that represents the profoundest depth of the self as well as the highest mutuality that spreads out on all sides without seeking any returns on the *quid pro quo* basis or the accommodation of interest to interest and of right to right that is essential in the conception of justice. The good society makes equality and solidarity rather than justice its highest moral ideal. Its aim is to seek the highest mutuality and communion. Both from the standpoint of the personality and from the standpoint of society, the highest ideal is love and unselfishness. The contradiction between individual and social morality, viz., that the moral ideal is progressively attenuated as it is applied to more and more intricate, indirect and collective human relations, which Niebuhr stresses, will accordingly disappear. "Where human relations are intimate (and love is fully effective only in intimate and personal relations), the way of love may be the only way to justice. Where rights and interests are closely interwoven, it is impossible to engage in a shrewd and prudent calculation of comparative rights. Where lives are closely intertwined, happiness is destroyed if it is not shared. Justice by assertion and counter-assertion therefore becomes impossible. The spirit of mutuality can be maintained only by a passion which does not estimate the personal advantages which are derived from mutuality too carefully. Love must strive for something purer than justice if it would attain justice."[5] Communion, equality or mutuality have to be distinguished from justice inhering in the relations of economic and political cooperation. The former are ends in themselves comprising trans-natural and trans-social aspirations of man, and, if secured, will make the cooperative life in an organised society easier. Justice on the other hand is a function of the structure of society and is difficult, if not impossible, on the basis of a mere rational calculation of competing interests, values and rights of individuals and groups. The "rightness" in human relationships really rests not on the accommodation or conciliation of conflicting values and interests but on the achievement of a real sharing of life or communion of understandings and values; and this is largely a problem of personality development and expression, not of rights, freedoms and legal relationships. The most perfect integration of society involves the sharing of life and effective mutuality of experience. As there is failure to achieve or to maintain such mutuality, there are constraint, limitation and obliteration by laws, codes and institutions that represent the penalties as well as the proofs of such failure. Accordingly it is not by multiplying laws, rights and institutions but by the effective mutuality of experience in the personal nexus that man can win the highest freedom and at the same time perfect organised co-operation in society. All these notions represent fundamental sociological and ethical principles guiding the destiny of man and society.

Relativity of Values and Virtues in Different Cultures

It is obvious that the lower and higher impulses and desires integrate themselves into the lower and higher values and goals. Rights are conditions, claims and opportunities safeguarded by society for each individual for the fulfilment of the essential goals and ideals of life, and the scale of rights follows the scale of values in every society. Rights also imply duties that are individual or collective—the duties of individual role, occupation, status and personality on the one hand, and the social obligations of continuity of the race and habitat, of justice and solidarity and of universal brotherhood, rising from the biological through the economic to the spiritual plane. Virtues are defined as the "values of conduct"—those traits of individual character that are inherent in the striving for and fulfilment of man's goals. To satisfy one's craving for food and sex is not a virtue; but fortitude in the fight for life against pain and disease and courage and ingenuity in the fight for self-preservation against destructive elemental forces are virtues. To earn livelihood for the family, to maintain its standard of living, or to save against the rainy day are not generally regarded as economic virtues; but to improve one's technical efficiency by systematic training during one's spare time, or to exhibit a marked ingenuity or inventive spirit in the use of machine tools and processes, and venture-someness and fortitude in pioneering enterprises are economic virtues. Thrift, prudence, foresight, trustworthiness and initiative are economic virtues. Honour, rectitude, fidelity, justice, tolerance and sweet reasonableness arc social virtues. But the highest virtues are those associated with the pursuit of knowledge, art and religion-disinterestedness, self-control, purity, wisdom, compassion and love. Thus there is a scale of virtues as there is a scale of values and of rights and duties.

The normal ordering of rights and duties, values and virtues is inherent in the very notions of values, duties and virtues. The individual not only acknowledges the above arrangement of values and virtues but finds himself under the obligation to choose according to this. Values and virtues imply exercise of will, judgment and preference. To have a will implies to subordinate the immediate biological and economic values to more stable ideal values, to harmonise present needs and satisfactions with long-run aims and goals. Man's self is fragmentary and temporary as it distributes itself among lower satisfactions and values; the realisation of the whole or ideal self rests on the proper orientation and integration of values at different levels through deliberation, appreciation and choice in which, of course, the individual is largely guided by the social and legal order. Civilisations have perished that have not exercised a wise preference of the higher values and virtues to the lower. Thus the hierarchy of human values and virtues has become ingrained in mankind's value meaning and value-configuration. Yet in the course of human history civilisations have shown a wide divergence in their basic ethos or core of values. The Indian and Chinese ideal of purity, humility, non-violence and humane, cooperative behaviour illustrates a characteristic ethos. The medieval European spirit of uncompromising denunciation of wealth, pleasures and values of the material world and concentration on the supernatural world as the true reality marks another. The modern Euro-American ideal of sturdy individualism, acquisitiveness, dominance and power manifestation represents a value system that is spreading to all corners of the globe with capitalistic-industrial economy. The ethos or pattern of type values of whole cultures, peoples and epochs comprises relatively generic preferential trends, attitudes and frames of reference that provide different foci for persons' sentiment and thought and furnish the background of differential racial behaviour. A recent interesting study of comparative moral judgment of the Chinese and Americans illustrates the possibilities of exploration of this virgin field. Several groups of Chinese students ranked 15 "vices" and 16 "ideals" in order of importance. A high degree of correspondence was found among the groups. Comparisons with earlier studies of American student groups yielded correlations '50 or higher. Both racial groups "were critical about sex irregularity, stealing and cheating and tolerant of smoking and dancing. Honesty was unanimously agreed upon as the most important ideal, while obedience, thrift and reverence were generally regarded as of small importance".[6]

Cultural anthropology and sociology should deal objectively with divergences in social and economic systems and systems of values and their effects upon individual motivations, attitudes and life-goals among different peoples. The widespread recognition of the relativity of various systems of culture with distinctive scales of values is the first step towards international amity and goodwill through an appreciation of the characteristic aspects of life and valuations of distant and strange peoples. While there are marked variations in the stress of certain values and virtues, the general ordering of the values of life in different civilisations remains the same, although these may differ much in implementing the hierarchy in actual social habits, behaviours and relationships.

Different Type of Ethics Based on Contrasted Personality Values

One of the striking differences in type-values between different cultures is represented by the values attached to personality. In modern Europe, ethics regards personality as the highest value but not as spiritual. Personality in European ethics is bound with its relations to society, and does not transcend the destiny of society. Or, society is regarded as the source of moral distinctions and valuations, and conscience as the voice of fellowmen. In this case the struggle for personality and its value share the vicissitudes, conflicts and frustrations of society. European ethics, individualistic and society-bound, has in large measure run counter to the preachings of Christianity. It must also be admitted that the Christian conception of the suffering and sacrifice of the Man of Sorrows is an apotheosis of the personal moral worth. Niebuhr observes: "The devotion of Christianity to the Cross is an unconscious glorification of the individual moral ideal. The Cross is the symbol of love triumphant in its own integrity but not triumphant in the world and society. Society in fact conspired the Cross."[7] In Christianity both metaphysics and ethics are based upon the doctrine of the Holy Trinity, which is a Trinity of Persons just because they presuppose one another and imply mutual love and intercommunion.

This uniformity of the scaling of values among the various forms of social culture in the world, as represented by the general subordination of the spiritual and idealistic to the economic and biological values, stands against the clear-cut contrast between the three permanent types of ideologies, the "ideational", the "sensate" and the "idealistic" type, which according to Sorokin underlie the historical development of cultures and societies.[8] No community or culture worth the name remains satisfied with or confines itself to the shell of the "sensate" existence. All cultures orient themselves toward some "super-sensory" reality-, and in fact such orientation leads to the stability of the social organisation. Magic, religion, art and myth import everywhere the "ideational" values and principles into the institutions and practices of peoples. The integrating and ordering principle of any society or culture is in fact represented by the "ideational" element. Sorokin's grammatically charted theory of cultural fluctuations is of course modified by his finding that hardly any culture in the history of mankind is totally integrated, and consequently the other contrasted ways of living and thinking live within a particular culture-pattern as "minor currents". All societies, however, exhibit in their religion, moral code, law and system of rights-and-duties, the process of recording the spiritual and the transcendent in the sensate and the rational. Man's spiritual or ideational values that are matters of his conscience, faith and belief express themselves not merely in his quest of the imponderables in religion, art and all imaginative construction and experience, but also in the quest of the good and the just in his social, legal and institutional forms. What is important for culture history is the *quality* or level of culture as determined by the specific blend of the ideational and sensate modes of living and thinking, that determines the composite culture system. The differences in quality or level of culture cannot be shown by any weighing of the items of cultural expression or by quantitative tables. Thus the 'ideational' cultures of India and China and of the early Middle Ages in Europe show both differences and resemblances, as also do the "sensate" cultures of Greece and Rome and of the Modern West; and both differences and resemblances have to be studied closely and appraised with respect to the formative economic or biological, social and religious factors. Such factors are operative everywhere, mutually acting and reacting upon one another in a complex, uncertain manner, determining dominant trends, minor fluctuations or sharp transitions in culture, none of which can be quantitatively expressed. The religious or ideational factors in one age or culture may be too regulative or repressive. In another it may stimulate progress in economic, artistic and social fields. There are also all sorts of lag, friction and maladjustment in the actual working of a social culture that as a system shows a viable balance between the so-called ideational, sensate and idealistic modes of thought. An economic catastrophe, a political invasion or conquest or the advent of a new leader or prophet may altogether change the value-configuration of a culture. There is no short cut to the classification and comparative study of cultural types. Sorokin's picture of cultural transformation as represented by the recurrence of his cultural types (with some minor variations) is too simply drawn.

An adequate social psychology and philosophy have first to clear up the roles of the economic, social, political and religious factors in the formations and mutations of a particular culture. The quantitative method of Sorokin obscures the fundamentals of a culture, the imponderables and the invisibles that can only be appreciated by sympathetic imagination and not weighed by mathematics. Then it will be the task of comparative sociology to formulate a classification of cultures, both in their static and evolutionary aspects. Different religions influence man's moral and social relations differently through their conceptions of personality-in-community, and it is over-simple to suggest that in all ideational cultures ethics and law are moulded after the same pattern, or that God and religion here control all social relationships and organisations. Such conclusions do not carry us far, besides being untrue. No doubt the clue to the interpretation of a given culture-pattern is provided by its dominant values, but the manner in which the ruling preferences determine the actual ways of living, relationships and institutions is too complex to yield to any socio-cultural dialectic or abstractionism. "The moral life of every individual person must be interpreted", observes Berdyaev, 'after the image of the Divine Tri-unity, reversed and reflected in the world. A person presupposes the existence of other persons and communion between them. Personality is the highest hierarchical value and never is merely a means. But it does not exist as a value apart from its relation to God, to other persons and human society. Personality must come out of itself, must transcend itself—this is the task set to it by God."[9] Similarly in certain forms of Oriental theistic mysticism ethics is personalistic but not individualistic, explaining the ethical life of every individual as a partnership with God in his Divine Sport, Love and Sacrifice reflected in the processes of the world. Here personality is regarded as eternal but at the same time impossible without love and sacrifice, without passing over to the Other, to the Suffering and the Sinful, to the Beloved. In the vision of Christ the kingdom of God on the earth is impossible of fulfilment except through the Divine grace. Thus society remains man's great defeat and frustration as it is the source of his sorrow and suffering in the pursuit of the moral ideal. In Oriental religion and ethics, however, society becomes the playground of reciprocal sport between the human and the Divine, a great fulfilment, realisation and bliss. The triumph of personality and establishment of the just and happy society come through the trans-human resources of love, knowledge and sacrifice of the individual restored to his true divinity. Oriental mysticism has also reached out to an impersonalism, to the Mind and Community of the Cosmos that transcends not merely self and society but also God as a Person, who in theistic mysticism pre-supposes his Other, another Person, and is Love, Sport and Sacrifice. In this case it is mystical insight that establishes an inward continuity of self and the universe as a whole including more than man and society. Here is an experience in which the "good" of action and the "true" of thought become inseparably fused. An impersonal mysticism produces a universalist ethics. It is thus that different social cultures and epochs with their different kinds of metaphysics have built up different types of ethical theory based on contrasted ideas of personality. In India, and generally speaking in the East, mysticism, whether of the personal or of the impersonal variety, generates reverence for all men and sentient creatures as creators and carriers of the super-personal values, whether God as the Person or the Mind of the Cosmic Community. It is this which largely explains the greater humanism, compassion and tenderness in social relations, characteristic of the East.

It is also probable that while the notion of personality as the image and likeness of God in man has helped towards the strengthening of the moral sentiments of love and sacrifice in the earlier stage of social development when man lived in familistic groups, an impersonal type of mysticism, such as familiar in the East, is more appropriate for the integration of human relationships and the transformation of society into a communion in the new social age. The present dominance of secondary groups, classes, states or nations in which men hardly know one another, and yet have to live in peace and concord, demands a kind of inter-communion that can only be assured by an insight into the Reality, the Universal Other that is not bound and limited by anthromorphic concepts, and yet penetrates into all human relations and experiences. Thus the Great Society can become the Supreme Communion, not as a philosophical abstraction but as a concrete spiritual reality in mutual Jove and sacrifice.

The Triumph of Personality and Communion

The affirmation of personality provides the clue to the hierarchy of values. Man's individuality is biological and social, connected with the history of the species and the development of society. Its growth and expansion demand the diversification and fulfilment of the biological, economic and social values. Personality is spiritual, and manifests itself only with the receding into the background of the biological self-assertion and self-centredness of human individuality, the power-manifestation of the social man and the subjugation of man's freedom and creativeness by the power of the state. Human personality is a great religious mystery. "To say that a man is a person", observes Jacques Maritain, "is to say that he is a minute fragment of matter that is at the same time a universe, a beggar who participates in the absolute being, mortal flesh whose value is eternal, and a bit of straw into which heaven enters. It is this metaphysical mystery that religious thought designates when it says that the person is the image of God. The value of the person, his dignity and rights belong to the order of things naturally sacred which bear the imprint of the Father of Being, and which have in him the end of their movement." Personality is immortal and is the creator and carrier of the enduring and supreme ideal values.

Max Scheler laid down the principles of permanence, indivisibility, dependence and axiological absoluteness in determining man's choice or preference among values, basing his ethics on the value of personality, highest in the hierarchy of values. All the principles, except the last are sociologically grounded. Society seeks permanent, durable satisfactions of life that bind man with fellow-man. Transient pleasures soon become boring and galling, while these are perennial sources of discord and conflict. Social experience thus gives preference to the permanent values, and also guides the individual how and where these are to be sought. Values are so much the higher, the less the quality of their carrier increases with its extension and decreases with its division. "Economic goods admit of being shared among persons only in as much as we divide them. Their value for the individual diminishes progressively with each division." Spiritual values are not in themselves capable of being divided, and in fact there is gain in depth of satisfaction with participation. Hartmann observes, "That the social conflict of interests depends upon material goods and not on spiritual, rests not in the nature of the interest directed towards them (not, as it were, in the greater intensity of this) but in the nature of the values."[10] Material goods separate the persons who share them; spiritual goods unite men in a common possession. Moral and spiritual values in a pre-eminent sense forge bonds between man and man. Knowledge, art and religion, pursued for their own sakes, are the major forces that humanise and socialise man, lead to the recognition of his supreme worth and majesty, and abolish the barriers that sunder classes and races. The evolution of society and human culture accompanies the progressive differentiation of human functions, interests and values that supervene upon mere biological and economic ones. Hunger, sex, work, play, protection, wealth, property, security—the entire field of biological and economic values is primarily instrumental rather than intrinsic. These are means of realisation of the social and spiritual values that supervene upon them. These are more self-sufficient and independent, at the same time the lower and the more elementary, while the social and spiritual values that are dependent are the higher. Much of the apparatus of human culture, education and social control is concerned with regulating the biological values of hunger, sex or play in such manner that the physical satisfaction, excitement or sport associated with them does not become an end in itself. Human culture fights against such *perversion* of values that results in personal disorganisation and social disruption, but uses the biological and economic values as instrumental to the realisation of social and personal values as well. This is as necessary for the realisation or perfection of the personality as for social integration and solidarity, In the course of social evolution, the system of values that records the experience of the race is developed in such manner that those values are highest which contribute most to total self-realisation, coherently energising and integrating life's functions and experiences at different levels and to the achievement in concrete social action of the identity of self and not-self. The pursuit of the highest values contains in it the potentiality of the fullest realisation of the personality and the fullest unity of men in a common participation of values. Both the triumph of personality and communion in the social group can, however, be perfected only as values existing in virtue of the super-personal values of the Divine personality and Communion, whence are derived the basic conditions of the life of man and society, which together with the freedom of the human personality explain human history. This is a religious, and not an ethical conception.

The system of values is not presented before the valuational consciousness as a set moral scheme or pattern. The individual is called upon to exercise his preferential trend in concrete social situations that may call for innumerable choices according to which of the values sought is taken as fixing the standard. Not merely do values at lower and higher levels, but different values of the same level engender antagonisms. Several values that are not opposed to one another are not all accessible simultaneously in a particular situation. The law of the ordering of values is too simple and abstract. In a concrete empirical situation every individual preference is unique, and touches every conceivable grade and variation of the values, and the richer and more highly individualised the personality, the greater is there room for variety of possibilities in axiological distinction and for uniqueness of preferences within of course the hierarchy of values that remains inviolable and absolute. In progressive communities the social and the legal pattern remains tolerant and flexible enough to provide ample scope for the variation of principles of precedence according to individual liking, together with the manifoldness in the moral order.

The Fundamental Ethical Principles of Solidarity

Spiritual values are actualised in the community life. The community life in so far as it is the matrix and foundation of all values is itself invested with the highest value. For if the community perishes all values in life are negatived. From one standpoint, the individual values of personality are the highest morally, and represent the entire congeries of the universal virtues and the perfection of the human ethos. From another standpoint, the solidarity of the community represents the perfection of the human ethos, since man basing his moral tasks as the builder of the community and the creator of law, tradition and convention and of the economic, social and legal order on the principles of 'each for all', 'all for each' and 'all with all' imports into all human relations the most absolute values conceivable in their universality. Without the mutuality and solidarity established through the principle of sacrifice of the present for the unborn generations in transmitting the heritage of race and region, through the principle of equi-marginal satisfaction and sacrifice in the allocation of scarce resources for the economic community, through the principle of justice in the social order: ("equal rights, equal duties with others, whether the individual or the whole of the community") and through the principle of universal love and brotherhood, the continuity of communal life cannot be ensured, nor man's egoism, fear, aggressiveness and will-to-power eliminated enabling him to outgrow himself, and reach his true destiny. (See Column D of *Table* 5.2.) Wise conservation of resources and the perpetuation of the family and of rational fruits of civilisation are an indispensable kind of solidarity just as equality and justice are. The former bear the race, and the latter bear the whole social structure on their shoulders. But the principle of universal personalism and communion is stronger and deeper than the solidarity of symbiosis, the solidarity of maximum satisfaction and the solidarity of justice, since it oversteps the boundaries of territories, nations or states and brings the whole of mankind into common participation of actions, joys and sufferings.

The international community of the future can only be built up on the basis of the four fundamental ethical principles of solidarity based at successive levels on ecology, economics, sociology and religion: husbandry of world resources, world economic optimum, freedom, equality and justice for all peoples of the earth and the spiritual oneness of mankind. This is man's evolutionary destiny to which his system of ethics gaining that universality that has so far been lacking leads. International law, conventions and agreements play an effective role in world integration on the basis of a new ethical system; a great deal depends upon the development of a new international honour and conscience that can rule the affairs of the world subjectively through the sense of discord or guilt and inner realization of the spiritual brotherhood of mankind that emanate from the world's most sensitive, international souls. It is not enough to have a sense of international honour and international conscience; there must be built-up such world institutions as the economic, political and juridical machinery of the U.N.O. and such world securities for individuals and minorities as an international bill of human rights that can safeguard the international community much in the same manner as the Rights of Man are guaranteed by the rule of law, juridical review and the written constitution in various countries.[11] But the evolution of juster international intercourse rests more upon a new conscience of humanity and faith in the oneness of the world than upon laws and codes.

References

1. See Sumner and Keller: *The Science of Society*, and A.M. Lee: Interest Criteria in Propaganda Analysis, *American Sociological Review*, April 1945.
2. *The Sociology of Law*, p. 146.
3. Is the Antithesis of "Mora Man" and "Immoral Society" True? *Philosophical Review*, Vol. 52, p. 54.
4. Mulseyee : *The Dynamics of Morals*, pp. 46-50.
5. See *Moral Man and Immoral Society*, Chap. X.
6. Lo: Moral Judgment of Chinese Students, *Journal of Abnormal and Social Psychology*, 1942, pp. 264-269.
7. *Moral Man and Immoral Society*, p. 32.
8. P Sorokin: *Social and Cultural Dynamics*.
9. *The Dtstiny of Man*, p. 71.
10. Hartmann : *Ethics*, Vol. 2.
11. See Laulerpachts : *An International Bill of the Rights of Man*.

6

LAUGHTER AS THE SOCIAL GESTURE OF VALUATION

The Instinctive Basis of Laughter

Society sets up a system of values for its members, and also develops processes and mechanism through which this system is maintained. These are both instinctive or informal, and conscious or formal. Man's character or behaviour is gradually trained and directed in such manner that on the habit and instinctive level he mechanically conforms to society's value judgments and approved patterns of behaviour. This is what we call social conditioning, education or socialisation. All cultures develop a variety of devices and techniques by which the individual habitually and instinctively conforms to the ideas, attitudes and valuations of the community. This method is so old and familiar that one can hardly guess what would happen to society if these be abolished for a time. Laughter represents a spontaneous, instinctive or informal device by which societies, backward or advanced, vigorously express their social valuation. The smile and laughter of scorn, ridicule, banter, praise or exaltation—the myriad ingenious forms of laughter-expression—work effectively in maintaining the ascendency of society by the method of quickly, sharply and adroitly attacking disapproved patterns of thought, feeling and behaviour.

Laughter is a heritable psycho-biological phenomenon. In the child it is the sunny expression of satiety and enjoyment, of a spill-over of superfluous physical and mental energy. It is also a social phenomenon arising in or out of the social situation that provides its occasion and objective. From the genetic viewpoint, laughter is rooted in the dispositions of play, gladness and sense of relief, and is by its nature happy and genial. It is chiefly, though not exclusively, a human phenomenon. The great apes all laugh. Jackdaws indulge in practical jokes with cats and dogs. My dog Gumti used to laugh as it stole my socks and frustrated the mad chase. Stephen Leacock mentions the laughing jackass and also the loon of the Canadian lakes which emits a sardonic laugh more mocking than anything human. Animals cannot show by their facial features that they laugh in the human way; in fact they laugh with their whole body. Both man and animal laugh in sport. Play and merriment are both spontaneous, expressive of the abundance of energy. Laughter is mainly the manifestation of physical enjoyment, delight or play, and in animals is best developed among gregarious, frolicksome apes on the basis of common gesture that enhances fellow-feeling and solidarity. Yerkes points out that the smile or laugh of the chimpanzee more frequently occurs in response to favourite foods and play. Both animal and human sounds indicating a pleasurable state of mind are also, as Darwin pointed out, associated with the union between the sexes or meeting between parents and offspring and other individuals in the family or larger social groups; or again with the overcoming of, or release from, an imminent peril. This is the true instinctive basis of laughter.

The Social Basis of Laughter

Genetically, therefore, there cannot be any single and simple explanation of laughter that with biological evolution is associated with several very different groups of ideas and feelings. Laughter originated in the human species not merely in the collective pleasure and indulgence after successful hunting or harvesting, as Carveth Read surmised, but also in group merriment, dance or sex orgy, or in the relief and triumph after a hard-fought battle and strenuous economic enterprise or expedition. In play and merriment or in sudden relief from danger and starvation, or the triumph of lust and aggression (laughter and sexual satisfaction or aggression helping each other), laughter, breaking out as the aftermath of violent collective feelings and experiences, establishes the physiological balance by quickly consuming within the body the surplus or pent-up energy. Laughter is comparable to sudden demobilisation, and, as Crile points out, substitutes for action *by* the body action *of* or *in* the body and thus consumes sugar and other associated secretions in the blood that have prepared the system for overt action that is, however, suddenly called off. Thus the body achieves its balance and euphoria of action through the happy convulsion of laughter converting a break or an interruption to an exhilaration. In human evolution the strong and spasmodic indulgences of the horde or tribe in rough sport, dance, sex, cruelty and aggression probably elicited the earliest *organised* laughter.

The Evolution of Laughter

With the development of social life man acquires the "laughing habit". The human child's laughter is part of his gregariousness, play and sense of relief and euphoria. Soon it acquires along with the laughter of relief and communicative gratification other types of laughter responding to a much greater variety of occasions and experiences than the offspring of the great apes. Already in the first year of the child's life the difference between smile and laughter becomes manifest. Washburn's experiments indicate that smiling seems to be much more a learned or conditioned response as the child nears the age of one year, and seems to be a communicative, adaptive response ; while laughing seems to be a more communicative form of behaviour, expressive of affective states.[1] Valentine and other observers record laughter of the child in response to the laughter or smile of another at about two or two and a half months,[2] an instance of social stimulation different from the laughter of contentment with food, good health, exuberance of spirits and play that the human child shares in common with a chimpanzee. Smile, born of the mere joy of social attention and communication, indeed, becomes so common that it is recognised as the index of greeting or reciprocative mood and relationship.

In the evolution of the human species various types of laughter are found simultaneously, its social meanings and values becoming more marked and accentuated with social development. Thus the significance of mature laughter as a social gesture, both natural and pretended, spontaneous and deliberate, is out of all proportion to the more primitive form of laughter, expressive of mere physical enjoyment and exhilaration. As a matter of fact even the laughter of mere physical delight and exuberance of spirits of children and young persons is much intensified in friendly company so that the role of gregariousness as it integrates with pleasurable excitement, play or delight or sense of relief becomes obvious. The child after his full feed and exhilarating bath indicates his pleasure to the mother or nurse, elicits reciprocative attention and affection, and gradually develops the smile as a social gesture for the stimulation of goodwill as manifest in the responsive smile of others surrounding him. With the mental development of child, the sources of pleasure or delight, of the sense of physical relief and enjoyment and mental poise and exhilaration are very much extended and variegated. The mature person laughs as he experiences joy and excitement in self-assertion and aggression, in the excitement of sex, in artistic creation or constructive activity of all kinds, and, finally, in the pursuit of the spiritual values. Throughout this development and elaboration of complex stimuli of laughter, different groups of ideas and feelings attach themselves to it; while the social note becomes more and more dominant in line with the general social trend. Gradually laughter develops its social values, stimulating and strengthening the 'consciousness of kind' by smile, uniting primitive tribes and folks in hunts, dances and corrobories by loud yell, and acting as an evaluative and corrective mechanism by disapproving and ridiculing marked divergence from normal types of social adaptation.

In man's social evolution the impulses of play or merriment, sense of relief or pleasure-gain accordingly blend inextricably with various other impulses such as sex, constructiveness, self-assertion, aggression, and above all, sympathy and sociability and thus there are socially conditioned various types and subtypes of laughter characterised by specific and varying affective notes, and evolving varied and subtle social functions. Particularly are the social note and conditioning stressed in what is an instinctive individual response, because the situations of play, relief, self-assertion or sympathy are eminently social situations uniting a group of individuals in common emotions. Yet the individual's own affective experience is of basic importance. With the evolution of mental life and the development of society the occasions of mature laughter, indeed, enormously multiply. Man in society shows a regimented, repressed and tense self. Laughter now emerges as a mechanism of defence against anxiety and tension and denial or mastery of unconscious fear, hate and aggression that are inhibited or stifled. Every sex incident of situation, every derogatory allusion to a person one hates, every obscene joke that gives relief to the mind suddenly release repression. The sudden and unexpected thrust of a joke eludes the censor, and the social disguise makes it more acceptable accompanied by pleasure-gain and laughter. Laughter dissolves a variety of repressed complexes, and liberates energy that would otherwise be expended to manifest control over motor and expressive behaviour. It is suggested that whereas unrestrained, automatic, imitative laughter represents a regression by offering full expression to the id, smiling at the other extreme signifies the complete triumph of the ego.[3] Thus laughter becomes enriched with a variety of feelings and ideas some of which are not discernible, rooted as these are in the depth of the unconscious. Without a significant role for both the psycho-biological life of the individual and for his social life, laughter could not have been such a universal gesture, extraordinarily rich in its possible meanings and implications. Laughter, to be sure, is of different species and varieties, carrying a variety of feelings, and these have to be genetically differentiated. It is both instinctive and socially conditioned, and its forms as well as social meanings differ from society to society. In each society the different forms and varieties also often merge in one another with an intermingling of the emotions, and it is not easy to distinguish them.

The Evaluative Functions of Laughter

In laughter the genial, the funny and the playful unconsciously blend with the serious, the reflective and the critical. It is thus that laughter develops evaluative and disciplinary functions with social evolution. Lloyd Morgan questions while examining Bergson's theory of laughter whether any such form of social utility has given to laughter its chief evolutionary value in social life. He considers it rather a secondary utility like that of the insect's sting which is derived from an organ of different ancestral value. This view is partial and unsatisfactory. For social evolution as continuing biological evolution utilises and transforms for social ends what is biologically valuable to human species as a nervous tonic—the laughter of pure gladness that braces up not only the individual, but also infects the group increasing the blood circulation and pressure of all. In human laughter the gladness and geniality are inseparable from the social situation and interaction of suggestion and sympathy; and thus as society develops, the thoughtful and playful laughter elements, pregnant with social meanings and values, blend and integrate, evolving a social gesture, In real life one or other element in laughter predominates or is found in isolation. The happiness, fun, gentleness and conviviality of laughter are absent in the grave, derisive, or disdainful smile, the scornful or cruel sardonic laughter, the loud exultant laughter or the "Homeric" laughter. This is the result of the social process or sophistication that excludes or attenuates the sheer joy of laughter that is genetically a universal instinctive response. It is not the malicious, derisive or sardonic laughter that is infectious. What attacks other individuals, no matter what their psychological condition, is,— whether they are pre-occupied, indisposed and irresponsive or not—is the merry laughter- A light, joyous laughter captures and transforms the dispositions of all persons nearby, who for the time being swim in the tide of merriment. Such an instinctive appeal of laughter is reduced or destroyed for other types that show a blending of social attitudes, interests and values and individual pleasure, prejudice and judgment that unlike the humorous emotion cannot be shared by all. This explains why reflective, disciplinary laughter cannot easily multiply.

Social evolution however gradually eschews aggression, cruelty and malice from the expression of laughter. The sunny, genial laughter that enshrines its true spirit serves as a wholesome tonic not only for the individual but also for the society in adversity or misfortune. The burden of the complex civilisation of today can be endured because of the practice of gentle, happy laughter in the home, and of the holiday of organised laughter and mirth at week-ends, on the sea-side and country-side or the daily amusement in the cinema house, dance-hall and theatre. Man's hilarious spirit in institutionalised holidays and carnivals, his casual and promiscuous jest, wit and humour in social converse and his deliberate composition of farce, skit, cartoon, parody and extravaganza that come under pure comedy, as distinguished from satire, alike testify to the universal instinctive appeal of sheer gladness of laughter in civilisation. No stress of the social functions of laughter can minimise the biological significance of laughter as a protective response against the misfits, maladjustments and incongruities that fall to the lot of every man. Some of these evoke sorrow, sighs and tears. But many may provoke laughter, that has now become efficacious, not merely in shielding both the body and the mind of the individual against any difficult or unpleasant social situation, but also as an evaluative and disciplinary social gesture correcting and punishing his failings and lapses. Such a function laughter can exercise through the salutary fear and sense of complete isolation it engenders in people. Both the spontaneous and the educative, the happy-go-lucky and the critical elements are found in laughter in various permutations and combinations, and this in both wordless gesture and in literature.

On the other hand, there is also abnormal laughter—the sneer of the scoffer, the snarl of the cynic, the exultaut laugh of the misanthrope, the sardonic laugh of the devilish, the nervous laugh of the diseased and the wild laugh of the insane. The neurotic is so ill at ease with the social situation due to the maladjustment between his behaviour and actual experience that he regards the proper behaviour of all persons as incongruous, and accordingly becomes the persistent victim of strained laughter. By way of contrast, there is the silent, half-expressed smile of the contemplative mind, expressive of inward joy and serenity that brightens the world for those who see it.

Mature laughter is society's spontaneous gesture, her simplest, quickest, and most economical technique for enforcing its valuation and judgment. As it is begotten of man's sociability, it conveys its social meaning and value through a variety of ways—a chorus of fun, ridicule, mockery, sarcasm or praise, either casual and spontaneous or reflective and concerted, and reaches its highest expression forms in the selective products of the fine arts. Custom and tradition come next to laughter as means of habituating the individual to group values and attitudes. Laws, institutions and codes come last as mechanisms of a more rational formal valuation by which society deliberately sets up standards, embodying moral and social values and provides sanctions, *i.e.*, rewards and punishments.

The Gay, Alert Constable of the Community

Custom, tradition and law may sleep, but laughter is ever-vigilant and watchful. Laughter intervenes where even the long hand of law does not reach. It is the gay constable of society. It anticipates the law made by the court and runs faster than any of its messengers. It is much more quickly operative than custom and law, nipping in the bud social and moral deviations that are not dealt with by the latter unless these develop into a social menace, into a positive illegality or crime. A. Michiels observes: "Conscience and the written laws form the two lines of ramparts against evil; the ludicrous is the third line of defence; it stops, brands and condemns the little misdeeds which the guards allowed to pass.... More precisely it is a special un-sociability, one which escapes all other penalties, which it is the function of laughter to reach. What can this unsociability be? It is the self-love in each of us in so far as it has anything disagreeable to others in it, an abstraction of every injurious and hateful element." The great American humourist, Mark Twain, thus aptly describes the efficacy of the weapon of laughter: "Your race in all its poverty has unquestionably one really effective weapon—laughter. Power, money, persuasion, supplication, persecution—these can lift a colossal humbug—push it a little-weaken it a little century by century; but only laughter can blow it to rags and atoms at a blast. Against the assault of laughter nothing can stand. You are always fussing and fighting with your other weapons. Do you ever use that one? No, you leave it lying rusting."[4]

When the entire community goes to sleep, and yet there are lapses, impertinences, cruelties and injustices of individuals and classes that cannot or do not come under the cognisance of law, and that yet flourish challenging the common faith, custom and tradition or the genuine goodness and fellow-feeling of men; laughter is fully awake and alert. By itself or by combining its resources with art, it quickly and skillfully checks and punishes individual unsociability and cruelty as well as social imperfection and injustice. There are, indeed, infinite lapses, failings and aberrations that threaten personal and social adaptation and that cause deep-rooted mental discomfort, anger and even rage but being mere signs and anticipations cannot be dealt with by law or custom but by the code of human converse, manners and etiquette. Laughter belongs to this code ; it is an evaluative device set up by man's long social discipline and experience, and it starts spontaneously to check and punish such aberrations and smooth the social process. Since it is instinctive and not conscious or deliberate, it does not often discriminate between individual cases of transgression nor is always characterised by goodwill and justice, nor sure of its target like law and custom that must hit the mark. Much depends unon the psychological make-up of the individual and the development of social converse and manners. There are ingrained in man along with human tenderness a streak of cruelty, malice and aggression that are responsible for sneer, mockery and sarcasm lacerating the flesh of human feeling.[5] Like the animal, man also has his grin and snarl, his cruel and malicious practical joke and sardonic and sadistic laughter. Here is an instance of a social mechanism being perverted in its use due to the wickedness of human nature and the immaturity of society.

But on the whole the education of man and society towards greater human kindliness and social justice makes laughter a most valuable tool in the hands of society for the protection and promotion of its values; while its cutting scissors' edge that abrades human feelings is blunted. Laughter divests itself of naked malice, callousness or sadism and cultivates detachment, pity and sympathy in order to scold and abase the transgressor; for rebuke and humiliate it must to succeed in its object, while remaining true to its essential spirit of sheer fun and lightness of heart. Laughter must have its sting though without its poison and abrasion. Satire is more devastating and paralysing than even the punishment of law. Social contumely and ostracism, the weapons that custom wields against the abnormal, the rebel and the innovator derive their strength from derisive smile and laughter. More than social disesteem and isolation what man fears is the loss of esteem to himself that is the result of laughter, pricking the bubble of his pretension and engendering an acute sense of inferiority. Laughter thus operates in social life by destroying both social status and self-status.

Classification of Causes of Laughter Safeguarding Values of Different Levels

Anthropologists have found that primitive peoples are peculiarly sensitive to humorous and derisive laughter and adverse public opinion, and that this more than anything else expresses and maintains the values or standards of the group. The social function of laughter is not fully appreciated by the psychologists, and their theories of laughter should be reoriented from the sociological point of view. Laughter, with all its various and ingenious expression modes, works in maintaining the normal social conditions and situations for the fulfilment of values and also the proper relation between different orders of values in society. The order of values and norms and the causes of laughter are briefly schematised in *Table* 6.1

Laughter is the readiest and most economical symbol of valuation and means of social control. Man's normal life and development express themselves in an individuality, personality or character. When he shows himself an automaton or robot, laughter is the result. This was stressed by Bergson who observed that "the attitude, gestures and movements of the human body are laughable in exact proportions as that body reminds us of a mere machine." Any kind of clumsy, incomplete or mechanical behaviour is the butt of ridicule. A pompous man is laughed at as he stumbles and falls, an officer dressed in uniform strutting mechanically like a puppet or performing duties like a machine

TABLE 6.1

Classification of Evaluative Functions of Laughter

Values	Norms	Sources of Laughter
Biological	Biological individuality	Deviation from physical, mental or moral attributes and features that indicate defective or abnormal personality and behaviour.
Economic	Standard of living	Disparity or incompatibility between wealth, income or skill and standard of living of the class or profession.
Social	Status	Disparity or incompatibility between ability or work and social power, status or prestige.
Spiritual	Character	Deviation from the moral norm or order; disparity or incompatibility between the biological and the higher values and the human traits and behaviour associated with these.

provokes mirth. All deformities and oddities, physical, mental or moral, that show departures from the moral standard, similarly excite laughter. In all such cases, the symbol complex of laughter expresses the value of normal human personality that eschews anything defective, unsymmetrical, incongrous, odd, mechanical or automatic. Man, however, no longer laughs at a broken limb or a natural hereditary bodily defect or abnormality. For if he goes against the common stock of goodwill, reason and common sense he cannot appeal to fellowman. Stephen Leacock says; "We of today would keep our 'Homeric laughter' for a man who had slipped on a banana field or limped with 'pins and needles', and wasn't really hurt. Humour has changed from a basis of injury or destruction to what one may describe as a basis of 'incongruity' or 'maladjustment'."[6]

Criticism of Bergson's Theory

The inadequacy of Bergson's explanation of laughter lies in this that he conceives only one kind of causes and situations for different types of laughter, one kind of incongruity or maladjustment as the spring of all laughter viz., what is rigid, mechanical or automatic encrusted on the living, imported into a situation that should develop on the higher vital plane. In fact he stretches the meaning of mechanism too far including in it ill-manneredness, logical inconsistency, absent-mindedness, lack of sociability and so on.[7] As a matter of fact his brilliant treatment of the various comic elements in social life often oversteps his single track explanation. Maladjustments and incongruities rise from level to level of social adaptation, and laughter results when consciousness is transferred all of a sudden to the perception of maladjustments that could be overcome normally. Not all episodic maladjustment is, however, laughable. There is an element of baulked or thwarted expectancy in laughter. Only that maladjustment or incongruity is laughable which social expectancy judges as easy and essential to get over, and at the same time the lapse does not cause severe individual pain or suffering. Laughter intervenes as a kindly or spiteful gesture of guidance toward the norm of social adjustment. The physical, mental and moral idiosyncracies of man, his breaches of order and discipline in society are also straightened out and made to conform to the norm by laughter. Equally with the physical defects and deformities like the protuberant belly, the squint eye, the flat or big nose, the uncertain clumsy gait or the unfinished movement, absent-mindedness or faltering, the foibles and vices of man, defects of intelligence and of sociability and character that do not show him up to the moral standard of the class or nation to which he belongs are responsible for much amusement and laughter. Similarly a departure from the standard of living of the on-looker or the social stratum and, again, a disharmony between man's role, status and prestige, and social expectancy produce laughter. When men are not companionable and do not hold or work together laughter suppresses the fissiparous tendency, and establishes proper men in their proper jobs, roles and categories, while pushing out the incompetent and the conceited. Laughter accordingly serves as a cement of the social structure. Finally, laughter safeguards devotion and consistency of endeavour and character in the pursuit of the spiritual values. Any the least deviation from the high standards laid down in man's search for knowledge, art and religion is sharply and quickly reproved by laughter.

Laughter as a Guardian of the Integrity of Personality and Society

The general formula that may be laid down is that a deviation from the physical, social and moral norm of the group or society or, in other words, contrariety to the values of personality development, rising from the biological and the economic to the moral level, is the determinant element in bringing about the feeling of the ludicrous and its expression in laughter. This also applies to the subtleties of humour and irony. There are unconscious desires of aggression, jealousy, hate and fear that cause constant troublesome tensions and anxieties and prevent social adaptation. When a fun or joke suddenly releases these repressed complexes, as by the recital of smutty or mock-heroic stories, man experiences artistic insight, and triumphs and laughs. All mature laughter rests on the release or dissolution of repressed complexes and the arousal of subconscious reserve energy, and hence is a source of inner poise. At the intellectual level, laughter is caused by an abrupt bridging of the difference between a man's pretension and his achievement, based on the sudden illumination of the ego. Humour accordingly is the way to sanity and earnestness in the achievement of one's goals and values of life, keeping clear of or overcoming one's own defects and deficiencies that he cannot see himself but are readily reported by others.

At the same time, laughter that is very infectious and quickly spreads in expanding joyous circles breaks down many barriers and conventions, promotes a unison of minds and solidifies the group. A smile of cheer enables a group of men to hold on in a most hazardous situation even unto death. Laughter fosters the desire for kindliness, fellow-feeling and sweet reasonableness, first in the primary groups and then in the secondary associations, and as such it is a great binder in human relations. The acerbities of dominance-subordination relationship in a stratified community are smoothed by smile or laughter. Smile or laughter makes one endure conditions of existence otherwise quite intolerable—the regimentation in the barrack or factory, the dull routine and drudgery in the office and the strict discipline in the church or temple. Laughter softens old enmities and animosities, dispels suspicions and is a great promoter of amity and friendliness. Many a deadlock in family circles, local communities and parliamentary assemblies is dissolved by laughter which prepares the ground for mutual tolerance and co-operation that did not exist before.

Gordon Allport thus explains why laughter is so disarming a pattern of expression. "It is a familiar experimental fact that a smiling face is judged as more intelligent than one that is serious and is credited with all social virtues and graces. Smiles arouse so favourable an affective attitude in observers that impartial judgment is virtually impossible. Conversely disfiguration and asymmetries of the face make for adverse judgments."[8] This is an instance of undue constraint found frequently in perceptual processes, whereby some single item in the field claims the observer's attention, and contributes disproportionately to the meaning aroused, quite eclipsing the evidence from surrounding cues.

Finally, laughter maintains and safeguards the integrity of society by shielding it against any abnormal or eccentric persons, ideas, feelings and forms of behaviour that may to the slightest extent threaten the smooth, harmonious working of its machinery. On the other hand, if the social machinery becomes too rigid and inelastic, and the status-power system becomes an enemy of the moral order, laughter is equally serviceable in attacking the social malformations and maladaptations and initiating the forces that bring about a more rational social organisation and system of values. An institution, rite or convention that outgrows its uses, becomes formal, inert or stereotyped or dissociated from the core of values that gave it birth is mirth-provoking. In all societies and civilisations laughter checks the rigidity of customs and institutions, the immobility of laws and moral codes and the formality of social rituals and manners. Laughter directs the human mind to the reality of its interests and values, and is the great enemy of any social camouflage, false appearance, transposition or perversion. It is the sly watchdog of sincerity and rectitude of social goals and values. It brooks neither social immobility nor hypocrisy nor illusion and is hence a sure guardian of social progress.

The Mental Laughter

Primitive and less advanced peoples roar in convulsive laughter or jump about, clap their hands and throw themselves on the ground unrestrainedly. In civilised society laughter is not boisterous at all, but is often suppressed and reduced to a smile and yet the smile, though stiff, artificial and empty as determined by social custom and etiquette, is no less potent in its social effects than laughter. More than laughter, smile establishes friendly rapport between civilised persons. One of the directions of the Earl of Chesterfield to his son was this: "I could heartily wish that you may often be seen to smile but never heard to laugh while you live."

Similarly we read in the Sanskrit text, Sahityadarpan : "That laughter is the best that is free from the shaking of body (akampa) and in which the eyes are slightly closed. Such laughter removes sin. Frequent laughter is blameworthy and this is met with in various forms in an insane person." There are six kinds of laughter according to Sanskrit literary critics. Of these the noblest persons have two, *viz.*, (1) smile with the eyes slightly opened and lips slightly quivering (smita) and (2) the teeth slightly visible (hasita); the middling persons have (1) melodious laughter (vihasita) and (2) laughter with the head and the face shaking (abahasita); for the lowly persons continuous, convulsive laughter is characterised by (I) tears coming out of the eyes (apahasita) and (2) and the limbs thrown about (atihasita). Laughter is described as an 'all or none' response correlated with impulses and emotions. These are functions of the thalamus and not of the higher cortex. Thus laughter is naturally boisterous and uncontrollable. Gradations of laughter are however, established by social and cultural habits and experience. These are to be attributed to the higher cortical influences. Civilisation abolishes the raucous haw-haw and guffaw of the gambling den and the card-table as also clownish jesting. The refinement of human converse and manners excludes all physical, convulsive gesture forms, and gives a premium to the gentle, dignified smile or the mental laughter that involves no squandering of energy.

The Spiritual Laughter

Laughter corrects and chastens society by detaching itself from it. But what would correct and chasten laughter itself? Does it not often become disruptive and repulsive by laughing at defects and imperfections without love, sympathy or goodwill, which "is a sign of pusillanimity" according to Hobbes ? "For", as he rightly observes, "of great minds one of the proper works is to help and free others from scorn and compare themselves only with the most able." Education, sense of human fellowship and genuine goodness remove the poison from the laughter. Thus man's intellectual, aesthetic and spiritual development raises both the level and efficiency of laughter as the bright illumination of the human spirit in the darkness, uncertainty and perplexity of life. The highest spiritual values are implied in the highest laughter, awakening man or society that falls into mental ineptness or moral turpitude into a sense of the values of life, and spurs it to action and achievement. There is an intimate relation between the highest laughter and spirituality in this that the man of laughter easily gets the better of the ordinary trials and travails of life, regarding them as something really trivial and amusing. This conviction of the triviality of life and of its occurrences is the bedrock of the religious quest. The man of religion, with his mind and heart entirely concentrated towards the eternal values, develops a profound sense of humour that infects every man, and brings home through a variety of anecdotes and parables a true apprehension of the vanity of human wishes. The Danish philosopher Kierkegaard places irony as the border-state between aesthetics and ethics, meaning by it not brutal, biting satire for its own sake, but the shock which is imparted to bring ignorance and folly to light, and also puts humour between ethics and religion. Every true mystic or religionist is endowed with an abundant kindly sense of humour that enables them to laugh at his own follies and smile benevolently on the follies of fellowmen.[9] Mankind had through the ages its education in the eternal verities and spiritual values through the appeal as much to the sense of the ludicrous as to the sense of the sublime.

The alliance between humour and spiritual contemplation is best illustrated in the lives and sayings of Lao Tsu and Chuang Tsu in China, of the Zen Buddhists in Japan and of the Bauls and Fakirs in India. Such elevation of the spirit of laughter is, however, rare. The Chinese among all peoples show the most abundant sense of humour in their attitude towards life, its disappointments and tribulations, misfortune and death. This is born of a profound realism, simplicity of life and thought, and conviction of the transitoriness of all things. Even a funeral procession among the Chinese is full of farcical elements, and cannot be easily distinguished from a marriage procession. In China much of administration, social reform, agrarian programme, flood and famine relief and even banditry and warfare become acceptable to people through lightness of touch and silvery laughter of the old rogue. It is the spiritual values made accessible to the people at large by Lao Tsu and Chuang Tsu, the rings of whose laughter have echoed through the ages, that enable the Chinese to carry the joke into all situations of life, however difficult, unpleasant and unfortunate.

The Interrelations between Society and Laughter

Social development itself implies the deepening of human sympathies so that cruel, cynical or malicious laughter that hurts without uplifting is gradually eschewed as bad taste. A society full of coercion, injustice and intolerance exhibits aggravated and malicious laughter. With the abolition of class barriers and social monopolies and privileges, social goodwill and fellow feeling thrive, and mitigate both the cruelty and the bitterness of laughter. The world's most infamous and malicious laughter is that of the Renaissance in Italy, when the new-born individualism and ambition of men, irrespective of means and consequences as well as luxury and profligacy were lashed by a poisonous brood of envious place-hunters and impotent railers, critics and scandal-mongers, who developed an easy-going contempt of everything and everybody. Burckhardt observes : "Italy became a school for scandal the like of which the world cannot show, not even in France at the time of Voltaire."[10] The world's most genial, kind-hearted laughter is perhaps that of the U.S.A. where it welds together different races and nationalities from the Old World echoing lustily in its wide open spaces. Referring to the American distrust of absolutism in philosophy and rejection of any important intrusions from 'The Absolute' into social culture, Max Eastman observes : "One of our chief virtues is that when we hear people say things like that we feel inclined to laugh, Laughter actually plays among us somewhat the role played in Germany by this same 'Absolute'. It enables us to carry on through the painful complications of the relative, the imperfect, in short the real facts—with buoyancy and courage. Our culture took its start from matter-of-fact knowledge and pioneer humour instead of mythical beliefs, solemn rituals of consolation."[11] In the U.S.A. humour in literature has largely contributed to sustain the tone and temper of a new civilisation in the pioneer region.

A society is known by its laughter, by the ways it laughs and the objects and persons it laughs at. With social progress, tolerance, solidarity, security and leisure all increase. Man's failures, misfits and misfortunes will now be attributed more to social handicaps and less to personal characteristics and attributes. This results in more genial and humaner laughter. The ignorant, irresponsible laughter that nips in the bud the inventor, the innovator or the prophet also disappears with intellectual progress. Laughter is the voice of the herd that is not always right in matters respecting intellectual tastes, beliefs and fashions. At the same time it is necessary that all innovations should stand the tests of fun and ridicule. Thus indirectly laughter protects society against the crazy, the obtuse and the conceited, and aids towards stability. In modern society good humoured laughter encourages self-criticism and self-knowledge that open the door to valuable novel ideas, beliefs and practices that gradually win the commendation of the people.

The preponderance of secondary groups and associations and abolition of face-to-face contacts also change both the character and expression modes of laughter. Frequent and loud laughter in the primary groups, such as the family, neighbourhood and rural community, with their circles of gossip, now becomes taboo. If the pathognomy of laughter has become less direct, rough and boisterous, there has been, to be sure, even a more profound change in motivations of laughter. This has been due both to the extensions and deepening of human tenderness and goodwill and the rise of literature that has taken the place of outbursts, gestures and pantomimes together with the cheers, jeers, yells, grunts and neighs of primitive peoples.

Literature is the usual method of communication of the secondary group world, and man laughs in literature among other art forms of laughter *en masse* in spite of separation by long distances in space and time through satire, humour and irony on the one hand, and pure comedy on the other. Mirth is characteristic of comedy in which laughter is relatively purposeless. But satire, humour and irony belong to the same genus though representing different species; these all expose with a consistency of purpose whatever is evil, anti-social and unprogressive in man and in society. Satire, humour and irony, all have their tremendous social usefulness in safeguarding and recording the values of life from age to age, and all have undergone on the whole a refining process gradually ridding itself of malice or the desire to inflict pain and suffering, and becoming kindlier, deeper and more complex as man himself has shown greater sensitiveness, self-esteem and fear of derision and sarcasm. Increase of population and perfection of means of communication have also raised the potential of satire as an instrument of ridicule. Thus it has become all the more essential that the art forms of laughter while showing greater keenness, pointedness and devastating skill are also characterised by greater sincerity and humanity. Such advance is, however, by no means uniform and consistent. Thus we have protean literary forms in this field that shade off into one another. An American writer, David Worcester has made a useful classification : "Satire begins where laughter enters. It need not be the tinkling laughter of drawing-room comedy. The grinning taunt is the lowest variety. The laughter of exultant victory, of scorn, of derision informs the most direct invective-satire. Following the other innumerable varieties of laughter, satire shades off into ridicule, light banter and irony which is a dry inner laughter, often at the expense of one-self."

The Art-forms of Laughter

All through the ages along with the different types and subtypes of laughter man has his written, literature of satire of different types whose stimulating and corroding effects are, indeed, reminiscent of those of the wordless humour of primitive peoples. As a literary critic, Hannay observes: "Horace leaves you wise; Juvenal, indignant but aspiring; Swift, angry but better ; Lindsay, amused and in good nature; Burns, tingling with rage but full of hope; Erasmus, improved and delighted. The great satirists have all a healthy effect."[12] The role of satire in bringing about revolutions in society is best illustrated by the influence of Aristophanes in discrediting the mythology of the older times, of Cervantes in undermining the foundations of feudalism and chivalry of medieval Europe, of Voltaire in disintegrating the ancient regime, and of Gogol in lashing sharply the Czarist administration in Russia. On the other hand, humour in which laughter mingles with tears, which does not humiliate or punish but is saturated by a profound goodwill, sympathy and pathos, also rises in literature to sublime heights, and binds class and class, man and man. The humour of Daumpier's and Gotz's sketches and cartoons, Mark Twain's Huckleberry Finn, James Barrie's Sentimental Tommy and Goodbye, Mr. Chipps, or Charlie Chaplin's Hard Times illustrate a profound appreciation of social values, tenderness for fellow-man and sensibility to thousand and one oppressions and injustices he is subjected to, like what Shelley experienced;

> Me, who am as a nerve over which do creep
> The else unfelt oppression of this earth.

Satire, humour, irony and comedy, journalism, painting and especially the stage and the cinema have become in modern civilisation the favoured media of expression of laughter, that organises more and more people under its ambit, gradually freeing itself from the techniques of gossip and the allusions and features of the local context. Choral laughter gives place, except in the stage, the cinema and the radio, to humour or individual laughter. Modern civilised man can laugh silently and by himself as has not been possible before. Yet the humourist's method and message 'hit the target' all right, through expanding circles of readers and auditors who all join in the laughter. A larger fund of social goodwill, optimism and tolerance in the modern age alters profoundly both the direction and attitude of laughter through the elimination of anything in the nature of cruelty, jealousy or malice, on the one hand, and of wry cynicism on the other. Laughter aids and is aided by man's moral improvement as its methods and technique are intimately related to his intellectual and aesthetic development. Man's collective gesture of evaluation has seized upon every available medium of expression, and also, as Lumley aptly observes, "invents where nothing suitable is already made; besides there are probably immense stores of laughter-energy unexpressed—an avalanche ready to fall on luckless mortals if a satisfactory outlet is ever discovered."[13] On the other hand, modern man, thwarted and frustrated in all ways, and losing all faith, belief and morality, laughs more at himself than ever before. Such cynicism, self-pity and sceptical irony have, indeed, become purposeful in modern literature that spreads these among the millions in a neurotic, restless and unhappy world. Once these rule, laughter that stifles and corrects, and cannot build up, will be more wasteful and devastating in its functions than is socially useful. Especially is such danger greater with the increase of the intellectual at the expense of the natural, joyous element in laughter. As long, however, as children and youths smile and laugh in hilarity, adult laughter will be there though gravitating towards wit, humour or individual laughter; while radio, television and other new instruments of the expression of laughter will foster social chorus especially for the less intellectual circles on a more expansive. scale than in the past. In the future the art forms as contrasted with the gesture forms of laughter will, it is expected, be more varied, subtler and more effectively planned and organised for both the cleansing and amusement of society. It is probable that there will be more laughter in the future than is heard now, due to the improvement of social goodwill and manners, increase of leisure, sharpening of the perception of incongruities and maladjustments and perfection of the techniques and instruments of social communication.

The Ordering of Goals and Values in Laughter

Laughter is frequently the result of the subordination of the lower to the higher values of life, of the biological and the economic to the spiritual values. A glutton or a philanderer is laughed at; each of them has made a fetish of physical value *per se*. Laughter accordingly promotes a right ordering of values. A boy who takes to all play and no work, a man who takes pleasure in coarse and unwholesome recreations is corrected by derisive, scornful laughter. Laughter castigates folly, foible, fool-hardiness and fanaticism, and all kinds of pose, pretension and extravagance as well as social aberration or deviation from the moral order. At the same time it unmasks hypocrisy or imposture. It promotes propriety in social relationship and behaviour by ridiculing extremes and mock heroics that men themselves know as laughable in others. It also fosters the appropriate selection of one's goals in life by unmasking inordinate aspiration and vanity on the one hand, and ignorance or incompetence in ambitious persons on the other. Laughter is a great social leveller. A man who is extravagant in dress and expenditure, a sponger, an idler or a spendthrifit, one who aspires to a higher standard of living, role or prestige than his training and abilities warrant is corrected by humorous laughter. The ostentatious display of wealth by the rich, of the pomp of power by the privileged, and the exhibition of pedantry by the learned are equally lashed by laughter. In fact one test of stability of the status-power system in any society is whether it can endure fun and laughter. A miser who cannot distinguish between intrinsic and instrumental values, between wealth as means and wealth as an end, provokes mirth in every society. Laughter, therefore, is, above all, evaluative. It puts values in their proper places and also persons in their proper roles and statuses. This is the truth underlying the "sudden glory" theory of laughter developed by Thomas Hobbes, Man laughs at somebody else's defects, imperfections, and infirmities because it leads to a sudden realisation of some superiority in himself. It thus serves the important function in society of adjusting man's status-power and prestige to his natural talents and capacities. The unworthy man occupying a superior role and status excites ludicrous laughter. "Men take heinously to be laughed at or derided, that is triumphed over", observes Hobbes. Bergson also stresses this point. "Laughter is, above all, a corrective. Being intended to humiliate, it must make a painful impression on the person against whom it is directed. By laughter, society avenges itself for the liberties taken with it. It would fail in its object if it bore the stamp of sympathy or kindness." On the other hand, laughter, springing as it does from self-complacency and self-esteem, is a spur to achievement and maintenance of status, the social goal of every individual.

As might be surmised from what has been observed, the fertile source of laughter is the anomaly or incongruity in a social situation in respect of the normal hierarchy of values. Any situation is ludicrous which draws the attention of the onlooker to the disharmony between the lower and the higher values and the human traits and behaviour associated with these. A plump widow or a priest fattened by offerings at the temple provokes fun much more than an old man wobbling like a child or wearing a young man's apparel. The former is a more serious misfit. A teacher who cares more for office and power, and a student who cares more for dress than for his study equally elicit amusement. The vulgarity, coarseness and hypocrisy of the rich are chastened by laughter. Any incompatibility between the physical and the moral side in a person or a situation concerned is as mirth-provoking as that between a person's status, privilege and power and his natural talents and capacity. Boris Sidis observes: "The significant and the insignificant, the noble and the ignoble, the grave and the gay, the heroic and the grotesque, the unusual and the usual, the superior and the inferior, when juxtaposed, raise laughter. Whatever reveals weakness in an object of superior standing and releases in the audience subconscious sources of hidden reserve energy is a fit subject for laughter and ridicule."[14]

Laughter is thus definitely conducive to rational expression and development of personality. Man's inconsistency in the pursuit of truth, his wavering in family duties and social obligations or his inconstancy of devotion in art and religion provoke much mirth and amusement, and engender necessary self-criticism. One cannot juxtapose the serious and the frivolous, the axiomatic and the incidental argument, the pious and the ugly, the austere and the gay in worship, and the beautiful and the ignoble in artistic creation without eliciting mirth and derision. Laughter safeguards the higher spiritual values of the personality by compelling self-examination, reflection, insight and consistency of character. On the other hand, a personality with marked insight is distinguished for its sense of humour. Allport observes: "The man who has the most complete sense of proportion concerning his own qualities is able to perceive their incongruities and absurdities in other than their customary frames of reference. Yet perspective does not mean superciliousness. Values have their place even though they be viewed at times in strange and incongruous settings where their pretensions and incongruities are disclosed."[15] True humour and irony enable a man to have a close view of his own drawbacks, deficiencies and eccentricities and open the surest road toward the recognition of the values of life and of the vanity of values. Affording a new perspective to life and the world, they enable him to conquer the accidents, disappointments and misfortunes of life with a lightness of heart that is sometimes truly amazing.

Laughter as an Aid to Social Re-valuation

If laughter is an effective but gentle reminder to individuals that they had better keep to roles and statuses for which they have natural talents and capacity, it exposes the injustice of a social and economic system and undermines social privilege and prestige where these are not due. Laughter works in society by isolating, frightening and demoralising. The stupefying, paralysing fear engendered in the upper social classes that enjoy privilege and power, but lose prestige due to organised loud laughter, is the first indispensable condition for their loss of structural status and power. On the other hand, the bitterness, pugnacity and determined opposition of the masses may be drained off along innocuous and even delightful channels by laughter through recreations and sports. All dictatorships down through the ages accordingly provide organised popular shows, circuses, parades and other entertainments that contribute to dissolve, at least for some time, the stiffness of resistance to tyranny. Laughter has accordingly both a conservative and revolutionary function. On one side, all re-valuation begins with a ring of scornful laughter, that is infectious and spreads among the masses as a prelude to new social and political adjustments. "Society is right," aptly observes Sully, "in her intuitive feeling that an unbridled laughter threatens her order and laws."[16] Revolutions are born and thrive in an orgy of derisive laughter. On the other side, revolutions are also forgotten by means of laughter, by a vacation of mirth.

The manifold social meanings expressed and conveyed by laughter are also borne out by the role played by it in myths, legends and cults. In various Hindu and Greek myths laughter is the symbol of the God's privilege, serenity and strength, conquering the forces of evil, while at the same time it is meant to be a gesture of rebellion of the races of men and titans. This is best illustrated in the world's religious art that records the higher spiritual values in all countries and ages. Contrasted with the aggressive loud, disdainful laughter (attahasa, as it is technically called) of Durga and Kali slaying the demon in Hindu art, are the tender, benignant smile of Gouri, the joyous, seductive smile of Siva-Parvati and Krishna-Radha, and the pure, understanding smile of Buddha, Bodhisattva, Vishnu and Siva. All these in their different nuances represent spiritual joy and competence—the triumph of the human spirit. The same spiritual mastery is revealed in the images of Jesus, Madonna and the Angels in the Cathedrals of the Middle Ages in Europe. The spiritual laughter of the gods in Oriental and medieval Christian art conveys unequivocably the supreme freedom and triumph of man over his life and destiny. Painting and sculpture as also the screen and the stage in modern times contribute towards stereotyping the gestures and symbols of laughter. Thus the higher experience of humanity has left its record in the many meanings that belong to the various art forms of laughter that became ascendent in certain epochs among many peoples.

The Institutionalisation of Laughter

Many societies utilise the feeling of the ridiculous and its expression in laughter in institutional forms for maintaining group standards and values. Crime and social deviation are frequently punished among primitive peoples by great ridicule that so shames the transgressor that he makes amends, leaves the community or even commits suicide. Paul Radin speaking of one of the American tribes observes: "Stated broadly, we may say that every mistake, every deviation from accepted opinion, every individual and purely personal interpretation, every peculiarity and eccentricity may call forth ridicule. It is ridicule and not indignation and horror that assails a man who attempts to change a detail in a ceremony, to tell a story in some new and original manner, or who acts counter to some definitely accepted belief and custom, and it is the same fundamentally ill-natured laughter that greets him when he becomes unwittingly the victim of some untoward accident. To avoid it a man will go to any length."[17] Appropriately does R. Maunier call laughter or ridicule the "satiric sanction" of social convention and conformity.

Among the Eskimos of Greenland, a couple of enemies, men or women, sing drum songs of accusation and ridicule against one another passionately in the open air under the summer sun or in winter within the huts. Such songs with their own melodies and refrains, burdened as these are with weighty reprimands and sneers, express the singer's wish to appear at their best to the audience. These are constantly improved and passing from mouth to mouth serve as a most useful device for abolishing misdoings among a people who are considered to be exceedingly touchy. Sometimes, however, such drum fight songs result in homicide (never during the drum fight itself).[18] In most primitive communities laughter is ritualistic and symbolical, and plays a large role in ceremonies and observances. Primitive as well as advanced peoples have the institution of the "joking relatives" (such as wife's brothers and sisters), who enjoy the license of ridiculing and criticising errors, shortcomings, foibles and vices of their kindred to an extent that serves as an effective deterrent for the offender. Another interesting instance of the institutionalisation of laughter for the purpose of education is afforded by the Australians who teach the youths at the time of their initiation into tribal life what to do by performing ludicrous pranks. The tribal initiation ceremonies through a mass excitement of the sense of the ridiculous set the standards for the community. All through the ages civilisation has enjoyed the burlesque, the comic festival or drama, the lampoon, the satire and the clown. Among the Pueblo Indians of New Mexico the clowns or "delight-makers" perform a valuable function for the whole community. Ruth Bunzel describes how they would stand before the various houses in Pueblo, calling the inmates by name in song, and twit-ling them for their stinginess, laziness, domestic infelicity, excessive fondness for American ways, and so forth. In India there are certain socio-religious festivals in which processions are taken out with clowns commenting on some social deviation or vice in terms of scathing ridicule that excite laughter among thousands of onlookers for a long while. The clown of the royal court and of the popular burlesque or festival in different countries and epochs is also an institution by itself, protecting kingdoms and peoples by his raillery and humour. In some of these processions as those of Dacca or Calcutta in connection with the Janmashtami and Charak Saṅkranti festivals there is an actual acting or mimicry of forms of behaviour that are sought to be censored, the entire city population participating in mass ridicule directed against the transgressions. Among the Chinese and the Japanese, "face-saving" is institutionalised, safeguarding the emotional security of the individual, who is early conditioned to regard mockery or sarcasm most seriously. Chinese diplomacy often depends upon its success in finding out ingenious devices of "face-saving" for all the leaders and parties concerned, sometimes irrespective of the major political issues. In Japan criticism from strangers is followed by punishment from parents and makes the sense of shame a more potent influence in behaviour than any sense of sin. The desire for "face-saving" underlies the well-known institution of hara-kiri or ceremonial suicide which is not only condoned but is approved as honourable conduct in this country.

Laughter, the Symbol of Glorification of the Normal and the Ideal

Men laugh on seeing other men laughing, although they are not aware of the particular tale, incident or situation that has caused the initial laughter. This indicates, as we have seen, the instinctive basis of laughter that has been widely harnessed in inter-personal relationships, traditions and institutions for valuation, social criticism and judgment in the form of mass physiological stimulation that raises the blood pressure, and promotes the circulation of blood and the vitality of people. Laughter provides an excellent tonic of physical, social and mental health, a hilarious social binder and an antidote to strain, worry and depression in difficult and distressing personal and social situations.

Laughter is the exhilarating, joyous, social gesture and symbol of glorification of the normal, the sane and the wholesome in the various levels of man's physical, social and moral adaptation. It uses and elaborates various media of expression, methods and techniques, all adapted to the stage of social and intellectual development of man and society, to its message and to the concrete social situation. Laughter, therefore, is unique or individualised for every group or community, being largely a function of its custom, social norms and values. "Our laughter is always the laughter of the group", Bergson observes. A stranger cannot join in the laughter, and is conscious of this inability, even regarding the laughter as senseless. On the other hand, one who belongs to the in-group can join even without being aware of the cause of the laughter and strengthens the group through his intoxication. A group becomes solidare by infectious laughter.[19] A person who cannot join in any laughter is a neurotic. A normal person is subject to attacks of group laughter because of his inadequate control of his motor and expressive behaviour. A normal society similarly enjoys jest and ridicule. It is only when social values are smothered or attenuated by a rigid framework of laws, institutions and traditions, when social relations become exploitative, or the regulation of the status-power system becomes too mechanical and oppressive that social satire or burlesque sharply lashes individuals and classes, the Church and the State, and society winces at the attacks of loud, devastating laughter spreading like an epidemic. Such laughter as that of Voltaire, Carlyle, Gogol or Bernard Shaw is not tender nor kind-hearted as it lays bare the impertinences and injustices of society. It is conceited, bitter, spiteful and even cruel; it spares none, attacking the innocent and the guilty alike, but it shows a curious blend of sympathy and malice, sadness and hilarity, and on the whole contributes towards the establishment of justice and solidarity.

Life and society demand of each man alertness and promptness of adaptation, physical, social and moral. It is laughter that serves as the constant gentle or sharp reminder to man and society of this. It is the ever-watchful, gay guardian of the values of life in the different levels of social adaptation. It restrains and eliminates all kinds of imperfections and lapses in adaptation that imperil man and society,— oddities or deformities in the biological individuality, blemishes, extravagances or deviations in the intellectual and moral personality, make-beliefs, improprieties and injustices in social relationships as well as errors and incongruities in value judgments and illogicalities and asymmetries in intellectual and artistic relations and products. Laughter makes man and society endeavour to reach or at least to simulate what they ought to be. Merriment, relief, sociability, social valuation and punishment and idealism are all seen to be the sources and occasions of laughter— life and society's most economical device for guiding and controlling progress. There is yet another species of laughter, not related to man's lapses and failings, repressed complexes and social conformities. That is the spiritual laughter of the alone to the Alone, which passeth all understanding, and does not multiply, but represents the most exquisite rarefaction of physiognomic expression that contributes towards building up the goodwill and solidarity of the human race. Laughter is the tender, angelic daughter of religion, the jolly, radiant companion of art, and the tell-tale, sensitive sister of morality, leading man and society merrily to the true, the good and the beautiful.

References

1. *Genetic Psychological Monograph*, 1229, 6.
2. Valentine : *The Psychology of Early Childhood.*
3. Kris: Laughter as an Expressive Process, *International Journal of psycho-analysis,* Vol. 11, p. 314.
4. *Mysterious Stranger*. For English and American humour see Kimmins : *The Springs of Laughter,* Chapter XI.
5. See. J. C. Gregory : *The Nature of Laughter,* p. 221.
6. *Humour and Humanity,* p. 27.
7. H. Bergson : *Laughter, An Essay on the Meaning of the Comic.*
8. *Personality*, p. 484.
9. *The Collected Works of Kierkegaard.*
10. *The Civilisation of the Renaissance in Italy, smaller edition*, p. 98.
11. Quoted in Beard : *The American Spirit*, p. 664.
12. *Satire and Satirists,* Preface.
13. *Means of Control*, pp. 262, 263.
14. *The Psychology of Laughter.*
15. *Personality,* pp. 222-24.
16. Sully : *An Essay on Laughter,*
17. *Primitive Man as Philosopher,* pp. 50-51.
18. Thomas: *Primitive Behaviour,* p. 544 ; See also Klineberg: *Social Psychology,* pp. 189-195.
19. The nature of 'infection' in laughter has been studied by Schilder in *The Image and Appearance of the Human Body,*

7

THE DEFINITION AND INTEGRATION OF VALUES IN THE FAMILISTIC GROUP

Mankind's First Lessons in Valuation in the Family

Man shows a similarity and fixity in the pattern of his basic urges, interests and values. Yet these are profoundly modified by social and cultural influences. Both values and the manner of their fulfilment are largely defined and moulded by the primary groups, of which the most familiar types are represented by the family, the clan, the caste, the kindred, the neighbourhood and the small rural community. The primary character of these groups or associations is due to several factors in man's evolution. These associations are as old as man himself, and are fundamental for the development of his social nature and training in habits of co-operation for millions of years all the world over. Mankind received its early lessons in fundamental habits and attitudes in these vital modes of association. Its valuation process was focused in these groups that not only defined, modified and refashioned the original impulses of man into socially approved interests and values, but also provided him with means for their fulfilment. For the major portion of the world's population the essential needs and values of life are still fulfilled through the mediation of these groups that are outgrowths of the family, the basic and the smallest unit of community life. This is the reason why primary groups and relationships are also called 'familistic'. The clan, the caste and the rural community grow by accretion and multiplication out of the family, and repeat and multiply for the individual the essential techniques of food-production, use of tools, protection and recreation as well as social and moral adaptation that are first learnt and taught in the family group. Thus the values, biological, economic, social and spiritual, as well as moral codes are carried over to the individual in a direct but informal process of daily intercourse in the primary groups.

Socialisation of the Child through Role-taking and Expectancy

The growing child in the family group is profoundly influenced in his search for all satisfactions and values and the modes of their fulfilment by his early contacts with the parents, siblings and others in the household. In the short period of a few childhood years the infant has in fact to recapitulate the entire history of civilisation for learning the standards of social behaviour. Thus Freud observes: "The difficulty of childhood consists in the fact that the child has in a short span of life to make its own the acquisitions of a cultural development which lias extended over tens of thousands of years. It can achieve part of this alteration through its own development; a great deal must be forced upon it by education."[1] This education through the influence of the family group is effective and pervasive, because it is interaction at a face-to-face level in which 'speech', 'touch', 'gestures', 'visual stimuli' and 'interplay' of emotions are all involved. Psychologists studying the language development of the child point out that the parents' fondling, talking and other stimuli are associated with the expanding range of his interactions and the acquirement by him of new cycles of activity. The desire for social approval as well as imitation are early discernible as stimulants of vocalisation, gesture and speech and later on of the cycle of daily activities. Gradually the child develops his ability at role-taking, acting first one part and then another as the direct result of his contact with those around him. This he does in both play and imagination. The adoption of roles, relations and values of different individuals from father, mother and sibling to worker, craftsman, clerk, soldier, teacher or priest and of "good", "adventurous" or "wicked" boy or girl is also associated with different wishes, wants or ideals that are placed before the child by the family group.[2] We, therefore, see imitation in a new light as a basic process of development of the child based on his conscious assumption of a series of roles and activities of others that are presented to him by the family. Each r6Ie is a focus of new values and phantasies and the child as he grows also gets an opportunity for reflection and preference. More than that. As he plays the roles that he delegates to himself, he disciplines and transforms his own ego-centric impulses and desires, and at the same time becomes painfully conscious of the difference between how he acts and how he ought to. Gradually the various roles, the reflected self and the moral and social expectancies of the group become "internalised".

"The self arises in conduct," observes G. H. Mead, "'when the individual becomes a social object in experience to himself." The child gradually becomes a social being in his own experience, and he acts towards himself in a manner analogous to that in which he acts towards others." It is the appraisals of others in the family group that clarify and select the child's wishes, roles and appropriate habits, attitudes and values. Out of a wide range of specific roles of others which the child has played, there emerges in time a generalised and a more or less integrated pattern of the total role of the child—"the generalised other," as it is called by Mead, corresponding to Freud's superego or conscience.[3]

On the one hand, the child through his wide variation of roles learns to reckon with the possible or anticipated roles of fellowmen in society, while at the same time maintaining a consistency and continuity in the behavior of the self. On the other hand, the attitudes, values and habits of the large and increasing number of persons that come in social contact with the child weave themselves into the child's self, hi the process of socialisation the child accepts not only a variety of social relations and roles but also a variety of adaptive behavior patterns—the economic, intellectual, moral and aesthetic traditions, values and ideals of the family group. Maxims, slogans, and shibboleths, whose use is largely restricted to the familistic social groups, with their appendage of emotional values and irrational implications, also provide stereotyped definitions of situations for members of these groups serving as an unquestionable guide to conduct in all situations that normally occur within society. Man's perception and understanding of the world is through what are called the "stereotypes" that are the results of social intelligence and communication. Both the "thinking as usual," to use Alfred Scheutz's term, that corresponds to Max Scheler's idea of the "relatively natural conception of the world" and "feeling as usual" as we may call it, relevant to the familistic group, enable the individual to adjust himself most easily to the social world with a minimum of effort. Man obtains from the familistic groups a ready-made standardised scheme of interpretation and expression of behaviour and values; his manifold adaptation to things and to fellow men becomes habitual, semiconscious. He hands this over to the next generation even if he may not understand its origin and full implication and meaning. The "tested and trustworthy recipes" for interpretation and utilisation of the milieu accordingly include language and intellectual tradition, the arts of utilisation and the economic tradition, and the aesthetic and moral tradition, all of which mingle harmoniously. Thus the familistic cultural pattern or way of living develops an adequate coherence, clarity and comprehensiveness to provide the individual guidance and security in all his possible adjustments. This also has profound significance for the effective expression and experience of the individual of the in-group. Daily intercourse in the circle of the family and kindred provides an opportunity for practical economic effort and organisation as well as for interchange of relevant ideas and moral sentiments and appreciative sympathy. All these engender mutual tenderness, friendship and intimacy in the primary-group world that give their meaning and value to the satisfaction of organic needs and that are themselves enlarged and enlivened at the same time.[4]

The Values of Personal Nexus

From the primary division of labour in the family of primitive hunters when the man foraged and hunted and the woman reared children to the deep personal attachment between man and woman in the civilised family, woven out of the threads of sex attraction, mutual understanding and appreciation and community of social purposes and ideals, there is a remarkable enrichment of the values of personal nexus. Every family group becomes the focus of meanings and standards of practical economic adjustment, intellectual apprehension and aesthetic understanding of the real world.[5] From savagery to civilisation there is gain in the family traditions of economic co-operation and intellectual, moral and aesthetic insight that have profound import for the growing child. There is also deepening of family affection, attachment or loyalty that directly contribute towards a more effective social conditioning of the child in the period of dependence and constant care. It is the adult example and pressure that initiate the growing individual's satisfaction of organic needs in approved ways, stimulate curiosity about the environment and its practical control by tools and appliances already operative in the family group, and also arouse religious and aesthetic sentiments as he participates in solemn festivals or ceremonies or joins in group games and recreations. The unfoldment of intellectual curiosity, of the interest in and capacity for manipulation of the environment, of aesthetic apprehension and of the sense of justice is, to be sure, possible only in a social atmosphere where there are interchange of ideas, practical cooperation in daily toil and imaginative sympathy.

Simultaneously in the course of daily expression and communication of significant ideals and sentiments as well as of utilitarian expedients there arise an appreciation and enjoyment of other personalities culminating in reciprocal love and devotion, weaving enduring ties that overreach the domestic and social scene. In the familistic group the individual not only reveals his total personality to the objects of his love, devotion, friendship and loyalty, but rises in the same process to the fullest development and appreciation of these ideal personal values. The familistic group thus cultivates and nurtures the great specific values of a living personality that pierce through the empirical personality, however imperfect, to his ideal essence and destiny. Here the ideal shines upon and transforms its imperfect carrier, the empirical individual with all his moral limitations. "Personal love", says Hartmann, "lives by faith in this highest that is within the loved one, which despite its inadequacy love senses prophetically. Such love is ethical divination in the pre-eminent sense of the word, not of course divination of a universal human ideal, but of the ideal of a particular individual. It sees the perfect in imperfection, infinitude in the finite."

What is true of the extension enlargement of ideal values is also true of moral and social values in the family setting. In the stimulating family milieu of unition and solidarity, the growing individual participates in family conviction and judgment, the appraisal of all motives and conduct on the basis of which he approves his own conduct. His norm and standard and those of the family coincide. He gains self-esteem or status as he wins love and admiration of other members of the family by conforming to the common norm and standard that he himself also aids in fashioning. Similarly approbation or disapprobation of the larger primary groups like the neighbourhood or the small village are backed up by warm and personal emotional support and security. It is thus that sentiment and emotion become intermixed with habits, mores and moral codes, defining fundamental values and methods of their satisfaction for individuals. Like the family, the other primary groups are also more or less permanent, controlling the individual over a sufficient period of time and facilitating the formation of habits, attitudes and values. Further, the primary groups afford a fairly permanent basis of adjustment of the individual not merely with reference to food, shelter, family-raising and security, but also in respect of occupation and economic role and status in the social order and also of intellectual, aesthetic and religious objects, interest in which is stimulated and often fulfilled by cultural products of the home, the creations of craftsmanship and art, decorative, pictorial or musical. All the major values of life can, indeed, be satisfied *integrally* in the primary groups in which the individual's interests and energies are more or less completely absorbed. An integral value experience for the individuals, whose social selves are not irregularly scattered among several groups claiming their interest, action and allegiance, is as helpful towards effective personality integration as the congeniality of mind and temperament and community of purposes and standards established between the individuals. Such integral value experience elicits a stable, spontaneous loyalty. Josiah Royce stresses the significance of loyalty as a source of insight to reality: "This central characteristic of the loyal spirit consists in the fact that it conceives and values its cause as a reality." This arises out of common understanding or communion and mutuality of interests and sentiments that create a new totality which comprehends and overreaches the meanings, preferences or goals of the individuals concerned. Royce illustrates this with reference to loyalty to friendship that "involves your willingness to actively and practically create and maintain a life which is to be the united life of yourself and your friend—not the life of your friend alone, nor the life of yourself and your friend as you exist apart but the common life, the life above and inclusive of your distinctions, the one life that you are to live as friends." All loyalties engendered in the familistic groups involve unique insights, exaltations and disciplines of a new creative, spiritual whole that is brought to birth in the process of or maturation of every major familial relationship.

The Familistie Group as Framework of Integral, Universal and Enduring Value-Experience

The primary groups are formed, grow and expand from the smallest unit of society spontaneously, bringing under their fold persons homogeneous in social composition and culture. In close, direct and continued association with one another within a small territory for the satisfaction of manifold fundamental demands, they develop mutual devotion, love, justice, fidelity and sacrifice that are essential familial values and virtues, carried over into wider fields of social interests and goals and taking in the total personality. The conflict between ends which are "intrinsic" or moral, and ends which are merely "instrumental", i.e., social, between loyalty to the family and loyalty to society is reduced or eliminated in the primary group world. As the values sought are such universal values as justice, love and goodness that are resolved into concrete face-to-face relations between man and man, such ideals cease to be abstract norms or sentiments but arouse ardent emotions and loyalties, and stimulate the moral action of each member of the group according to his place in the system. Simultaneously the desires and emotions are set at rest in bonds of reciprocal understanding and appreciation of persons that like the values themselves are regarded as eternal, beyond-human. Dewey observes: "There is something deep within human nature itself which pulls towards settled relationships. Inertia and the tendency toward stability belong to emotions and desires as well as to masses and molecules. That happiness which is full of content and peace is found only in enduring ties with others which reach to such depths that they go below the surface of conscious experience to form its undisturbed foundation".[6] The norms derived from the vital, steady and deep relationships of a good family thus permeate the whole of collective life and interests. The members of the clan, caste or rural community are designated "brothers and sisters". Even when strangers are introduced into the village community they are adopted as "earth-brothers" in imitation of the practice of adoption of kinsmen in the absence of natural sons as heirs by the joint family. In each case the acquisition of status and privilege rests on the recognition of kinship. Just as the patriarch and the elders rule the family, so the village, the tribe and the folk are governed by patriarchs and elders who mete out familistic justice to all irrespective of blood relationship. "In agriculture the farmer, fully alive to the needs of the future generation, conserves soil resources; he is "his brother's keeper",—the brother of tomorrow. In arts, handicrafts and the professions a certain standard of service to the community is maintained. Occuptions mark the man who conforms to certain standards of social expectancy. Each group sets up its norm or pattern of conduct for the individual, defines the role for each member, and invests it with a certain status.

The definition of norms and the laying out of various roles and statuses in all primary groups follow the familial situation in which the dominating spirit is a sense of solidarity. The family expands into the clan or caste; the clan or the caste expands into the village or group of villages, that become somewhat mixed in blood and culture but all persons are closely welded together by the ties of kinship, vicinal association, neighbourhood attachment or participation in ritual observance or worship at the common shrine for the village god or ancestor. The ascendency of the absolute values over individual goals and of the social obligations over individual preferences has been established in the past, and is established today more effectively and more universally by the primary group than by any other type of group. The types of primary groups are affiliated to one another, one comprehending the other in the form of concentric circles so that all interests and values, biological, economic, social and spiritual, are satisfied integrally, and certain universal patterns of ideas, sentiments and values evolve. The lives of all are fully integrated with the collective purpose and ethos that find expression in the smooth, harmonious inter-personal relations in the village community, the joint family, the caste, the religious, social and economic brotherhoods. The small stable community gives every individual a share in determining the occupational role, status and character of all the other individuals. Moral judgment, censure or approbation are universal processes which all share and in which all are equally concerned. The values of a face-to-face community are worked out and shaped for all by all; they become easily the universals of a culture.

Family or any other primary group loyalty often blocks the expansion of the self, and endangers higher loyalties in many countries and states of social development. In the Orient this danger is sought to be averted by integrating the family with the clan, the caste and the neighbourhood that all present the individual with opportunities of devotion and sacrifice in larger social groups above the family. At the same time the code of ethics transforms family virtues into universal virtues, extending the spirit of love and devotion in familial relations to larger and more complex collective relations; while the stress of the ascetic ideal keeps family virtues in their true place. Thus the mutuality attained within the family circle expands from lesser and parochial to higher and more inclusive loyalties in the community, borrowing from the family all its vivid symbols for exciting devotion and sacrifice in the wider social groups. The absence of class cleavage and of disparity of power and privilege and the greater solidarity of the community in the Orient also help towards the ascription of universal values to larger social units that do not come in conflict with other groups or units, but express themselves harmoniously and altruistically in the total life of human community.

The Family and Caste—Starting Points for the Cultivation of Universal Values and Virtues in the Orient

No wonder that in Chinese ethics the five eternal ideals,—humaneness, uprightness, propriety, insight and faith—are based upon the principle of child obedience in the family. From child obedience are also derived the four forms of moral obligation: filial piety, brotherliness, loyalty and fidelity. The "five cardinal human relationships" are all occupied with the family. They are the relationships between king and subjects, between father and son, between husband and wife, and those between brothers and between friends. The last relationship between friends may be identified with the family, because friends are those who can be included in the family circle—"family friends".[7] The family thus becomes the basis and the starting point for the cultivation of all virtues. Confucius has explained this, "The reason why the gentleman teaches filial piety is not because it is to be seen in the home and every-day life. He teaches filial piety in order that man may respect all those who are fathers in the world. He teaches brotherliness in the younger brother, in order that man may respect all those who are elder brothers in the world. He teaches the duty of the subject, in order that man may respect all who are rulers in the world." And, again, when Ta T'ung or world brotherhood is realised, man, according to Confucius, will not love his own parents to the exclusion of parents of others, nor his own sons to the exclusion of sons of others. He will provide sustenance to the aged as long as they live, employment to the able-bodied, opportunity for development to the young, friendly care to widows, orphans, childless men and the disabled, for each man a task and for each woman a home.[8] Thus "filial virtue is the basis of virtue and the origin of culture." The Chinese word for 'culture' is derived from the word for 'filial piety'. In Chinese society we find, indeed, a superb example of the values of primary groups moulded into universal values, virtues, beauties and proprieties that have fashioned a most enduring and humane civilisation.

Indian civilisation has worked somewhat differently. India, which is less family-minded than China, has chosen another primary group, *viz.*, the occupational or functional caste and transformed its values and virtues into the universals of her culture. "Better to die in one's role than to imitate the ways and functions of the superior!" lays down the Indian scripture. There are dignity, honour and esteem for all in their roles or occupations, however sinful or wrong, as those of the butcher and the hunter. For it is God who resides in every person and incites every activity. There is thus universal value achieved in the duties of one's role, occupation or station undertaken from a pure sense of duty. Disinterestedness, detachment and devotion in one's narrow circumscribed position and status are the universal virtues that constitute the very basis of ethos in India. A religion of universal personalism has smoothed the acerbities of an immobile occupational structure and rigid caste gradation, and explains the humane, non-violent and peaceful character of Indian civilisation.

In both China and India the magnification of familial and occupational values and virtues into the universal patterns of culture is due to the definiteness and endurance of the family, the clan or the caste as endogamous cultural groups in the respective civilisations, to the intensity of emotional inter-stimulation in these face-to-face groups supported by age-old myths and legends, and to the total participation of individuals in these groups that satisfy manifold interests and values, economic, social, aesthetic and religious, and that offer more or less inclusive foci of thought and activity.

The Ethics of the Family

The familistic groups are interested in the family and homestead land, in work, security and status, and in character and co-operativeness. These comprise the major values of life. In each case man becomes the carrier and transmitter of absolute values. Land becomes a prized possession, and cultivation not a business but a profession, a school of virtues,—foresight, prudence, fortitude and a belief in divine providence. Even in the United States of America, "the acquisition of land has motivated rural peoples of our nation from the time of its founding. It remains today a major interest. About this goal centred first; enterprise, security, status, drive and ambition." The American pioneer-farmer replenished his family, but dissipated land resources. He was dominated by the spirit of business and speculation in his agricultural enterprise that led him on from homestead to homestead in feverish pursuit of profit and wander-lust. Life and labour in connection with the land in such ancient and sedentary rural civilisations as China and India are dominated by the collective purposes of perpetuating the family and the clan, and transmitting to posterity the heritage of the soil and homestead unimpaired through a kind of 'permanent agriculture' or 'circular farming'. In China a peculiar type of rural mysticism also transforms the toil of the peasant in the fields into a communion with the Spirit of Heaven. Without a commingling of the spirits of Earth and Heaven, the Yen (female) and Yang (male) principles, crops cannot grow and ripen. The toil of the Chinese farmer in the fields brings about this sacred consummation and perpetuates the patrimony, worship and tradition of the family. Thus absolute values forge the bonds between work and worship, between Earth and Heaven.

Another set of basic values are centred round work, security and social status. In rural society a person obtains status by hard and honest toil. The man who obtains the richest harvest or forges the best steel for the plough ascends in social esteem. Strenuous toil is the road to security. The idler and the pauper are looked down upon in all rural societies, while the nature of production is such as to rule out exploitation since the tools and implements belong to the worker himself. Universal values are imported by social myths into work as a supreme virtue. In familistic ethics the motto is, 'each according to his needs'. This principle is extended as far as practicable to all other primary groups that fight against social and economic cleavage that landlordism and capitalistic farming have introduced as new features. Personal misfortunes and accidents often reduce sufficiency into poverty and insecurity. But the primary groups — the family, the clan and the kindred—support and protect the disabled, the infirm and the destitute. This along with warm, intimate responsiveness on the part of others prevents demoralisation. The primary groups assure to everybody the general conditions of fulfilment of one's role, however limited and circumscribed the sphere of life and interests, in order to assure him status and self-esteem, the indispensable pre-requisite of emotional security and support of personality value.

Social cohesiveness and solidarity, fidelities in the relations of men and of groups, co-operativeness in labour in the fields from season to season, and the sharing in common of family joys and sorrows illustrate how the absolute values of mutual love, devotion and sacrifice seek to guide the relationship of man to man. The greatest emphasis in the primary groups is put on the value of character. Neither by age nor by efficiency nor by learning but by character one gains status and community respect. Nor is there an exaggerated sense of individuality. In rural civilisations spiritual discipline widens self-consciousness into collective consciousness. The individual personality obtains realisation by identification with the collectivity.

Familial Relationships as Religious Symbols

Religion and philosophy, art and ethics, all serve one aim, *viz.*, the manifestation of the absolute values of truth, goodness and beauty in the empirical world including the relationship between man and man. Every major human relationship, such as the parent-child relation, the relation of companionship and the man-woman relation, is seized and transfigured by myth, art and religion into an approach to the deity. Thus not merely man but every human relationship become symbols of the ultimate values. The Deity as the Father, the Mother, the Friend or Companion, the Chief and the Beloved becomes the apotheosis of the familistic attachments and attitudes that direct man's emotional ecstasy and insight into the absolute and transcendental.[9] Man uses symbolic ritual means when he deals with the realm of the transcendental. Symbolic action or relationship does not show any intrinsic connection with the transcendental end. The fundamental values of family relationship are closely related to the absolute values; these have an exalting metaphysical element and cannot be judged by the rational rules of *quid pro quo* or contract but by transcendental meanings, attitudes and values that these express. As a matter of fact an importation of the idea of contract or calculation of mutual services and rewards into the conjugal or any other familial relationship entirely repudiates the nature of such relationship, and is regarded as some kind of perversion. In most countries of the world the notion of marriage as a sacrament, accordingly, stresses the duties and obligations of the partners beyond individual ends and purposes, and directs these into a communion of life and mind that extend beyond the finite lives of the individual. A destiny is fulfilled in and through the partner's individual happiness and unhappiness that is greater than their actual ethical being, the revelation of a life of another order than that of the empirical man and woman—of a deep transcendence and permeation from person to person of eternal values and creative insights that give an ultimate meaning to empirical life. Hence it is that the major familial relationships become themselves symbolic. Obedience to the parents, piety for the ancestors, attachment between the married couple and tenderness for the young ones, all partake of the nature of rituals, sanctified by religion, ennobled by art and conserved by tradition. Just as art and religion impregnate family relationships with transcendental feelings and attitudes, the familistic groups supply to religion some of its major symbols of loyalty or approach to the divinity derived from man's primary experiences and values. These bring about the intensification of and canalisation of human loves and affections that deepen and widen, overreaching the bounds of human aspirations and the contexts of the domestic setting, and making accessible to man and woman engaged in their daily routine of domestic duties, joys and insights that are trans-natural and trans-human.

Interchange between Religion and Family

Religious consciousness in which the human and the divine love patterns easily slip into each other largely strengthens familistic values and virtues, contributing to reinforce all social bonds and aid social integration. Religion gives back to society through the infinite ideal variegation and enrichment of satisfactions and values and integration and fixation of norms of social relationships more than it obtains from the familiar and universal domestic values and virtues. Chastity, fidelity, conjugal love, brotherliness, compassion, obedience and sacrifice become sacred not merely as human loyalties—the sublimest flowers of rural civilisation, but also as the ultimate values beckoning and directing human beings to the Beyond. Such trans-human values become inexhaustible in each single relationship with infinite range and depth that over-reach man's lives; while, springing as these do from different human relationships, these merge together as in an ocean of undifferentiated joy and love freed from any human or social context. They become universal loyalties and symbols, saturated with deep emotions that guide primary experiences and produce balanced, integrated personalities, who are in peace and harmony with the universe and at the same time enjoy the ecstasy and enlightenment of mystic detachment. The supreme achievement of a culture is to bridge the gulf between the empirical and the absolute, between the transcendental and the concrete, between the One and the Many. The familistic types of groups and relations bear the possibility of conditioning and moulding man to the supreme revelation that his empirical values are but one aspect of the infinitely richer values. A man becomes holy, the torch-bearer of the supreme values, irrespective of age, class, personal capacity and social status; he cannot be used as a mere means for something or somebody. The relationship of man to man also becomes holy. This builds up an ethical system in which the struggle between individual and social loyalties, between individual and supra-individual values is set at rest. Through its intellectual and emotional comprehension of the relation of the individual to mankind, it attains a universality and at the same time a constructive significance and dynamism for the personality and social order that have been hard to combine in man's ethical codes.

References

1. *New Introductory Lectures*, p. 137.
2. Young: *Personality and Problems of Adjustment,* pp. 168-173; also Handbook of Social Psychology, pp. 110, 133-142; Nimkoff: *Personality Development in Encyclopedia of Psychology,* 194-196.
3. See Mead : *Mind, Self and Society,* pp. 177-186 ; Murray and others : *Explorations in Personality,* chapter II.
4. See especially Toennies' book translated by Loomis : *Fundamental Concepts of Sociology*, Chapin : *Contemporary American Institutions* and may *Man and His Habitation, and Social Ecology* for analysis and implications of the cultural and social aspects of group phenomena.
5. See Gardner Murphy : *Personality*, pp, 855-857.
6. *The Public and its Problems.*
7. Lin Yutang, *My Country and My People,* p. 170; also *The Wisdom of China and India,* pp. 853-860.
8. Confucius, *The Book of Rites*, VII.
9. See *my Theory and Art of Mysticism.*

8

THE DIFFERENTIATION AND CONFLICT OF VALUES IN THE INTEREST-GROUP

The Superficiality and unstability of Values in the Interest Group

Social progress implies the differentiation of man's interests and functions. The differentiation of values accompanies this process. Man's mind attains greater flexibility, and adapts itself to new social experiences of specialised interests and orders of activity by inhibition and specification of satisfactions and values. Simultaneously he forms groups deliberately and consciously on the basis of specific interests, satisfactions and values. Such groups are called by sociologists special-interest groups, secondary, ecological, impersonal and derivative groups, representing principally fractional and specialised needs, interests and values. Man never seeks values in isolation. Just as his life is entirely lived and comprehended within the range of primary or familistic and secondary or interest-groups, that exhaust all his social interaction, so all his values accrue in the course of his participation in the primary groups, especially the family and the neighbourhood, and the secondary groups, especially the occupational groups, the trade union, the class, the political party and the state.

All secondary or interest-groups depend for their stability and continuity not necessarily on face-to-face contacts and emotional attitudes and ideas arising there from, but on rational consideration or calculation of interests and satisfactions and on indirect, mechanical means of social interaction and communication extending over the postal system, the press and other means of long-range communication. The primary or familistic groups, depending on direct relations, are confined to a limited ecological and social space. The secondary or interest-groups may develop into secondary "communities" that extend beyond the geographical boundaries of peoples and nations, as, for instance, class, race, empire and the Communist International. For this reason the intensity and range of man's intercourse with fellow-men in such groups diminish, in spite of the contacts established by the modern newspaper. "Vision is a spectator; hearing is a participator", observes Dewey. Publication is partial and the public which results is partially informed and formed until the meanings it purveys pass from mouth to mouth. In the secondary-group world, where communications are broken, inarticulate and faint, social intelligence and emotions no doubt become restricted in their operations and effects. The scale of satisfactions and values diminishes in ardour and intensity. Such values are, indeed, thin and surface-rooted, not being earth-bound nor derived from primary experiences in the relations of personal intercourse. They are also distinctly intellectual, men being drawn together *en masse* by the newspaper and the press on the basis of economic interests, political loyalties, and tastes and preferences in aesthetic or recreational matters. Men are here of interest to one another, not as persons but for the work they do, their contribution towards fulfilling the large variety of their economic needs and abstract intellectual interests through the large and expanding network of mechanically intermediated social intercourse. They rise, to be sure, far above family exclusiveness, parochialism and narrow loyalties to the kindred, the caste, the occupational group and even the nation, and extend their activities on a scale unknown before. But personal friendships, loyalties and attachments wane. In the secondary groupings men live in a social vacuum; sentiment and emotion are much less interfused with the fundamental habits, attitudes and moral codes that are rooted in ties of mutual understanding and appreciation of persons, but these have an impersonality facilitating easy assimilation into covenants, pacts and laws. The secondary group world is knit by formal laws and regulations, that however cannot replace deep attachments and transcendental loyalties. But such secondary groups that are insecure and live dangerously, such as the criminal gang, the secret society and the revolutionary political party, claim the whole individuality of their members. Like the familistic groups these develop rituals and symbols for their consolidation, and apply sanctions familiar in the primary group world, *viz.*, social ostracism and psychological pressure to combat disloyalty and defection. The secondary group organisation of society is also characterised by the multiplicity and shifting character of groups which reform, subdivide and reintegrate, satisfying the many "social selves" of the individual, his various fractional needs and values, that separate and blend more freely.

The temple or church ritual serves religious, aesthetic and intellectual values; with the decline of religious interest a considerable proportion of the religious body seeks satisfactions in associations like clubs, societies for the cultivation of science, art, social welfare, drama, etc., or habitually visits cinema houses and theatres. Cheap dancing halls and cabarets satisfy those among the cinema and theatre-goers who seek coarse recreations rather than aesthetic and intellectual delights. The clientele of dance halls are, again, brought together into night clubs and brothels when they drift into yet unwholesome pleasures. In each case secondary groups are constituted by persons who resemble one another in parts of their motivations, goals and lives, and who also belong to other groups that persistently claim a different part of their interests and satisfactions. As persons change in their patterns of dominating interests and values, secondary groups change their circles of adherents, who, however, differ in some measure in respect of the satisfactions derived since all groups fulfil several interests and values at the same time. The multiplicity and viability of secondary groupings reflect the unstable and fractional character of satisfactions and values they fulfil. With the dominance or weakening of a set of motives and values, secondary groupings thus continually change in their pattern and membership.

The Ethics of the Secondary Groups

In the secondary-group organisation of society the individual's and the group's scale of values hardly coincides. Man ceaselessly strives to fit his scheme of life and goals into the group norms that show considerable flexibility, or he becomes a rebel, an innovator or an outcaste, affiliating himself with groupings that have segregated, exclusive, even anti-social goals. More commonly he becomes a misfit in another way. Man's values, attitudes and social habits have been in the course of human evolution shaped and selected by his primary-group world. With his earth-bound affections and primary experiences still dominating his nature, he cannot adjust himself to innumerable, invisible groups that demand his allegiances clamorously through the press, the pulpit and the platform. He becomes volatile in his opinions and attitudes and in his judgment of values. Full of whims and caprices, unable to frame a life-plan of his own out of the medley and confusion of values that different groups present before his consciousness, and the subtle lure and illusive technique of propaganda adopted by them, he loses his sense of values. If he does not love, honour and obey as in the primary-group world, he cannot expect to escape coercion by group pressures, and seduction by group suggestions and propaganda. His search for values becomes an illusion and a snare.

The secondary-group organisation of the urban world is interested not in the family and homestead land, but in romantic satisfaction, money and mobility, not in work, security and status, but in conspicuous idleness and consumption and social ascent, not in character and co-operativeness but in individualism and power. Such difference in major goals between the primary-group and the secondary-group worlds is dynamic with implications in social habits, moral norms and personality patterns. For in each case man becomes the bearer of empirical, instrumental and fractional rather than absolute, intrinsic and integral values of the primary-group world. The former fit into a social pattern, characterised by the compartmentalisation of interests, functions and values, interchangeability of roles, jobs and statuses, and all-engrossing pursuit of money as a dominating end in itself, procuring not merely material goods but also purchasing and manipulating the higher values of life.

Formal and impersonal groupings for the procurement of fractional and instrumental values are as old as civilisation itself. Along with the tribes, folks and kinship groups modified by adoption and other fictions, early societies also saw, especially in the cities, the formation of influential groups of traders, money-lenders and scribes who introduced legalism and contract into the primary-group world. Ancient urban communities, based on money economy, developed a good deal of compartmentalisation of interests and values, and moved away from the major values of the rural primary-group world towards the artificial, sophisticated ideal. But it is in the urban-industrial world of today that this movement has seen its perfection. Machine technology uproots vast masses of men from the land and the countryside, and keeps them on the move from town to town and from factory to factory. It brings about the disintegration of many primary groups and destroys many fundamental values, attitudes and habits, connected with land, work, family-raising and the neighbourhood that motivate rural peoples.[1] A people uprooted from their homestead and kindred do not show any keen desire for property and home-building, for transmitting the family possession, faith and tradition to posterity, and even for perpetuating the family itself. It loses thrift, home-spun prudence, fortitude, faith in a long scheme of things and other ancient virtues of a rural primary-group world, and by wasting soil resources for the sake of quick and transitory gains impoverishes the future generations. The new values of the secondary-group world centre round money and conspicuous consumption, quick movement from place to place and status to status and individual ambition and power-manifestation.

The Class Personality

Specialisation of functions and interests and minute division of labour in the urban-industrial world imprison men's values within the limited sphere of their occupations, professions and jobs that mould their minds internally even more than externally. Pareto observes: "Living in a given group impresses the mind with certain concepts, certain ways of thinking and doing, certain prejudices, certain beliefs which endure in time and acquire psuedo-objective individuality." Minds are so compartmented and values so fractionalized that the common ground of values, attitudes and habits is narrowed to an extreme, limiting the opportunities for collective thought and action. Thus class interests, attitudes and values emerge, breaking up the solidarity of the community and the integrity of the universal of its culture. The individual's scale of living, including his aesthetic and spiritual values, approximates to the standard of living of his social class. The class standard of comfort that is an external norm is measured by one's material goods and visible satisfactions—food, apparel, apartment, car and the amount of leisure and the class of recreations that he can afford, and that elicit social approbation or admiration and improve status.[2]

The delights of family-raising and rearing and the higher intellectual, aesthetic and religious values are subordinated to the desire to attain the standard of comfort of the class or of the next higher social grade, that is conceived in materialistic terms, since a constant upward social movement should be assisted by visibility through conspicuous enjoyment or ostentatious display. Often the effort to procure costly and luxurious furniture, car and woman's apparel for maintaining the class standards that bring status disorganises the lives of individuals and families, and also keeps social classes on the move to discover and crave all that glitters. The standard of living is now a symbol of class status, a means of maintaining the social distance between the classes. Not food in general, but the kind of food, not dress in general, but the style of clothing, not shelter in general, but the special kind of flat, apartment or mansion, not recreations in general but the special class of entertainments, associated with a particular social class, have become economic values for the winning of status. Not the standard of living but the *display* of the standard of living has become an economic imperative for the maintenance of class status. Man develops an 'occupation' or 'class personality', with his habits, attitudes and values differentiated as if he belongs to a different nation in the bosom of the same community.

Depreciation of the Values of Social Consensus and Communion

With the increase of social and economic cleavage the values that the individual as a member of a particular social class seeks become more rational and abstract, on the one hand, and segregated from the community interests and welfare and the universals of a culture on the other. These embody themselves in such goals as power, privilege and prestige manifestations. The basic community standards of equality, justice and solidarity are challenged. Dewey observes : "Each class is rigidly sure of the rightness of its own ends and hence not over-scrupulous about the means of attaining them. One side proclaims the ultimacy of order—that of some old order which conduces to its own interest. The other side proclaims its rights to freedom, and identifies justice with its submerged claims. There is no common ground, no moral understanding, no agreed-upon standard of appeal."[3] The rural primary-group world metes our justice in social relations through the age-old emphasis of the sacredness of man and of all human relationships, interpreted according to the norm of the familistic relationships that become the seats of the supreme values. In the urban secondary-group world, equality, justice and solidarity have to be implemented through the legal formulation of the Rights of Man and of the various freedoms that mitigate the dangers of social cleavage and of coercion and exploitation of one class by another through the use of the machinery of the state that as a secondary grouping eclipses the power of the class. Both political and economic Rights of Man of the 18th century, as reformulated in the 20th, and the freedoms from want and economic insecurity, of self-organisation and expression of opinion represent the objectification of certain supreme values in human relations based on the infinite spiritual worth and dignity of the individual. The supreme value of a democracy is the majesty and sacredness of the individual. From this have flowed the rights and freedoms of the person, and the notion of integrity and solidarity of society that is superior to and larger than the class or the state. Unfortunately both the stress of individualism that infected the Western mind with what Hocking calls the disease of Rights-without-Duties[4] and the excessive impersonality and fractionalisation of interests, activities and values sought by the economic class that has become the most powerful and best organised among the social groups prevent a full appreciation of the values of consensus and communion that society embodies, and that no other secondary groups in industrial civilisation can embody. Thus instead of rounded, integrated personalities, group selves characterised by psychic dissociation and conflict emerge. Instead of the growth solidarity within the community, social classes with sharply segregated interests and values grow in power and violence. Industrial civilisation with its machine technology, its minute division of labour, its interchangeability of jobs, its ascendancy of secondary groupings in terms of special interests and its excessive mobility has profound implications for man's scale of values and social harmony.

The Supremacy of Pecuniary and Instrumental over Imponderable and Absolute Values

The law of substitution obtains supremacy in the urban, secondary-group world. Men's jobs, positions and roles exchange for one another. Thus their jobs, positions and roles become more significant than their intrinsic qualities, their efficiency than they themselves. This encourages a rationality, impersonality and casualness of relationships that ramify through almost all contacts, and that are integrated and organised into a vast, complicated institution, called the "market".[5] The market that is the predominant institution in an industrial civilisation is not merely the field of exchange of visible and divisible economic values; but it also standardises, purchases and sells many values of a non-pecuniary character through the use of money. The power of money to regulate social activities and interests, entirely free from economic considerations, rests on the casualness, immediacy and rationality of human relationships in the secondary-group organisation of society. Transitory, deliberate and contractual relationships supplant the enduring, integral and personal relationships that are bearers of the absolute values in the familistic group world. The casualised and specialised relationships in the secondary-group organisation of society become carriers of the empirical and instrumental values now promoted to the rank of the supreme values and reducible to pecuniary terms. Such relationships, rather than personal loyalty and personal service, are bought and sold in the market by money that far oversteps the economic sphere, and becomes the quasi-universal nexus of man-to-man dealing.

In a certain state of secondary-group organisation of society, money is sought in the abstract as an end in itself without invoking in imagination the varied satisfactions and values it can procure. Money in modern industrial civilisation is the "Open Sesame" key that opens the door to many values that are considered outside the pecuniary realm by other civilisations. Man's self-esteem, honour and status frequently depend upon money. Factors in personality development come to be governed by his pecuniary status. Even his cultivation of the arts and pursuit of goodness in philanthropic service in some measure rest on money power. Such pervasive influence of money is silent, insidious and unsuspected, and is derived from the entire background of modern machine technology and group organisation and the ascendency of empirical and instrumental values. The secondary-group world no doubt yields unsuspectingly to the principle that 'everything has its price'. Money holds, according to G. Simmel, a privileged position in virtue of the very indeterminateness of the satisfactions it can procure and the possibility of alternate choices. Money is the unrivalled tool, the pure means; and this is precisely why it passes to the foreground of desire and concentrating on itself the multitude of efforts set up as a dominating end.[6] Money is the most appropriate and adaptable value medium of a community that applies the law of substitution of jobs, roles and positions over a widening and interdependent territory and sphere of human relationship. It can best activate the secondary-group organisation, and best express and integrate its empirical and instrumental goals. It serves as a most efficacious implement of reciprocity, a powerful social binder in the secondary-group world.

The imperfection of money as an implement arises not as a medium, but in extending the use of this medium to indivisible, common and absolute values, in reducing such values into divisible and instrumental values, and thus bringing them within the pecuniary sphere. This is a moral problem, concerned with what is called the 'perversion of values'. The way to fight economism and money power is not to treat the pecuniary sphere as sordid and base; but to strictly delimit its boundaries, and at the same time to introduce into it the supreme values so that the latter may as far as practicable mingle with the money values, and modify the working of the market and mere pecuniary relationships. The pecuniary system must be subjected to constant criticism and revision, based on moral judgments. The transactions of the market should be humanised and moralised, so that these might not run counter to the higher ethical aims of the personality and society through the transformation of instrumental and intermediate into intrinsic and ultimate ends. Excessive differentiation and substitution of jobs and roles, proliferation of groupings, occupations and functions as well as preference of instrumental and empirical values are all facilitated by the intermediacy of money as the abstract and pure means universally accepted as a dominating social purpose. The twin laws of substitution and intermediacy in the secondary-group world of machine technology continuously remove the means farther and farther from the ends. The ever-variegated, ramifying pursuit of economic and biological values, not as means of realising the social and spiritual values but as dominating ends themselves, receives no check. This is the familiar law of 'transfer' by which instrumental values become promoted to end values. The interplay of the principles of substitution, intermediacy and transfer alters the absolute moral order that subordinates the biological and economic to social and spiritual values. The conflict between the absolute hierarchy of values and the order of values that is culturally conditioned by the regime or secondary groups denotes a serious moral crisis for the individual that forms the background of widespread personal distress and disorganisation in modern urban communities.

The Fractionalisation of Self, Values and Society

Gradually the outlook of the impersonal, special interest, secondary groupings and the habits and cultural values and practices associated with them invades the family, neighbourhood and the rural community, and this leads to the disappearance of many of the personal, intimate and integral reactions in these groups, and their accompanying values. In this manner the secondary-group organisation and its associated habits, attitudes and values destroy the universals of a culture and produce psychic conflicts and tensions within the individual, due to the antagonism between the integral attitudes and values represented by the ancient and familiar primary-group contacts and the segmental and specific attitudes and values built up by the new secondary groups. On the one hand, the individual is regimented by machine technology into a machine hand, the man with his 'job' whose vocational training fits him psychologically and physiologically to the type of job that requires a particular combination of abilities and aptitudes. It is according to the latter that man is classified and appraised. His personality becomes the sum total of reaction patterns expected by society from willing individuals. It is stereotyped and segmented with dependable, uniform, psychological responses and action patterns. Man's thoughts, feelings and attitudes, all become assimilated to a general standardised pattern demanded by science and technology. He cannot build up integral values and experiences. His values are not his, and his instincts and desires become, therefore, possessive, exclusive and aggressive. It is the starvation and impoverishment of normal desires and emotions as the result of mechanisation, standardisation and irrationality of the technological apparatus that make these morbid, violent and antagonistic. On the other hand, the loss of self leads to the substitution of automaton conformity for the real self. The individual merges his frustrated self into the secondary group, and the secondary group becomes transformed into the mass or crowd with uniform thoughts, emotions and action patterns, uniform not only in the offices, workshops and factories but also in the sphere of amusement and recreation. The secondary group promotes a dead and deadening uniformity in man's schedule of interests, values and living. Such a social situation in which thousands of individuals are gripped is the chief cause of psychic tensions and neuroses, resulting in both split personalities and split masses or crowds.

The various "social selves" of the individual accordingly seek satisfactions at random and disharmoniously; and the divergent and opposed interests, values and forms of overt conduct prevent the development of integrated personalities. In many ways the differentiation of societal groupings met with in the modern world accompanies a process of splitting up of human personalities, due to the lack of harmony between the divergent satisfactions and values of the social selves, and the incapacity of the self to take the roles, attitudes and values of persons belonging to other groups. The rise of secondary groupings in the modern world that has been facilitated by an evolution connected with industrial division of labour, specialisation, machine technology, the growth of cities and the pecuniary scale of valuation leads to individual and social neurosis and revolt and social unrest due to the profound contrast between the frustration of the values of the individual and the apparent fullness and lavish promises of his secondary-group environment.

The crisis in modern industrial civilisation is concerned with both the personal life organisation and scheme of values and the pattern and function of group organisation. The secondary groupings with their advantages of detailed specialisation, inter-changeability of functions and standardisation and reduction of a wide range of values into the pecuniary measure have come to stay in modern industrial communities. Loyalties to the family group, the neighbourhood, the clan, the guild and the region have shown a narrowness and exclusiveness that are incompatible with the procedures of big business and liberal democracy or with the values of natural liberty, freedom of initiative and enterprise and voluntary co-operation that they have prized. But these secondary groupings must not be permitted to bring about personal insecurity and deviation and disruption of the unity of society. The social solidarity of modern communities was promoted in the early stage of industrialisation by the improvement of transport and communication, the comprehensive use of money as expressing, integrating and energising personal and social values and the formation of all sorts of secondary groupings on the basis of rational, contractual relations. At the present social stage this solidarity instead of being furthered is profoundly disturbed by the economic sphere, with its pecuniary measure, regulating large spheres of social activities and relationships and setting up ends that do not fit harmoniously with comprehensive social and ethical ends, by the development of economic relationships on the basis of exploitation rather than of reciprocal service, and by the rise of the class as a powerful secondary grouping overshadowing other secondary groups. The class has sought property, privilege and wealth and used these against the rest of the society, subordinating the key values of equality and justice to class power and privilege. Neither laws, nor formal regulations and conventions of the secondary groups, nor public opinion have been able to combat and control this effectively.

How to refashion the secondary groupings so that they may fulfil integral and comprehensive, and not specialised and segregated interests and values, and arouse the intimate responsiveness and idealism of the primary groups is the crucial task of modern culture. Inseparably dovetailed into it is the task of restoring solidarity to the highly fractionalised society of today through the stress of social values and virtues and universals of culture, and of re-integrating the personality and his internal value system that may function in bringing to a focus more integrative and more adaptive types of societal groups and relations within the framework of a highly complex, mechanised industrial civilisation. One thing is clear. If we wish to alter fundamentally the secondary group organisation and cognate social habits and institutions of industrial civilisation, we have to begin with changes in the series of tables of values erected by the latter. The realm of values is the invisible workshop in which man discovers and fashions the raw materials, energies and mechanisms for remaking his visible environment.

Great multitudes in modern industrial communities are deprived today of the adequate use even of their normal emotions and intellectual faculties in the daily toil of life. Only a small section of the population can function creatively on the higher level of culture, enjoying the values of appreciation in the realms of truth, beauty and goodness. The toil, the burden and the risk of industrial civilisation are disproportionately borne by the rest of the population condemned to the life of mechanics. is only a free collective industrial enterprise in which the masses of industrial workers may participate, not as cogs in a vast chain of complicated production which they do not understand nor appreciate, but as co-owners, co-managers and co-sharers, fixing and achieving the goal of industrial production in its larger aspects that can arouse thought and emotional experience. The worker's intellectual interests are fully awakened as he ceases to be "a mere hand drawn from the pool of labour," but apprehends the co-ordinated activity of the factory or the system of industrial production as a whole. Only as a co-producer in a great cooperative venture, a worker can become an artist. A recent writer, E. E. Ericksen, observes: "Work in industry without social realisation is banal and deadly. The consequence of such detachment is an extremely artificial bifurcation. So it is most unfortunate that the philosophy of modern economics has so generally assumed that industry and the economic process develop independent of human evaluation and thinking."[7] If the perspective could be changed from the individual to the collective, from the fractional and isolated to that of a whole collective endeavour, industry can satisfy social, intellectual and aesthetic values. Thus Whitehead aptly remarks, "A factory with its machinery, its community of operatives, its social service to the general population, its dependence upon organizing and designing genius, its potentialities as a source of wealth to the holders of its stocks, is an organism exhibiting a variety of vivid values. What we want to train is the habit of apprehending such an organism in its completeness." It is largely through the remaking of the structure of industry that modern civilized man can achieve greater social integration since it is industry that engrosses man's interests, thoughts and emotions. As long, therefore, as industrial civilisation cannot make accessible to all its material as well as its cultural values, nor can nurture the social and cultural level of living for all, society cannot experience the profound depths of intellectual, emotional or moral rapport or communion.

Crowd, Interest-association Society and Commonalty—Ascending Degrees of Social Participation

The distinction between Crowd, Interest-association, Society and Commonalty, representing the ascending degrees of social participation, is of great significance in sociology and ethics. Modern civilisation with its sharp division of social classes and class attitudes and lack of social integration is characterised by crowd phenomena and experiences. The unity or rapport noticed in crowd life obtains mainly in the sphere of instinctive behaviour, emotion and imagination. The affective life in crowd life is reduced to the more primitive emotions, the cognition to the images, and the life of instincts to action. Crowd unity is based on man's primordial, psycho-physical nature obtaining the upper hand. The Crowd is the most unstable, emotional and fitful of all social groups, and is the greatest danger today to industrial peace, political action and social solidarity. It is the crowd psychology that through the press, the radio and the platform is now exercising the strongest pressure towards shaping public opinion in the direction of sectionalism, schism and division in every field, splitting up the unity of modern democratic culture.

Thus democratic society faces the difficult task of maintaining the stability of social relations and institutions against mass outbursts and attacks, whether those of the unemployed and the poor, the political malcontents, the alien-baiters or the mass of newspaper readers, reacting in the same anti-social manner to certain events and situations. Wars, revolutions, schisms, strikes and persecutions, all contribute towards the segmentation of groups, and the movement away from real sociality or universality. Commonalty represents the highest degree of sociality through the interpenetration of minds and behaviours at their highest levels. Usually such Commonalty is restricted in society to family groups, nations, parties, gangs or any other groups in mortal danger and to religious sects and congregations and intellectual and aesthetic groups. The social integration characteristic of Commonalty is based less on the rapport of instincts and emotions or unity of economic interests, and more on common ideals, beliefs and faiths that are embodied in moral patterns, ideals and symbols. Commonalty represents a promise not a consummation. It is Commonalty that represents the perfection of "we-feeling," the acme of identification of individual consciousness with the collective consciousness.

Corresponding Depth-levels of the Self

Corresponding to the four degrees of intensity of social participation there are, as Gurvitch aptly points out, four depth-levels of the self.[8] There is the empty, suggestible primal self of the individual merged in the mad Crowd, the superficial, fractionalised "self" of the individual, participating in the special Interest-association, the more profound "self", participating in Commonalty. The ethical problems of society arise out of the superficial levels of the self, giving rise to individual feelings, attitudes and behaviours that are egoistic, narrow and disintegrative, and to group experience and behaviour at the instinctive level that are equally disruptive. On the other hand, social and moral values and ideals spring from the deeper levels of the self, characterised by both identity consciousness and supremacy of rational intelligence over the instinctive life, seeking to establish equality, co-operation and interdependence of individuals in society, and the most profound "self" participating in society. The deepening of the self is marked by the supremacy of the social or universal over the individual or restricted aspect of the self, by the expansion of social attitudes to the universal life and consciousness. It is only the saint, the poet, the artist, the genius and the hero, who can reveal to society the higher possibilities of the self through intense participation in the collective life and mind. For them the collective is no external milieu to which they are bound by herd suggestion or impulsive imitation as in the Crowd, nor by group egoism or selfishness as in the Interest-association, nor, again, by the uncreative, superficial bonds of habit and passive conformity as in Society. The collective sends its tap roots into the innermost depths of their being. It is they who are fully social in the sense that with the interpenetration of the individual selves and attitudes with the universal they gain at once the highest freedom and responsibility of the self and the transcendental enthusiasm of the social. No doubt the collective institutions and aspirations can be enormously aided and stimulated by a theory of human personality that identifies the self with the universe and the universe with the self.

Non-theistic Mystical Symbolism in the Secondary Group World

The above is a mystical conception without which neither truth values and moral and aesthetic values that are significant for the community can be created, enlarging and deepening communion, nor the invisible bonds between men in the secondary-group world to-day grasped and experienced in what Dewey calls the miracle of a shared life. Bergson rightly insists that individuals can arrive at communion only through the mystic way. The mystics prove themselves to be great men of action: "That which they have allowed to flow into them is a stream flowing down and seeking through them to reach their fellowmen; the necessity to spread around them what they have received affects them like an onslaught of love."[9] It is religion that furnishes the supreme guidance and perspective for all values. In fact religious values are truth values and moral and aesthetic values enhanced, deepened or widened, raised to their highest supra-human or transcendental possibilities.

Mysticism which is the core of religion can, indeed, properly reorient the scale of values and redefine the relationships between invisible and anonymous fellow-humans in the secondary groups by the creation of new, significant symbols and gestures of full and moving human communion and solidarity in the Great Commonalty. Man as a member of the primary groups obeyed the omnipresent, omniscient and omnipotent patriarch, magician, hero or king. His conception of the Personal God was an expansion and elevation of the Father, the Mother, the Patriarch, the Hero, the Sage, the

Guardian, the good Shepherd, the Leader of the Caravan, or the Lord. He aspired after these human values and ideals that religion provided and charged with deep emotions and intuitions of the depths of life. This not only wove the pattern of social integration, but also provided the ethical development of mankind in the primary-group world. It is a non-theistic mysticism that can now make the principle of neighbourhood relationships and loyalties the principle of extensive large-scale organisation through its comprehension of one Cosmic Life and Mind as a vast continuum embracing all men and groups, feelings and concepts, spaces and times, events and lives. A neighbourhood community gave to mankind the conceptions of creating, regulating and destroying personal Divinities, Gods or Spirits, and fixed the pattern of its religious consciousness in terms of the emotionally charged relationships in the family and other primary groups that have become the familiar symbols of worship and communion. Such a small local community of the agricultural world that fashioned not merely the major values and virtues of life but also symbols of approach to the deity in a personal religion have now expanded into a world community of the industrial and commercial world. A personal religion can no longer furnish the abstract principles of loyalty or brotherhood in the modern age of casual and indirect contacts and of impersonal relationships. The failure of religion to fulfil its social role of supplying the requisite symbols for cementing impersonal relationships, due to religious dogma prohibiting readjustment in the conception of the deity, is largely responsible for the profound religious crisis and loss of faith of a considerable section of humanity of this age. This has been recently stressed by a distinguished biologist, Prof. Wood Jones : "The misfortune that has overtaken the spiritual outlook of man is that as his universe expanded his conception of the deity did not expand with it. The tragedy arose through the fact that though there were no limits imposed upon the enlargement of man's conception of the universe as his knowledge of it increased, strict and implicit limits were placed upon any alternations of his conception of the deity. The result has been that, while all the sublime and spiritual revelations of the working of nature become grander with the passage of the centuries, this one—potentially the most sublime and spiritual of them all—has shrunk so far as to be completely incapable to fulfilling the role for which it was conceived. Man of necessity made his deity too small and now is disappointed because this thing that he originally made too small and has not permitted to grow, has failed him."[10]

An elevated type of mysticism gets over the difficulty of transferring the concept of personality to the Absolute, the Beyond, and reaches out to the Mind of the Universe that transcends but includes man's mind and morality; and this need not imply any sacrifice of its ethical possibilities, as is so often assumed by Western ethicists. Moral values that develop most sensitively in inter-personal relationships are viewed here from a transcendental perspective differently from personal religion. These embrace duties towards humanity, past, present, and future, so that human progress both in the sense of the evolution of superior biological types, and the miracle of an increasingly shared life or communion can give man the necessary faith for service and sacrifice that devotion to will of the more personal God of revealed religions now provides. For the ardent mystics of all higher religions, the sense of identity of self with the not-self is often so strong that the desire for personal immortality is overcome, and becomes merged in the silence of supra-human order or the supreme devotion to work for humanity as worship. The archetypal images of the Divine Father and Mother have through the ages supported the spiritual feelings of the brotherhood or solidarity of man. But the notion of God not as the First Person but as the Total It, the third Person Singular, released from the limitations of the idea of human personality, can satisfy his intellect, provided he cultivates sufficient philosophical exaltation, serenity and detachment. And, indeed, in a universe, conceived by science as inevitably advancing through degradation of energy towards annihilation in bleak space, oblivious of human sufferings and aspirations, his utter loneliness and impotence demand moral attitudes that should he purer and more detached, rooted in an acosmic transcendental order or law, the intuition of which may be the abiding source of infinite love and sacrifice in our little dwindling, dying world. It is possible for an impersonal mysticism to contemplate the Absolute in terms of man's own highest ethical aspirations without loading them however with connotations derived from the sense limitations of human personality, to discover the ground of morality in the heart of both the Infinite as well as of the inner life without the risks of any faulty moral insights that may arise from anthropomorphic conceptions of the deity.

Lao Tsu observes: "All things go through their processes of activity and return to the Root. This is what we call the State of

Quiet, and this stillness is the reporting that they have fulfilled their eternal end. To know the Infinite is to be perceptive, to ignore it leads to wild movements and evil issues. To know the Law is to be great of soul, and to be great of soul leads to sympathy with all things. From this sympathy comes the ruling soul, from rulership comes spirituality. In spirituality the Way (the Law) is possessed. He who possesses it endures long, and is not liable to decay." As non-theistic mysticism effaces the distinctions between self and all sentient creatures and all things that are here the goals of life, morality becomes an episode in the establishment of the unity—a pattern of the transcendental cosmic order. The world and human society or Becoming are embraced in one comprehensive Relationship, one all-pervasive Value in Being. There emerges one Life, one Form, one Relationship through nature and the processes of world and society. Through a complete identification between the self and the not-self, each representing the infinitude and majesty of the ail-pervasive cosmic consciousness, man's moral attributes become invested with supreme purity and detachment, transcendence and power, and he can find in the anonymous, invisible secondary-group world of today the manifestation of the supreme religious values. "In the mind of the Eternal spirit there is a Grand Symbiosis of the cosmos in which every part, however insignificant, knows what other distant parts are doing and acts accordingly. There is also an abiding human symbiosis in the spirit behind our direct apprehension which leads us to truth and righteousness and enkindles love, faith, and sacrifice."[11]

The Transcendental Enthusiasm of the Social

Such a religious, trans-social ideal will resolve the present conflict between the egoism, coercion and conflict of secondary groups and personal moral idealism in contemporary society that Niebuhr laments as irreconcilable.[12] It will moralise the vast collectives and values and relate them to the ideal of a total harmony of all life. It will enable classes, nations and other secondary groups to approximate the principles of justic and love and create the international mind and international conscience corresponding to the international economic community built up by modern technological civilisation. Thus the tenderest emotions, beliefs and faiths of mankind will grow to cope with the social and moral situation ushered by the advances of science and technology.

Certain phases of mysticism, whether Oriental or Western, have stressed the impersonal and transcendent aspects of the deity and developed a metaphysics that may furnish the foundations of a modern social ethics. There is here an identification of man's consciousness and the deity from which well forth an infinite pity, compassion or love, cosmic in their sweep and inclusiveness. Or, again, the view of the deity as "the self-transcending transcender of all," imperfect and suffering with all the evil and the pain of the world in the self-surrender of love, becomes temporalistic or ethical, more in keeping with modern metaphysical conceptions than the traditional view of the perfection, self-sufficiency, independence and absoluteness of the Creator. The finite man is here regarded as necessary for God's creative achievement, a partner and friend from whom he expects responsive love. Such types of non-theistic mysticism, with their insights of Cosmic Life, Mind and Purpose and their raptures of unity of consciousness with the processes of the world, might furnish the cosmic pattern of moral principles, symbols and concepts that could effectively regulate the abstract, impersonal, mechanically intermediated social relations in the world of large-scale institutions and vast secondary groups and associations of to-day. These might stimulate an expansive idealism and humanism that could fight for the freedom and equality of economic and political rights of all men and approximation of standards of living of all peoples of the globe. The true foundations thus might be laid of world ethics and world citizenship, emotionally charged and directed by a living religion socially operative in man's enlarged and anonymous environment of today. The new forms of social idealism and humanism stimulated whether by the Hindu conception of the pure Overself that is everywhere and in all men and yet transcendent, or the Buddhist conception of the Buddha nature that is in all sentient creatures and in all the grains of sand of the Ganges, or the modern Christian notion of the "reflexive transcendence" of the deity might accordingly permeate and redefine the anonymous, abstract relationships and values of the secondary group world of to-day.[13] These would, indeed, elicit from man the same continuous and ardent loyalty, devotion and sacrifice for the strange, invisible or unborn fellow-human of the modern city, nation or world organisation as he had shown at the earlier social stage within the bounds of the family, the kindred and the neighbourhood. Modern science shows life as a vast continuum. Modern social and political and economic organisation manifests a global integrity and wholeness.

May not the spiritual vision of man in the anonymous world of the modern city with his vital contacts extending over the expanse of a big state or over international relations make him solidare with the Great Mind and Community of the Universe as the atom is today discerned as solidare with the universe, with him and with all things? But unlike the atom he is conscious and deliberately cooperative and communicative. He ardently seeks the Great Mind and Community of the Universe through the realisation of Truth, Power, Goodness or Charity. Such realisation is the striving of each man for all fellow-humans as the Cosmic Mind and Community in which all live, work and suffer in inexhaustible communion with one another.

References

1. See Webr : *The Protestant Ethic.*
2. Compare Zimmermarn : *Consumption and Standards of Living.*
3. *Human Nature and Conduct*, p. 83.
4. *The Lasting Elements of Individualism*, p, 5.
5. See Max Weber; *Theory of Social and Economic Organisation* pp. 167-171.
6. Quoted in Bougse: *Exclusion of Values*, p. 77. See also Simi and *Le salaire, l' evolution sociale et le monnaie and my Institutional Theory of Economics*, pp. 198-199.
7. Materialism in Democracy, *The Philosophical Review*, Vol. 51, No. 2.
8. Gurvitch distinguishes between Mass, Community and Communion as different states of collective mind. But with him even a group of gangsters may "commune" in a very intense fashion or a religious sect commune in the brief of the value of perverse or even criminal rites. This is contrary to the general usage of the term. Nor is Communion a state of "collective ecstasy"; it is rather an intense sense of awareness that accompanies creativeness in the realms of truth, beauty and goodness. In Communion we deal with a species of interpenetration or fusion of minds in which tertiary values, social symbols and ideals that involve collective judgments. and moral patterns intensify, sustain and rationalise the group unity. Both man's reason and sentiment, his emotional ecstasy and intellectual clarity here obtain their full freedom and universality. (See. *Gurvitch : Mass, Community, Communion, Journal of Philosophy,* Vol. 38.).
9. *The Two Sources of Morality and Religion*, p. 81.
10. *Design and Purpose*, pp. 75-76.
11. *Theory and Art of Mysticism.*
12. *Moral Man and Immoral Society.*
13. See my *Theory and Art of Mysticism*, pp. 272-282.

9

THE ORDER OF VALUES IN THE STATUS SYSTEM

Stratification, its Biological and Ethical Function

The human community maintains its solidarity through participation of its members in certain common traditions, meanings and values. Such participation involves an integration of the activities of individuals in the social structure in terms of some scheme or order of values or ends. Society implies a gradation of roles, statuses and strata organised around fundamental interests and values that individuals seek through the mediation of groups. Both the hierarchy of groups and group values and corresponding prestige scale of a country record its system of values and ends. Status is both ecological and social. The solidarity of plant and animal communities is established by stratification. Stratification in the human level corresponds to the division of species of a forest community into dominants, sub-dominants and subordinates that form tiers or strata of diminishing rank in the world of vegetation. In rain-forests of the tropics, tiers of vegetation rise upon tiers, and the hierarchy is biologically useful for the effective collective exploitation of soil, sunshine and rainfall by different species of plants that most minutely adapt themselves to each stratum or level. Similarly an animal community is stratified into dominant and subordinate species determined by links in the food-chain, niches and occupations. Such niches, grades and differentiations restrict competition among individual animals to each stratum, and assure collective subsistence for the various species of animals in the ecological order that represents a system of reciprocally interdependent and balanced growth of all. What is position or role in the ecological hierarchy of a plant or an animal community, status is in the human community.

In the social organisation of a particular animal species there is also discernible an order of dominance and subordination as represented by the pecking, biting, bullying or mounting hierarchy. This is achieved by coercion or show of coercion, depending largely on the age, sex, strength, intelligence and temperament of the animals.[1] No doubt creatures with a developed mental organisation like the great apes and elephants, can alone show a variety of unregulated behaviour; for the pattern of subordination in a band, colony, troop or herd is, biologically speaking, much simpler and easier. Allport calls this tendency of domination and subordination "a law of polarity in social contact". In human stratification, tradition, behavioural pattern, law, institution and society's ethical judgment of the individual's or the group's participation. in the common values of the community come in. Alike in prehuman and human evolution, division of labour, specialisation and segregation bring about social stratification as a fundamental mechanism of social adaptation of organisms that are of different types and species or vary in fundamental traits, functions and capacities. Stratification introduces a constancy in social evolution and a variability of individual units as these exploit the limited resources of the same environment in different ways. In human society stratification, due to the unique development of speech, tradition and training develops into an integration of habits, interests and behaviour and a communion of sentiments, meanings and values. It serves the important moral objective of providing an orderly framework of mutual service and cooperation of various social strata, and of aiding society in maintaining its collective interests, purposes and scale of values, unhampered by the lapse or ineptitude of the less efficient members. Ortega rightly points out: "As long as there is any doubt as to who commands and who obeys, all the rest will be imperfect and ineffective. Even the very conscience of men, apart from special exceptions, will be disturbed and falsified."[2] Each social stratum plans the life, social habits and values of the individuals. Man's social adaptation through specialisation of functions, attitudes and values thus includes the evolution of personality types and behaviour patterns of individuals. Statuses and strata in man's social organisation are as much individual as cultural achievements. In other words, status is the institutionally defined position or role of the individual, that is supported by the individual's personal qualities, attitudes and evaluation. Status is recognised and safeguarded by society through legal privilege, economic monopoly and social distance. Status depends upon past status and sometimes becomes hereditary. But each person gains status through struggle, or at least has to fulfil the minimal obligations of a status through concrete behaviour that must win the prestige associated with that status.

Full or Limited Participation of Values in Class or Caste

Status may now be defined as a cluster of "rights" which the individual together with his group and the society recognises as due to him in his particular position or role in the community's scheme of differentiation of functions, interests and values. Such rights of individuals are those in respect of biological and economic values, such as protection, leisure, property, standard of living and security, and social values, such as mobility, freedom, power, honour and prestige. The term 'stratum' signifies a group of persons enjoying roughly the same status. A class or a caste is a stratum; it enjoys certain total "rights" as special-interest or functional groups that are recognised and supported by the entire social structure. The difference between a class and caste lies in this that in the latter status or the ensemble of "rights" or conditions of access to certain values are limited by birth and kinship to groups, and remain fixed for life irrespective of individual efforts; while in the former status or the structural rights accrue as a result of individual achievement that throws the door open to a larger and larger range of values which the culture emulates. In most societies of the world classes that have attained a high favourable status seek different ways to transmit it to their descendants, thus assuring them certain economic and social values, more or less exclusively; but these become castes only when improvement of status is entirely shut out for individual ambitions but assigned largely or wholly as the result of family ancestry and custom. In the caste the unit of social mobility is the endogamous territorial group; in the class it is the struggling, aspiring individual. The rights of individuals or of strata, whether class or caste groups, in any society also carry with them certain "duties" that the community expects of them and that they tend to fulfil.

Any social structure may thus be viewed as a status, prestige and power system, of which the scale corresponds as clearly as possible to the community's scale of values, absolute or specialised, intrinsic or intermediate. Status represents the social interaction, prestige the subjective attitude, and power the formal legal relation. In the familistic groups the status of the patriarch is determined by birth, age and kinship, and prestige accrues as the result of custom and tradition that engender the deferential attitude. In the Roman family the structural status of the *Pater familias* depended on law to be transformed into structural power. To the Hindu caste hierarchy the structural status of the Brahman also depended upon the protection of his privilege and prestige by the king upon whom was enjoined the duty of enforcing the conformity of the people to the Varna-asrama-dharma. Privileged social strata in order to keep such values that all seek but cannot be shared, viz., wealth, property and office-holding exclusively for themselves use the authority of both social convention and law. Thus both social prestige and legal power serve to maintain and support a high social status. There are other values that may be shared in common and yet set men apart as superior, *viz.*, learning, goodness and purity. In this case also the stratum, priestly class or caste, may try to ensure vested interests for their descendants through bequeathing temples, monasteries, wealth and property. But since these values are common shared possessions, these cannot be fenced off from the multitude by law and discriminatory patterns of behaviour without injuring the values themselves. Social systems that have placed at the top of the prestige scale an elite comprising the wise and the holy can only succeed through the enforcement of a self-denying or ascetic ideal for the group and customary accession of new individuals through the acquisition of the same personal worth and capacity. Throughout history the priestly class, however, has mixed up the economic with the intellectual and religious goals, and sought to enjoy the monopoly of their superior spiritual wisdom, even the reading and possession of the sacred texts that is supported by ecclesiastical power, social deference and material possession. Thus the sacred values of knowledge, character and religion have been profaned by being transformed into the instrumental values for a privileged class that like any other group has sought to protect its tangible interests, even at the expense of other groups. This perversion of values undermines their structural prestige, and finally leads to the loss of their structural status and power. Changes in social gradation in all societies reflect changes in the invisible world of values.

The Major Status System as the Record of Social Valuation

The scale of values of a society reflects not only its dominant interests and pursuits but also the degree of social cohesion or integration. Ruth Benedict characterises types of American Indian cultures as Apollonian and Dionysian with differences in dominant values and in the cultural imperatives that mould and govern behaviour and personality. Though the psychological characterisation of a whole people by a stereotype, or catch-phrase is neither scientific nor truly objective, Ruth Benedict's method of defining the cultural norms as the frame of reference for analysing or interpreting a culture as an integral whole has now won wide recognition and scientific support.[3] Similarly M.E. Opler has profitably employed what he calls themes or postulates that serve as the stimuli for beliefs, or rationalisation and behaviour for the interpretation of a particular culture. The themes are considered as the broadest directives of a unified nature implicit in a culture.[4] Here again the emphasis is on focal attitudes, values and purposes that not only can explain the clan, flavour and unique organisation of a particular culture but also lead to a better appreciation and understanding of its practical, technic and objective facets. Again E.H. Spicer devotes attention to the description and analysis of the value-system of a culture, (the Yaqui Indians) and applies the term "foci" to those values or attitudes around which interest is centred in Yaqui society and which seems to stimulate and guide activity. It is thus abundantly clear that the functional school of anthropology have seen the necessity for discovering dominant values, interests and attitudes and widely shared beliefs that make more vivid and understandable a particular culture. Their point of departure is the warm, normative subjective aspects of the culture rather than its natural resources, technology and other practical aspects that almost monopolise the attention of orthodox anthropology. In sociological analysis the significance of common values and goals as underlying the unity of a social group or community has not, however, received similar stress. An active cross-fertilisation between anthropology, sociology and social psychology will reveal the social ethos of a particular culture (after the integration of Dilthey and Scheler) and its situational and general imperatives as well as the social structures, functions, hierarchies of values and imperatives common to primitive, peasant and urban-industrial communities in different stages of social development. Perhaps the necessary coordination and synthesis of the results may be achieved by sociology.

Social and economic changes in historical cultures are associated with shift in human valuations and rise of a different status-power system. In ancient India the social stratification was based upon the supremacy of the Aryan peoples over the indigenous inhabitants of the country, the Dravidians, whom they subjugated. The highest rank was accorded to the Kshatriya group comprising the rulers, warriors and landholders and the lowest to the cattle-breeders, cultivators and traders—the Vaishyas. Below them, outside the pale of the Aryan Society, were assigned manual labour and craftsmanship, and the Dasyus or Dasas representing the wild aboriginal, hunting, fishing and other groups. After a few centuries the scale of values with the ranking of spiritual knowledge and priesthood at the top represented by the Brahman, of military power in the middle represented by the Kshatriya and of wealth and economic toil at the bottom represented by the Vaishya and Sudra commonalty established itself.

This shift in valuation was the outcome of two factors: first the Brahmans asserted themselves throughout the Aryan culture as teachers, law-givers and statesmen, and were accorded the highest rank and prestige, higher than even the ruling noble and land-owning class, the Kshatriyas. This happened probably in the 6th century B.C. as a reaction against the upsurge of Buddhism that represented in its genesis a Kshatriya movement in its opposition to ritualism and priesthood. At the time of Buddha the status of the Brahmans was somewhat lower than that of the Kshatriyas, who also proved their intellectual worth by formulating various metaphysical doctrines, including those of Buddha and Mahavira. But the Brahman-born, whom Buddha criticised, gradually asserted their supremacy. There were probably bloody Kshatriya-Brahman conflicts as included in the legendary battles between Vasistha and Visvamitra, between the Brahmans and Janamejaya, between Arjuna and Bhrigu and in the killings of Parasurama. Both Buddhism and Jainism led to the prominence of the ascetic-mendicant or wandering orders as contrasted with the Brahman forest-dwelling hermits and of monachism and large-scale desertion of households for the celebate and contemplative life. Hindu society reacted to this peril through the stress of the Brahmanical intellectual standards and of the obligation to the householder to lead the contemplative life of the sage (*muni*) in old age. But the decline of the Kshatriya or warrior group was soon to be speeded up by the invasions of successive hordes of invaders such as the Sakas, Yavanas, Palhavas, Kushans and Huns for well-nigh seven centuries beginning from the third century B.C. in the course of which the old Kshatriya group was totally exterminated. Foreign Saka and Hun tribes took advantage of their political power to obtain recognition as new Kshatriya groups by affiliating themselves with ancient Kshatriya clans and accepting the traditional rituals of coronation and horse-sacrifice. Foreign immigration and invasion led to the Varnas getting considerably intermixed as recorded in an Andhra inscription of the second century A.D. During the same period we find king Satavahana Pulumayi of foreign extraction being extolled for his success in preventing the admixture of the four varnas. New castes were, however, continuously formed as the result of the assimilation of the Aryan groups with the invading tribes. Such new castes, products of admixture (varnasankara), included the Mlecchas and the Ajivas (artisan groups) according to the Vayu Purana (not later than 500 A.D.) as well as the Vratyas and Vrisalas in Manu's classification, dated about 400 A.D.

Secondly, there was even greater racial admixture at the bottom of the Aryan society while the occupations of the Vaisya and of the Sudra from the Dravidian rank also merged in one another. Neither the Vaisya nor the Sudra is mentioned as a separate caste in either the Vedic or the Buddhist literature. The Vaisyas formed the Aryan common people, while the Sudras who were described as timid, miserable, servile and owning no property in the Puranas and the Mahabharata were the indigenous inhabitants of India, subjugated by the Aryans and assigned low status in Aryan society in exchange of manual labour and servitude. The Dasyus, obviously the primitive tribes of the forests who ate the flesh of dogs and killed and ate cows, were given a yet lower status.

There was a fresh attempt at social gradation at the bottom even in the more liberal Buddhist period, when at lowest rungs of the social ladder were allocated Hina-sippani, or low trades, such as those of the weaver, the potter, the barber and the tanner, and the Hina-jatiyo, or low tribes, who were recruited obviously from the forest folks or Dasyus and followed such occupations as hunting, fishing, fowling and scavenging. Both these categories corresponded to the varanasankaras or mixed groups below the Sudra caste as described later by Manu.

Hindu society expanded across the centuries in India through a gradual process of social assimilation of aboriginal and forest folks rather than through subjugation and expropriation. These were included in the Hindu fold as they gave up impure animal foods, abandoned nomadism and pillage in favour of agriculture, tanning, leather work or farm labour and adopted certain customs in respect of marriage and worship. But in this process of absorption many lagged behind. These were gathered into castes that were regarded as low and unclean in the Hindu social scale.

We accordingly see that there have been striking shifts in valuation. One was obviously associated with the ascendency of the Brahman caste over the Kshatriya nobility occupying formerly the highest rank and with the emphasis of knowledge and spirituality throwing the door open for all castes to the highest status in the age of Hindu liberalism. Another shift is related to the social recognition of the Sudras who rose to be kings and also high state officials in the beginning of the Christian era as recorded in the Puranas. Not merely the Ramayana and the Mahabharata (especially the Bhagavad Gita) but also particularly, the several Puranas were composed with the special objective of general education of the Sudras and the womenfolk of India. The Sudra varna gradually split up into a large number of functional castes, all ranked below the Vaisya, their social status and role being largely determined according to Brahmanical predilections. The Sudra is now used as a general appellation for all social groups of lower status than that of the Vaisya. A third shift in valuation is connected with the gradual advance and absorption of primitive tribes as the result of their economic uplift and social progress and their relegation to the lowest rank as the process of assimilation was left incomplete. In the static and well-knit Hindu social hierarchy, it was the Brahmanical intellectual group that through the centuries set the accepted pattern of values and determined among them the social prestige of different occupations. Outside the range of this social ranking, dominated by ritualised intellectual standards of the Brahmans, the gradation of the occupation groups, that today form the considerable majority of the Hindu castes, largely depends upon the economic and social progress from hunters, fishers, food-gatherers, nomads, thieves and beggars into permanent and settled cultivators and artisans, and in the artisan groups from the adoption of improved craft methods and techniques of trading, It is thus even in static society economic improvement is associated with the improvement of social rank based on the valuation of labour, wealth and sedentariness. Such is the existing caste gradation in India dominated by the stress of both ancient, ritualised, and intellectual and modern, flexible and economic standards that have tended to mix together in the densely populated plains of India, subjected to a long series of immigrations and racial and cultural assimilation of peaceful folks living side by side for centuries.

Karl Mannheim refers to the similar remarkable change which the Germanic tribes, formerly cattle-breeding nomads, experienced in their valuations and social gradation in the course of their great migrations. As the tribes split up into warrior groups and princes during their invasion of foreign territories, an entirely new set of values and attitudes stressing individualism, bravery, domination and pillage replaced social conformity, co-operativeness and value of labour. Societies welded by the sword and organised for violence have shown in all epochs and regions a different scale of values and status system from those societies that have grown by peaceful integration and assimilation and are organised for labour and co-operation. It is well known how with the expansion of Rome and her conquest of the Italian peoples, the wholesale desertion of the fields and rise of the *latifundia* were accompanied by the degradation of the status of yeomen farmers and agricultural labourers and glorification of soldiers and warrior groups. A revolution in the scale of values was experienced in Italy of the Renaissance that suddenly increased luxury, leisure and glory for the merchant and bourgeoise classes. The Industrial and Commercial Revolution in nineteenth century Europe similarly led to the dominance of a moneyed leisured class and created the distinction between the professions and the vocations associated with a new gradation of values concerning kinds of work.

Group Values, Counter-Values and Dis-Values

Through all such shifts in values, society progressively adjusts itself to new conditions and forces of the environment. Social valuation is, indeed, a most vital, integrative function of the community associated with its capacity for collective reaction in the evolutionary process. The scale of values integrates or binds together a whole tribe, people or nation. But all values cannot be equally shared among the different social strata or economic classes. Where there is much social distance between the groups that remain satisfied with a limited enjoyment of the goals and values of life, we call such society a caste society. But even in a rigid caste society, bound hand and foot by regulations that stereotype unequal opportunities and freedoms, the majority of the population that is exploited or subjugated and that has low social status, must have access to enjoyment of the essential values of labour, property and freedom. Otherwise there is social dissolution. Societies greatly differ in the proximity and communication between the different social strata. Thus the scales of values of the different social strata coalesce or clash, depending on the process of social integration. In a society where certain social groups are superimposed upon others, enjoy monopolies and privileges, and exclude a considerable section of the community from essential values and amenities of life, their superior attitudes and valuations give rise to counter-values and attitudes of competing or exploited groups. Society in such a case becomes split up into discordant group minds, and the results often are social disintegration as well as personal disorganisation. Counter-values often bring in their train disvalues of diseased and unorganised groups and minds. Society is a changing, compound structure in various levels of social cohesion. Its scales of values constantly shift and intermingle; there are always individuals and groups rising and falling in the social scale by approximating to or deviating from the highest prestige values. Individuals and groups also constantly create by their enterprise new patterns of values that win social esteem by successfully challenging the prestige values and social ranking of the elite groups. Besides the social classes, such primary groups as the family, the neighbourhood and the rural community, and such associations as the club, the university and the sports ground that cut across social and economic frontiers set their own patterns of values and attitudes that also claim allegiance in the individual mind. Thus valuations proceeding from groups of various kinds compete with one another in man's social milieu. Their assimilation or segregation depends on the nature of the groups and the fundamental social processes of competition and co-operation that give rise to the group forms themselves and set up distinctive human attitudes and activities. Each set of values, whether the established ritualised pattern or one created by adventurous individuals or groups, is to be judged in relation to the evolutionary process that is gradually developing the more organic, socially integrated minds, groups and institutions. In a harmonious society which has established some integration and balance, the scale of values of the elite groups becomes representative of the whole community, and provides an orderly framework of co-operation and co-ordination between the different groups. The change from Interest-groups into Commonalty, indeed, marks the merging of separate standards and attitudes into an integrated, universal system of values.

There develops within each normal and progressive society an integrated system of values. Certain values and ends are absolute, others are relative; some values and ends are intrinsic, others are instrumental. Those which are regarded as relative, specific and instrumental are subordinate to others that are conceived as intrinsic, absolute and universal in human experience. This moral judgment both of society and individuals holds the key to stratification of which the essence is the unequal evaluation of different roles and positions. A society's dominant evaluation is reflected in its major status system, with its institutionally defined values and ends to which individuals conform, and which are divergent for the different strata. Such divergence of values and ends of different statuses and strata is of course the outcome of differences of function, and is associated with a system of rights and duties. Both the status system and scheme of rights and duties that belong to particular roles and positions of individuals in the social structure objectify and implement the society's series of tables of values, subordinating the biological and economic to the moral and spiritual values, and the relative, instrumental and intermediate to the absolute, intrinsic and ultimate ends. The community's broad agreement in respect of the hierarchy of values is accordingly expressed in the relative gradation of statuses and strata that ensures co-operation and reciprocity between the social classes on the one hand, and enables individuals in their divergent roles and possessions to participate in the common purposes, on the other. Through the status system of the society, the values and ends of the biological individuality, the "occupation" and the "status personality" are socialised, and become integrated with the ultimate and absolute common values, with which is associated the total development of the personality. The individual conforms to certain standards and submits to certain discipline pertaining to his status; and is at the same time assisted in his role and position by certain rights, prestige, social distance and influence. In a peaceful, solidaristic society the relative ranking of the key statuses commands general assent, recording as it does the subordination of the intermediate and specialised values and ends to the values and ends prized as supreme and common by the community. Thus the moral order implicit in the status system that evolves in the judgment of a particular community serves to hold together the complex social structure with its highly specialised, stratified statuses, roles and positions of individuals.

Social Status and Self-Status as Measuring Achievement of Specialized Values

Man shows in the complex civilization of today only a limited participation in the values and goals of life. His values and goals are largely decided for him by the role and status that belong to him. Such role and status are the products of the adaptation between his organic and cultural equipment and the limited social space which he appropriates, and from which he obtains his quota of satisfactions and values. These values are associated with each role and status and may be regarded as external goals set for him. These limit no doubt his aspirations and achievements. At the same time they chalk out the boundaries of his social action and lead to economy, specialisation and concentration of effort, free from the distraction of disharmonious wishes and interests. Since these goals and values are common to other individuals belonging to the same social stratum, society discovers and lays down the mechanisms of competition and co-operation in the pursuit of ends that may be shared or are mutually exclusive. On the whole, the differentiation of values between strata in society helps the individual in the appropriation of his own values through institutionalisation of his role and position, winning for him a particular status in his organised group that maintains continuity on the basis of the spontaneous participation of all members in its particular goals. Society gains, in the first place, as the institutional role and position select those qualities and potentialities of persons that fit with the requirements and goals of the social culture, and integrates these in an ordered system of rank, prestige and power for social ends and ideals. Secondly, award or punishment for proper or deviant behaviour is distributed between the legitimate authorities of several institutions that can appeal more easily and effectively to the sense of honour and moral obligation of individuals than the state which is accordingly released for other legitimate functions. Each social stratum or class group that presents the individual with certain specialised goals and values, not shared by others, develops a unity and solidarity of its own that are strengthened by the possession of common property and knowledge, discriminatory tradition and cult, social prestige and power. It develops "rights" against other groups and against its own members who do not conform to its own standards. It has its leaders, chiefs, elders etc. who guide the activities of the co-operating individuals. In each social stratum there are different categories of members, each with a different role, status and set of "duties". The distribution of status and power rewards the individual in his obligatory, active participation in groups and institutions. This serves a double function: the pursuit of exclusive goals and values by each stratum in a regime of social co-operation that defines and limits the pursuit of such specialised and intermediate values within a scheme of common and ultimate values of the community ; and the appropriation of personal values by stratum members who are guaranteed certain rights or conditions of fulfilment of such values with which are also associated certain duties normatively standardised and classified by the stratum or class group.

On the other hand, the goals and values of the status personality are internalised and made one's own. Man's normal self-status or self-esteem depends upon the prestige the stratum or class group accords him on a scale of importance. The expectancies of one's fellowmen make one live fully up to one's role and corresponding status, accepting their approbation or disapprobation as 'efficient' or 'incompetent', 'satisfactory" or 'worthless'. This is as significant for the efficiency and welfare of society as for proper integration of habits, attitudes and behaviours of the individual directed to certain social values.[5] The assignment of status and definition of prestige, with its minimal code of obligations corresponding to it, serve the all-important social purpose of presenting a clear goal and norm of behaviour to the individual with reference to individuals of other statuses and positions, and hence in evolving meaningful personality differentiations in society's scheme of fulfilment of values. As the individual strives after and reaches the goals which his stratum holds dear, he raises himself in self-esteem that aids him in imposing on his circle his independent standards of how his role should be played ; as he recedes from them he suffers loss of self-status. The latter involves personality deterioration. Into the texture of man's personality are interwoven his social impulses, standards and values that govern his psychic life and behaviour as much as his sex, hunger and other egoistic impulses. Man's mental adaptation comprises the integration and co-ordination of his elemental impulses and desires as these are moulded and modified by his environment, on the one hand, and his social dispositions and feelings with which mingle social expectancies and values, on the other. Thus can he find peace and sanity within the self, handing over to the next generation the fruits of organic and mental heredity, and at the same time achieve his due role, status and prestige in the social community, enriching the social heritage by making his proper individual contribution to the society, while at the same time deriving support from it.

Personality Integration and Development in Status-Gaining

In the differentiation and development of the psychogenetic and social personality both human nature and society record their full development and purpose. In man's adjustment in the social milieu, the blending and interplay of his own impulses and desires and of social attitudes and judgments on his role and status are implied. His personality equilibrium is a matter at once of harmony of drives, desires and aspirations within the inner self and of his orderly position, status and prestige in the social community, that not only give full play to his special endowments, aptitudes and tastes, but also engender self-esteem or self-status without which he feels himself a complete misfit and a non-entity. The equilibrium of personality is dynamic, not static, and involves the interaction of the shifting dominance of man's urges, interests and values, on the one hand, and his changing role, status and prestige in the community, on the other. In the lives of leaders, prophets, and social reformers, of those great personalities who are the "makers and shakers of society" it is hardly possible to distinguish in their roles between their impulses of self-assertion and domination and their altruism and deliberate pursuit of the social weal. Often man's unconscious, repressed impulses, that stand out rebellious, motivate great drives either for community well-being or for crime and social deviation, resulting in profound changes in his role, position and prestige. It is through finding prestige and power which society at first denies him or (through suffering, humiliation of status and position and loss of affection and social ostracism that he may resolve inner conflicts. A leader, through his zeal for social and economic reform, may disturb social relations and institutions to the extent of forfeiting his cherished status and privilege, but in doing so he may contribute materially to social values, and at the same time bring about a poise in his inner self through the satisfaction of his cravings for self-assertion and his intense social feelings blended together in harmony. What may be an apparent loss of social prestige may be profoundly conducive towards the relief of inner tensions. Man's personality equilibrium is thus a single integral whole, the self recording its inner poise or tension in man's social status and mobility in the changing social world and endless pattern of his group relations. A criminal similarly embraces loss of status and prestige (partly compensated however by social recognition in his own gang or group) by going against the established social and moral order ; his egoistic impulses and craving for power refuse any compromise with the social impulses that are much weaker, and demand fulfilment at the cost of social contumely or ostracism.

Distribution of the Social Self in Various Statuses

A man enjoys several statuses as member of different groups. His role and position may be high in one group, and low in another. He may be a kind father, an honest citizen, an unscrupulous businessman, an unsocial clubman and a pious Church-goer. By the process of integration, the esteem or blame that attaches to man's various segmented roles and positions in society builds up the pattern of his personality on the basis of reorganisation of his entire social experience. Thus personality is defined by Kimball Young as the more or less organised or integrated ideas, traits, attitudes, frames of reference and habits, built up into roles and statuses which revolve around the central concept and sense of self-hood or ego esteem. "This self-organisation,", he observes, "depends upon the capacity of the individual to take the role of others, to adapt them to his own inner drives, and further to view his own role in terms of the ideas and attitudes of others towards him, that is, to more or less accept the status they accord him."

Certain statuses concerned with fundamental goals and values of life such as sex, marriage and family largely, however, shape the personality pattern. The loss of self-status in love, the sadistic or masochistic tendencies in one's nature implicated in the love relation or, again, the bullying or humiliation and encounter with incompatible or contradictory norms or standards of conduct from unstable, quarrelsome or over-indulgent parents in childhood supply the clue to the individual's struggle for role and status and to his aims and aspirations. It is the child's basic habits and attitudes learnt in the family, the play group and the neighbourhood that largely govern whether a person is able to fully accept the role and status accorded to him by others, or whether he takes a submissive or dominant attitude in his position. Biological factors account for the characteristic types of behaviour of the young child, aggressive and dominant or helpless and submissive, that are stereotyped by social expectancy when the contrasted behaviours obtain appropriate epithets from the family members around him. Both appellations and expectations of the adults chalk out the roles of the "selfish", "cruel," "nice" or "quiet" child. Given a certain psycho-genetic status, the child plays successfully certain roles in the various fields of social activity in keeping with this status. Thus the bully will become the leader of his gang, the town "bad boy", the high pressure salesman, the tough labour-boss etc. Similarly the "nice" or "quiet" boy will become the diligent student, the docile industrial worker, the submissive adherent of the sect or political party and the law-abiding citizen. He also develops, as he matures, appropriate "habits" or predisposing tendencies that may adapt him to meet certain situations associated with his role as well as characteristic "attitudes," enabling him to respond in certain ways to meaningful social experiences which come to represent social values. An aggressive role may lead to attitudes and sentiments favourable towards war, direct action and capital punishment,[6] and unfavourable towards feminism, philanthropy and collectivism. At the same time the society's valuations and attitudes, its scales of values and goals are constantly and indelibly impressed upon the growing child through the primary groups.

Social stratification, based on the order of values, is not, however, sacrosanct, but is scrutinised and evaluated afresh by each maturing individual, who challenges each time through his own experience and effort the social expectation or judgment in respect of his own worth, role or position. From this springs the individual's rejection of fixity of his position or status and his effort to impose the ends and values that he prizes as superior over the ends and values implicit in the status scheme and in the general customs governing conformity or devotion to duty. The fundamental training in the familistic groups determines his conformity or lack of conformity to the major prestige system of the society.

It will be of interest in this connection to refer to the inflexible status-prestige scheme of the East Indian Balinese, who have been culturally conditioned and accustomed to it by a variety of institutional and symbolic devices that have left an indelible impress on their character and temperament. In very early childhood, at the knee-baby stage, the Balinese are subjected to severe frustration, beginning with excessive teasing, denial of affection and complete rejection by adults in the family unknown in any civilised community. For the Balinese are really a highly cultured and artistic people. After initially reacting to such frustrations by cries and temper tantrums, the Balinese child gradually learns by imitation to be indifferent to any affection and interest from anybody. Apathy and avoidance become the norms that govern daily social intercourse. Thus the Balinese, as they mature, develop a schizoid personality with marked features of dissociation, narcissism and withdrawal.[7] Even anger and fear are socially expressed by them by placidity and indifference, accompanied "by greater smoothness of speech." People react to accidents and other critical situations in a dreamy, stupefied manner—"not talking, not looking, but nodding." "A thief whose case is being tried slowly falls asleep." No narcotic or drug is in use. Social adaptation is facilitated, however, by the mechanism of symbolic activities as represented by communal shadow-shows, dances and ceremonials that are exceedingly popular and in which participation is taught early. The roles of the actors playing the parts of heroes and devils of the epics and legends, derived largely from Indian sources, are the periodic occasions for emotional releases of self-assertion, aggression, anger or fear. Worship in the open, with plenty of feasting, flowers and music and with young maidens playing a leading part, also provides an agreeable stimulating source of sublimation and symbolisation that serve as delicate means of graduating the emotions. The established folk-ways of social and economic co-operation in work in the fields with reciprocal obligations of giving and sharing also discourage egoism and selfishness. Due to various rigid social taboos, sex and marriage problems appear to be also rare, and there is smooth tenor of family life. Balinese society is caste-ridden and immobile, with four major castes like those of India, and is dominated by an elaborate round of group rites and observances that interpolating with the ordinary routine of life are largely responsible for bringing about emotional integration and poise. The common vogue and practice of the histrionic art in a variety of dances, dramatic performances and cermonials, where the roles of good and evil powers, gods, demons, and witches are enacted and re-enacted with great zest, not experienced in actual life, no doubt help the people to maintain psychic compartmentalisation or divorce between wish and conduct without grave disturbances to the personality. Although cases of dissociation and hysteria are not infrequent among the adults, these are not considered 'pathological.' It thus appears that the caste and priest-ridden social structure prizes a scheme of values in the island of Bali far different from what is normally adopted. Through early religious indoctrination in the Brahmanical ideology of the caste system and in the Indian doctrine of Karma and alternation of the cycle of life between religious and mundane activities, Balinese culture in spite of its rationalisations and compartmentalisation shows a high degree of accommodation and consistency, and creates and maintains a stylised form of life and conduct of the individual and harmonious group co-operation with little play of self-assertion and rivalry, contributing toward social amity and solidarity of a docile, easy-going, highly artistic and pleasant people. The system of focal values, goals and norms of Balinese society is novel, but is the sheet-anchor of its rigorous status-prestige system, with its pre-ordained fixity of roles, positions and obligations of individuals ; it nourishes certain personality traits, attitudes and reactions that cannot be called abnormal, but thoroughly conform to what Kardiner calls "the basic personality-structure" of the social culture.[8]

Personality Disorders as Outcome of Lack of Integration

Man's segmented "social selves," distributed between different roles and statuses in the social structure, are reintegrated in the sense of self-hood, total self-status or personality. These divided selves become harmonious or incompatible according as the interests and values of the different groups that claim his allegiance overlap and blend with one another. The disparity of roles and statuses in different positions and spheres of life endanger man's psychic unity and brings about personality disorders. Especially is man's status in the fundamental unit of social life, *viz.*, the family, important. If he loses esteem and suffers distress or humiliation in the family relation, his personality is warped to the extent of making him a misfit in his roles and positions in other groupings. On the other hand, for some persons, intrinsic interest of their tasks or the self-expression, prestige and power that these bring, compensate for frustrations in love and family life. For many, again, the job in the complex industrial system bears little relation to their special aptitudes, tastes and interests, and thwarts the creative impulses. The individual's role in modern occupations is frequently so depressing to his self-esteem and morale that he reacts by indulging himself in unwholesome, erotic day-dreams during work and in coarse recreations during leisure. This results in both personal disorganisation and social neurosis, characterised by resentment not only against the repetitive tasks in the industry but also against the entire social and economic structure. Man's roles in industrial civilisation hardly give full expression to his many-sided nature or even assure him self-esteem and security; while these are too often incompatible or antagonistic. For many in modern culture the different roles and statuses, seeking specialised and intermediate rather than common and ultimate ends and values, represent a system of water-tight compartments permitting no intermingling of ends and values. The absolute or supreme values are not permitted to overstep the barriers of the "ideal" world, and trespass into the spheres of vocation or business. But all cannot easily acquiesce in this lack of life-organisation. Many individuals, who suffer from a sense of inferiority, due to being less favoured by parents than other children in the family or bullied by the foreman or manager in the factory or, again, thwarted in their fundamental wishes for security and for status develop a strong, generalised resistance against any system of industry, any status system, any given order of values. The loss of normal or expected status in the family, industry or profession may lead a few to a new evaluation and self-fulfilment in life, a sort of superior harmony of values in the personality. Or due to bad training and social habits or wrong company, they may select goals not approved by society, and become criminals and delinquents. Following the methods, techniques and traditions that the gang approves, they gain their esteem, self-respect and security, and evolve a status system in the underworld with its distinctive mores and patterns determining their delinquent roles and positions, and based on aims and aspirations that repudiate the society's system of values. Criminial groups seek the same values that people in general seek, *viz.*, wealth, property, security and power, but their specialised roles and statuses are a complete negation of the moral code of society, the accepted means-ends scheme. More fortunate and gifted individuals brought up under happier conditions in the home, business or profession may develop strong social affections that in the mature personalities become the bearers of the supreme values. In their case the assurance of status in the family and in the business circle and economic security, and hence the sense of self-security and self-reliance are associated with such an imperative sense of superiority of the ultimate values that truth, religion, and morality refuse to concede to the intermediate and specialised values of their business or occupation roles. They succeed in living up to the highest moral standards and even in introducing these to the various roles of life, occupation, art, business and politics.

Man's psychic stress, conflict and misery in his particular role and position in the social structure are, as we have seen, the fertile causes of personality maladjustment. Often the causes are of a more general and persistent character, connected with the frustration of the desires for constructiveness, gregariousness, response, recognition (status) and security that the present industrial system cannot adequately fulfil. Sometimes, especially in periods of rapid industrial and technological change, the rapid change of jobs and excessive mobility make quick, inner adjustment difficult, especially in the case of the marginal man who has come from the countryside, or from a different cultural milieu. Man may have worked out his group adjustment smoothly and efficiently, but his group conformity may itself be a cause of tension if the group stands for goals and values that are not organically assimilated with those of other groups and with the society as a whole. Again the social culture as a whole may show a chaos, conflict and perversion of values which aggravate the unbalance, inconsistency and conflict in the individual personality. Discord, struggle and revolution in the status-power structure have their reflection in the neuroticism and psychic conflict and segregation of individuals. On the other hand, peace and harmony between the classes, races and nations provide the opportunities for stable internal security and freedom, indispensable for the smooth balance and inclusive, rational integration of the personality. The more the groups, between which man's social selves are distributed, become consistently integrated with one another and with the external world, the more is he able to achieve his internal consistency, balance and freedom. There is an intimate correspondence between the integration of society and of the individual with homologous contained imperatives. This has been ably demonstrated by J. W. Woodward, in both human infancy and in primitive culture, Woodward shows the earliest attempts at integration cannot escape being incomplete, inconsistent, and emotional in character. "This at the cultural level, gives the control culture initial dominance, resisting over millenia-long periods the freeing of the inductive and aesthetic-expressive cultures from its repressive controls. As emotional integrations, the earliest-formed organisation of personality, of social organisation, and of culture tend to handle problems emotionally, repressing readily and resisting the necessary transitional break-ups incident to achieving mature and inclusive rational integration. The earliest occurring social organisation thus overemphasizes status, caste and the like; that of culture, the forms of repressive control. And the earliest (infantile) organisation of personality thus tends to create fixations, regressive patterns and unassimilated nuclei through whose emotional pattern further experiences are filtered in a vicious circle whose cumulative working may carry on to neuroticism."[9] So far as the sanity, happiness and rational integration of personality are concerned, civilisation has not yet out-grown its early childhood. The super-ego is still tyrannical, inconsistent and mutilating. Civilisation attempts at integration by downright repression or by rationalisation, symbolisation and compartmentalisation, leading to split personalities with their fears, defence mechanisms and obsessions or their thwarted impulses in open rebellion against the society that further uses more severe, repressive and arbitrary modes of control. For stable social and personal adjustment, society must develop modes of reconciliation of conflicting interests, goals and values of various statuses and strata by collective criticism and discussion in a free, open atmosphere of tolerance and forbearance, untainted by propaganda and suppression of opinions, beliefs and faiths. Class biases, racial attitudes and rational prejudices everywhere prevent a genuinely rational, fair and open discussion of conflicting interests and goals. Prejudices are mass adjustive mechanisms, analogous to the hysteria of neurotic individuals, that grow out of and persist in situations of repression, insecurity and conflict and serve to make crowds, groups and strata solidare. These are dissipated as soon as there is real advance towards freedom from exploitation and insecurity, towards some equitable accommodation of the inevitable antagonisms in the status-power structure and towards communal harmony and morale. The orderly resolution of struggles and antagonisms in the status-power structure stimulates understandability and rational and wide-minded rather than narrow, emotional, and dogmatic ways of thinking. This aids towards further building up mutuality, morale and solidarity. Culture gradually curtails its fields of both irrational thought and action and emotional, repressive regimentation. With greater sanity, consistency and freedom, the personality can now reach finer integrations through reconciliation of the divergent outlooks, interests and instrumental values of the various statuses and strata in society, through ideal creativeness and moral initiative, and also perhaps through a fundamental revision of the current scale of values that by placing the means above the ends and the subsidiary, superficial and instrumental above the fundamental, ultimate and intrinsic values aggravates ambivalence and functional inappropriateness in all the three levels, personal, social and cultural. In such manner the individual, the society and the culture can achieve a comprehensive singleness of social meanings and values.

Need of Proper Orientation of the Statuses and Values of Life

The great majority of individuals in modern industrial, civiiisation suffer from either confusion or contradiction of values and ends of the various statuses and strata. This is because the particular ends and values of the various statuses and strata have become ultimate rather than instrumental ends and values. The supreme and ultimate values recognise and call for divergent values between strata and statuses, associated with differences of function and conditions of social adaptation, so long as these remain instrumental and intermediate rather than intrinsic and absolute.

The ideal social order is one in which the status system is integrated on the basis of the supremacy of the intrinsic, common and ultimate values and of the intermingling of instrumental values in a scheme of morally approved ends and means for both individuals and groups; the instrumental values in the specialised roles and statuses neither replacing nor invading the sphere of the intrinsic and absolute values. This can give to the individual, whatever his status and station may be, full opportunity of his total personality in his concrete and specialised role and positional personality.

Civilisations differ in respect of the subordination of the instrumental and intermediate values to the intrinsic and ultimate values. Oriental social systems with their emphasis of family statuses, values and virtues, their absence of minute division of labour and specialisation of functions, and their conferment of the highest honour and prestige on persons of learning, wisdom and spirituality, irrespective of age and birth, have succeeded well in ordering the statuses, values and virtues of life. The ultimate values and goals stand out clearly and consistently, and have their say as to the whole of life, the part it is necessary to concede to other values, their place in the hierarchy. The socially sanctioned intermediate values and goals are reduced to their proper proportion. With proper orientation of values every individual would undertake the culture of the specialised and intermediate values of his role and status that are accessible or applicable to him and to him alone in the right moral attitude. Scheler rightly observes: "To every phase and every moment of development belongs a specific relation to value that will never recur, involving rights and duties that belong in the nexus of the objective order to just this moment, and if unfulfilled are lost for ever." Thus the values of an individual's role and status, belonging to him exclusively, are the highest that he can achieve in his own particular station in life, whatever this may be. With one's vigilant individual judgment ever re-shuffling in his own life the order of values given by social tradition and ethical code, and a fully aroused conscience yielding moral insight in his particular role and situation on the basis of his own experience and effort, the role or status personality evolves into the spiritual personality and the particular values and ends of the various statuses and strata become universal and absolute values.

References

1. See my *Social Ecology*, Chap. III
2. *The Revolt of the Masses*, p. 155.
3. Ruth Benedict: *Patterns of Culture* ; See also Mead : The Cultural Approach to Personality in *Encyclopedia of Psychology* and Gardner Munphy : *Personality*, pp. 796, 816.
4. M.E. Opler : *Cultural Anthropology : An Applicatian of the Theory of Themes in Culture*. See also Union: *Cultural Basis of Personality* and Kluckhohn and *Murray : Personality*.
5. See R. F. Cregan : The Sociology of Personal Behaviour, *American Journal of Sociology*, 1945 ; also Gardner Murphy: *Personality*, pp. 516-517, 559.
6. Bloch : The Social Individual as a Primary Datum in Sociology, *American Sociological Review*, October 1943.
7. Bateson and Msad: *Balinese Character*. See also Research on Primitive Children in Carmichel (Ed.) : *Manual of Child Psychology*.
8. Abram Kardiner : *The Individual and His Society* ; See also Gardner Murphy : *Personality*, pp. 814-817.
9. See his chapter on Social Psychology in *Twentieth Century Sociology*, also The Relation of Personality Structure to the Structure of Culture, *American Sociological Review*, 1930.

10

THE SOCIAL MECHANISMS OF RE-VALUATION

The Psychological Basis of Disobedience and Aggression

Man's personality externally is multiple-structured, resident in his various roles and statuses in different groups. Similarly internally his normal personality also is complex and multiple-structured, comprising, according to the Freudian analysis, the ego, the id and the super-ego. The ego is what is in common parlance described as the self or conscious percipient. The id is the driving mechanism directing the ego towards the satisfaction of the libido in which the ambivalent instincts of life and death, love and hatred are equally operative. The super-ego is the voice of societal norms and values imposed on the ego in the process of its maturation and socialisation. In the normal, mature adult personality the super-ego is no longer in conflict with the id, nor stultifies it, but comes more or less in harmony with it-Thus the super-ego regulation that had a blind, compulsive character gives place to regulation by the ego which becomes more independent of the super-ego and enlarges its field of perception. A few Freudians who have developed a theory of criminology hold that some individuals fail altogether to develop the super-ego that makes for the socialisation of the self. For the majority the super-ego in childhood is a harsh tyrant, demanding compulsive submission to the 'Thou shalts,' and 'Thou shalt nots' of the family and society, and is in conflict with the rest of the self which recoils from it with terror and suffering, aggression and hate that are stimulated by frustration. The super-ego, however, seeks quick revenge and retribution that are supported by the individual's revulsion against his own aggression—the tendency to self-censure in which is rooted the conscience. The above analysis explains not only the universal revolt against an established moral code and table of values but also the profound thrill and delight associated with the sense of shame and guilt and feeling of remorse, of which the basis is the super-ego. Yet the individual restrains his rebellious and aggressive tendencies; since in giving full play to these he destroys both his parents and himself, the parents having become in his mind an integral part of the self, *viz.*, the super-ego. Thus with hatred love, with rebellion reparation, with destruction creation are equally discernible as fundamental unconscious tendencies. The impulses of life and love, of the creation of enduring goodness and wholeness and the social impulse spring from a common root, and are directed overwhelmingly to restrain one's own dangerous aggression and hatred. In the process of the mind's growth, the "moral" becomes the restitution of those objects threatened or injured in phantasy by the individual's aggression and hatred. The 'immoral' becomes his aggression and hatred against his own beloved objects. Man thus obtains profound satisfaction both from breaking the ethical code that is rooted in aggression and revenge against the parents whom he first loved and hated, and from whom this code is originally derived, as well as from reconstituting the ethical code by which in his unconscious mind he can reconcile himself through the sense of remorse with the objects of his love.

The normal growth and harmonious maturation of the personality show the self-integrating the ego and the super-ego and eliminating its early conflicts and frustrations. The development of the super-ego implies both the fulfilment of the demands of society and the achievement of poise within the self when the conscious and unconscious, forces of the mind can freely intermingle. The biological function of the ethical code or the law, then, is that it provides the smooth-working machinery by which the taboos, prohibitions and values directing man's social evolution are generalised and "internalised" and assimilated in the self as the super-ego in early childhood, so as to prevent the waste of psychic energy arising from inner conflicts that are normal and habitual only in the case of the human species; while at the same time the repression of the libidinal and aggressive tendencies that is the cost of socialisation of man does not become severe or mutilating. An undue frustration of the libidinal tendencies injures personal health and happiness, while that of the aggressive tendencies especially endangers the social organisation through occasional outbursts of rage and destructiveness that may be stabilised as a social neurosis like crime or war as an institution. It has been impossible for any ethical code to keep the balance between expression and repression even though what is repressed is kept away from the main field of consciousness.

Man's disobedience of which the impetus is derived from his frustrations and conflicts is equally insistent as his obedience, the categorical imperative of the requirements of society that he has made a part of his unconscious self as the compulsive super-ego. In early civilisation while the ethical code forbade and punished aggression and murder, revenge and cruelty, incest and adultery, myths and legends often portrayed gods and goddesses, heroes and heroines indulging in the forbidden and unusual conduct in a somewhat supernatural setting, thus appeasing the unconscious that recoils in suffering from the super-ego. Similarly both ancient and primitive codes of morality often emanated from some gifted or chosen individuals, who through drink or use of some narcotics fell into a trance or inspiration. In 'inspiration' the impulses, wishes and phantasies derived from the unconscious were as a rule attributed to the god, ancestor or hero. It is in various ways that the ethical code establishes, indeed, a compromise between the aggressive tendencies of the ego and the admonitary, warning voice of society that receives from the individual the allegiance necessary in order that he can develop a super-ego. With the maturation of the race, the individual accepts repression and frustration with less distress, due perhaps to his greater social adaptability, while the various mechanisms, such as sublimation and phantasy-making, enable the mind to get more easily over the insistent and yet discordant urges that cannot bear the light of consciousness in the world of reality. The development of culture opens up the possibilities of sublimated satisfactions in a much more varied and complex manner than were available for primitive peoples. At the same time the social structure with its status-power system imposes less rigid and arbitrary barriers that can be more easily got over by the individual; while the individual life is less repressed and regimented with the progress of civilisation. Thus the ground is ready for less drastic violation of the ethical code, for more peaceful social change.

Yet the tendency of all social structures with their status system is to drift towards inflexibility. Thus individuals and classes find life unbearable and the restraints of the social and moral code galling. The moral order recurrently submits to revision. For the stability of society, obedience and disobedience are equally essential, both being equally rooted in the unconscious tendencies of the mind, as our previous analysis has shown. The cause of revolutions is the thwarting, repression or perversion of what people consider as entirely legitimate major values of life. Every revolution has a moral aspect, since it seeks to remove glaring social and economic injustices. These are brought to a focus by the unadaptability of the institutional set-up and power relation, the overhauling of which is presented as an inescapable moral issue for the community. Every revolution has also its ideological aspect, since it records the failure of the dominant social strata to condition the masses either to the established status-power system or to new social and economic changes. A new ideology, coming from without or evolving within the society, illumines and enkindles it for revolution, phantasy, hope and faith, Every revolution is the intellectual offspring of a social myth, that not only provides a rational or psuedo-rational explanation with great clarity and directness, told in fulfilment of the elemental urges and values of life, but also mobilises the masses for practical action through its aesthetic imagery and moral imperative. Myth is taken not as a symbol or a phantasy, but as a living social reality to which men adjust themselves as they do to living persons and moving events. Believed as such, a revolutionary myth becomes an unerring beacon-fire or signal that guides the path of a country-wide mass movement or revolution. "Liberty, Equality and Fraternity" put in a nutshell the social myth of revolutionary France, just as "the Dictatorship of the Proletariat" embodied the myth of Russian Revolution.

The Elements of a Revolution

In a static society individuals develop social habits and attitudes in conformity with the prevailing hierarchy of values. The relative gradation of the key roles, statuses and strata obtains universal assent. The barriers between the social classes are sacrosanct. The hierarchy of values of both individuals and groups as well as the attachments and loyalties associated with them are relatively unperturbed. The community life is characterised by harmony and integrity, and individuals generally are not disturbed by issues demanding their decision and choice for or against any predominant loyalties. Obedience is instinctive and unconscious, firmly entrenched in the intellectual and emotional heritage of the community, conditioned by symbols of respect and formulas of command as well as by lies and pretensions, myths and rituals that accustom the people to fixed ways of thinking and action. The evolution of new habits of thought and behaviour is also checked by the all-pervasive, tremendous pressure of tradition on the one hand, and self-deception and social and moral inertia of the under-privileged strata, on the other. The exaggerated stress of tradition is fostered in different ways by vested interests, and stands in the way of any kind of institutional change.

But before long there emerge non-conformists, reformers, and rebels who want to improve their roles and statuses. They are those persons whose instincts of domination are strong and those of subordination weak or who cannot identify their scale of values with the present hierarchy of statuses, groups, and norms. They consider the judgment of the society on their worth, role and position unfair. They protest that means are not available for the people for self-improvement, and appeal to the ideals of freedom, equality and justice. They preach that the people's scale of values is no longer embodied in the status-power system, and thus challenge the abstract moral principles underlying the power relation. They clarify the moral principles and norms underlying the good life and the good society, and rationalise both the present stresses and strains and the new values, beliefs and moral cravings in the form of social myths, slogans and catch-words. They are the dreamers, the prophets and the agitators—the leaders without whom revolutions become abortive, miscarry or are perverted. It is the leaders who not only verbalise the emotions and aspirations of the masses in the form of social myths and shibboleths that circulate, but also establish and consolidate the "ideological" group with distinct feelings and attitudes and welldefined plots, policies and programmes. When they recall traditional principles and norms, their revolt appears as conformity to society's ends and norms. Thus Pareto observes : "Assailants of the social order, the better to destroy it, try to take advantage of the forces engendered by that order and therefore make every effort to show that acts which are undoubtedly acts of revolt are legal and therefore ought not to and cannot be punished by the defenders of the order."[1] The masses that were hitherto unable to explain the changes in social values and in the social-economic structure now obtain clarification in respect of the society's legitimate ends and values, and soon develop new group loyalties that are derived from their social heritage and that command them from above. Such new loyalties of course are enriched and enkindled by new social myths, symbols and shibboleths that establish a compulsive, rigid and intolerant group opinion and belief. The group is gradually prepared for mass action by symbolism or the manipulation of certain familiar words and phrases, events and personalities for attacking the established set of values, by agitation and demonstration, by the force of leadership or, again, by the artificial creation of the so-called "'scapegoats". These latter appeal to old passions and prejudices and bring about a solidarity of the people on an instinctive level. It is thus that large masses of men who may not be cemented by a new system of values and idealistic attitudes and beliefs are mobilised through skilful handling of the elements of the national pattern of human values for social upheavals. Social history also gives evidence that in times of crisis a social class threatened with loss of status and power seeks the support of any group or section of society that promises effective opposition to its enemies. Many non-commital groups for some time simulate the ideology of one or other of the struggling groups, intending to return to their original social role and power when the crisis passes. But as the struggle deepens these can no longer 'sit on the fence,' but are either liquidated or attach themselves to the dominant groups. Much also depends upon the total sociological situation that must include the economic roles and reserves of the different classes as well as the forms of group and ideological warfare, resting on the country's political institutions, traditions and procedures. The power-relationship and processes, whether in a democracy or autocracy, largely determine the methods of resistance, both unorganised or passive, and organised or active. Democracy resists the murmur or grumbling of revolt by talk and propaganda—persuasion. Autocracy resists it by soldiers and machine guns. But it is social and political traditions such as those of slow, legal and constitutional change or quick, spasmodic revision or coup, the disparity of power between the social classes and the freedom of social mobility that permits the absorption of fresh and active elements into the power-structure that determine the combination of persuasive or violent methods and techniques used both by the actual power-groups and the revolutionaries. As a matter of fact constitutionalism or orderly change and direct action or revolution for the transformation of the status-power structure represent two alternative policies that are rooted in the temperament of peoples and their traditional mechanisms of association and social control.[2]

The Role of Moral Power

Behind the social and political structure, conventions and mechanisms is of course exerted the silent, unobtrusive and spontaneous moral power of the just against the unjust, of the weak against the strong that everywhere feeds the smouldering flame of protest, resistance or revolution.

Moral power is social intelligence, feeling and will in their highest fighting potential, brought out in an unjust, insufferable social situation. The social consciousness at white heat can be operative only in the individual mind, that in its complete rapport with society takes up vigorously and uncompromisingly the challenge to the higher values prized by society and the individual. Thus moral power is the revelation also of the spiritual initiative and creative and social endeavour of the individual at their highest. It is for this reason that in India this has been identified with 'soul force' of which Mahatma Gandhi has been the apostle and symbol in the present age.[3] The communion of the self with not-self and society releases human intelligence, moral courage and social sympathy to an extent undreamt of before. In fact man's energies transcend themselves, and, like invisible angels, take over the generalship of the host of man's baffled values and aspirations in an unrighteous, unhappy and chaotic society. What the social mind is committed to as must be done is the basis of moral power of the individual, and it may not be the wise men but the commonalty that may lay hold of this, inspiring a new social vision and faith in the abstract, and leading the community in its concrete stupendous, even unattainable task for the common weal. Moral power is the only hope of the weak against the all-powerful, the solace of the vanquished against the victors, the pride of the outcaste against the elite. It is the impregnable steel armour of the non-violent in the irrevocable fight for the higher social values, when these are denied or usurped by the powers that be. The fight may go away; but since moral power is the solidarity of man and society at its highest tension, it renews the fight in the hearts of man as long as he aspires after the freedom, majesty and dignity of manhood, and society dreams of the brotherhood of man or the kingdom of God on the earth. Thus moral power establishes the superiority of unarmed hands against the armed might of machine guns, of mangled corpses against powerful battalions. In humiliation, suffering and death, moral power raises the dignity of man and the values of society to new levels. Moral power, springing as it does from the navel-cord between the individual and the community, that is the warm vehicle of all values of life, is the source of all social re-valuation and the prime lever of all moral achievement and social progress. It is irrepressible, indestructible and irresistible. To challenge moral power is to challenge simultaneously the very foundation of society and the spiritual worth of the individual.

Might is never formidable enough to defy or neglect the definition of right and wrong in the conscience of a few martyrs or great multitudes, backed as this may be by their moral power. Might endeavours to appear legal, formal and punctilious in the uss of the scales of justice. It uses patronage and designs propaganda of lies and false claims in order to win approval of the masses for its action patterns and values. But a few men of 'soul force,' active and defiant, are enough to keep alive the supreme sentiment and value that the might which over-awes and subjugates them is wrong, and therefore its claims are morally intolerable. Thus alternative action patterns and values, stemming from their virginal definitions of human justice and solidarity, challenge might in action. More than the overt, formal challenge, the informal, silent, non-violent challenge of moral power is indomitable. For its strength lies in its complete dissociation from physical force, in its appeal to both the conscience and experience of all men and of all ages that right alone makes might. Moral power owes its supreme power to the profoundest depth of the human personality and the most complete experience of human justice, equality and solidarity accessible to it. Moral power can quickly mobilise great multitudes; because its criticisms, passions and imperatives have a detachment and universality derived from man's true conception of the self and of the teleological nature of the universe. Moral power is the Form and Idea of the True, the Good and the Just which the multitudes seem to recollect. It is the Triune God's supramundane action pattern of creation, preservation and destruction, that multiplies in myriad human minds and hearts stirred by the Divine purpose and passion. It makes itself manifest each time that the world goes wrong, unjust and chaotic, and each time it recalls it to justice, goodness and solidarity as the external law of man's history, prophetic of the Kingdom of God.

If moral power be continuously opposed and flouted, the power-groups inevitably lose their morale and are unable to defend their privileged status and interests with the same degree of self-complacence and self-deception as before. Might is easiest to defeat by moral power when it is based on property, wealth, and the physical force of the executive, police and army, that are freely transferable through change of opinion and sentiment or loss of morale. It is most formidable as it entrenches itself in the habits, standards and vested interests of groups and classes. For nothing individuals and groups hold dear than class or sectional monopolies and privileges, with the power of custom and sentiment, illusion and rationalisation behind them. Against these are, however, pitted the social insights and passion of the wise, the just and the good that daily grow in volume, and remind the community of the true meaning of justice and solidarity or the age-long struggle for freedom and equality. It is their moral power that destroys at once the over-weening self-confidence of the privileged groups as well as the moral torpor of the community. As long as moral power makes itself felt as a force, the social structure perpetually renews itself through the adoption and embodiment of new scales of values and interests and abandonment or modification of outworn ones.

The Struggle for a New Order of Values

One of the inevitable drawbacks of the struggle for a new status system is that new active centres of discontent and revolution do not emerge simultaneously in all sectors of society. Their emergence at different times enables the existing power-system to subdue the revolt before a general upheaval occurs. But such sporadic movements, though stamped out, influence public opinion in the direction of resistance, and gradually lead to the assertion of moral power that becomes the hope and the faith of the community. In different social fields more and more of resistance occurs in the form of strike, sabotage and defection in the army and the police or the rise of rebellious leaders from among the power-holding classes. Such nuclei of resistance in different sectors of the social field soon integrate themselves into an illicit or revolutionary stratum that refuses to accept the existing status system, and even the hierarchy of values on which it is based. It develops a new group ideology and order of values, putting an end to the supremacy of certain specialised and intermediate values that have run counter to the common and absolute values. The revolutionary movement that focuses the aspiration for new values, and functions as the builder of the new social order is associated generally in history with evolutionary and counter-revolutionary mass movements. Each social transition or crisis evolves its own orientation and alignment of ideological groups, revolutionary, evolutionary or counter-revolutionary, that all seek to obtain the sanction of the masses. The success or failure of a revolution depends upon the depth, intensity and universality of appeal of the new values, the effectiveness of the new social symbolism and leadership, and strength of resistance of the social class, holding key statuses, roles and power.

A far-reaching change in the status, prestige and power system in a community *i.e.*, a revolution is the outcome of group pressures and individual repressions, conflicts and revolts when the solidarity of society breaks up due to the old hierarchy of values, implied in the status system, becoming altogether unacceptable. Throughout history the rise and fall of social classes are connected with the community suddenly becoming aware of certain common values, that call for a new power-system, and demand precedence over certain specialised and instrumental values as these latter have entrenched themselves behind a rigid social framework and have been fenced off by selected classes and castes for their exclusive enjoyment. Social anomie inevitably results from the distance between the social strata becoming too rigid and over-bearing. This is supported by the dominance of certain specialised and instrumental values in society that is challenged by an enlightened social conscience. Individuals and groups feel that they are fixed in cramped social and moral space, with circumscribed goals and restricted opportunities for self-improvement. Thus the revolt proceeds from the depths of the personality that surfers chronic distress from repression and frustration and cannot internalise the social norms and prohibitions.

The Steps of a Revolution

A revolution begins with satire, ridicule and decline of prestige of a privileged social stratum. From smile, sneer and scowl to resentful mass, jeer and scornful laughter, from the burning of effigy to organised boycott and non-cooperation without violence, a revolution employs various symbolical devices, sometimes artistic, to establish itself without word or sign. All such symbols express sacrifice, resistance and aggression and gradually indoctrinate the masses with the militant ideals and axioms of the revolutionary group, while inculcating enmity and contempt for the rival groups or the existing social order. Next in order come the vocal protest, gossip, lampooning, mustering and demonstration in which the student's slogan, song or pamphlet and the leader's oratory mingle to arouse the mass. The use of naked violence by the power groups is always effectively counteracted by an appeal to abstract notions, and to a system of higher values side by side with an exposition of hollowness of the creed of the powers that be. This is the stage of myth-making, of the construction of a new pattern of ideas, beliefs and moral norms that is advanced in opposition to the prevailing one. Without a myth and an ideology the masses cannot be moved into revolutionary action. The mythology of a revolution is usually born in the cities where the contact of many minds and the suggestibility of the masses, especially youths, are taken full advantages of by a propagandist press for the integration, organisation and dissemination of the revolutionary credo. It is fashioned out of the frustrations, aspirations and hopes of the masses always by the intellectuals, the talkers, the writers and the demagogues who are the real pre-revolutionaries. An era of revolution is always preceded by a literature of revolt, ridiculing, humiliating and abusing the roles, statuses and credenda of the superior strata, decrying the injustice of the social structure, and also envisioning a new moral order. The distinction between legitimate and illegitimate status and prestige becomes now sharply drawn, individuals who felt the pangs of conscience in departing from established social habits and attitudes and the prevalent social norms now feel a moral obligation to revolt and resist. Non-conformist groups are formed, harnessing the unconscious tendencies of hatred and aggression. These also set up, as the sense of remorse and guilt is overcome, a less tyrannical super-ego, a new order of values, a new type of controls. Soon the new group builds up a constructive but disapproved, illicit or revolutionary prestige system, based on a novel but persistent scale of values and pattern of attaining strongly cherished instrumental ends. A new table of values breaks up the old prestige scale and establishes fresh goals and values for individuals and classes. Thus the way is prepared for a change in the major power system as social deference and law no longer bolster up the ascribed status. The real impotence of power lies in its derivation from outside the perennial system of social values. The non-conformist and the rebel build their own myth, creed and symbolism in the darkness of the prison cell; or as they sing before the executioner on the scaffold, whence these electrify and sweep through the community, enormously reinforced by the moral challenge of suffering and death. Power is feeblest in society when it brings itself down to the level of brute force. It is most easily conquered when its final challenge of life is met by that of death. On one side, authority is organised, firmly entrenched in law, tradition and symbolism and supported in the last resort by naked violence. Against it are pitted the conscience and moral power of the soul, the faith and insight that give to the community a new creed, formula and scale of values, and the new idealism that teaches life to defy suffering, torture and death. In human experience the latter are often found to win their greatest victories in moments of their deepest endurance and humiliation. Moral power, faith and idealism are invincible, not physical power. For these are immortal, lived and re-lived in the minds and actions of a generation of dreamers, rebels and leaders who arise to carry on the same protest; while physical power, always disunited, vacillating and demoralised, cannot easily reproduce itself in the next generation. Those who refuse to obey authority for ideal and social rather than personal aspirations serve the indispensable function in every society of envisioning a new type of community, a new system of economic and social relations and a new scheme of values. Bertrand Russell observes, "An individual may perceive a way of life, or a method of social organization, by which more of the desires of mankind could be satisfied than under the existing method. If he perceives truly, and can persuade men to adopt his reform, he is justified. Without rebellion, mankind would stagnate, and injustice would be irremediable."[4] A rebellion succeeds finally by a new structural status, embodying a new scale of prestige and power and a new system of societal valuation. As a new cultural, religious or economic movement sweeps through the land, the new status and power-system easily assimilates into the new scheme of social interests and values and preferment that it brings with it. A revolution is to be distinguished from a rebellion. The former implies the advent of a new system of values, of morale, social recognition and stratification. The latter may begin and end merely with a seizure of the power structure and has no implications on the cultural, economic and other aspects of life.

Real or Faked Table of Values

In a changing social world when the established social values are overthrown, new groups suddenly crop up and integrate on the basis of organised greed and self-assertion, and take advantage of the confusion and the strife to capture the key statuses in society, initiating a regime that may be quite as severe and repressive in its way as the old. Thus the social changes in a revolutionary situation can hardly be anticipated. A new order of values is no doubt set up, but once the familiar status system with its appropriate institutions, habits and attitudes is forsaken there is loosening of all controls and inhibitions. The change in the power system initiates changes in such fundamental social institutions as family and property, and if the period of transition be one of turmoil and struggle, the accompanying famine, disease, murder and rapine accompany an unbridled license, a veritable revolutionary debauch. A revolution may have derived its drive from a new scale of common values for the masses, but due to the repressed explosive forces of aggression and hate let loose in all spheres of life, the super-ego is completely silenced, and there prevails the reign of the more elemental patterns or segments of the self—the id—that ordinarily are repressed in Russia during the course of the Red Revolution when the individual reverted to the more primitive forms of action in different social relations, as is vividly portrayed by Sorokin. 'The conduct of the masses, swayed now (during revolution) only by elemental unconditioned reflexes, grows to be anarchic: one unconditioned reflex is opposed and overridden by the other; one individual oppresses and overrides the other. Famine increases, instead of decreasing, consequently ; the reflexes of nutrition are still more oppressed. Personal safety grows more insecure; the death rate rises tremendously, thanks to murders, famine and epidemics. Therefore, the reflexes of self-preservation are more and more oppressed. Confiscations of wealth taken away first from the rich, later on from the whole population under the guise of ever-heavier requisition and taxes oppress proprietorial instincts. The growth of sexual license oppresses sexual reflexes. The arbitrariness of the governing class oppresses the reflexes of liberty etc. In short, with but few exceptions, whatever group of fundamental reflexes we touch upon in each one of them, the oppression has increased not diminished; the more so, the more profound the revolution has been. In this primitive chaos *beellum ominium contra omnes*, a general oppression of all fundamental reflexes takes place."

Peaceful social change, as contrasted with a revolution, effects the transition from old to new types of status and power in a smooth, easy manner. In democratic societies, not exposed to sudden gusts of mass excitement, the periodical change in the personnel of the cabinet or the executive and also of the composition of the legislature takes the place of an alteration in the power system. Rival political parties who struggle for political power may present before the country different ideals and programmes, but on the whole their assumption of power does not mean any change in the status system. The American democrat, Jefferson, observed that a country required a revolution every twenty years in order to keep alive the spirit of liberty. Parliamentary institutions working under the party system have on the whole proved their capacity to adapt themselves to changes in the industrial structure and the distribution of wealth among the economic classes without any sudden shifts in power-relation. It is only when a political party wants to alter the basic institutions of property, competition and capitalism that the status-power system undergoes a fundamental change. Such change is violent, and affects not merely key statuses but also every phase of group relations, inspired as it is by a new order of values, an enlightened social conscience that overthrows many old privileges, many accustomed barriers, many established values. But times of revolt and reconstruction, while these are ushered by dreamers and idealists, are taken advantage of by scoundrels, gangsters and morons thrown to the top by a revolutionary upheaval. Thus the system of new values becomes a fraud. Men are compelled to practise outlandish new rituals or profess lies to save their skin. A cloak of hypocrisies covers the new table of values.

Such are some of the social mechanisms through which the changing pattern of values manifests itself in man's group relations and patterns of behaviour. In every society the status system is the key to the understanding of the major values and goals of the people. It varies as the cultural values and goals themselves vary. It is a dynamic organisation which reflects the periodic changes in the community's value judgment, sudden arousal or revulsion as well as slow and gradual enlightenment.

References

1. Pareto: *Mind and Society*, p. 1079.
2. The sociology of revolutions is treated by Sorokin, Brinton and Merriam and recently by Berirand Russel in his *Power and by Timasheff in The Sociology of Law*.
3. See G. N. Dhawan : *The Political Philosophy of Mahatma Gandhi*, pp. 70-71. According to Mahatma Gandhi soul-force, truth and non-violence are identical—these are never-failing remedies—direct, ceaseless and inexhaustible. 'The hardest heart and the grossest ignorance," he observes, "must" disappear before the rising sun of suffering without anger and without malice." Mahatma Gandhi has experimented with the techniques of applications of truth and non-violence in mass movements in politics, and created appropriate organisations and trained personnel in asramas for the purpose of a revolution through collective mass Satyagraha (i.e., the collective strategy of civil disobedience for the sake of truth). See also *History of the Congress*, p. 665.
4. *Power*, p. 263.

11

THE CONSERVATION AND SYNTHESIS OF VALUES: TRADITIONS, INSTITUTIONS AND SYMBOLS

Difference Between Groups, Traditions and Institutions as Nuclei of the Major Values

Man, as he is physically endowed and as a social being, seeks values not singly but collectively. He forms groups and institutions that represent methods and mechanisms for the satisfaction, promotion and transmission of values. Every basic interest and value of mankind constitute the nucleus of formation of groups and institutions. Groups grow up as individuals cohere together for the satisfaction of the basic values; while the mass of institutions is called into being for standardising, organising and directing group relationships and activities for the satisfaction and fostering of these values. Groups are episodes in man's adaptation emerging out of the ordering and fulfilment of specific human values that become the common ends or goals of the associated individuals. As the system of values becomes stable and continuous, groups crystallise into institutions by which we understand social relationships, attitudes and habits that are more or less enduring, and have obtained social approval. Institutions accordingly represent the more definite, formal and sanctioned social relationships and behaviours, the more stable integrations of both values and adaptation techniques that provide the standardised ideas, attitudes and purposive controls for the fulfilment and promotion of values.

Institutions are embodiments of the major values of man and society. They give definition and meaning to values for the individual, who can mature his self only in so far as he can reflect these in his social activities and relationships. It is in this manner that values become a part of the structure of man's developed and organised self. Groups may be temporary and group values may be shifting; but in so far as groups develop into institutions group values are tested, renewed and consolidated by the experience of generations. Institutions combine the results of deliberation, memory, organisation and judgment on individual and social experience for generations, and thus generate ideal values. Such ideal values of institutions outlast the lives of both individuals and groups; at the same time these may be infinitely enriched by the contributions of the latter. Values are defined by institutions in a broad and general manner, leaving ample scope for the variety and flexibility of individual strivings and behaviours. In fact the mind of the individual, socially fashioned as it is, constantly recreates and modifies the pattern of social values in terms of the self. Institutional values are also systematically assisted in their fulfilment in daily life by she fixation and elaboration of means and programmes, conventions, habits, morals and schemes of action for the individual, involving specific rights and duties according to his role, position and status. Man's interests, values and ideals are made definite and permanent as his duties in life and character stabilised by finding his role and position in institutional life. He can enter into and fully participate in the totality of values, both concrete and ideal, of a society and culture only in and through institutions, that are embodiments of social experience of generations guiding him in his evolutionary advance. This is the biological significance of institutions.

Concretely institutions are the agencies for the fulfilment of the essential and universal biological values, such as food, marriage, family and protection; economic values such as wealth, property, standard of living and security, social values such as status, honour and prestige, and spiritual values, such as aesthetic appreciation, knowledge and security amidst the uncertain and the inexplicable. It is because man can fulfil and foster values mainly through the instrumentality of institutions that these latter possess authority and sanctity. Giddings, therefore, is entirely wrong when he suggests that any social organisation or relation that has grown up unperceived by the public becomes an 'institution' when the attention of the state is called to it, and the state then permits it to exist, thereby authorising it.[1] It is the imperative, universal and persistent character of the values that underlie and inhere in institutions that give them their authority and sanction.

In the beginning of social evolution values did not crystallise, nor became definite or differentiated. These therefore inhered in a loosely blended mass of traditions, customs and folkways that did not have any specific internal unity or organisation. With the specification of interests and values, tradition and custom and their cognate ideas and sentiments developed into an institution, characterised by a definite rational and practical content and purpose. The difference between an institution and tradition is that the former not merely shows a greater clarity, coherence and unity of purpose and value, but also a more definite prescription of behaviour pattern that endures through groups created for the specific fulfilment of the value. It is the tradition element of an institution that apparently gives the latter authority that stands the test of social selection and survival; but the real authority springs from the urgency and universality of the values that institutions embody and foster. If society be regarded as a spacious mansion of values, its traditions, customs and folkways would be the brick, the lime and the mortar, and institutions would be the pillars, concrete and steel, the strong and rigid framework without which neither society can function, nor values can be operative. The state is only one of these institutions in society, fulfilling values centring round order, protection and security. Institutions are what they are, not because of the fiats of rulers but because of social sentiments and judgments in respect of the values they create, order and guarantee and that are tested by social experience.

Human Values are Derived Social Values

Man is mentally so constituted that his major urges and desires blend with one another and with his social dispositions. Thus most values integrate desires and interests at different levels with the social urge. Human values are essentially social products. These can be satisfied only in and through man's groups and institutions. "Nearly all human values," observes Joseph Mayer, "are 'social' values, except possibly a few biological ones which man shares with the brutes or those implied in the unrealistic metaphysical doctrine of solipsism."[2] The values that groups and institutions fulfil do not represent ego-centric, primary desires in the raw, such as food, sex and aggression but are secondary or derived values. Institutions stand for a certain discipline and control of man's primitive impulses and desires, a certain degree of socialisation that transforms his blind, explosive and disruptive urges into large and stable interests and values. It is not the mere sexual values that create the family and marriage institutions. Sexual and parental desires, hunger and food, play and repose, all intermingle in the composite, secondary values of the family that also extend into and overlap, due to the interplay of the social impulses, with the values of kinship. Similarly, economic values are secondary and derived values, not to be attributed to the operation of single primary drives like food-getting, appropriation, and possession, curiosity or constructiveness. All these mingle together and also with the social impulses in combinations that enormously vary, and that are often difficult to trace, comprising the permanent, derivative economic values of economic adequacy and standard of living, security and power. Similarly, man's primary tendencies of aggression and sympathy, dommance and subordination merge together for fashioning the derivative social values of status and prestige. Here also institutions embody large and universal derived values. Finally, in the case of the values connected with the aesthetic, religious and ecclesiastical institutions, it is even more difficult to single out the threads which connect them with the elemental urges of human nature. Such institutions are integrations and ordered expressions of the impulses of play, creation, assertion and gregariousness, but in the imaginative values arising out of the harmonies of sound, colour, matter and movement as in art, and in those arising out of man's ordered relationships with the unknown and the bewildering, these elemental human nature satisfactions are very much in the background.

Human Values Involve Orderly Relationships of Persons and Objects

All institutions accordingly give fulfilment to secondary or derived values in which some definite ordering or integration of the primary urges and interests is implied for the sake of their durable satisfaction in man's social setting. By blending, ranking, and harmonising, satisfactions and values become relatively stable. On the other hand, the same process involves orderly relationships of persons and objects. Underlying the institution of the family are both the integration of sex with the food-getting, parental and social urges and the idea of ordered relations of the sexes and the family groups. In wealth, property and other economic institutions we have the pattern of fundamental human urges, such as those of food-getting, appropriation, possession, aggression and constructiveness mingled in different combinations, and the notion of orderly economic relationships and transactions of the regulation of competition and cooperation and of ownership or control of material resources and implements of production and distribution and exchange. In status there are similarly a definite integration and combination of the impulses of aggression and sympathy, dominance and submission as well the notion of systematic distribution of social rank, power and prestige relationships. Every institution, accordingly, both stereotypes values and sentiments, and standardises forms of social relationship and activity. In other words, the institutional values are the only values, the institutional relations the legitimate relations, and the institutional ways of action the moral ways in society.

Thus arises what is called the 'institutional fallacy' according to which man hides his conscience behind the institutional feeling, belief and habit. The chief reasons why the institutional fallacy persists in all societies are the institutional determination of his attitudes and social actions and relations, and his rationalisation in respect of his own behaviour and institutional standards that saves him from psychic conflicts. Due to the chronic antagonism between individual wishes or scale of preferences and the institutional values, he sometimes both adores and condemns, extols and decries the institution. For there is no escape for the average man from the institution, since he finds reward, convenience and self-status in institutional conformity. On the other hand, the institution lays down norms and standards only in a general manner permitting some amount of divergence of individual behaviour and mode of fulfilment of values.

Institutions Derive their Stability from Integration of Biological, Social and Ideal Values

Man's values that are concentrated and integrated in institutions, as these become his goals, lead him away from the mere physical values that are disapproved, and come under various taboos and prohibitions in life and society. The familial values standardise and stabilise the desires and satisfactions of sex that no longer run the tumultuous course of brutal lust. The biological, the economic, the social and the ideal values fuse and interpenetrate. The result is that even such an explosive and disruptive impulse like sex, that also constantly changes in. its aim and direction, develops into a deep, stable and tender attachment that becomes the seat of realisation of many ideal values. In economic and social values that are ordered and guaranteed by economic and social institutions, the values that are fixed in the minds of people and determine their goals and activities grow out of primary and universal urges as well, but the biological urges and values are here hardly recognisable. Hunger, the desires for appropriation and possession, curiosity and constructiveness are hardly manifest in the vast complex economic apparatus, providing for the production, acquisition and distribution of food and other necessary economic goods and services that ensure economic sufficiency ; yet these original impulses furnish the drives for the newly fashioned, derived economic values of standard of living, wealth, property and economic power, mingling as they do now with the social impulses and the interests of social order, security and efficiency. Man's social values are even more varied and complex, woven as these are by threads of various kinds and grades of urges and satisfactions. Among the most important of these are gregariousness, sympathy, protection, dominance and submission, that are, however, not found in the raw but blend and integrate with one another and with the various types of biological as well as ideal values. The process of valuation, then, is undoubtedly the work of man's groups and institutions that create derived or secondary values through (1) the ordering and integration of the biological, the social and the ideal satisfactions in each case, thereby giving values both intensity and stability, and (2) the ordering and standardisation of the activities and relationships of the persons and groups concerned.

Institutional values lose their stability and unity, and disintegrate, contributing also to the break-up of the solidarity of the group, as the biological, the social and the ideal phases of satisfaction fail to cohere or dissociate themselves. The familial values lapse and the family group sunders as a result of brutal lust and aggression, unchecked by the social impulses or any ideal satisfactions. On the other hand, where the sex impulses, home-making and other interests cannot obtain adequate fulfilment due to the dominance of economic values and the desire to maintain an artificial standard of living for the class as an economic goal, there is a similar dissociation of the familial values. Economic values lapse at the time of an extreme food crisis or famine, due to the magnification of the hunger impulse among the famine-stricken masses that excitedly hunt for and seize food, unmindful of social and even familial relationships and obligations. These are extreme instances of the pursuit of mere biological values to the exclusion of the social and ideal values, spelling social un-settlement and disruption. Abnormal social conditions marked by the unstability of group and institutional life are associated with the persistence of pathological institutions that evade the laws and social codes, such as the brothel, the saloon, the gambling den, the black market. These foci of "disvalues" are fairly common in all societies. The solidarity of society depends upon the network of institutional values surrounding human life and behaviour, and fixing in human minds social habits or ways of living in which biological values no longer fulfil themselves in brutal ego-centric satisfactions but coalesce with the social and the ideal values. Man's social advance is possible only on the foundation of relatively fixed habits, attitudes and ways of living that make his choice of subordination of lower to higher values easy and automatic involving scarcely any mental effort.

The Evolution of Tertiary, Universalised Values of Institutions : Familism, Economism and Nationalism

Over and above the secondary or derived values that institutions embody and integrate, institutions foster *tertiary* values. There are several sets of values that institutions fulfil and promote. These are interdependent. Their synthesis generates a new tertiary value. Furthermore, the institution becoming the necessary condition and requisite for the satisfaction of these various sets of values acquires a new tertiary value. Tertiary values are composite, emergent and ideal values, and often grow out of a constellation of value-systems that are harmonised and merge in one another. The familial institutions of India and China, like the joint household, the clan, the gotra, the kindred and the generations tied with one another to the hearth, the home and the soil by ancestor-worship merge their values in the great tertiary values of "familism," centred round the peace, continuity and solidarity of man in his generations. Such is the supremacy of the tertiary values of the family in the Orient that these embrace most of the values of life, and direct the all-round, complete unfolding of Oriental character and personality in the family setting. Similarly in the modern industrial West "economism" comprises the tertiary values represented by the system of industry and business organisation, property and the class. Here, again, the synthesis of economic values generates new tertiary values, centred

TABLE 11.1

Classification of the Major Institutions as Foci of Universal Social Values and Ideals

A *Institution*	B *Primary and Secondary Values*	C *Tertiary Values*	D *Ideals and Symbols*
I. Family	Values arising out of integration Of the primary satisfactions of sex, hunger, and parental and gregarious impulses. Love, Affection, Parental respect, Brotherliness, Neighbourliness.	Familism : Devotion and loyally to family and the kinship group, faith and tradition, Propriety of manners. Continuity and Solidarity of patrimony, race and culture and Sacrifice of one generation for another.	Devotion to abstract principles, and symbols of Kindness, Reciprocity, fidelity, Chastity, Loyalty, Humaneness, Chivalry, Truthfulness, Justice, Love, Solidarity.
II. Economic and Industrial Institutions.	Values arising out of integration of the primary impulses of appropriation, possession, and constructiveness. Security, Thrift, Workmanship, Adventure, Enterprise, Inventiveness, Recognition.	Economism : Devotion and loyalty to class, job, occupation, profession, and standard of living of the social stratum. Mobility, Competition, Power and Privilege of Classes, Conflict, Co-operation.	Devotion to abstract principles and symbols of Fair Play, Contract, Justice, Progress.
III. Political Institutions.	Values arising out of the integration of the primary impulses of protection, domination and subordination.	State-ism : Devotion and loyalty to territory, tribe (folk) and culture. Tribalism. Patriotism, Nationalism, Imperialism, Racism.	Devotion to abstract principles and symbols of Law, Order. Liberty, Equality, Fraternity, Humanitarianism, Internationalism. The Four Freedoms.
IV. Religious Institutions.	Values arising out of integration of the primary impulses of fear, self-abasement, self-assertion, regariousness, creative impulses, etc.	Holiness : Devotion and loyalty to deities, rituals, and priesthoods, Bigotry, Asceticism, Other-worldliness.	Devotion to abstract principles and symbols of Truth, Gondness, Wholeness, Universal Humanism, Persocalism.

round individualism, equality and freedom of mobility that have represented abstract conditions favourable for the development of a particular type of character and personality and their distinctive contribution to civilisation. The state that comprises the system of institutions, promoting and safeguarding the essential values of life and security, order and peace, freedom and justice, education, social welfare and culture, becomes the pre-condition for the pursuit of most of the ends and values by other groups and institutions upon which it imposes regulatory measures. It thus embodies and fosters universal tertiary values that may for want of better terms be called stateism, legalism and nationalism. These have elicited the devotion and adoration of citizens of vast, continuous empires held together by a common, ideal legacy of justice, liberty, equality or an aggressive cultural mission. All through the ages, the religious organisation, the monkhood, the church and the ascetic order also have in different countries often developed great tertiary values centred round purity, wisdom and ministration of the poor that have given to the world some of its greatest and lovable personalities. The ensemble of virtues and quality of personalities developed in different civilisations are largely the outcome of tertiary values of characteristic institutions in different patterns of culture, stimulating and eliciting the noblest toil, devotion and sacrifice of individuals.

All tertiary values of institutions go back to certain conditions of social history and cumulative influences of region, race and tradition embodied in some special phases of development of such institutions. Familism in the Orient draws its character from the ancient co-operation of the large household and the kindred in rice agriculture, the unchequered, peaceful history of the autonomous village communities in the vast river basins and the peculiar development of the worship of ancestors, household, clan and caste deities and of local gods and godlings in Indian and Chinese polytheism. The pecuniary tertiary values of the Western industrial organisations can be easily traced to the peculiar social and geographical conditions in Western Europe, the expropriation of the village communities and rise of the big estates, the wholesale migration from the villages to the towns, the rise of Protestantism and the series of scientific inventions and discoveries associated with the utilisation of coal and steam. Similarly the significant tertiary values of state-ism and legalism embodied in the political institutions of the Roman and the British Empires grew out of the peculiar history of Rome as one of the Latin republics expanding in the Mediterranean region, and of an island empire that obtained supremacy over the entire globe by its sudden increase of industry and commerce, requiring liberal institutions for their expansion among different peoples, obeying strange customs and laws. All peoples and cultures develop their familial, economic, religious or political institutions, but under special conditions these have given rise to a special system of values in the Orient and in the West that have attained relative permanence and universality. As a matter of fact all the above sets of institutions, familial, economic or industrial, political and religious, have always tended to develop on the basis of larger and more stable relationships and universal values towards a universal social order. Familism moulded the entire Chinese empire into a functional pattern working out universalised familial values and virtues, and transforming the family code of ethics into a universal socio-political code. The Chinese ideal is a social order, grounded on certain universal moral obligations that first emerge in the family but apply to every relation of life. Not only social organisation, industry and the state but also religion and philosophy have their roots in the family ethos. The economic organisation easily expands into an international society on the basis of an impersonal, rational division of labour and abstract social relationship of exchange and freedom of competition and contract. In different countries and epochs the state, welding together different peoples through the power of the sword, has developed universal ideals of a larger world community than an empire, organised in terms of social and spiritual mission rather than of might. Similarly religion through the ages has striven to establish an abstract universal human community or social order through the doctrine of the spiritual brotherhood of man or the worthlessness of all men before the Divine will and power. It is in this manner that the major institutions under special social and historical conditions have attained in different countries a universality and uniformity of interests and values, knitting together masses of people into some kind of a rational or abstract universal society. This expansiveness or universality of institutions is of course due to the development of abstract philosophical notions and social relationships, gestures or symbols that attach themselves to institutions engendering and developing universal attitudes and values.

The Role of Myth and Ideology in the Organisation and Dissemination of Ideal Tertiary values

The tertiary values of institutions, indeed, carry with them a headlight of abstract concepts or ideas organised into a consistent myth, symbolism and philosophy. Behind the largeness and universality of the tertiary values one can sense a pattern of basic ideas and emotions that engender characteristic mental attitudes towards the set of institutions, social relationships and ways of living. Man's values and habits, aspirations and hopes adjust themselves to what Lippmann calls "stereotypes" that comprise "an ordered, more or less consistent picture of the world" for him. This is not a full and complete picture but one to which man is adapted, just as he selects certain accessible or possible values out of the world. He feels at home in this ordered world; he finds here the charm of the familiar, the normal, the dependable. Its grooves and shapes are what he is accustomed to find them.[3] The ingredients of a stereotype, like those of a myth, are logical concepts, imageries, emotions and phantasies. In a value-situation a good deal of practical common sense as well as primary instincts, repressed complexes and emotions are involved; these are all canalised into socially expected and approved channels in order that man may get on smoothly with fellowman. Stereotypes represent the verbal symbolic equipment of man that directs his value-seeking and achievement, and especially originate from and centre round all kinds of critical human situations that arouse great pleasures and pains, expectancies and anxieties. Stereotypes, that also include in the same category catch-phrases, maxims and slogans, obtain currency in every society and briefly embody and transmit the fundamental beliefs and moral and institutional preferences and values of a community or group. There are rich prestige suggestions of such comprehensive, emotionally loaded stereotype terms and phrases as Chastity in body and mind, Compassion to all sentient creatures, and Chivalry to both friend and enemy-tertiary familial values; Freedom of competition and social mobility—tertiary economic values; or Liberalism, Nationalism, Totalitarianism and Imperialism—tertiary political values. "Be like Savitri" (the wife of Satyavan, the noblest model of chastity), with which Indian women greet one another, "The brothers are like Rama-Lakshman," "In adoring the parents, you adore all the gods," "Look upon every woman as thy mother" or "Every woman is a part of the Divine Mother",—"Every child is the playful infant, Lord Krishna"—these few stereotypes represent abbreviated phrases of popular speech that through pregnant ideas, images and sentiments quickly define moral situations, and serve as symbols of social and moral norms in Hindu culture. Similarly "Workers of the world unite," "Three acres and a cow," "Land belongs to the tillers of the soil", "Akhand Hindustan" (undivided India) represent emotionally saturated slogans that indicate for the masses under different circumstances certain distinct sets of values, and define courses of political action. These form part of a wider system of social ideology and myth. Stereotypes and slogans are a species of the genus social ideology and myth that go round in the primary and secondary groups of all cultures, and serve to orient both individuals and groups to culturally accepted ideals, norms and wish-fulfillments.

Stereotypes, myths, legends, slogans and other verbal symbolic devices organise themselves into a harmonious pattern known as an ideology which functions as a tool in man's endeavours to achieve value fulfilment. According to Pareto, ideology constitutes the structure of fine rationalisations, the acceptance of which enables man to do what he does. Much of his conduct and motivations cannot be accepted at their face value. He acts in consonance with his verbalisations that are called "derivations" by Pareto and that rather than pure motives determine behaviour. It is in this way that values gather round them a structure of ideology, a tissue of fictions and rationalisations that are yet of great dynamic significance for his social habits and actions, his capacities and aspirations. This idea is also conveyed by the recognition of the social myth especially in Marxism. Many Socialist writers, beginning with Sorel, have stressed that the myth focusses all the values and hopes of the working class movement, and gives these a precision and rigidity that no other method of thought could have given. But apart from the emphasis of the functional role of economic myths in modern industrial society, myths that are obviously designated as such have an important social-psychological function. Myths and legends are imaginative reconstructions of primordial and great happenings, of the deeds of ancestors and heroes and of the genesis of institutions, mores and norms. Without these social life and interaction lose much of their meaning and significance for most individuals, who will also experience serious stresses and strains in adjusting themselves in emotional crises and difficult social situations. Myths deal with love, marriage, parenthood and death, with past and future life, with the origins of family, tribe and community, with law and punishment. These have their basis in all kinds of difficult predicaments that man must have to face in his physical and social milieu, and the fears and anxieties associated with them. All major myths of the human race exhibit the gradual growth, maturation and socialisation of the self—the integration of the ego with the super-ego or voice of the social group, and embody the interplay of the ambivalent unconscious instincts of aggression and love, destruction and restitution. They are characterised by an aesthetic element of 'social disguise' by virtue of which man obtains a profound satisfaction from the violation of taboos and injunctions, social and moral norms in an imaginary distant world. Such happiness is rooted in his aggression and revenge against his parents in the infantile consciousness. But equally is he stirred in his unconscious by his sense of guilt and self-censure and restoration of wholeness or goodness. Owing to the factor of 'disguise,' myths profoundly stir the imagination and give pleasure through the expression of the libidinal and aggressive tendencies in the aesthetic creations of heroes and situations that are thus kept away from the major field of consciousness. At the same time these safeguard and enforce beliefs and social and moral codes of the community by reconciling the individual to these without too severe or mutilating repression. The reason why myth is not believed as false or fictitious is the balance it maintains through artistic disguise between the fundamental tendencies of expression and repression in the unconscious.[4] A myth or legend is not a story or an idle tale, but a vivid, emotionally charged "description of what the people regard as a true happening in terms of their deep-felt cravings, beliefs and phantasies. Among all peoples myths and legends enhance and strengthen significant interests, beliefs and social values, safeguard and enforce meanings and morals by giving them the seal of sanctity and antiquity, and also guide man's behaviour patterns and manners according to certain practical rules and codes. In fact myths and legends largely account for the continuity of culture and moral values and virtues from generation to generation. Myths are still being made. Instead of clustering round the situations and relationships of the primary-group world, myths now arise from the severe economic stresses and strains that present the more imperative emotional problems for solution, and articulate the demands for economic security and equality, justice and power. Myth and ideology in the modern industrial communities reflect the political and economic cleavages within a nation as well as the conflicts in racial and international relations. Since myth and ideology have to do with emotional adjustment and moral action, a culture with its associated set of values, virtues and personality traits is best discerned and judged from its myth and ideology. Science has usurped the place of many nature myths, but social myths cannot be superseded by the social sciences. As long as man experiences emotional crisis and remains a value-seeking and value-achieving animal, social myths will continue to play an important role in assuring the individual poise and sanity in the midst of his strains and conflicts and also safeguarding the stability and continuity of social culture. So far as the relation between myths and legends and a particular social institution is concerned, the former create and maintain the latter through their linkage with the basic value content and imaginal core of institution. It is in this manner that a distinctive stereotype in respect of social relations and activilies, a myth, an ideology or philosophy of order, a faith in respect of certain specific personal traits and virtues and a set of symbols attach themselves to the tertiary values and motivate man and society. The chief reason why men adhere so tenaciously to the cluster of institutions that develop the more basic, more co-ordinated, stabler and subtler tertiary values is the cumulative influence of stereotype, ideology, myth and symbol that all become fixtures in the people's minds.

The Heritage of Symbol Patterns

The emergent and ideal tertiary values of institutions are expressed also through symbols that are substitutive devices for condensed expression of abstract principles, values and social relationships or ways of living that groups and institutions embody. A symbol is an object, person, activity or situation or its representation by any sign (such as gesture, sound, colour or writing) that through mental imagery by a kind of abbreviated reasoning monopolises attention and emotions and points easily, quickly and unerringly to a conclusion. Besides object symbols that society fashions for its economic and technical manipulation and mastery of the environment, there is a whole array of connotative or evaluating and meaningful symbols that every society needs for facilitating adjustments between man and fellowman, covering the entire field of social control, including mores, manners, conventions, morals and laws. Man's conformity to social culture is achieved by a host of control devices among which social symbols that easily and immediately arrest attention and arouse a train of appropriate attitudes, emotions and phantasies are most efficacious. The fiat of the law-giver, the threat of the police, the indication of the traffic-controller, the persuasion of the artist, writer or preacher and the suggestion of the propagandist are all short-circuited by the use of a variety of symbols that replace the objects of attention and yet elicit the appropriate responses. Such supersession is due to the emotional accretion and suggestiveness of the symbols that achieve a deeper insight into reality than mere perception through effective concentration on the relevant and the meaningful, in which art usually comes to the aid of symbolic representation. Basic social institutions like the state, the family, the church and the economic class cannot indeed carry on the ordinary routine of their activities without the adroit manipulation of a wide variety of symbols in their distinctive fields that are well understood by the people, and taken as living social realities, and express and enhance their common faith, belief and norm of behaviour. Men respond to the summons and decrees of the law court, the baton of the policeman, the whistle of the train, the traffic signal on the road and the toll of the temple bells in much the same manner as if they are dealing with living and dominating persons, state-officials, police-men, engine-drivers, traffic-regulators, and priests, commanding, directing, warning and expostulating.

It is well worth pausing to consider whether modern man does not sometimes suffer from the over-elaboration and abuse of symbols. Man's symbols are now independently organised in a virtually autonomous system so that often his attitudes, emotions and behaviour elicited by these symbols lose connection with his primary desires and elemental activities; while there is also a profound gap between his natural feelings and emotions their social expressions. Instance is afforded by his need of training even in the arts of sexual love and reproduction; such is the mastery of purely artificial symbols or word-signs with their associated partial meanings and values over human conduct.[5] According to F.H. Allport, "not only are our feelings conditioned through the use of symbols but our processes of thinking and imagining as well. There is, furthermore, a deep-seated tendency to rationalize a symbol, that is to discover some logical reason for feeling towards it as we do. We love the flag, therefore, not as a mere fetish, but because it stands for our country...Thus do we build up a belief in the reality of the things for which our symbols stand. These "projected" realities are not regarded as the product of our emotions, but as something existing quite apart from us and above us. They are not created by faith, but they themselves create faith in that they are regarded as its justification. Without belief in them all rational support for our attachment to their symbols would be lost."

Through the symbols of the marriage ring and garland, the domestic ritual and ceremony, the family altar, crest and coat of arms, the integrity and solidarity of the family from generation co generation are expressed. Such symbols are full of emotional potency and unconscious meaning and suggestion, Similarly the tertiary values of industry and business organisation clustering round the impersonality and expansiveness of mass standardised production and quickness of movement of men, goods and services have found their appropriate symbols in the trade-mark and form of advertisement, patent sign, money and the cheque book. The tertiary values of states and empires seek emotionally charged symbolic expression in flags, national anthems, seals, pictures of leaders, national holidays, ceremonial regalia and slogans, all associated with abstract political principles, emotional attitudes and ways of political behaviour. Religious groups and institutions exhibit the most complex and variegated patterns of symbols, due to the fact that the tertiary values here reveal the deepest levels of human experience. Such, for instance, are the trident, the cross, the temple, the idol, the hymn, the mantra, the posture and gesture of meditation and the religious rite and ceremony, all of which provide some meaning or interpretation of the supernatural. Educational institutions, universities, colleges and scientific associations use the academic robes, titles of distinction and other symbols of expectancy, satisfaction and award to promote the interests and values of higher learning. All groups and institutions offer titles of high status or position, prizes, awards or certificates of merit—symbols of social appreciation of the role of the individual in his participation in group activities. Symbols like the marriage ring, the domestic hearth and the ancestral temple familiar in the family; money, cheque and bill of exchange in economic life; the national flag, holiday parade and festival in political life; the costume, degree and ceremonial in academic life; and titles of dignity, distinction or pre-eminence in all major institutions; the idol, prayer and ritual in religious life serve in different fields as gestures and methods of human communication and valuation. These bring together masses of men separated by vast distances into uniform attitudes and habits, and build up a deeper spiritual unison just as language and the fine arts do in their own fields.

Symbols may be not merely objects but also mythical or imaginary persons of children's fairy stories, popular tales and legends, whose memory is adored by the community, and who become the personifications of community values. Max Scheler strongly stressed the significance of "the social ideal images," types of social personality, that inspire and orient the conduct of a society in terms of its cherished goals and ideals. These images may embody the perfections of individual personality of different categories, such as the hero, the saint and the genius, or belong to the various professions and occupations, stimulating the development of character and group ways of living and service. The family in all cultures attempts to inculcate ideals of chastity, devotion and humaneness of the highest order through folk-songs, nursery tales and ditties. Ballads, epics and historical legends set forth the courage and sacrifice of great national heroes, saints or ancestors, who serve as symbolic models for noble conduct. The heroes of the Jatakas, the Ramayana, the Mahabharata and the Bhaktamala form the basis for the projection of a multitude of religious values and virtues in India. In Europe the characters of Theophrastus, the Lives of Plutarch, the Bible and the biographies of the medieval saints have similarly served as symbolic norms of perfection. All through the centuries the cherished ideals and aspirations of a culture are embodied in its mythical heroes who serve as symbols and assist individuals in their progress towards their life goals. In the Orient, where society is relatively static, and the behaviour of the heroes of a by-gone age may be effectual and significant for today, such heroes still receive worship in the temples as directing spirits for the community. Literature, painting, sculpture, music, dance, cinema and propaganda, all illustrate the enormous significance and potentialities of symbolism for patternising the habits, virtues and values of the multitude. All symbolisms play the important role of recording and disseminating in most economical and simplified forms significant value systems and attitudes of the community for the guidance of both individuals and groups. They serve as familiar and eloquent sign-posts, recalling and directing special attention to the major values and virtues that are cherished by a particular culture, and as a matter of fact themselves become substitute forms of emotional expression, creative foci of value experience.

Myths, legends, stereotypes and symbols focusing round such major institutions as the family, the system of industry, the economic class, the church or the state engender a firm belief in their reality and continuity transcending the lives, needs and experiences of the individuals. This is no group illusion or fiction, as F.W. Allport would regard it.[6] In fact it is because of the universal convictions about their supra-personal reality, due to endowment with a vast, ever-expanding content of meaning and values, that institutions function as most powerful agencies for individual guidance and control, selection and survival. These are also responsible for the attribution of a "moral" and a "judicial" personality to institutions—dynamic, immortal systems with their distinctive values, meanings, moral usages, instruments and sanctions.

The Definition of Ideals in Conflict Situations

Men have various group and institutional selves. They seek values, secondary or tertiary, through a variety of groups and institutions whose harmonious fusion and economical reconciliation characterise social evolution as much as the complexity and differentiation of associations and institutions, and of the values they create and promote. Values develop into 'ideals' in conflict situations that call for deliberation, criticism, judgment and choice of values competing with one another for securing man's loyalty and allegiance. It is in the ideal that man finds a reconciliation of the diverse and conflicting sets of values, crystallised in different institutions demanding his loyalties. The ideal is the outcome of clarification, criticism, judgment and systematisation by which all the values involved in a conflict may be conserved so as to reconstruct the world, and by which, therefore, human nature is expressed more completely in relation to the situation. Man's life in the concrete world is beset by opposition not merely between particular individual aims and institutional goals, but also between the higher values, that always pushes him forward to co-ordination and synthesis in the shape of the ideal. The ideal takes all relevant values into account, and rests upon and expresses specific orderly relations between persons in given conflict situations. Without the ideal man cannot reshape his life nor rearrange his conduct and social relations, since his choice is concerned not merely between right and wrong ends and values, but also more often between several absolutely valid institutional values that have to be brought somehow in harmony with one another in actual life in order that the latter may be meaningful and worthwhile. It is the necessity of a fuller and more vital social living whence the ideal derives its authority, if it is not to be mere idle and vague sentiment, nor a superimposed command. Gradually the ideal becomes assimilated to the self as habit, and not merely has adjustment value for the temporary psychological situation but also for effective adaptation through life. In a static social system, however, the ideal may be regarded as pre-conceived pattern, acquired by the individual from society for his adaptation to a more or less stable life situation. Every society, indeed, develops in the individual some generic ideals that are psychologically and socially satisfying, leaving the individual to work out slight changes within the ideal pattern. Thus within the orbit of the ideal he adjusts himself to the social realities. Or, if he finds the ideal incompatible with the latter, he passes through much stress and strain, and reshapes and reformulates the ideal. Not seldom he fails to piece together his pre-conception and the life-style and suffers from maladjustment.

The Ideal, the Link between the Concrete and the Transcendental

The ideal not only represents a greater degree of abstraction and intellectualization than the value, either derivative or tertiary, but is also more effective and constructive in its moral aspect, grading and integrating man's urges into one harmonious whole, arousing the will and quickening the effort to realise the 'ideal' relations and behaviour in life. Gurvitch observes that an ideal type of moral conduct transcends the general norms or prescriptions of society and is valued very highly. Another French scholar, Bayat, also points out: "One of the most instructive aspects of social morality is the ideal type of collective conduct which a group or society formulates: for instance, the warrior, sage, stoic, gentleman, citizen, etc. The sublime collective virtues expressed in these terms are not prescribed as duty or obligation. The society proposes them to its members only as an acme of perfection, the achievement of which while attended with infinite difficulties, nevertheless transcends all other social merits." The ideal at once relates itself to a timeless, universal principle like equality, freedom, justice and solidarity, and is continuous with the social reality that exists here and now. Further, the ideal being a subject of rational deliberation, judgment and communication, society is enriched by both individual and social experience. Society and individual may be recurrently defeated in the achievement of their goals and purposes, but it is the ideal that keeps their resolve and effort at the highest potential in the midst of humiliation, suffering and disillusionment. And in fact the greater the defeat, the more effective and uncompromising is the challenge of the ideal, burning at white heat, fed by the fuel of the majesty and dignity of manhood and collective intelligence, courage and sympathy. The ideal imports into an institution, social habit and way of living that constantly change, a "practical absolute" beyond the flux of circumstances. The institution is the link between the transcendental principle or ideal and the society in which it is embodied and stabilised. Not all abstract principles and ideals, however, can be expressed by institutions. It is significant that in the field of aesthetic value and experience there is no institution. Aesthetic values and ideals express themselves through individual works of art that appeal directly to the percipient. Art cannot be institutionalised because the aesthetic qualities of harmony of sounds and words, colours and movements in space and time charm the audience or spectators by themselves. The mediation of any other agency is unnecessary, although conformity to an aesthetic tradition is helpful towards appreciation that varies from mind to mind. On the other hand, familial, economic, political and religious values require and create their institutions in order that, these may become effective in the social world. Institutions in so far as they seek either instrumental or intrinsic values also show striking differences in their choice of means for their attainment, and hence also in their efforts upon the cultivation of virtues and of personality.

Intrinsic Values of Institutions easily develop into Universal Social Ideals

Due to the modern exaggeration of division of labour in both economic and social fields, and development of machine technology, means and ends, instrumental and intrinsic values are now sundered farther and farther from each other, and more and more of the values that men seek become instrumental values. Man's jobs, occupations and professions now imprison his mind for better or worse. He identifies himself with the standards of his job, profession or occupation that organises the entirety of his life interests and values. Each successful man in the modern community—the worker, the businessman, the politician, the lawyer or the editor—develops an occupation 'personality' lacking in that richness of life that the progress of modern civilisation should place at its door. In the modern social structure the growth of certain institutions, such as industrial and political, has become lop-sided, and institutions do not co-operate or fit harmoniously into one another, but create and promote highly differentiated systems of instrumental values within their conventional social areas and procedures. Industry, labour, family, politics, education, science, art and religion, each epitomises and concentrates specific values that represent the function of special social and economic groups, classes or categories of people, and are often found to be incompatible with one another. Furthermore, many of these instrumental values, limited within the range of specialised institutions and their special personnel, are developed and manipulated in such manner as to be conducive towards the advantage and aggrandisement of segregated groups, classes and professions. These values come to be separated from the totality of social values—pecuniary and economic values, family values, political values, military values, legal values, recreational values and so on, inhibiting the growth of the total personality whose urges and values cannot be fulfilled except by traversing over several groups and institutional fields and their systems of values. Within each institutional field, man's virtues are tested or appraised in strict accordance with the successful undertaking of his specific task in a given job, profession or occupation. His role, position and status are accordingly determined not with reference to his general intelligence, social dispositions and character, but by his fitness for specified tasks that are standardised in a vast complicated scheme of division of social labour. The upward or downward movement from one social stratum to another is now dependent not on the general qualities and virtues of the individual, but upon his specialised talents and capacities that open the avenues for the satisfaction of highly differentiated values. Such values and virtues cannot, therefore, develop into ideals—channels of expression of the overflowing human mind and effort reaching towards something universal and eternal.

It is much easier for the intrinsic values of the familial institutions to develop into comprehensive social ideals. The reasons are not far to seek. The human personality has the surest claims to intrinsic worth. Thus great intrinsic values centre round the relations in the family—the parental relation, the conjugal relation, the fraternal relation, the kinship relation. In each case the ground of valuation comprises the fact that each of the different kinds of personality, of different ages and degrees of relationship, fulfils quite a variety of impulses and satisfactions that all blend together and are projected to the individual. Thus the human personality that is maintained in the relations of love, tenderness and sacrifice comes to be regarded at the most supreme value. In the Indian ideal of familism, the various types of family relationship lead the developing self with tenderness, devotion and loyalty to the loved one, to the companion, to the master, to the Person of Persons. The narrow egoism and clannishness in the family or other primary groups ruin personality. Against this Oriental familism has set the individual the task of seizing the relationships of mutual love and intercommunion in the family as abstract symbols, illustrated by such phrases as the Divine Mother, the Eternal Bride, the Holy Child, the Sweet Companion or generically the Person of Persons, for transcending the personality by passing over to the Supreme Person. It is in this manner that the primary-group and institutional world of the Orient has intellectualised the basic emotional attitudes and values, developed in primary group relationships, and created abstract moral and religious symbols and ideals for the true understanding of human relationship and uplifting and assimilating these to the Beyond-human.

Instrumental Values of Secondary Groups Vitiate Morality

The secondary group like the class and the state because of its largeness, rationality, calculated pursuit of ends, irrespective of means and techniques used, and impersonal character satisfies only one set of impulses and interests and thus cannot possess intrinsic values. It becomes the nucleus of instrumental values. As the secondary groups expand and multiply indefinitely, and more and more of human relationships become abstract, rational, pecuniary and impersonal, institutional valuation becomes principally the function of special social groups and classes which create and foster instrumental values for their special interest, enhancement and power. Such institutional valuation of course inhibits the free and diverse self-expression of the individuals. Many individuals and groups come habitually to instrumental values for their own sake, and the institutions also become huge machines and ends in themselves.

The gifted individual as the politician subordinates patriotism to partisanship; as the common worker or the professional man he regards his job or profession as the end for which the economic system exists; as the successful lawyer he sacrifices truth and righteousness to legalism; and so the entire range of individual tasks and goals disregards the normal hierarchy of values.

All institutional values are functional in character, i.e., these form part and parcel of the vital processes of individual and social adaptation. In the institutional situation as it has developed today in industrial civilisation, economic and political values overshadow all other values; these have become so clamorous, insistent and imperative that no morality is observed in respect of the techniques and means used in their attainment. Economic and political values are instrumental values which, due to the loss of the impact of the family and the Church and of the intellectual and spiritual side of life, nurture a technique and tradition of power and violence rather than of moral and spiritual nourishment, while diverting to themselves more and more social energy. Their pursuit by individuals and groups that show little moral responsibility in the choice of means in industrial and political conflicts corrodes both individual and social morality. In the struggle for power of the industrial proletariat, the Marxian tactics of class struggle and revolution is heedless of the principle of moral responsibility in the choice of the techniques or weapons that may be used to bring about the classless society. Similarly patriotism is an unsatisfactory religion because, in Bertrand Russell's words, "it lacks universality and infinity". Thus in power politics any insistence upon justice, law and honour has become out of date. Machiavellianism in politics is as rampant as direct action and sabotage in Communist struggle, reinforcing the tendency towards abrogation of the rule of law and constitutional method that express the principle of ethical responsibility in the choice of means in inter-group struggles. Industrial and political institutions that represent the ruling institutions in civilisation today are thus largely responsible for the disintegration of character due to their acceptance of a dual code of morality. But, as William Alexander Percy has observed, "it is sophistry to speak of two sets of virtues, there is but one ; virtue is an end itself, the survival virtues are means, not ends. Honour and honesty, compassion and truth are good even if they kill you, for they alone give life its dignity and worth."

The entire trend of modern civilisation has been, to be sure, to promote a disbalance between different kinds of institutions with their specialised instrumental values in discord with one another, and their techniques and procedures no longer relying upon the continuous total life of groups and institutions informed by the spirit of reciprocity, and justice. Even the progressive ideals of social equality, justice and humanitarianism are harnessed by Socialism and Communism as mere techniques or weapons in the class struggle. Thus in the revolutionary institutional situation the familial groups and their old world ideals of honesty, integrity, compassion and solidarity lapse ; while the secondary groups, actuated by the unilateral struggle for power and privilege, become larger and more mechanical and ruthless in their pursuit of instrumental values, without any communications in respect of their techniques and means, and vitiate the morality of whole societies.

Need of Revaluation in the Secondary-Group World

The instrumental values of the impersonally organised secondary-group world of today can only be corrected and subordinated to the ultimate values in two ways. There should be, first, a re-orientation of groups, classes and states. Only a restoration of the immediacy of relationship and of community life and personality through neighbourhood, regional or cultural groups can bring about balance and normality in the value patterns. Regionalism and functionalism may transform the Leviathan which, however democratically it may be controlled, is bound to become stratified. The establishment of regional autonomy in definite culture areas and self-government of factories, workshops, co-operatives and agricultural associations may give a chance to the average man to find self-expression and hold his own against mass-opinions and standards. The pattern of group organisation and the dominance of intrinsic or institutional values are linked with each other.

No revaluation is possible in the mechanical and the secondary-group world of today without renewing it in its foundations through the restoration in some measure of small groups, neighbourhoods and community activities that differ in species but belong to the sams genus which humanised mankind from the earliest times in the horde, the tribe, the family and the village. New agencies of social work, propaganda, education, religion and the fine arts should be utilised for the resuscitation of the community life and personality as the nucleus of integral and universal rather than segmented and specific interests and values. Secondly, there should also be a transformation from within. As man's contacts with fellowmen have become impersonal, indirect and derivative, for the development of his personality in modern political and industrial institutions he should, after an intellectual analysis of social relationships and behaviour, discover, assimilate and adore certain abstract spiritual principles and symbols that may lead to the transcending of his self, rehabilitating personal and primary values and ideals that have now languished.

Symbolism stands for both the primacy of the spiritual values and of the reality of this world as the embodiment or incarnation of such values. Symbolism holds the key in the secondary-group organisation of society of today for transforming the primary-group attitudes and values in every field, shot through with emotions, into abstract tertiary values, ideals and concepts of common welfare, justice and solidarity of the invisible man. The transformation through an emphasis of impersonal attitudes and ideas and symbolical projected constructs is indicated in Column D of Table 11.1. Such abstract spiritual symbols would be represented in the abstractly organised social environment of today by justice, equality and fraternity that would help to link society with the world of spiritual values that really exists. The highest spiritual values and experience can be expressed in human language only symbolically. These relate to Personality or Being that always remains inexhaustible and mysterious, hidden beyond the world, and yet gives symbolical expression to Itself in the travails and sorrows of the work-a-day world. The human values and ways of action that develop out of primary-group relations, such as love, tenderness and solidarity, become infinite, inexhaustible and prophetic in the Being, who transcends society and the world as He infils them and all human relationships. Thus these become constructive symbols of love, justice and fraternity that seek the infinite, inexhaustible expansion, depth and perfection of the Being's love, justice and fraternity, and lead to a real transfiguration of society and human relations. Such transfiguration rests only on the mystical way of thinking and action that identifies the divine mind with the mind of man, the mind of all men and of the universe. In metaphysics God is too often posited as the absolute, the perfect, the whole or the self-sufficient Being. On the other hand, mystical experience through the ages regards the Being as the absolute and at the same time the concrete universal Person, reciprocating man's all-too-human feelings and attachments. Perfection and imperfection, transcendence and immanence become both necessary in the mystical experience. In India in the Bengal School of Vaishnavism, for instance, the antinomies of perfection and imperfection disappear. It is maintained that God is infinite and at the same time a Person. The limitation of personality does not apply to the case of God whose infinitude of excellence, power and love can be felt by every finite creature. On the other hand, the communion of love demands a sympathetic and synthetic response. Thus the finite being becomes as much a requirement for God, as God is for the finite being. Here concrete religious significance is retained in spite of the traditional monistic position.[7] In Western metaphysics it is only recently that Whitehead, Montague and Hartshorne, among others, have defined absolutism and completeness of the Divine in such manner that neither pantheism, panentheism or (universal) personalism is blindly rejected, nor man's rational need to contribute something quite as concrete and individual as himself to the divine experience disregarded.[8] Hartshorne stresses in almost Bengal Vaishnavic category that, in its true concept, the "perfect" is "the self-transcending transcender of all"; it is reflexive instead of irreflexive transcendence, and to reflexive transcendence contributions in the literal sense are possible.[9] Thus there is no longer any incompatibility between perfection and the status of the cosmic group mind or the concrete unity of things and values. It is this concrete group mind conception of God that may enable man in the secondary-group world of today to transcend the national or any other human group mind, the dangerous myth of which has jettisoned human freedom, and sacrificed it in favour of abstract collectivism. Freedom will no doubt be restored to modern man in abundant measure by his inclusion in the divine group mind, transcending the nation in both space and time and in concreteness and integrity.

The Role of Abstract Symbolism in the Rehabilitation of the Ultimate Values in Society

The new Leviathan or the nation, taken mystically as the super-whole, reduces in value the human individual to its political aspect. On the other hand, the mind of the cosmic community, concrete and integral, is the matrix within which man's spiritual values and aspirations and the cosmic laws of justice, freedom and solidarity from which are derived the basic conditions of his life are born and bred. It grants complete freedom to the individual and keeps alive his devotion and sacrifice for the invisible man and the universe in an infinitely continuing cosmic drama of love. In interpreting the divine group mind, modern man has, to be sure, the aid of mystical tradition and experience of which he has not made adequate use. Let us quote two well-known Indian traditions in this respect. "God beholds creatures crossing the sea of the world in the frail boat of the flesh, and says to himself: T will be their boat, and I, even I, *will* be tossed about and buffeted by the waves of that sea." Here is the same resolution of antinomy of monism and dualism, perfection and imperfection in the conception of the divine life. Or, again, in the words of a charming Bengali folk-song : "It goes on blossoming for ages, the soul lotus, in which I am bound, as well as thou, without escape. There is no end to the opening of its petals, and the honey in it has such sweetness that thou, like an enchanted bee can't never desert it, and therefore thou art bound and I am, and salvation is nowhere."[10]

These passing references are enough to indicate the significance of both mystical experience and metaphysical speculation in evolving the notion of the mind of the cosmic community that alone can supply the adequate ground of moral obligation in modern man's world of indirect and invisible social contacts and relationships. Democracy, industry, all human arrangements and institutions will be transformed by the transfer of cosmic imagination, thought and emotion to human relations that in spite of their impersonality and invisibility will be rectified and reinforced from the beyond-human channels, Walter Lippmann rightly makes a distinction between mystical and literal democracy : "There is no way of proving the doctrine that all souls are precious in the eyes of God, or, as Dean Inge recently put it, that 'the personality of every man and woman is sacred and inviolable.' The doctrine proceeds from a mystical intuition. There is felt to be a spiritual reality behind and independent of the visible character and behaviour of a man. The doctrine of ultimate human equality cannot be tested in human experience; it rests on a faith which transcends experience. The mystics (from Christ and Buddha to St. Francis and Whitman) had attained a sense of equality by transcending and renouncing all the standards with which we measure inequality. The populace retained its appetites and its standards and then sought to deny the inequalities which they produced and revealed." In the literal democracy of today the universal search for instrumental values, "gold and precious stones" that are claimed by everybody, has meant not that all personalities have infinite worth and are equal before the throne of God, but that "all men are equally good biologists," and that the counting of individuals, opinions, minds and souls is the final arbiter of all values. Democracy by a false sense of equality that it has attained by accepting that the worth of a soul can be measured, and by its complete reliance on the process of adding up souls for arbitrament abolishes the order of values. Personality is the highest in the hierarchy of values. The more the modern democratic state is saturated with the significance of the majesty and dignity of the human personality, the more surely can it secure the abstract, formal and far-reaching types of social forms and relationships that promote justice, equality and fraternity in man's wider, invisible social contacts. Thus the democratic relationships and institutions can become the vehicles of realisation of the supreme values. Many democratic communities through their social services among the handicapped, the unfortunate and the under-privileged, and their cultural mission among the backward races and peoples are now seen to be profoundly influenced by humanistic ideals that stand in clear contrast with the ideals of power politics, economic imperialism and race dominance of the previous epoch. Not merely political institutions but economic and industrial institutions as well may be the channels of expression and ordering of the supreme values, and assume positive, spiritual and idealistic tasks on the basis of abstract or symbolical understanding of all relationships in terms of the supreme worth of the personality. Thus the civilised man's mastery of abstract, intellectual symbolism, that is the core of the mystical consciousness, may enable him to achieve the ultimate values in and through the indirect and impersonal relationships of the secondary-group and institutional world.

The deeper integrations of the self, such as represented by Commonalty in the social world, are the result as much of feelings and sentiments as of abstract intellectual and symbolical processes. Man's rescue from the psychosis and immorality of either crowds and masses or the vast secondary groups of today is to be sought from his cultivation of transcendental supra-human notions and ideals that may make him solidare with invisible men and groups in the Great Society. Sociology in the first decades of the twentieth century emphasised gregarious instincts and collective feelings and institutions as means of social integration and progress. The new sociology should re-interpret the functions of reason in society as arousing and disseminating the meaningfulness and values of community life; it should stress the ideal tendencies of man's nature—his intellectual systematisation and aesthetic symbolism—for building up institutional values and ideals in order to achieve sanity, goodness and wholeness of social living. The construction and reinforcement of socially adaptive metaphysical concepts, ideals and symbols are the means by which society can rise from the instinctive and automatic to the reflective level, and subordinate diseased and unorganised minds, groups and institutions to the dominant, infinite and eternal values of justice, equality and solidarity at their highest potentials, set far above the instrumental values of power, utility and distance.

References

1. *Descriptive and Historical Sociology*, p. 431.
2. *Social Science Principles*, p. 250.
3. Lippraann : *Public Opinion*, p. 95.
4. See my *The Social Function of Art*.
5. This has been emphasised by *Burrow in his The Biology of Human Conflict*.
6. F.W. Allport: *Institutional Behaviour*, pp. 141, 142.
7. Mukerjee : *Theory and Art of Mysticism*, pp. 137, 159 and 160.
8. Whitehead : *Process and Reality* ; Hartshorne : *Man's Vision of God and The Logic of Theism*.
9. Elements of Truth in the Group Mind Concept, *Social Research*, May 1942.
10. Translation by Rabindranath Tagore.

12

THE SHARING OF VALUES—FROM NATURAL RIGHTS TO SOCIAL IDEALS

Rights and Duties as Aids to Value Fulfilment

Valuation is an essential phase of man's social life. Groups and institutions define, integrate and order values, create the conditions for their fulfilment, and also elaborate the means to be chosen by the individual for it. Groups or institutions with their respective valuations compete or cooperate with one another. It is the community that ultimately selects, approves and orders the values, so that the various activities of individuals and groups may be linked together and harmonised in given social situations. Out of its deliberation and criticism of values arise norms, ideals and virtues. Out of its adaptations of means and ends arise rights and duties. It is the *duty* of every man to work out the meaning and ideal for his life in its individuality and contribution to society through his particular role, position and status in institutional life; and just for this reason that he has this duty he has also the *right* to the conditions of its fulfilment that are guaranteed by the community or the state. All rights define both an ideal and programme of social action for every man, and invest him with freedom and power for carrying it out either in cooperation or in conflict with other men. All rights have costs; There are duties attached to all rights. Family, marriage, occupation, school, union, religious group and club, each of them fulfils certain values for the individual, and in the context of his specific role, duty and social relations he obtains from the community help, forbearance and power in the form of rights for value satisfaction.

Behind the maintenance of all rights there is the recognition of the supreme value of the human personality and its promotion and cultivation upon an equalitarian rather than a differential principle in spite of the various and unequal qualities and capacities of individuals. All civilisations nourish notions of human equality and dignity that give spiritual connotation to human rights and liberties. But societies and civilisations differ in respect of the order of significance of rights that correspond to their scheme of social values. Rights thrive best in democracies that breathe the essential and inalienable dignity of all men, and distribute fairly among the expanding range of the common values of civilisation. "Every man," runs the H.G. Wells Declaration of the Rights of Man, "is a joint inheritor of all the natural resources, and of the powers, inventions and possibilities accumulated by our forerunners." And further: "Notwithstanding the various and unequal qualities of individuals, all men shall be deemed absolutely equal in the eyes of the law, equally important in the *social* life and equally entitled to the respect of their fellowmen."

Rights and Social History

The accrual of rights has differed among different peoples and cultures, and has been connected with social history. In Oriental societies in spite of the fact that institutions have shown a greater fixity, rights have been safeguarded by groups and institutions such as the family, the clan, the caste, the guild, the village community, the brotherhood and the profession whose jurisdiction in respect of specific interests and values within the community has been largely recognised and protected by the state. In the local and functional self-government of the Orient, rights have been maintained less by the state and more by the various local and functional bodies. In ancient Hellas, in spite of the glaring contradiction of slavery and certain oligarchic elements in society, the moral equality of man was proclaimed; while in Rome the extension of the Empire that embraced strange territories and peoples of different degrees of civilisation was favourable to the idea of the essential unity of mankind. The Stoics who believed in pantheism maintained that all men were akin by nature, formed of the same elements and having the same purpose on the earth. All this humane tradition merged in Christianity that was, as Harold Laski points out, "in its original phase essentially a society of the disinherited to whom the idea of the inherent dignity or human personality as such would make an urgent appeal." In England the Puritan Revolution re-formulated with pious fervour the Christian notions of man's "innate natural freedom, property and liberty." On the other hand, Calvinism, with its dogma of pre-destination, by inculcating the individual's worthlessness at a time when the dissolution of feudal society and guild system of Europe threatened his security, prepared him for the acceptance of his subservient role in capitalistic society. Eighteenth century Europe believed in Nature and Reason. The current of pagan and Christian idealism was now reinforced by the intellectual movement for an examination of feudal, monarchical and ecclesiastic institutions and the struggle for human dignity and liberty. It is significant that at the time of the Sophists, and again in the 18th century, the tendency was discernible to view institutions as man-made and as artificial, restraining the individual from the normal pursuit of the values of life. Thus demands for the restoration of usurped rights were formulated. Similarly in the twentieth century with governments either becoming state collectivisms or passing under the sway of monopolistic productive and financial organisations there has been great encroachment upon liberty, particularly liberty of thought. Thus a great number of people under the leadership of H. G. Wells have drawn up a Declaration of the Rights of Man, the list being adapted to the changed social and economic conditions of to-day. In the preamble we read: "The history of the Western peoples has a lesson for all mankind. It has been the practice of what are called the democratic or Parliamentary countries to meet every enhancement and centralisation of power in the past by a definite and vigorous re-assertion of the individual rights of man. Never before has the demand to revive that precedent been so urgent as it is now."[1] What is attributed to European democratic tradition really goes back to the heritage of the pagan and the Christian religious vision. Reinhold Niebuhr rightly observes: "The modern communist's dream of a completely equalitarian society is a secularised, but still essentially religious version of the classical religious dream. Its secularisation is partly a reaction to the unrealistic sentimentality into which the religious social hope degenerated in the middle-class religious community; partly it is the inevitable consequence of the mechanisation of modern life and the destruction of religious imagination."[2] No doubt all formulation of the rights of people in the twentieth century has been profoundly influenced by the equalitarian ideal of Soviet Russia that has largely replaced Christianity as the fundamental faith of the common man in the world. In Germany the Constitution of 1919 incorporated a large number of fundamental rights and duties that represent some kind of a compromise between Western individualism and liberalism and Russian collectivism. In both Soviet Russia and the Weimar Republic certain basic duties were also emphasised contrary to the Western liberal tradition, and in fact the obligations of private property, the duty to work and universal labour service in both the Russian and German Constitutions represent the establishment of new principles in the economic structure of society. The Soviet Constitution of course definitely lays down as its fundamental aims the abolition of all exploitation of man by man and of the division of society into classes and the establishment of a socialistic organisation of society. It is well known, however, how the latter political developments in both Soviet Russia and Germany have made of the constitutionally protected rights of the citizens a nullity.

Rights and Values in Their Institutional Setting

In spite of the fact that the content of rights has remarkably changed from epoch to epoch through the vicissitudes of man's social and political history, civilisation has on the whole shown a large measure of consensus in respect of man's rights as essential conditions of the pursuit and fulfilment of his values, and the observance of certain duties for the realisation of his personality. Institutions have been, in spite of Rousseau, aids and means for the realisation of values and rights rather than obstacles and interferences, though specific institutions can never be the full expression of them. From level to level of man's social adaptation institutions have been the conditions under which the fulfilment of the biological, social and economic values has been possible. As these have changed from country to country, they have provided rights and claims, status and power for individuals in an ever varying vital process of social, moral and intellectual accommodation. As a matter of fact the changing content of values and rights of institutions keeps alive the human spirit, as the fixity of institutions however good in themselves is one of its tragedies. As Karl Barth has explained: "The more successfully the good and the right assume concrete form, the more they become evil and wrong, *summon jus, summum injuria.* This theocratic dream comes abruptly to an end when we discover that it is the Devil who approaches Jesus and offers Him all the kingdoms of this world. It ends also with Dostoevesky's picture of the Grand Inquisitor," Men have no right to possess objective right against other men. In man's social history, groups and institutions, such as families, castes, village communities, trade unions, cooperatives and professions, have themselves acquired certain rights, privileges and prestige that have under different social conditions served as a serious hindrance or bulwark of the rights of individuals and protection against an all-embracing centralisation and concentration of power by governments or economic and financial organisations.

In ancient India governments down the centuries recognised the precedence of the village communities by treating them "more or less on terms of equality" and by paying great deference to the village headmen. A gens or community, guild or corporation had its collective rights and code of duties (dharma), checked of course by the larger and higher community and ultimately by the state. Narada observed: "Family meetings (kula), corporations (sreni), village assemblies (gana), one appointed by the king, and the king himself, are invested with the power to decide law-suits; and of these each succeeding is superior to the one preceding it in order." Thus in Hindu law the rights of families, kinship groups, village communities, guilds and mercantile corporations contributed not a little towards the effective protection of trade and industry, religion and education against the enhancement and centralisation of power of dictatorial monarchs or groups. Gautama, Manu and Brihaspati and other codifiers in ancient India mention that "rules of their own profession" were recognised by the state for cultivators or peasants and farmers, artisans such as carpenters or others, artists, money-lenders, companies of tradesmen, dancers, persons wearing the token of a religious order and even robbers. In a static society the safeguarding of the rights and privileges of rural communes, guilds of craftsmen and artists, religious, mercantile and educational corporations were also associated with the formulation of an inviolable and rigid code of duties (swadharma) of different classes, occupations and professions. In Hindu political theory there are no rights and privileges without corresponding duties or dharma, and it is enjoined that each person should be kept in his proper role and duties by the state enforcing "terrible" *danda* or punishment for social deviation. The doctrine of dharma or code of duties makes the Hindu state somewhat similar to the Greek conception of the state as fostering the highest good of the citizens. Oriental peoples like those of China and India are, as Bertrand Russel once put it, the least governed in the world.

A large number of independent or semi-independent groupings developed an autonomous, juridical and economic organisation not subjected to the tutelage of the state, and created what George Gurvitch has called "social law".[3] Social law possesses different degrees of flexibility and security depending upon types of groups and modes of acknowledgment or voluntary traditions of social co-operation and regulation. The conception of law based not on coercion but on the correlation—socially guaranteed—between claims and expectations on the one hand and duties and obligations of groups on the other, developed by the Russian scholar, Petrazitzky, and the French scholar, Gurvitch, is more applicable to Oriental countries that have maintained a large amount of autonomous and genuine sociality of groups and associations cooperating as equal units than in the West, where conquest, expropriation and domination of one class over another have gone to the making of a tyrannical state, engulfing all economic and social groups and substituting for social law the law of subordination which finally changes into the law of coercion.

Class Struggle and Rights

In Europe, due largely to her political unstability and series of wars, conquests and expropriations, the virtue-state of the Greek philosophers was transformed, to be sure, into the class state, and political evolution became largely a history of struggles of different classes for rights wrested from the state through revolutions. The memorable struggle of the Roman Plebs has its various counterparts in later European history. The army, the ecclesiastics, the nobility, the middle class, the traders and the working class have each in turn tried to dominate with consequent revolutions and struggles. Such is the story of the Magna Charta, of the several bills of rights of the seventeenth century, of the bills of rights of America, of the Declaration of Rights in France and of the later written constitutions, followed in their wake by labour upheavals leading to recent formulations of the economic rights of workers. The content of the Rights of Man in modern Europe is largely the outcome of the Industrial Revolution in England and the need of expansion of the new exchange economy based on security of transactions and property and the newly-won freedom of the worker, no longer a chattel of the landlord but selling his labour to the highest bidder. Roscoe Pound has well observed that the legal rights of the eighteenth century Englishmen came down to us as the rights of man. The English traders, merchants and entrepreneurs who were the pioneer liberals laid the foundations of the new theory that the rights of contract and property were inalienable and inviolable, derived from the laws of nature and nature's God, and hence beyond the realm of human enquiry or debate. According to the Declaration of Rights in Virginia in the United States these ""inherent" rights are "the enjoyment of life and liberty, with the means of acquiring and possessing property and pursuing and obtaining happiness and safety."

Early Western liberalism spread the notion of inalienable rights without the counterpart of any duties. Such unconditional and costless rights of which a person could not be deprived, no matter whatever his attitudes and behaviour were towards himself or towards fellowmen, was largely responsible for an exaggerated individualism and the loosening of social and moral tissues in the industrial age that was breaking down old institutions, social habits, scales of values. The result was that the liberal creed became altogether a misfit and an anachronism as the modern democratic state had to implement a series of measures for social amelioration and organised social services, filling the gap created by a ruthless dehumanised economic system. The need of reformulation of the rights of man became, indeed, imperative as the basic rights and freedoms of liberal democratic society ceased to be operative or relevant in the modern industrial situation with its pulses of economic fluctuation, chronic unemployment and distress for the majority of the population. Throughout the 18th and 19th centuries liberalism helped to build up the secondary-group organisation of society by breaking up ancient feudal privileges and rigid social arrangements and unsettling even the primary groups; but it could not furnish a new principle of social integration, and as a matter of fact its dissociation of duty from right, of service from power, was altogther fatal to social justice and solidarity, as the disparity of wealth and social and economic opportunities withheld "natural liberty" from an increasing section of people. The natural liberty of European liberalism had its roots in the Christian stress of the supreme worth of the human personality, in the law of nature of Stoic philosophy and the Roman jurists, in the revolutionary movement that overthrew absolute monarchy as well as in the natural law philosophy of the Encyclopaedists of the French Revolution. But in the face of the ruthless and devastating forces of Big Business modern man fled in terror, and in his spiritual isolation and economic destitution sought refuge in the collective. If he was deprived of his property, initiative and enterprise, he gave up his own conscience, associated himself with the mass and imposed a compulsory, regimenied life. The way was thus prepared for socialism as liberalism lost its old religious and metaphysical moorings and became materialistic and positivistic.

In Marxism, proposed as an alternative creed, the questions of personality and of rights-and-duties found scant consideration. For Marx, after formulating that the masses of workers are deprived by the industrial system of the produce of their labour which is their own by right, does not stress the problem of justice in distribution, but believes in the dialectic march of industrial events through class struggle for the ethical consummation, viz., the classless society in which there will be no class of parasites and idlers with illegitimate earnings. The driving force behind the social transformation is the unity of class interests, not the sense of social injustice that might call into the struggle groups and individuals not strictly belonging to the proletariat. Marxism in its stress on the forces of economics altogether ignores the divergence of man's goals and values, and even regards his abstract ideas and moral values that have a history of their own as originating from and being fashioned only by economic events and interests. Thus Marxism is even more frankly materialistic than the later phase of European liberalism. The tactic of class struggle in Marxian sociology is divested of any moral or spiritual elements. Man is no rational creature conscious of his destiny or even the course of events. In the dialectic of history he is irresistibly carried along as a wisp of straw. Yet in a larger sense Marxism through its vivid recognition of the degradation of the worker to the "level of an appendage of a machine" and his "mutilation into the fragment" of a personality in the capitalistic system, where "the worker's life time is transformed into working time and he is estranged from the intellectual potentialities of the labour process" appeals to the sense of ethical justice of the people in a manner as few social philosophies have done. As a matter of fact even though the Christian meaning of liberty is now eclipsed, Marxian sociology has stood up as a most effective guardian of human dignity against exploitation and abuse in the industrialised age.

Whether socialism has captured the citadel of the state or not, the conviction has gained ground in the industrial West that the classical political rights are infructuous, unless these are buttressed by new economic rights—rights to work, to a living wage, to freedom of association, collective bargaining and strike, to protection against old age, widowhood and other forms of disablement and to holidays with pay; and new social rights-rights to health and parenthood, freedom of speech, worship and education, rights to cheap and decent housing and right to easy, cheap and wholesome enjoyment of leisure. The present generation has been in fact rather liberal in the formulation or promotion of new social and economic rights, uprooted as these have been from their supernatural or metaphysical foundation. God or Nature may have been niggardly, but the modern democratic state, responsive to the wishes of the people, has become lavish in its gifts of human rights to fulfil the demands of human equality and justice.

The Postulate of Social Equality

Since the time of Plato and Aristotle equality and justice have often been identified, and in epochs such as the present, when there are undeserved social discriminations and injustices meted out to certain classes and social or racial groups or minorities, the demand of equality has expressed a fundamental aspect of social existence.[4] The postulate of human equality rests on the demands of justice that requires the accrual of equal opportunity for the fulfilment of the values of life for all individuals, equally deserving as men for human shelter, clothing and nourishment, for education and for protection against disease, disablement and undeserved misfortune in society. Due to the accident of birth each man starts differently due to the difference in hereditary equipment. Then the family, the social stratum or the class largely "condition" his development, determining his role, position and status, thus accentuating artificially the difference due to the inequality of birth and fate. Each man at least consciously feels that he is born into his station, high or low, irrespective of his native endowments and capacities. This makes it a fundamental ethical requirement that all privileges, discriminations and handicaps that hinder social mobility and assignment of rank and status according to worth or capacity should be abolished or minimised. This is from the point of view of the individual. From the point of view of society, men, even if they are not actually equal, should be treated as equals in order to promote social co-operation or solidarity. For, as T.V. Smith observes, "it will hardly be thought to demand argument that men work together better when they regard themselves as substantially equal." Man's natal inequalities are sought to be eliminated by eugenic policy and legislation adopted by many modern states that reduce materially the number of births of hereditarily defective, diseased and handicapped individuals. In childhood many modern states guarantee equality of opportunity to all individuals through the rights of nourishment, covering, medical care and education. As individuals reach adulthood the postulate of equality calls for far-reaching social security measures. The recent development of rights to work and protection against disablement and unemployment, to living wage, old age pension, comfortable housing and cheap and wholesome leisure seeks to provide the under-privileged advantages and benefits that would make their status equivalent to that of the privileged classes. On the other hand, undeserved gains and privileges demand equalisation or redress that restores the balance, as illustrated by the imposition of heavy death duty, capital levy, excess profit tax, surtax and other forms of progressive taxation and by forms of public expenditure and social services of all kinds directed largely or exclusively to the benefit of the under-privileged classes. All these promote an equitable distribution of wealth. In modern planned economy the programme of social equality looms large having its source in two emotions—social jealousy or resentment and social compassion or justice.

The application of the principle of social equality differs in different countries according to different stages of industrial development, social habits and sentiments and ideology. "The programme of social equality of a materialist type is related rather to the sense of resentment, that of an idealist type to the sense of justice," observes Zweig.[5] The Soviet collectivist experiment illustrates the idealist type. In the light of this, the masses of the population in every industrial country claim more and more not absolute but reasonable equality measured by the standards of efficiency and security. The most important objectives appear to be free access to facilities of education of all grades, free opportunity of social and economic promotion and free social and medical hygiene and protection. At the same time the range of income is also restricted on the basis of the principle of equality of sacinrifice by drastic taxation of higher incomes, compulsory saving and rationing. No society can progress on the basis of a mechanical equalisation that promotes adult, mediocre culture of mass products, and works against a qualitative democracy adjusted to differential aptitudes, talents and capacities of individuals. Nothing will be gained, for instance, by heavily taxing the rich and the privileged and depriving them of certain intellectual or aesthetic advantages in order to offer facilities of physical satisfaction and welfare for the under-privileged. On the other hand, a minimum human standard of living, security and welfare, rising progressively with the improvement of national income, should be safeguarded by rights in law and by institutional and administrative services and welfare measures whose cost should be met by progressive taxation. The equalisation of income on some functional basis strengthens the moral foundation of democracy, and enlarges and extends the democratic process. All this has been greatly aided by the development of a large variety of social and economic rights grounded on the democratic postulate of human equality. It must, however, be pointed out that outside Soviet Russia the rights of private ownership are not yet redefined and recast to meet the demands of a new industrial ethos. The process will not be dalayed as a necessary requisite of a free industrial society.

The *Raison d'etre* of the Right to Social Security

As a matter of fact the origin of these new economic and social rights that may be subsumed under the single, comprehensive right to security is to be attributed to the general failure of modern economic and industrial institutions to fulfil certain common values that claim universal validity as being indispensable for every man's welfare and self-realisation. The present industrial system has, above everything else, failed to provide security for the mass of the population, and thus the right of security has now come in the foreground of political consciousness as an incentive to social efficiency, harmony and justice. Specifically the essential constituent of the right of security is the right to work, which is the corrective of the rights of property and freedom of contract or bargaining that have now become altogether disruptive of society. It is not merely a question of a man of property without an adequate sense of duty destroying the conditions of his own self-realisation, on which ground indeed the claim to property asserts itself, but of the right to property in the tools and implements of large-scale production becoming the right to economic power, whose abuse can prevent work-the fountain head of personality expression and growth for the most considerable section of the population. Thus in all industrial communities the essential or key industries are coming under the ownership or management of society; while the right to work is considered as fundamental as the right to life, and is gradually implemented through a steady job or unemployment benefit. The right to work supported by rights to a living wage, to protection against sickness, disablement and decrepitude and to marriage and family allowances becomes the right to security, which expresses the aspiration of an industrial community to equitably distribute among all classes the hazards of the industrial system. The longer the postponement of an effective overhauling of the industrial structure and of the right of industrial property, the more strongly does the right of security seem to become entrenched. For in a modern industrial community only few enjoy a sense of security, and that precariously. This is indirectly conducive to a gross exaggeration of acquisitiveness, pride and vain-gloriousness on the one hand and the greed, resentment and impulse to aggression and destruction on the other. If the sense of security could be universalised, society would gain from an undreamt-of liberation of man's social impulses. Democracy has now shifted from an agricultural to an industrial base ; with this far-reaching economic change the distribution of the gains of industrial economy through the mass of the community that now looms large as the social ideal can be effectively insured only by the right to security. The quest for security that has now the greatest "marginal utility" of all public goods is the strongest social trend that points towards social and economic planning.[6] Thus most democratic countries today through systematic planning aim at social security and equitable distribution of the purchasing power so that with industrial progress the proportionate gain for the masses might be larger than the increment of the national income as a whole. Along with social security, social equality is posited as a definite goal attained by drastic taxation of the higher incomes, compulsory saving and rationing. President Roosevelt proposed in a massage to Congress in April 1942 that "no American citizen ought to have a net income, after he has paid taxes, of more than $25,000 a year." Planned economy is creating the right to social equality as a primary claim that impresses large sections of the population in modern democratic states.

Viewing the social situation as a whole, the multiplication of economic and social rights along with the classical political rights has been largely due to its various tensions, to individual and collective maladjustments, to the unrestrained and chaotic relations of institutions to institutions, of institutions to individuals and of individuals to individuals; all this implicating the dissociation of rights from duties in every field.[7] Thus has arisen a vicious circle. Bad institutions promote unfreedom, insecurity and unhappiness, and lead to the creation of new rights. New rights-without duties, without common understandings and attitudes, call for yet fresh rights that are advocated largely because of certain advantages that special interest-groups, trade union leaders or demagogues will reap, once new organisations for administering new duties are created. Thus the grant of equal rights to all citizens does not often mean more freedom and happiness, nor tempers the inequality of power. It leads to fresh tension, resentment and resistance. As Merriam aptly observes: "Rights may be defended by ideologies, by patterns of concrete interests, by institutional contrivances and procedures designed to hold back the arbitrary, but liberty is still more deeply entrenched. Naked hand and empty pockets may obstruct and antagonize the action of authority and with means which can scarcely be successfully opposed without destroying the basis of human association itself. These forms of resistance are understood almost as well by the ignorant as by the learned—indeed, sometimes more perfectly—and their action may be spontaneous, unorganised, unled in emergencies," New rights are born out of such deep-seated, instinctive oppositions.

The Integration of Rights-and-Duties in a Value System

The following table shows the large variety of human rights that are now formulated or safeguarded by the state for the fulfilment and promotion of the common values and good things of life regarded as indispensable for every individual in the present state of economy.

Rights are multifarious and differentiated, representing aids and conditions of encouragement of specialised values of individuals accepted as social ends or goals. Thus all rights would not be of interest or significance equally to everybody, and in fact rights are worked out by individuals according to their qualities and capacities. Where rights, equally operative for all citizens, create fresh inequalities of power, such rights become a misnomer. For it is the function of rights to equalise opportunities for all, or to mitigate inequalities due to differences in natural endowments and abilities, while utilising

TABLE 12.1

Classification of Rights-and-Duties as Aids to Value Fulfilment and Participation

Values	*Rights*	*Social*
Biological	Rights to life and personal freedom and security; "Right to the nourishment, covering and medical care needed to realise man's full possibilities of physical and mental development from birth to death"; Right of preservation from accident or any form of premature death; Rights to marriage and parenthood; Right to an easy, cheap and wholesome enjoyment of leisure; Right to holidays with pay; and Right to cheap and comfortable housing.	Familial obligations: Duties to obey essential rules of hygiene, personal protection and cleanliness; Duties to guard dangerous machinery and to obey sanitary, housing and other regulations; Duty to defend the country against military aggression.
Economic	Rights of property, inheritance and profits; Right to work; Right to a living wage; Right to protection against old age, widowhood and other forms of disablement; Right to social security.	Obligations to pay taxes and refrain from the use of property, skill and labour in a manner detrimental to society.
Social	Right to maintain the group or institution of which one is a member or the right of association ; Rights of freedom of expression, discussion and movement; Right of protection against physical ill-treatment, mis-representation, humiliation or mental distress; Right of protection against restraint, detention or imprisonment without trial; Right of protection against social, economic or any other discrimination for reasons of birth, age, sex, race or religion ; Right to share-all-alike the natural and cultural heritage, irrespective of distinctions of race, colour or professed belief or opinion, or the Right to social equality.	Moral, social and political obligations. "Duty to contribute such service to the community as will ensure the performance of those necessary tasks for which the incentievs which will operate in a free society do not provide."
Spiritual	Right to a certain field of free activity for the discretion of the individual or Right of freedom of action ; Right of resistance against the encroachment of personal liberties by unwarranted or unconstitutional laws or governmental procedures. Right to free education ; Right to freedom of worship ; Right of protection against exhibition of ugliness and immorality ; Right of protection against false propaganda.	Intelligent, aesthic and religious obligations.

these latter for the enrichment of the community. Many rights become common possessions; others are not adequately attained, while a few more are emerging social ideals constantly striven for. Rights cohere and integrate with one another into a pattern, representing a characteristic value system. In the West due to the political and economic circumstances during the last three centuries two contrasted systems of rights are clearly discernible, *viz*., (1) based on the egalitarian social ideal stressing social equality and intruding upon personal liberties for the attainment of social harmony and justice; and (2) based on the libertarian social ideal, cherishing civil rights above everything else, grounded on the faith that the free individual and the free society are greater than the state. Such difference indeed is rooted in differences in the value system as it concerns itself with the personal life organisation and the structure of the state. The former emphasises the ideal of harmony and solidarity of the community, and builds up a functional social individualism within the framework of compulsive group obligations. The latter emphasises the ideal of maximum individuality and personal expression purchased at the expense of social inefficiency and even injustice. Throughout the world the struggle between the Democratic and Marxian philosophical and economic doctrines is reflected in an ambivalence and tension between different kinds of rights. This is inevitable because mankind in this epoch has lost its absolute scale of values and its ultimate criterion of judgment of the roots of man's freedom and self-actualization, derived as these are from something higher than the economic and political community. Man, no doubt, strives after political and economic equality and human brotherhood and solidarity, but at the same time in the depth of his being orders his personality not to the society but to the universal, the infinite and the eternal. Therein lie, he insists, his authentic freedom, honour and dignity. Co-ordination and reconciliation rather than competition and conflict, interweaving and interpenetration rather than reduction and exclusion of rights are possible only when society pays due attention to the intrinsicalities rather than the instrumentalities of life and to virtues, duties and idea's rather than claims, immunities and rights in every sphere. Duties, virtues and values provide the frameworks of man's true self-actualization and freedom and can establish balance and harmony in the acknowledgment and exercise of all human rights, whether in Democracy or in Communism. No state is wholly controlled by the above contrasted principles of social organisation and freedom as ideal ends, but one or other is emphasised due to social and historical factors and the influence of philosophical and economic doctrines.

The Sanctions of Rights

The rights of man, political, economic and social, aid one another and are aided by the observance of corresponding duties and efforts of individuals. Society, through the collective focus of attention and reflection, transforms man's vital urges and fundamental interests and experiences into values, virtues and ideals, and also guarantees his success in appropriating values and cultivating duties and virtues by providing various types and forms of assistance, encouragement or forbearance through the enforcement of political, economic and social rights. There is interdependence between rights and liberties, but there may also be conflict among them. It is one of the basic functions of the state to ensure a balance and reciprocal adaptation of rights so that chronic or severe oppositions between them might not frustrate any major values nor warp personality expression and growth. Historically different cultures have differed in giving precedence to one or another set of rights based on a stress of one or other of the major value systems. In the totalitarian states in Europe all the rights of workers have, for instance, been extinguished at the same moment that the right to security or "economic liberty" has been made effective. Workers have lost their freedom of self-organisation, collective bargaining, strike and movement from one job to another as they are under the obligation to work in a given industrial establishment. There is severe discipline (as the introduction of labour books implies), while freedom of speech and discussion is also severely controlled. Totalitarianism has no doubt meant governmental intervention and encroachment in many directions upon man's personality that is disregarded in the multiplication of laws, rules and procedures.

From a larger perspective, it is society's familial and institutional relations, its pattern of group organisation and its social and moral norms that determine a country's system of basic rights and duties—the outcome of centuries of human effort and application. Rights do not fall like manna from heaven. Rights demand not merely the inclination and capacity of men for self-assertion, but also an institutional set-up within which such rights have a meaning. No right can in fact be operative unless the people develop the particular group organisation or institution necessary for its promotion and enforcement. Most rights depend for their effective guarantee on group application and institutional mediation. The rights of freedom of expression and discussion can be best fostered by universities and other educational institutions, jealous of their intellectual privileges, as the Churches and religious groups and organisations safeguard freedom of worship. Similarly trade unions safeguard the rights of self-organisation, collective bargaining, minimum wages and living and housing standards. Accordingly it is often groups and institutions that provide the necessary setting within which abstract rights of individuals can be operative; and as a matter of fact groups and institutions themselves become invested with corporate rights or claims that often pre-condition, extend and amplify the rights of individuals whose status is constantly being challenged and endangered. In a liberal democratic state the basic rights of diverse groups, classes, professions and institutions are not encroached upon, nor whittled down. These protect individuals from invasion by the state of the domain of the personal life, and at the same time ensure effective organisation of many of the abstract rights of individuals. The totalitarian state tries, on the contrary, either to abolish or to assimilate to itself every other form of association—trade union, industry, cultural association and even the Church. The bolstering up of government as the major interest of the community, and the subordination of all other groups and institutions that crystallise and foster other interests and values of life may change the cultural pattern for the time being, but no state can afford to ignore the realities of associated life. Merriam points out that if the modern totalitarian state actually succeeds in over-riding all other values than its own, "what would happen within the shell of the new totalitarianism would be the rise of value systems under other names but performing like functions. Men might salute the state or even wear the uniform, but the soul would be another soul and the spirit another spirit. The state itself would find it convenient to encourage independent centres of spontaneity even on its own. The reconciliation of other value systems and their co-ordination in a growing concern may be and usually is one of the most perplexing problems of statesmanship but it may also be said that for this hour came they into the kingdom."

The Moral Scale of Rights

It is only by appeal to the scale of moral values that free individuals, groups and institutions can sit in judgment over the exaggerated emphasis of certain interests and values by the state, its concentration of political power and obliteration of personal liberties. In a democratic state the right to work may not abolish or hinder other rights, if, along with public ownership and management of the basic industries and a framework of economic security and welfare, there is also maintained a wide variety of functional and regional groups, associations and institutions that can rescue the individual from the encroachment of the state on the one hand, and ensure the promotion of individual and corporate liberties of many modes and tenses on the other. Functional, regional, occupational and cultural groups of widely varying forms and purposes are maintained and thrive in all multi-group societies that do not come under an aristocratic or absolutistic system of political organisation.[8] As these develop corporate rights the state cannot easily expand its area of social action invading the area of free choices. The corporate rights of myriad groups and associations with their expanding or contracting ranges of free life, allocated or recognised by the state, also imply their corresponding duties and obligations like the rights of individuals. For if the groups do not inhere together in an order of social co-operation, neither the rights of individuals nor the rights of the intermediate groupings, can be more than formal.

Further, in the intimate personal relationships (Gemein-schaft) which are engendered in all vital groups and modes of association we find the association of rights with duties that ensures social co-operation as through custom and tradition without the intervention of the formal authoritative decrees of the state. As a matter of fact, it is the silent force of tradition and morale of these intermediate groups which still forms the nexus of the various interests, values and objectives in diverse professions and occupations, assuring a solidarity and continuity which are endangered by the stress of formal rights both of the individual and of the state. It is the institutional morale that not only transforms formal or abstract rights of individuals into socially useful power and enjoyment, but also prevents one set of human rights and value systems to swallow up or nullify other rights and value systems. Such eclipse or invalidation detracts from the infinite worth and dignity of man.

Without an ordering of inviolable or superior and auxiliary or inferior rights, society lacks not only an essential principle of organisation but may actually turn away from freedom. The ordering principle for the system of rights can be furnished only by the hierarchy of values according to which society determines the relative priorities of its ideals,—freedom, justice, order or equality—and of the several basic rights of individuals as channels of social guidance and assistance. Hocking observes: "We still find the 'right to life' relatively 'sacred' as compared with the right of property; and freedom for honest religious expression still held more vital than freedom of association. The scale of values and rights is to be determined by the closeness of their bearing on the development of mental power in individuals. It would be futile for philosophy to offer a formula for the guidance of law without some such scale of quantitative measure."[9] In brief, the working out of the scale of importance of rights rests on their significance in relation to the absolute order of values or the development of human personality. Such ordering of rights becomes much easier, leading towards harmony and interweaving of rights in various ways and forms rather than their opposition, as society pays due attention to duties corresponding to rights in every sphere, and develops outside the system of rights provided in the political setting institutions and other social and cultural frameworks of avowed common meanings, understandings and values that are the best guarantors of complete freedom, dignity and happiness for all. Democratic liberalism is wrong when it insists that rights exist by reason of the nature of the individual independent of the society and the state. Communism is equally wrong when it stresses that everything in the nature of man is within the state and there is nothing beyond it. All human social systems and states exist for the sake of achievement of man's perfect freedom and self-actualization and society's perfect freedom and self-actualization—the consummation of Commonalty of the cosmos. The two are linked with each other in the unfoldment of the human self in relation.

It is the transformation of society into Commonalty that can secure the largest amount of freedom and self-fulfilment for its members, involving as it does the primacy of communal relationship that eschews any kind of domination or tyranny of man over man, of class over class and of nation over nation, and the consequent constraint of individuals, groups and peoples. John Macmurray has recently stressed that there can be no technique for achieving freedom and that mere political or economic organisation cannot achieve or defend freedom. The "tightness" in personal relationship is accordingly achieved or lost "not in the field of economics or politics, of committees and rules, but rather in the domain of religion." It is man's abundant love, charity and goodness that, indeed, can best create and maintain freedom and equality in his varied relationships in society, that become surcharged by religion with the infinite or the absolute values in terms of the relation of the finite person to the eternal and infinite Person of Persons. For the good society it is more important to form good habits, understandings and ideals than to frame good laws and rights. No good society is possible without good men; and only good men understand, energise and implement the true spiritual meaning of rights that connote a real sharing of life, an effective mutuality of experience. The latter cannot be secured simply by laws and institutions, but reach beyond these and are pitted against them as the possible valid judgment over them that comes from the nature of the universe.

References

1. H. G. Wells : *The Outlook for Homo Sapiens*, p. 143; see also Fried-mann: *The Rights of Man.*
2. *Moral Man and Immoral Society*, p, 62; see also his *The Children of Light and The Children of Darkness*, pp. 90-96.
3. See my *Democracies of the East*; also Mookerji; *Local Government in Ancient India and Gurvitch : The Sociology of Law.*
4. See Maritain : *The Rights of Man and Natural Law and Freedom in the Modern World.*
5. *The Planning of Free Societies*, p. 73.
6. Zweig: *The Planning of Free Societies*, p. 38.
7. Compare Rallen (Ed.): *Freedom in the Modern World*, and Anshen (Ed.): *Freedom : Its Meaning.*
8. See MacIver : *The Web of Government*, pp. 436-439 and T. V. Smith : *The Democratic Way of Life.*
9. *The Philosophy of Law and of Rights*, p. 32.

13

THE PROTECTION AND APPRAISAL OF VALUES—FROM CRIMINAL LAW TO LEGAL DUTY

The Social-psychological Basis of Law and Punishment

Society develops common habits, institutions and values, the violation of which produces a profound inner discord in the individual and an antipathy in the group. The internal discord or unpleasant feeling arises because of man's strong social impulse, the social conditioning from childhood and the power of suggestion of the group that largely determines the contents of individual consciousness. The antipathy of the group against deviation is an emotional outburst rooted in the conditions of social selection and survival. Many gregarious mammals are seen to expel or to bite rebellious, abnormal or diseased individuals that show variations from type. In such situations a herd of cattle, bisons, antelopes and horses exhibits a collective aggressiveness towards the deviation from the biological norm. Aggression or its opposite impulse, sympathy, in the case of man is rooted more in the genetic history of the individual than in herd reaction.

Modern psycho-analysis has shown the significance of the instincts of aggression, destruction or death in the human individual that are ambivalent with the instincts of life, love and restitution. An individual's primal hostility and revenge against the parents in infancy express themselves in aggression against his group or the whole community, whose controls and prohibitions stimulate and aggravate such revenge. On the other hand, the individual also obtains profound satisfaction from his obedience to his conscience as well as the moral and the legal order that represent the super-ego, and by which he reconciles himself through the sense of guilt and remorse with the objects of his love. The prime biological function of law, then, is to "internalise" social norms and prohibitions and assimilate these in the self as the super ego.[1] The urge to confession that is universally met with in the offender signifies that the super-ego comes to assert itself, and that the offender who fears the possibility of losing his love-object hopes to regain it by confession. The offender feels the unconscious urge to confession so as to restore himself to the group against which he has committed his aggression. Confession or self-censure is the first step towards the reconciliation of the ego with the norms and standards of society that law stands for. W. I. Thomas gives a large number of instances of the offender's resort to confession and his confident anticipation of salvation in primitive society. He observes, "The development of confession as a pattern of control is associated with the concept that conscience is a symptom of spiritual displeasure at the violation of tabus, and is an anticipation of spiritual punishment. Disasters will further happen to the whole group if the individual offender is not regulated, and this regulation consists of a purification. This may be in the form of a physical purgation through an emetic, but usually the verbal confession is a purification, and sometimes the confession of an evil practice, say destructive magic, may be all that society requires. This point is referred to by Parsons in a comparison of Zuni and Aztec practices."[2] Confession and clearing of conscience are first steps in the restoration of the offender's mental equilibrium. These are associated with the assertion of the superego. Law functions as much by bringing the ego under the surveillance and judgment of the super-ego that represents conscience or the social norm as through the threat of an external punishment.

But law in performing this function sometimes effects too severe a repression of man's libidinal and aggressive tendencies in order to socialise him. This provokes in him the desire to 'get even', rage and destructiveness—crime and social deviation in all its forms that, as Freud observes, give mental relief. At the same time, in the processes of the mind's maturation and socialisation, he develops the normal super-ego, and accepts the punishment of law within his own self with profound delight, derived from the satisfaction of the fundamental unconscious tendencies of love, reparation and restitution that are ambivalent with hatred and aggression. In the community consciousness due to social discussion, it is the desires for self-censure, reparation and creation that reconcile the guilty person, through the feeling of shame and remorse, with those objects threatened by his dangerous aggression and hatred, and underlie the sentiment of 'justice' for the reparation of any breach of custom and social habit or violation of the social or moral order. Modern psychology shows that man's fundamental tendencies are blended with one another in an intimate way, and that some are in the foreground and others in the background of consciousness. In the manifestations of law and punishment there is the play of the unconscious tendencies of remorse, restitution and self-censure in the libido. But in the foreground the desires of gregariousness, self-assertion, possession, freedom and submission are all involved directly. The core of the interest of social control is represented by the tendencies of gregariousness, freedom and submission that is enriched from different levels of the psyche. Experimental studies indicate that if the normal course of impulses or desires be checked, these impulses increase in force and become dominating. The impulse to overcome the source of external resistance becomes an integral part of behaviour; while a change of the situation represented by the diminution of resistance usually reduces the intensity of the impulse. Further, when the strong desire is left unfulfilled, the sense of guilt or lemorse is not felt, but is restored to the full or even to an abnormal extent when the desire is removed. Other experiments show the growth of the retributive tendencies in children which have thrown much light on their juridical mentality and experience. These have been undertaken by Piaget and Caruso.

The Ethical Principle of Reciprocity and Retriubtion in Law

Society normally exhibits are ore or less pronounced emotional disturbance that becomes contagious, and provokes revenge attitudes in the case of socio-ethical violation. Such primary attitudes are rooted in the herd desires of love, reparation or restitution pitted squarely and evenly against those of hatred, rage or destruction. Primitive justice is retributive justice, and this is based on the socio-ethical principle of adequacy according to which the punishment of crime closely corresponds to the degree of collective dissatisfaction, with reference of course to the social and moral order of the people or the age, caused by the particular crime. Anthropologists who have studied primitive crime emphasise the principle of reciprocity, according to which the punishment differential is determined so as to give full expression to the retributive emotion. Malinowski in particular points out that the binding forces of law are to be found in a whole series of rebukes, reprisals and dis-services that accompany deviation from custom and law as well aş rewards in the shape of counter services for obedience. "Reciprocity", observes Malinowski, "is not as a rule a mere tit for tat, but it is graded, transmitted, shared or relayed, over a much wider circuit."[3] It is the well-balanced system of reciprocities in the household, the kinship group, the guild or the tribe that accounts for the strength of the retributive tendency in primitive justice. If the punishment for disobedience is less severe in degree than that indicated by the general law of reciprocity, there is a tendency on the part of the interested persons to take the law into their own hands. It cannot be gainsaid that retributive justice which represents the basis of primitive law and ethics, and is rooted in man's innate dispositions is one of the important and universal social defence mechanisms for the elimination of social deviation and crime.

Hans Kelsen, the jurist, in tracing the development of the principle of retribution points out that primitive man did not qualitatively distinguish between himself and any plant, animal or inanimate object in nature, but viewed all things and events under the aspect of social norms. The chief of these norms was retribution according to which evil deeds were compensated with evil and good deeds with good: The sea, the thunder-storm, the carnivore and the poison were all looked upon as persons and related to social happenings, and thus natural phenomena, failures in hunting or fishing, murder or accident, were interpreted as punishment for violations of the social order. Retribution was the central principle determining not merely man's sense of justice and morality in the social organisation but also reciprocal inter-relationship and behaviour between man and nature in primitive culture.

In civilised societies retributive tendencies, shorn of the aggressive and sadistic feeling for revenge, form essential elements of morals, law and custom, and still play their role successfully for subordinating individual behaviour to social patterns. The principle of reciprocity and retribution in primitive law is the collective tribal expression of the fundamental unconscious tendencies of reparation and restitution in the case of guilt or crime. Many primitive communities have shed the emotional attitudes of aggression and pugnacity in revenge, but lean on reciprocity in reparative behaviour that has undoubtedly a biological basis. An Eskimo who is wronged challenges his enemy to a public singing contest in which there is an exchange of abuse, mockery and humiliation, the spectators deciding who wins. Through the song and the rhythm 'there is sublimation of the feeling of hatred and revenge, but there is at the same time adequate compensation for injury done as judged by the public who hear the rivals, it may be, many times. Among the Indians of the northwest coast in America the reparation for wrong is through a public feast or potlatch at which the enemy is humbled by lavish gift or destruction of property. The latter loses status that can be regained only by similar feasting and ostentatious display. A Kwakiutl chief once said : "The white man fights with his hands, but we fight with property."[4] Thus the culture pattern governs the specific type of reparative behaviour as well as the application of the principle of reciprocity that constitutes the psycho-biological basis of punishment, fulfilling the revulsion against aggression and crime felt both by the community and the offender himself.

The Sense of Guilt and Law-abidingness

Man's mind, however, finds in the mechanisms of rationalisation, pathological lying and amnesia or selective forgetfulness of inconvenient facts one of its whole series of methods by which suffering and the sense of shame and feeling of guilt and remorse may be avoided. As it has been well observed: "The human mind is endowed with a machinery for maintaining self-respect, but none for making accurate moral judgments in the face of emotion. Self-respect is maintained by factual distortions attained by the psychological processes of fantasy, identification, rationalisation, repudiation and projection. The process serves the double purpose of the exoneration of self and theincrimination of others, and cumulatively leads to justification of objective deterioration of personal conduct in respect of others."[5] The inevitable consequence is that the system of law has to be supported by ordeals and oaths and by elaborate procedures for sifting the truth from falsehood, misrepresentation or distortion that spring from both the unconscious and conscious forces of the mind. On the other hand, the large majority of individuals in society exhibit law-abidingness or sense of order and veracity, rooted in the gregarious impulse that is developed as the effect of sex activity and of the relationships in the family horde, tribe and other primary groups. Man's life becomes easier and more secure in various primary groups that are necessary for defence, food production, ritual ceremony and trade and exchange of goods. Thus the gregarious impulse may have originated from family life but extended beyond it, due to the complete dependence of the individual upon the group for the satisfaction of bodily needs under conditions of culture. Obedience to law and veracity are derived from gregariousness, and become entrenched as means for the realisation of the major values of life in man's social setting. A man's social contact and participation are enlarged and his personality is culturally moulded. "Most men at most times wish to obey the law."[5]

Social integration implies the fixation of habits, the rigidity of institutions and the standardisation of a common system of values as factors of social stability and progress. There is a general tendency of the society justifying and sanctifying group convictions, habits and patterns of behaviour as right and just as the result of exercise of collective reason and judgment. This is what Jellinek calls "the normative tendency of the actual". All established social facts and relations that actually embody biological, economic and social satisfactions or values, and are sanctioned by custom, institution and law become also carriers of moral values and ideals. As a matter of fact, it is this "satisfaction" that underlies man's happiness in his acceptance of obligations imposed by the social, legal and institutional framework. Man's obedience even to a galling custom or tyrannical law carries with it moral obligation when such custom or law is recognised as just.

The Major Values of Life—the Roots of Law

It is in this manner that the essential function of law is focussed towards normative goals—the protection, delimitation, gradation and integration of human values both by the active status-power system and by the unorganised social community. Law is not a particular order of social activity and relationship, such as familial, economic, moral or religious. Law is the manner in which all such social activities must be carried out for the fulfilment of various kinds and grades of values. Law stereotypes and structuralises human relations in order that through definite and stable forms of relationship and patterns of behaviour the different kinds and grades of values could be satisfied by individuals in a manner compatible with similar satisfaction of such values by other individuals. With reference to the *biological* values that are most imperative, law enforces protection of life, and safeguards the mores of marriage and parenthood and the interests of the children for the continuity of society. With regard to the *economic* values, the law gives a definite form to *economic* transactions, creates and regulates the various kinds of property, and lays down the legal rules of competition and contract, and the employment of labour, capital and tools. The main objective of all such economic regulations is to safeguard justice in respect of the relations between economic costs and satisfactions, sacrifices and awards so as to maintain the conditions of a progressive standard of living for the community. With reference to *social* values, law supports the status-prestige system of the community, with which are indissolubly connected order, peace and social development. A legalised power-structure with its rules and regulations in respect of property and economic power and privilege is an essential element in orderly social progress. An arbitrary power-structure that tends towards injustice, on the contrary, leads to social chaos and dissolution. Moral, aesthetic and *spiritual* values also come to be protected and enforced by law, as such values command social approval to the extent of being transformed into social norms.[6] It is only at a late stage in the development of law that the higher values have become the roots of law. Recognition and protection of biological values, *viz.*, protection against murder, injury or ill-treatment of the individual, *i.e.*, order and security providing the necessary condition for the fulfilment of all values and safeguarding of the family, the tribe and the race; creation of freedom and organisation for the fulfilment of economic and social values and assurance for each individual of his role, position and status in institutional life; and, finally, the transformation of the ideal values into laws: such may be considered to be the successive stages in the development of law. For purposes of summary *Table* 13.1 will be found useful.

Protection of both Personality and Social Solidarity—the Ends of Law

Roscoe Pound observes: "For the purpose of understanding the law of to-day I am content with the picture of satisfying as much of the whole body of human wants as we may with the least sacrifice." This is a significant though a rather loose statement. It is only when human wants are transformed into values and ideals that are social products, and that become subjects of society's communication, discussion and judgment that they become the ends of law. Thus law does not attempt to protect and foster "the

TABLE 13.1

Stages in the Evolution of Social Norms and Laws

Prolection of Successive Orders of Values	Stages in Legal Development
I. Biological values.	(1) Protection of life and bodily security and preservation of peace and order. Punishment for man-slaughter, assault, battery, theft, robbery, etc. Enforcement of customs in respect of marriage, marital fidelity, parenthood and care of children. Protection against impiety and violation of social customs and taboos that are considered to bring about natural calamity, disease and death.
II. Socio-economic values.	(2) Enforcement of the status-power system. Regulation of property and' contract, freedom and organisation. Regulation of the condition of labour, employment, distribution and exchange. Protection of the major social, economic and other groups and institutions.
III. Ideal values.	(3] Transformation of ideal values into laws and subordination of the biological and socio-economic values to the ideal values.

whole body of human wants," but only those that are fashioned into approved social interests, values and ideals. Law keeps itself in intimate touch with all social relationships, interests and values that have obtained social sanction and are sustained and promoted by institutions. The security of the major social relationships, values and institutions is the task of law. Thus does law serve the ends of; *Kultur*, as Kohler stresses, and differ in every different culture in order to realise the major values of that culture.[7] Such values, as we have observed, are common for all peoples and could roughly be classified into two broad categories: values connected with the development of the human personality, and those connected with the solidarity of the community. Thus the broad outlines of legal development follow the *individual* norms of recognition and protection of the human personality, on the one hand, and the *collective* norms of social equality, justice and solidarity, on the other. In a particular system of culture the development of law largely follows the closeness of its connection with the basic interests and values in social evolution.

Legal Development in Relation to the Evolution of Moral Norms

No society can carry on unless the *biological* values are safeguarded. This is the reason why criminal law represents the first stage in the development of law and justice. Its importance has not diminished. Criminal law is the "basic law", supplying the foundation on which all other legal norms and injunctions are built. The second stage of development of law is that represented by legal rules and procedures defining and enforcing the *economic* and *social* values of the community through the regulation of status and privilege, wealth and property, freedom and organisation. The function of law here is to support the active status-power system or the social stratification by the moral order. Legal security is conducive not only to social solidarity by working for the advantage of the status structure, but also assures freedom and power to the individual as he has the right to act up to the very limits of acts prohibited by law. So much so that law is called the Magna Charta of criminals, "of all actual or potential offenders" would be a more adequate expression, adds Timasheff. Within the ambit of a vast number of laws, rules and procedures, the individual enjoys a good deal of freedom that fosters the development of his personality and also license that may turn him out to be a law-breaker. Further, legal security creates not only freedom and power for the individual but also organisation. The vast net-work of secondary groups and institutions in modern civilisation cannot work smoothly without the formulation of legal rules and procedures that minimise friction and conflict between individuals who cannot overstep their proper roles and positions. The secondary-group world of to-day with its casual, indirect human contacts cannot be sustained without the creation and multiplication of new laws and regulations that are growing more and more elaborate. The final stage of the development of law is represented by the transformation of *ideal* values, *i.e.*, moral aesthetic and religious norms and principles into laws and the enforcement of the absolute hierarchy of values, *i.e.*, the moral order by the legal order.

One of the chief aims of modern legislation has been to safeguard the supreme values of personality, and defend honour, honesty, loyalty and veracity. All these personal values in case of any conflicts in law represent the spiritual base on which the law rests. "The scope of legal duty", observes Allen, "has expanded in obedience to the urge of morals." He briefly summarises the trend of modern court decisions in this regard. We discern this moral urge in decisions that charge an owner of land with special duties to the young and heedless. We see it in the inroad made by recent cases upon the concept of an infant's disability where injustice would be wrought if the concept were maintained in all its rigorous simplicity. We see it in a tendency still almost in embryo, and yet perceptible, to enlarge the duties owing to licensees and even trespassers by a gradual extension of the class of invitees. We see it in the striking growth of the concept of duress, a concept broad enough to-day to supply a remedy against unfairness and oppression in forms long ranked as guiltless. At times, indeed, the movement has been helped by legislation. The land-owner was without redress at common law if his neighbour cut off his light and air for the mere purpose of annoyance. Statutes against spite fences have made neighbourliness a duty. Yet there are fields not far removed where statutes have been needless. In economic rivalry, the trader or the merchant has been ungenerous towards his competitor to promote his own advancement. He goes too far if the animating motive is unadulterated malice, the mere desire to destroy.

There is also the tendency of subordinating economic values to aesthetic values, as may be illustrated by the legal protection of the community against ugly, outdoor placards and advertisements, and the recent development of legislation in respect of town and regional planning. Roscoe Pound observes in this connection: "In the United States, courts and legislatures were long engaged in a sharp struggle over bill board laws and laws against hideous forms of outdoor advertising. For a time also the interest pressed in another way in connection with town planning legislation. It is significant that the courts are now ready to admit a policy in favour of the aesthetic as reasonable and constitutionally permissible." Similarly law is also protecting cultural and religious values. The freedom of arts, science, letters and religion is being slowly and gradually won through the decisions of courts that are called upon to adjudicate in conflicts or supposed conflicts between modern science, knowledge, technique and expression and the security of social and economic institutions. Law protects free thought, artistic expression and religious belief and worship, and also promotes education, learning, religion and culture that are institutionalised through promulgating a variety of legal rules and procedures. Finally, law not only protects economic values but also subordinates these to the larger interests and ideals of social security and equality. It is coming to be recognised in modern juristic thought that every individual can claim or demand certain minimum human standards, and also that such standards should be reasonable or even equal. The entire trend of economic legislation and court decision has been to secure social security and equality by social and health insurances, by the regulation of agreements and contracts of individual employers and control or abolition of combines and trusts that become too powerful in a country's economic structure. Modern law has indeed been radically transformed from a system of threats and punishments that menace the individual to a flexible code of moral rules that guide his conduct towards social harmony and solidarity under the complex social and institutional conditions of to-day.

The Scope and Mechanisms of Law and Morality

On the whole, as Roscoe Pound observes, "legal precepts are almost certain to lag behind public opinion whenever the latter is active and growing." The differences between law and morality are obvious. Law contains an element of external authority or force that is altogether excluded from the moral realm. Unlike law morality is autonomous, and obeys no authority except that which springs from within. Law always implies in human relations the indissoluble linking together of two parties, one of which fulfils an obligation, while the other has the right of demanding its fulfilment. In morality one fulfils a duty, but nobody can presume or claim that a duty must be performed. Thus charity blesses him that gives and him that takes. But no destitutes or unfortunates impose any claims upon the charitable person. Charity is a virtue and not an obligatory duty. In charity there is no correspondence guaranteed by society between the claims of the Have-nots and the duties of the Haves. The sanction of moral duties is a vague and fluctuating social expectation; legal duties are not only precise but are also enforceable by compulsion. All moral behaviour, i.e., social action in conformity with moral and not legal precepts, becomes tinged with emotional attitudes because of its uncertainty and lack of uniformity. When such action becomes common and habitual in society, the emotional attitude is attenuated or it disappears, it is then that the rule of conduct assumes a positive character, and the notion of justice supersedes the notion of morality, two parties emerging in the legal transaction, one performing a duty and the other claiming its fulfilment as a matter of right.[8]

The social-psychological mechanism, then, that transforms moral norms into laws is represented by the force of public opinion that brings about an approximation of the conduct of large numbers of individuals to the moral norm, with a strong feeling of social disapproval against conduct deviating from the norm. It is then that law supports and implements existing moral principles, and gives these legal sanction, provided that the active status-power system of the community can be influenced by the new moral group conviction. In this way law invades the field of morality. In every country or age social conventionality and law protect the *minimum* social values indispensable for the life of man in society. Law, as is said, comprises an ethical minimum. One lapses from the moral ideal if he takes advantage of every law or presses his legal rights to the extreme limit in any field. There is a large zone of freedom of action for the individual granted by law within which it is morals that become the guide to proper conduct and orientation to one's claims and obligations that are different from, but nevertheless interwoven with, legal rights and duties.

Moreover, certain values and virtues that are entirely personal cannot come under the suzerainty of law. The scope of law is limited by practicability and expediency for the society and the individual respectively. Law cannot invade the entire realm of the individual's character, but so far as his external relations and conduct are concerned, law is his first school-master. Law strengthens, fortifies and improves the individual conscience that, however, must transcend the law in order that it can reach its true freedom and nobility. The law of the individual conscience is the original source of the man-made law; it is juster and more universal than the latter, and in case of a conflict between law and law, it becomes the sole arbiter. No law is just that smothers the individual conscience. Law can command and progress only by safeguarding and unfolding the individual conscience. On the other hand, the conscience of the individual is sustained in its growth and maturation by imbibing the goodness and truth in laws, customs and traditions that surround and penetrate into his consciousness. Morals and law must work hand in hand and in close amity for the full development of the human personality. Without the aid of law, man cannot be a social creature, a citizen or a person. With only the regulation of law and his conscience stifled, man becomes a robot, and the society a regimented beehive where life is sacrificed to mechanism.

Horvath, discussing the relation of law and morals, of 'is' and 'ought to be,' observes that every legal precept which exists as an item of the positive law is in its application an activity towards a pattern of what 'ought to be' and every 'ought to be' pursues its purpose or end in the form of one or more positive precepts. Thus, according to Horvath, law relates facts of nature to norms.[9] Here is, therefore, the standard by which one can appraise any laws and rules applied in the courts in particular field according to the model or pattern of 'the ought to be' underlying the former.

In some respects the system of law that sustains and conserves the vague and inarticulate mass of traditions, customs and cultural norms, beliefs and agreements represents the necessary condition for morality. On the other hand, law as well as its complicated procedure, formalism and parade of precedents obtain their true meaning only with reference to moral values. In fact laws that have become inflexible are embodiment of stereotyped valuations of a given culture, conditioned by the accumulated force of social and legal history and tradition. Yet, since morality is primarily a matter of conscience for the individual, and aims at the universal beyond the passing panorama of historical factors and circumstances, it is its hierarchy of values that guides Jaw in its new understanding of old principles, purposes and ideals or acceptance of new ones. Thus morals and law, like twin sisters, advance step by step in unison, not in discord or incoherence that spells personal disorganisation and social maladjustment. All great social and moral transformations have been recorded in new laws that are more just, humane or universal than the previous ones.

Metaphysical Individualism and the Law

The development of juristic theory in the West from the 17th century was characterised by the emphasis of certain abstract, metaphysical rights of the individual. Such stress was connected with the peculiar circumstances of social and economic development of Europe that was emerging out of the ruins of feudalism in economics, mercantilism in trade and absolute monarchy in politics. Later on, under the influence of Hegel, legal history was viewed largely as the development in human experience of liberty, as an outcome of the clash of individual freewill, leading to the discovery of the indivisible bounds within which each might realise a maximum of self-realisation.[10] On the whole legal philosophy in the 19th century regarded every rule of law as an evil in itself, being an impairment of human liberty. Carter observes, "Liberty is the supreme object; every abridgement of it demands an excuse, and the only good excuse is the necessity of preserving it."[11] The social goal was envisaged by jurisprudence largely in terms of security of freedom of the individual coexisting with the similar freedom enjoyed by other individuals. This whole trend was entirely congruent with the metaphysical individualism in all branches of social thinking and of unlimited freedom of competition, industry, trade, enterprise and rise of prosperity and wealth in 19th century Europe. Just as in economic theory the economists in judging social policies argued about "economic friction" and were weighed by considerations of "interferences" with, or obstacles to, freedom of contract and enterprise, so in juristic theory, dominated by the conception of natural rights, "often the weighing of social interests was disguised," as Pound observes, "by reasoning about causation or by the drawing of what seem on their face arbitrary distinctions."[12] The naive faith in the inalienable human liberties, that is the basis of much of economic, political and legal thinking, still stands in the way of the development of adequate legal norms in respect of collective welfare and formulation of a clear policy behind the growing volume of constructive social and economic legislation, and the establishment of various agencies of social administration for implementing the laws.

Need of Emphasis on Collective Ethical Norms in New Fields

Thus in juristic theory the conceptions of social justice, harmony and solidarity have not been adequately worked out. The transformation of collective moral norms into laws, such as the principles of conservation of resources and the continuity of the race in the realm of ecological adaptation, the principle of minimum sacrifice in economic adaptation, and the principle of social equality and solidarity in the field of social adaptation, represents a phase that still meets with legal resistance. The implementing by laws and regulations of ethical norms in respect of the maximum harmony and solidarity of community life has, to be sure, lagged far behind the implementing by laws and regulations of ethical norms concerned with the maximum self-assertion of the individual. This will be evident from a scrutiny of the various items of laws in the last column, Table 10, that are yet to obtain full acceptance in several civilised countries. As functional sociological jurisprudence replaces older metaphysical theories, the above trend will no doubt be supported and strengthened. In modern economic society the scope of generally asserted demands with respect to social equality and justice has definitely enlarged; and juristic theory through the recognition and protection of these demands should facilitate social and institutional adaptation to new needs and ideals. This would be the result much less of the conflict and accommodation between divergent and hostile social interests as of rational deliberation of the just and the unjust out of which emerge new rural principles and policies of public weal.

The Role al Social Ideals in Law-Making

Rescoe Pound bases his sociological jurisprudence on a theory of social interests taking his cue from Jhering's classification of interests into individual interests, public interests and social interests.[13] This sounds as Marxian and makes the development of law a phase of the economic interpretation of culture, to which, of course, Pound does not subscribe. Law is something more than a mere record of the interests and attitudes of the dominant social classes with the waning of which it is doomed to neglect and decay. Man through the ages has defined and used the law according to comprehensive and relatively permanent human and social ideals for shaping the course of development. In the contemporary age this idealistic aspect underlies not merely constructive legislation but also the formulation of policy and development of innumerable autonomous bodies and organisations, concerned with public welfare and service. Roscoe Pound's theory entirely disregards the role of the ideal in law-making. A more adequate foundation of legal philosophy would be represented by a theory of social values and ideals, as envisaged above, rather than a theory of social interests that stresses conflict as the basic social process, as in the sociology of Albion Small, who following Gumplowicz and Ratzenhofer first developed the notion of social interests, and sociology.[14] The task of law is less to reconcile conflicting claims and interests between individuals or to safeguard social interests that different groups and social classes understand and interpret differently, and more to recognise and safeguard social values and also ideals that are shaping and insistently claiming to become an integral part of constructive legislation and social policy. In the complex social world of to-day true justice can hardly be reached on the basis of a careful calculation of competing and conflicting interests, values and moral rights. It is the moral and social ideal, based as it is on the mutuality of interests and rights of individuals and groups in society, that truly

TABLE 13.1

Classification of Social Ideals Underlying Modern Legislation

Order of Values	*A* *Ideal End of Law*	*B* *Individual*		*C* *Collective*	
		Moral Norm	*Law*	*Moral Norm*	*Law*
Biological	Recognition and promotion of human individuality.	Improvement and survival of the psychogenetic personality.	Laws providing protection against physical ill-treatment, injury and restraint. Laws abolishing debt-bondage, slavery and peonage. Laws providing for care and training of minors, orphans, dependents, destitutes, insanes or idiots. Laws for the provision of safely-devices and guards against dangerous machinery in buildings, Traffic Laws.	Bio ecologic co-operation for continuity of race and habitat.	Laws concerned with public order and peace, general health and morals. Laws of conservation of natural resources, soil, water, gas and oil, of protection of forests and pastures against indiscriminate felling and grazing. Legal planning for agriculture, forestry and mining. Laws against abortion or dissemination of information in respect of birth control. Law providing payment of marriage and family allowances. Law providing payment for unmarried wives of soldiers. Law providing protection for the unmarried mother and the illegitimate child.
Economic	Recognition and promotion of standard of living and security-	Development of occupation personality.	Laws regulating hours of labour and conditions of employment, Child labour laws. Laws providing holidays with pay and cheap and wholesome recreations. Laws for the encouragement of invention. Law forbidding agreements not to exercise the calling for which one has trained himself.	Maximum aggregate satisfaction and minimum aggregate sacrifice.	Laws providing work and a living wage. Law providing payment of unemployment and maternity benefits, old age pensions etc. Social security and equality laws. Rent, small loan and usury laws. Law against monopolies and trusts. Laws for limitation of incomes.

D *Order of Values*	E *Ideal End of Law*	F *Individual*		G *Collective*	
		Moral Norm	*Law*	*Moral Norm*	*Law*
Social	Recognition and promotion of status.	Development of status personality.	Laws providing protection against misrepresentation, humiliation or mental distress. Law abolishing social, economic or political discrimination of any kind due to birth, age, sex, race or religion.	Equality and solidarity.	Law providing for nourishment, covering and medical care for every citizen from birth to death. Laws of conscription and labour service.
Spiritual	Recognition and promotion of character.	Development of spiritual personality.	Law dealing with sexual honour (rape, etc.), with unnatural sexual practices (bestiality, sodomy, etc.). Laws protecting the indissolubility of marriage (against adultery, bigamy, etc.) and governing legal separation and divorce. Laws against libel and slander. Laws to recover for alienation of affection and consequent humiliation. Laws of *bona fides*. Laws against forgery and perjury. Trust and insolvency laws. Laws dealing with free and compulsory education. Laws providing protection against interference in religion, worship and ritual. Laws against blasphemy and misdemeanour. Laws providing protection against the display of immorality, vice and ugliness as a nuisance.	Universal personalism.	International laws underlying faithful observance of undertakings resting upon moral law.

represents the validity of justice. The dangers of accepting a theory of reconciliation of competing social interests in law-making are legal inertia and opportunism on the one hand, and the definition of justice in terms of the interests of the stronger pressure groups on the other. Not that the note of ethical idealism is entirely absent in Roscoe Pound, who is inconsistent. For he has recently observed: "As one reads the recent reports and studies recent legislation, it becomes apparent that we are attaining *a new measure of values*, whether the jurists help in the process or not. Nothing, then, is gained by taking refuge from this difficult problem in a doctrine of irreducible antinomies, or in a skeptical realism, or in a relativist legalism, inviting every one to take his own starting point, or in an analytical jurisprudence confined to the authoritative legal materials as they use and postulating that the judicial process in action accords with them."[15] Pound commits himself here to a theory of judicial idealism, as Moses J. Aronson points out.[16] It is in the recognition and enforcement of values and ideals that law can, indeed, truly judge and implement the right in "public policy" that looks beyond the present to the future. The emphasis of interests would keep law and judge largely bound to the present circumstances and conditions, marked by struggles, conflicts and pressures of different groups and classes. The emphasis of ideals would on the contrary keep them moving beyond the present scene of struggle to the vistas of the future, in which the values and ideals that civilisation cherishes most will be brought to bear upon the reconciliation and integration of conflicting or overlapping interests and values.

Law as Implementing Emerging Social Ideals

Modern sociological analysis has discarded the figment of the individual as a detached, self-contained entity on the one hand and the metaphysical notion of society as an un differentiated mass with its 'social mind' on the other. It finds different individuals, groups and institutions understanding and working for 'social interests' in divergent ways, and posits as fundamental the issue of adjustment, integration and balance of overlapping and conflicting interests that can only be achieved through the formation and assimilation of social norms and 'ideals'. E. Jordan rightly observes: "In our legal procedures, as well as in the theory of law, for the most part the person is merely a centre of reference for interests. But this only means that the law has abdicated to the law merchant. Besides being, as a theory of interests, a totally inadequate representation of the nature of the person, our law overlooks the more tragically important fact that interests cannot be made matter of law without denying and frustrating the very possibility of law in any sense except the mere expression of a command as a power to compel. And this is law giving way to force."[17] The role of law is to contribute towards maintaining a definite balance between individual and social interests and social control. Its prime method is to transform individual or group interests into goals that, through the impact of collective discussion and judgment, are converted into social ideals and norms. Ideals are of universal significance, and are yet continuous with and developed out of present social experience ; thus these can rule masses of men in societies. It is ideals that lead legal rights and duties from the selfishness and unreason of the present to the more desirable future where the conflicts of interests are resolved. Ideals in law-making look to something beyond and above interests and the use of external pressure, that underlies the true rational and universal value of law. Law is not merely satisfied with fashioning ideals, i.e., envisaging the better society, but it also institutionalises ideals by settingup various independent or semi-independent bodies for carrying out functions aud services for the public good in accordance with such ideals. In every modern country law is supported by a whole host of administrative orders and procedures—price and wage regulations, allocations, decrees—that are far removed from the abstract rights of the individual implemented by the old civil and criminal law. It is official or semiofficial planning Boards and Commissions that on the basis of social and economic research work out the patterns of social or public policy so that these may best embody emerging social ideals. In fact it is such Board decisions or specialized orders of the administration that represent somewhat continuous intervention of the state in the transformation of individual and group interests into community values and ideals. More and more law no longer solves single problems on the basis of either precedents or civil and criminal notions, but integrates groups and individuals towards supreme common values or objectives and implements moral norms and social ideals moulded in the matrix of community discussion, prognosis and judgment.

The survey of the legal order and inventory of the social values and ideals, which have pressed upon law for protection as given in the preceding table, shows to what extent law has delayed in the recognition of moral norms and ideals from the social or collective point of view, and also the trend towards which it is now moving. Taking a long perspective in the history of law, religious ideals still dominate the making of marriage and family laws in most parts of the world. In the 17th and 18th centuries the ethical ideal of individualism fashioned the foundations of modern civil, industrial and mercantile law of the West. In the twentieth century the humanitarian ideal has expanded and deepened, and underlies the change in the criminal law and treatment of crime and the legal protection of the destitute, the dependent and the insane. It yields the extending series of laws for the protection of woman and child labour in the fields, factories and mines, the regulation of conditions of employment and for social security and equality that assure a minimum human standard for all citizens. It is also responsible for the present chequered development of the law of nations.

Interpenetration of Morality, Conscience and Law

It is thus that ethical ideals that move masses of men, including the judiciary, accelerate the pace of law, making definite and stable what is uncertain and vacillating. In that dim twilight of community consciousness where moral judgment has not articulated itself into moral norm, and public opinion oscillates or tends to be obscured in the struggle among pressure groups or classes with antagonistic or overlapping interests and claims, law which is in the making finds its essential raw material for the transformation of moral into legal rules and valuations that become acceptable for the whole society. The function of law is to assure the social order the permanence and perfection of all ideal values that groups and institutions grope after and occasionally, incompletely and indistinctly experience. In the categorical judgment of the right and enactment of the just in the law, the individual and society find their strivings and struggles in the temporal social scene perfectly stilled as these are assimilated to the eternal, ultimate values. There is something absolute and transcendental in every law and its indication of rights and duties, that make these logically superior to the human situation whose limits these overstep. Herein lie the eternal meaning and value of law. On the other hand, law does not know anything of the struggles of conscience of the inner man. Thus law in implementing the moral judgments of the society, of the majority or of the mass may warp or thwart the creative life of personality. Law may prevent society from learning from the unique, virginal moral judgments of the individual, undeflected or undeterred by pre-conceived norms and beliefs of the state and society. Man is an integral whole like the social and the legal order in which he lives and moves. His conscience, truth and the ultimate values as well as institutions and laws are creations of his mind that interpenetrate and are mutually interdependent. The good society promotes and perfects this interpenetration. Not before religion and humanism reunite with operative legal and political theory can law play to the full its role in ushering in the good society, the kingdom of God on earth.

References

1. Compare Ranyard West: A Psychological Theory of Law in Sayre (Ed.): Interpretations of Modem Legal Philosophies.
2. Primitive Behaviour, p, 599.
3. See Malinowski: Introduction in Hogbin: Law and Order Polynesia.
4. Quoted by Klineberg : Social Psychology, p. 85.
5. See Timasheff : The Sociology of Law.
6. Compare Cardozo: The Growth of the Law; also Hocking: The Philosophy of Law and of Rights, p. 95.
7. See Kohter's Philosophy of Law; also Max Weber : Rechtssoziologie in Wfrtschaft und Gesellschaft.
8. Compare Sorokin: Society, Culture and Personality, pp. 83-85.
9. Quoted by Roscoe Pound in his chapter on Sociology of Law, Twentieth Century Sociology, p. 315; See also his Law and Morals and Llewellyn 3nd Hoebel: The Cheyenne Way.
10. Savigny,
11. Law : Its Origin, Growth and Function.
12. Pound; A Survey of Social Interests; Harvard Law Review, October 1943.
13. See Pound's paper in Proceedings of the American Sociological Society. 1921, later on re-written and published in Harvard Law Review, October 1943.
14. In this chapter in Twentieth Century Sociology Roscoe Puund refers to the influence of Ross and Small on his thinking.
15. American Juristic Thinking in the Twentieth Century in A Century of Social Thought, pp. 170-171 (Italics mine). Aronson considers that a jurispmdence which spurs the study of ethical values is like a soldier s hand whose triggsr finger is deliberately permitted to atrophy. See his article, Roscoe Pound and Juristic Idealism in Journal of Social Philosophy, October 1940.
16. In his Social Control through Law, pp. 14-16, 118-122, Pound again stresses the influence of an ideal social order and of newly pressing ideas and values on law.
17. The Role of Philosophy in Social Crisis, Ethics, vol. LI, 1940-41.

14

EDUCATION IN NEW VALUES

The Biological Basis and Role of Education

Mankind begins its education in values anew in each generation. Man's equipment of inborn instincts and impulses remains almost the same from generation to generation. Thus unlike any other animal he has to acquire knowledge afresh for the purpose of adaptation to his natural and social milieu. This is the objective of education, the biological background of which is furnished by the prolonged period of human infancy, plasticity of the human brain and man's capacity to communicate with fellowman. All these factors give unique opportunities to the human species to transmit tradition, knowledge and experience to the next generation. Many species of social animals enregister their racial gains and experiences on their permanent collective products, such as the ants' nests, bee-hives and termitaries and the ingenious habitations used by beavers and prairie dogs, and again on the marvellous devices used for obtaining food for themselves and their offspring. But man's external social legacy is much more complex and permanent. The acquisition by the human infant of habits of behaviour and norms of living from the family group begins education that is extended and amplified by the entire institutional framework, the moral and legal code, religion and the fine arts. Even though human nature has remained unchanged in most respects since man began his career on the earth twenty-five thousand years ago, man has thus gained knowledge and wisdom that have brought increasing control over the environment, his fellow creatures and himself. The social insects' external legacy of the colony or nest and their cooperative habits have been the same for millions of years. Thus they excel men both in their social solidarity and in their marvellous technical undertakings, albeit carried on in stereotyped manner and under favourable natural conditions from generation to generation. But their life and education are instinct-bound. Man's instincts are much less sharply defined and specialised for his adjustment, and accordingly he depends much more on his institutional framework and his education. This has its biological and social advantages as well as perils. With the development of language man is able to extend, amplify and transmit his traditions, experiences and values to future generations. The knowledge, experience and values of previous ages are at the disposal of the human individual from his years of constant dependence and nurture ; he can build on past achievement and wisdom. This explains his use of more and more effective appliances and techniques for subjugating the physical environment and his greater capacity of utilising its forces and materials for the satisfaction of his manifold desires, interests and values. He also inherits an imaginative world of values—the product of morality and religion, literature and the fine arts—that has extended the bounds of his material world and emancipated him from the limitations imposed by it. Man's twofold derivative environment—the institutional world and the world of values— that he superimposes upon the physical environment differs profoundly in space and time, and is consciously moulded and transformed to suit his needs, aspirations and experiences. Thus he builds up the culture complex, which is not only the repository of his values and ideals, but is also an agency of education, in the broad sense of the term, moulding the personality and implanting deep-set patterns of behaviour. Formal education, in a restricted sense, follows the pattern and trend of the culture complex and ethos of a people. The biological function of formal education is to take advantage of and control plastic childhood and instil habits and ways of living according to plan, so that the child can develop his individuality and at the same time contribute towards the efficiency and welfare of society through his individual role, position and status in the later years. All education serves this dual biological purpose: the development of human individuality and personality, on the one hand, and the maintenance and evolution of the race and social and cultural heritage, on the other.

Limitations of Education

Every education, whatever means and methods it uses, aims at fitting the growing individual for his special role and position in society so as to elicit the best out of him, and at the same time socialising him, through development of proper habits, attitudes and values, so that he enriches and strengthens the culture pattern. Herein lies also the essential limitation of education as a social function, *viz.*, that it is not apt to move with the times nor facilitates social change, but often resists it by stressing patterns of thought, values and ideals belonging to the past, and in its specialised aspects cannot quickly adjust itself to the constantly changing needs of economy, science and technology. Mostly education looks back rather than anticipates the future. Further, the training of individuals and groups must differ according to the differences of their aptitudes and capacities. It is often that, due to factors connected with social and economic cleavage, the educational system fails to provide a balanced training for different sections of the population, the elite or the governing class, the technicians and mechanics and the general mass. Thus education fails to secure and improve all-round social efficiency in the context of particular social needs and institutional situations. No country can progress when the educational system cannot adequately and effectively train especially the elite for progressive social ideals and institutions of the community. The subtleness and delicacy of the biological task of education consists in its marching at an even or even quicker pace with the development of the apparatus of human technology and system of values, on the one hand, and social or institutional change, on the other, and at the same time in re-shaping the instincts and habits of children and youth so that they may measure up to the demands of the latter.

Man's instincts and desires have not been adequately transformed or re-directed to keep pace with the progress not merely of his invisible world of values, but also of his visible technical skills, weapons and implements. Nature is harnessed more and more effectively and subtly for human needs and requirements; but human relations have deteriorated and enduring human values have been attenuated or sacrificed in the process. Since each generation of man has to learn anew quickly to adapt itself to the secondary man-made environment that increases in its complexity and its mechanical, rigid character, and also encounters him with conflicting standards and scales of preferences, the process of learning or education is often left incomplete and imperfect. The result is an alarming increase of the proportion of the retarded, emotionally maladjusted and delinquent persons that measures the failure of education. It is not merely the educational system but the entire institutional and group pattern conditioning the young generation that is responsible for misfits, complexes and maladjustments, and the increase of personal disorganisation. Education is a part of the more comprehensive system of social control. Its methods grow out of the general techniques of social control operative in a given society. In fact the evolution of social techniques from tribal magic, legend, myth, initiation, ritual and dormitory discipline to the school system and propaganda by means of the cinema and radio has determined the function and methods of formal education through the centuries.

Lack of Adaptation of Educational Techniques and Ideals to Social Life

The adjustment of educational techniques to changes in science and technology is the *sine qua non* of educational progress. The modern industrial system will collapse unless proper skills, habits and routines are not learnt by the young generation. The growth of modern cities and towns demands education in hygiene and sanitation without which epidemics will decimate thousands. Finance, commerce, agriculture and the professions call for specialised capacities that can only be the result of years of training. The numerous specialised functions in the Great Society of today cannot also be performed adequately and effectively unless there is an educated public. The world-wide change, associated with the transition from agriculture to large-scale industrialisation, often leaves the school system in the backwaters. Hogben's phrase, 'the spark gap is mightier than the pen', reminds persons in charge of education all over the world of the school system and outlook still dominated by academic instruction and out of touch with the realities of the industrial age. In few coutries in the world, too, is there equal opportunity of education for all. The adjustment of education to special talents or aptitudes or to physical or mental defects and drawbacks has also not made much progress. Recent advances in psychology definitely indicate that if these could be adequately and effectively assimilated to education, man would be able to live a saner and happier life with less value conflicts and frustrations and less open to indoctrination and propaganda from different quarters.

More significant than the techniques of education are the educational ideals that would naturally vary from culture to culture and from age to age. Brahmanical, Buddhist, Greek and medieval European education had each its different educational and ethical ideals, its characteristic emphasis of certain values and virtues, and its promotion of certain definite types of personality. In different epochs and countries, the family, the church, the elite and the guild were responsible for education and training. Here and there education is still the chief responsibility of one or other of such groups or institutions. The rise of nationalism, the development of commerce and transport and of mass standardised production, the extension of franchise and the increase of centralisation in Europe demanded a uniform type of education, physical, mental and moral, for the fullest development of manpower for both factories and battle-fields. The change was far-reaching in its import. The social transformation implied by the democratic and scientific movements in the world was carried out largely through the agency of the public school system that stood for universal enlightenment and efficiency. In no other epoch did the organised schools assume such responsibility for universal education; never, however, was the school utilised in such manner as the agency of the state for the regimentation of the thinking of peoples.

Especially the totalitarian states in Europe frankly have avowed political indoctrination as the aim of the educational system that is a fundamental part of the political organisation. Thus instead of fully expressing and developing the youth's personality, the school system has lulled freedom of thought and expression to sleep, made them docile subjects or robots shaped to fit into the prevailing system of ideology and values. Outside the totalitarian states, educational aims have wavered in different countries, and education has often preferred a specialised vocational instruction to creative social thinking and fostered class attitudes and cultivated snobbery or bourgeois selfishness and self-complacence, heedless of the conflicts of the social world. On the one hand, there is one kind of education for the masses of the people represented by the three R's and a modicum of liberal education in science, history and the classics that has no vital meaning for them in their hard, narrow and sordid social milieu; and another kind of education for the elite, stressing the humanities and neglecting applied sciences and technology as well as the social sciences that can successfully tackle the insistent problems of the work-a-day environment. The former type of education expands into specialised technical and professional education of various sorts, but is always considered as somewhat inferior to the latter. On the other hand, education in public schools and universities that provide the superior type has become so expensive, or entry into the latter so dependent upon wealth and prestige, rather than upon merit or upon ability of a particular over-literary kind, that instead of engendering social solidarity and social-consciousness it stereotypes class sentiments. Even in such a democratic country like the U.S.A., the land par excellence of educational experiments, the educational system is not adequately integrated with the life of society. In other countries the gulf between the values inside the public and technical schools and universities and the values of the world outside is even greater. This engenders a serious distrust of education among the majority of the people and impedes social integration. John Dewey thus speaks about American education: "If our public school system merely turns out efficient industrial fodder and citizenship fodder in a state controlled by pecuniary industry, as other school in other nations have turned out efficient cannon fodder, it is not helping to solve the problem of building up a distinctive American culture; it is only aggravating the problem. The distinguishing trait of the American student body in our higher schools is a kind of intellectual immaturity. This immaturity is mainly due to their enforced mental seclusion; there is, in their schooling, little free and disinterested concern with the underlying social problems of our civilization."[1]

The Prevailing Educational Practice as the Bulwark of Outworn Ideology and Values

The fact is that the economic and political struggles outside invade the school system; and public schools for the promotion of aristocratic privilege, middle-class schools for the cultivation of a self-centred social outlook, and the working men schools for the promotion of class antagonism, exist side by side, and take charge of different strata of the population, shaping habits and attitudes in the youth that conform to class standards and ideals. Thus the goals of education come to stress more class or status personality than total personality, and class prejudice than a gospel of democracy or social equality and justice, or, else, a sociologically colourless and standardised type of education is imparted in which any criticism or re-valuation of industrial or political institutions or re-examination of the motives of profit-seeking acquisitiveness and adventurousness is tabooed. Everywhere a rigid authoritarian discipline that stifles every kind of creative expression and an appeal to the dominant motives of fear and rivalry warp the development of the child's character. In an atmosphere of orderliness, repression and egoistic competition, inferiority neuroses are apt to develop that lead some to social deviation in later life; while for the many the traits of envy, jealousy and aggression become so firmly implanted in the school age that it becomes difficult, if not impossible, to modify social groups and institutions according to the newer ideals of social justice, equality and co-operativeness. It is only recently that the Montessori Method, the Dalton Plan or the Project Method, with their variegated techniques adapted to the natural instincts and interests of the children, have gained wide acceptance. These and other pedagogical practices have received scientific support from the new psychological movement led by Freud, Jung and Adler. But the glorification of competitiveness in the school dies hard in an industrial age.

It is only in Soviet Russia that the educational system has abandoned competitive methods eliciting interest and effort, and successfully fostered team spirit in intellectual and practical enterprise in a stimulating social atmosphere. Boys who are self-assertive and intelligent help their less gifted fellows for the work of the school class which becomes the responsibility of every member. Thus the competition between different classes, groups or teams that supersedes individual competition becomes an incentive to improvement of quality and output. No society can develop equality and co-operativeness in which the school stresses only the rewards of competition for the children at the top, and disregards the paralysing effects of frustration and defeat on the temperament of the many. Competition in the school-going age is the worst enemy of budding creative, explorative or co-operative impulses; it drains away all energies into the conventional ruts of self-assertion and self-display on a mediocre level. If the function of education is to anticipate the mental traits of adulthood of the next generation, the studious up-bringing of the child on the master motive of competition is an anachronism fraught with risks for both the individual and society. Creative expression and activity of all kinds from the making of mud-pies, toys and machines to literary composition, painting and dramatics are now increasingly assimilated into the educational system as providing channels of expression for many repressed complexes and baffled desires of childrern. Cognate in importance are the boy-scout movement, youth excursion and youth service organisation in forms useful to the people at large, that play an important role for overcoming distortion, repression and diffidence, and engendering self-esteem and self-reliance of the young, especially of the more sensitive and gifted type that is invariably pushed down by the callous, bullying and noisy type in most spheres of life. It is in this manner that the public school now attempts everywhere to build up a sane emotional-ethical structure for the adolescents who are often handicapped by the frustration of their parents, and fear, anxiety and insecurity in their homes. But so long as the majority of the population does not enjoy social security the new educational practices do not carry us very far.

Prevailing Conflicts in Social Ideology and System of Values

The conflict in educational ideals goes even deeper. In industrial civilisation there is no co-ordination between the major institutions and the values these fulfil and the standards these stand for. The moral codes and injunctions of religion are adjusted to the primary-group world, and do not fit well into the latest age of society. There is also a profound discord between the values of mutual help, brotherliness and neighbourliness that the family, the rural community and the small town inculcate and implant, and the traits and patterns of conduct dominated by self-assertion, cunning and greed favoured by the industrial institutions. Karen Horney rightly points out that many neuroses own their persistent and widespread character to the social and institutional situation. The incompatibility or even antagonism between family and industrial ethics is at the roots of lack of integration of impulses, habits and roles towards socially accepted goals. Further, the family ethics lays down many superfluous taboos in respect of auto-erotic practices and restrictions on sexual expression that engender serious worries and anxieties, and foster guilt and inferiority feeling. Thus many individuals develop psychoses and neuroses or revert to childish seeking of safety and security in place of normal struggle and achievement. The large part that the social and institutional factors now play in the development of neuroses indicates the need of an altogether different approach in the entire problem of mental hygiene.

Significance of Social Psychotherapy

Recent experiments with mental patients have shown the great possibilities of group psychotherapy extended not merely to the constellation of the family but also to the whole configuration of social institutions.[2] The patient shows less resistance when examined in the group, and establishes easier contact with the psycho-analyst that may gradually develop into a kind of transference. The treatment of an entire neurotic family has also proved of great value in bringing about the emotional readjustment of a neurotic child. Even more important than the family is the set or the gang in its effects on the emotional life of a young delinquent. Thrasher finds teaching or admonition of no aid in bringing about reform in this case. Success may be obtained through recognition of the role or position of the boy in the gang, and through setting before the gang itself a new, socially accepted task that may improve its prestige in the larger society. Thus the same group influences that consolidate and augment crime may be used as powerful levers of rehabilitation. The re-education of the individual according to modern psychiatry is easier not in isolation, but as a member of the family, the gang, the neighbourhood or the occupational group through control of the emotional tensions arising therefrom. Every individual is surrounded in society by a host of compulsives, faiths, beliefs and prejudices. He owes his motivations and values in respect of sex and love, self-assertion and service, status and prestige to the order of values or ideology of the community. In some countries and at a certain stage of social development a rational discussion of the prevailing economic or political opinions and beliefs is shut out for the sake of safety of the state or of vested interests. It is in such a mental climate that a large number of individuals show neurotic manifestations, and cannot orient themselves through co-ordination of impulses, habits and attitudes towards some central goals in life. Under such circumstances an analysis of ideologies revealing their roots in unconscious inhibitions, fears or obsessions is exceedingly helpful for individual re-adjustment. More and more the neurotic manifestations of individuals exhibit their intimate connection with social tensions and pressures, with the institutional, economic and political crisis. Thus the psychoanalytic treatment in the modern educational technique should fruitfully extend from the individual to the examination of group ideologies, emotions and interests as a preparation for both individual and group rehabilitation. Educational techniques follow social techniques, just as the values and attitudes sought to be imparted by formal education follow the pattern of values of the larger system of society. Unfortunately in the countries that are subjected to social repressions and frustrations, the educational system, controlled and regulated by the state, hardly gives any room for the psychological examination of social alternatives; and thus education becomes narrow-minded and single-tracked. Whether it is a pugnacious nationalism, war, military preparedness, a materialistic conception of history, hatred against Jews, socialists or communists or collectivism, strict and systematic indoctrination in the field of social affairs becomes the established practice in the educational system. This is largely the result of the social-historical situation in which a new regime has established itself in different countries by a coup or revolution and must win prestige and consolidate power through the re-education of the young generation, who are pliant and prepared. Not generic human motives or universal notions, but the motives and notions of a class, a clique or regime are inculcated in both society and the school; and the result is the increase of emotional tension and neurotic manifestation. The antithesis between Liberal Democracy and Communism, Freedom and Organization and Rights and Order in contemporary culture is responsible for many psychological tensions and contradictions in the educational system. Educational techniques, like the social structure, arts and religion, have to pass through an empirical dialectic experimenting with the extremes of values as well as with the golden mean so that these can explore and utilize the potential values of contrasted social attitudes and experiences. In very few countries, however, such openness of mind in respect of educational experimentation finds public support.

Religion as the Revelation of Perfect Social Values in Integrated Society

In an integrated society there are neither conflicts between the major institutions and the values these crystallise, nor does one set of values and ideology oust or suppress other values and ideologies. The mental climate is one of harmonisation and permeation of values and ideologies, all subject to common judgment and participation. The value pattern of the economic and political institutions and of the family, of religion and the fine arts, blend and integrate, so that the social culture in its totality becomes an embodiment of the absolute order of values. There is such a thing as the ethos of a culture, a super-individual spiritual reality, a unique and harmonious organisation of values and value-seeking activities in and through which the individuals of a particular epoch or culture express and fulfil themselves. Civilisation thus speaks in different tongues through various social cultures that differ from one another according to the major values that its dominant groups and institutions, its laws and its system of rights and duties, its moralities and manners focus, protect and augment. For each historical culture, such as that of Buddhist and Gupta India, Sung China, Periclean Athens, Hellenistic Culture, European Renaissance, and medieval European Church, there are an unique social structure of values, a distinctive experience and fulfilment of the major values for individual persons in the particular country or age.

Religion is the faith in the participation and permanence of values. It supplies the true and stable ground and intense zest for the ultimate values, rooted as these are in the universal superhuman order. It is the ever-vigilant guardian of the hegemony of the spiritual over the biological and social values. It thus directs the individual and society to their true destiny. In the vicissitudes of culture that comprise the historical process of humanity, religion deepens, uplifts and equalises the abiding values or goods, while art conserves, intensifies and transmits them. For both religion and art the ultimate values or goods must belong to all in order to be the ultimate and the good. Thus religion raises man's strivings after goodness, love and beauty to the highest potentiality by opening out a beyond-human channel for them. Values, then, reach their highest power and most comprehensive sharing as these come under the protection and direction of religion and art. Between religion and art, on the one hand, and social values, on the other, there is a reciprocity which has no end. Man projects into the Beyond the fullest and richest personal and the most expansive social values he can imagine in his social world. As the radiation of human love and goodness renews the vital flame of his mystic and artistic vision, the latter sheds its rays upon his social values and experiences, making human life and society continuous with the eternal and infinite.

True religion and art transform human relationships and values as channels of the expression of the absolute and the eternal through archetypes, symbols, myths, parables and pictures. It is thus that religion and art educate. In primitive culture myths and legends created primordial animal symbols and archetypes, dragons, serpents and monsters as well as fairies or demonic women that drained the subconscious and externalised man's sanguine instincts and impulses.[3] With the progress of civilisation the archetypal images came to be represented by fairies, gods and heroes that still released the unconscious, but now also expressed and symbolised human and social values, man's views of the universe and of his relations to it. Many are these archetypal images, different in different social and ethnic setting, that have been naively articulated by myth, beautified by art, cherished by morality and adored by religion, directing the life experience of peoples through the centuries. Such, for instance, are the theo-morphic images of Egypt and India, the fairies, the Heroes, the Saints, the Sinners; or, dominating the realm of Buddhist imagination, the various Buddhas and Bodhisattvas, Lokanath, Maitreya, Manjusri and Tara; the Hindu images of the various gods and their respective Saktis; or, again, the Christian images of the Good Shepherd, the Man of Sorrows, the Madonna, the Angels, the Annunciation, the Crucifixion and the Resurrection. Through the ages such images in different lands have supplied the organising principles of personality integration, and at the same time served as beacon-lights for social solidarity and the collective inspiration and effort of individuals. Apart from these primordial archetypes, art and religion through the ages have also fashioned symbols, legends and parables whose educative and unifying power has also sustained cultures. In the Buddhist world the parables of the Buddha's nativity, renunciation, enlightenment and charity to all sentient creatures have served for millions of Asiatics as sources of revelation of the true meaning of human life and destiny. Similarly in the realm of Hindu imagination the legends and parables of the struggle between the Devas and Asuras, the conjugal love of Savitri conquering Yama or Death, the sufferings of Ramachandra and his consort in obedience to the father's wish and the fight of Arjuna against his kinsmen in the cause of righteousness represent generic human episodes in which right conduct is interpreted and directed from the scale of the ultimate values.

What has happened to Western culture, when there are no "paradigmatic experiences" nor archetypes for setting forth the ends and climaxes of individual conduct or for co-ordinating social action, is trenchantly pointed out by Karl Mannheim. "The religious focus is not a moral or ethical experience, nor a way of regulating behaviour and conduct, but a way of interpreting life from the centre of some paradigmatic experience. One may discuss whether the basic Christian experience is original sin, redemption, the liberating and creative power of love or the Cross, the deeper meaning of suffering. It is from these foci of experience that the adjustment patterns of right behaviour and conduct are always reinterpreted. If these paradigmatic experiences evaporate, as in secularized European history, it is obvious that the problem of values contains nothing but the adjustment character of human conduct. Right or wrong only means efficiency, and there is no answer to the question: Efficiency for what? Regulations and values are considered solely as means, and their ends are lost sight of. The only relevant criterion of right and wrong that remains can be deduced from the need for reconciling individual and group adjustment."[4]

The Scale of Values as the Measure of Progress

Both individual and social adjustment has to be judged from the scale of values. Progress implies the enhancement of the values of life, which involves both the ordering of the levels of value and integration or harmony of value experience. As we rise from the biological and economic values to the realm of ideal values, the criteria of social progress are two-fold : one from the individual and the other from the collective viewpoint; first, society is progressive as it offers increase of opportunities for the harmonious fulfilment of the basic satisfaction values and capacities, and hence for the perfection of the human personality in all its members; secondly, society is progressive as there is increase of equality, solidarity and sociableness. The above is intrinsic progress. Any other progress, technological, economic or institutional, is simply instrumental to democratic personality fulfilment, equality and solidarity. The characterisation of the optima of progress as given in Table 14.1 is broad and comprehensive, and is based on the evolutionary conception of successive orders and levels of man's environment, and the three-fold movement of both individuals and of society as a whole. The hierarchy of values closely approximates to the itemised statements as presented in the table. It comprehends the items and indices of progress laid down by Willcox, Nicefero, Dellepiane, Hertzler and Clarence Case.

Progress is the outcome of improvement of the heritage and endowment of the race, of economic and technological improvement, and finally, of social evaluation, i.e. of the enlightened and deliberate societal subordination of the social processes and values in the biological and economic levels by those in the moral and spiritual. Progress is defined, guided and judged by man's ideal values. The

TABLE 14.1

Optima of Progress

Factors of progress	Ecological Level	Economic Level	Sociological Level
Habitat, Race and social Inheritance	Maximum Density of Population and Continuity of Habitat, Race and Culture (Measurable)	Maximum Technological Efficiency and Social Capital (Measurable)	Equalny, Justice and Solidarity, Syncretic Art and Religion.
Individual Acquisition.	Maximum Average Expectation of Life, Intelligence, Plasticity, Mobility and Sociability (Measurable)	Maximum Average Efficiency, Income, Leisure and Consumption (Measurable)	Harmonious Development of Human Personality and Character. Appreciation of the Ultimate Values—Truth, Power, Beauty and Communion.

ends of man's biological and economic adaptation are particular and instrumental ends, and work in subordination to the intrinsic values and standards worked out within the realm of appreciation and evaluation by the human personality. To the extent man's personality achieves the ideal values, he is linked with fellowmen in a commonalty of thought, emotions and achievement.

Man's progress, therefore, is biological, economic and ethical, one and at the same time: an improvement in the societal organisation and efficiency and in the equitable social distribution of the advantages of culture, from the collective standpoint, and a qualitative improvement of the individual, physically, occupationally and spiritually. The distinction between different levels of progress is a matter of convenience; for both individual and collective experience is single and integral. Thus the promotion of equality, justice and solidarity is possible only on the basis of renovation of the scale of values that underlies any existing economic and social situation. This is the fundamental task of education that in the last resort is nothing more and nothing less than the appreciation of the ultimate meaning and purpose of both the personal and collective life. A sound sense of valuation, that is the core of the educational process, fosters economic, technological or institutional efficiency and organisation, while the latter serve as means for the embodiment of the ethos or type-values of the social culture. "The surest way to the real is often through the Ideal." Man's discovery and realisation of the ideal values carries society irresistibly forward towards greater integration, efficiency and harmony. The progressive unfoldment of the individual personality and the organisation and enrichment of a spiritual commonalty go hand in hand. This abstract formula, applicable to the experience of mankind, is also applicable to any concrete social situation. Each social situation has its own measure and dimension of progress, a movement from inefficiency and poverty to efficiency, wealth and leisure; from conflict and inequality to harmony, justice and equality; from monotony, inflexibility and restriction to variety, expansion and enrichment. Progress is the constant transformation of the present due to the recurrent challenge of the ideal. But, as Dewey observes, "we find our clues to direction in the projected recollections of definite experienced goods not in vague anticipations, even when we label the vagueness perfection, the Ideal, and proceed to manipulate its definition with dry dialectic logic."

The Synoptic Character of Progress

Progress, then, is characterised by the enrichment of individuals and society in three successive levels along the lines of quantitative and qualitative elaboration of the optima set forth, the movement in the realm of cultural and spiritual values guiding and democratising, and hence enlarging, deepening and accelerating the whole process. An uplift of morals, the cultivation of temperance, honesty and truthfulness improve the physical and psychological health, efficiency and sociability. A refinement of appreciational life promotes mental creativeness, enterprise and endurance. A moral sense of continuity with the generations yet unborn checks spendthrift management of national resources and promotes long-run economic efficiency and progress. The only method of checking the present fall in birth-rate that threatens the continuity of culture in large organised industrial communities is to promote a sense of obligation of the family towards the maintenance and transmission of the social and cultural heritage. Social security and justice are the only means of improving social efficiency and harmony through a fair sharing of the hazards of the industrial system and through an abolition of violent and terrorist methods on the part of the discontented working class whose radical change of temper is a symptom of both personal and social disorganisation. Democratic equality, justice and solidarity are projections to the organisational plane of the moral and religious principles of equality and fraternity and the supreme worth of the human personality.

Progress is integral and synoptic. Degeneration accompanies fractional, one-sided development or specialisation in one level of life and value experience. Industrial civilisation shows, no doubt, progress in technological efficiency and accmulation of social capital, but it also recklessly dissipates natural resources. The ecological base of the industrial community of the future alarmingly shrinks. There is, no doubt, gain in the reduction of average mortality and increase of average longevity, but diseases of middle and old ages and individual and social neuroses have shown an increase. Above all, industrial civilisation is unable to utilise its science and technology for bringing about more harmonious human relations or increasing man's co-operativeness and fellow-feeling. According to Herrick : "That social stability upon which the survival and comfort of the individual depend and that moral satisfaction upon which his equanimity, poised stability of character depend arise from the maintenance of relations with his fellowmen which are mutually advantageous." Ethics, sociology and psychopathology agree in affirming that human progress has its fundamental psychic basis and background in the amity and congeniality of human relationships, and community of standards and values established between individuals. Industrial civilisation, due largely to the fact that its benefits and hazards are unequally distributed among the different social classes, menaces the security and well-being of the individual as its disharmonious, exploitative social relationships endanger the stability and development of his personality, and arouse mass emotional outbursts on the primitive plane. The sense of economic insecurity and social jealousy and resentment, both of which are aggravated by ostentatious enjoyment, become more and more widely diffused. Larger and larger sections of the population in modern industrial communities cease to have any aesthetic or spiritual interests, and exhibit the dominance of the primitive instincts and herd or mass reactions. Thus industrial and technical progress is associated with moral and spiritual deterioration, and in some phases and countries with even the decline of average health and physical degeneration.

Progress as Equalisation of the Values of Life

Progress is a complex, diversified, multitudinous process in which the optima of the different levels of adaptation are harmoniously blended and integrated. Each such integration is baffling in its complexity, since each social situation constitutes problems of adjustment of different levels of value and experience that are themselves of great number and subtlety. Such integration, to be sure, is guided by the scale of values. It is an increasing appreciation and refinement of the ultimate values of life that determine and promote the complicated tasks of equalisation and social justice. A false sense of the relative values of things would introduce a wrong kind of equality that would not tend towards the organisation and enrichment of life. On the other hand, a denial of social equality and justice itself jeopardises the appreciation of the ultimate values among a considerable proportion of the population, and this hinders social progress. This is the chief reason why the Greek philosophers regarded morality and justice as functions of the ideal society, inhering in the entire system of social and economic relations. The "good" life is not possible except in the moral social order. On the other hand, man's sense of social justice underlies through the ages his efforts towards achieving a "natural order" or rational social organisation that embodies his cravings for goodness and resentment against wrong. The revision of the scale of values among the mystics, philosophers, social reformers and prophets supplies the drive behind equalisation, justice and solidarity. Their sense of appreciation of the worth of personality, their insight into the absolute values, the indissoluble human trinity of truth, beauty and goodness, is the abiding stimulus to the shared living that alone can prevent the inequalities of man from becoming handicaps to efficiency and organisation, to social progress.

Man is not a solitary explorer of the universe. His objective world of the senses and his imaginative world are largely defined, selected and organised for him by his cultural equipment and heritage—the intellectual, aesthetic and practical experiences of fellowmen that speak to him through literature, science and the fine arts. His realm of meanings and values also is a realm not of individual but of associated intelligence and sentiment; while his creative expression and experience add new facets of meaning and value of the world to the experience of all individuals. Each new vision of truth and beauty, each great aspiration for goodness augments the value content of society that is a progressively expanding source of insights, loves and aspirations of men. Man's pursuit of truth in science, philosophy and art, as it is grounded on a society of inter-communicating intelligent individuals, achieves a closer spiritual communion in society. His artistic vision and expression bind together members of a society in sympathy and common imaginative experience. His advance in economic power and control over the environment also increase comradeship and fellow-feeling in productive enterprise. Thus do his original intuitions of truth, power and goodness, grounded in the universal nature of human personality, enhance equality and oneness between man and man through deepening common understandings, sympathies and endeavours. Progress is multi-dimensional. This implies that in spite of a marked divergence of the pattern of ways of living, values and institutions, as determined by regional and historical factors and circumstances, society shows in the broad the working of the dialectic of individual fulfilment and social integration, freedom and control, mobility and status, equality and order, and self-actualization and self-transcendence at the successive dimensions of life, society and transcendence. The dialectic of individual and community with its varied practical tensions and contradictions becomes even more significant and meaningful through inclusion within ever wider environment and enlargement of experience—the greater harmony and order of the vast unending community, including the world of living and non-living, cells, atoms, stars and galaxies, [to which the matured, contemplative individual ties himself. Neither the order and harmony of community nor the richness and uniqueness of the individual have any limits. Progress has no bounds either.

We reach the grand vision of sociology that the functioning of human individuals and societies is embodied in ever enlarged and more harmonious and integrated forms or patterns that connect the minor careers of men and communities within a larger history of community of communities without limits.

Human progress, in the first place, is marked by the ever increasing order, harmony and integration of the human community passing over into the eternal and cosmic community—the community of communities or *communitatus communitatum.*

Human progress, in the second place, due to the ever increasing uniqueness and creativeness of the individual is marked by a multiple dialectic, the dialectical pulsation of thesis, antithesis and unstable synthesis on many lines and at different tempo. Sometimes the antithesis and struggle between Freedom and Organization, Liberalism and Communism, Classicism and Romanticism, Naturalism-Humanism and Transhuman Myticism coincide and are vigorously continued in different sectors of life —in the political and social organization, in education and the arts, and in religion and worship. Sometimes due to unpredictable individual experimenting and stress of one polarity in a relatively heterogeneous and inconsistent but highly creative epoch, the march of the dialectic with its essential attractions and repulsions is uneven. Yet the working of the dialectical rhythm in the most comprehensive category of the struggle between self-actualization and self-transcendence is too basic and integral a part of human development to be wholly missed. The empirical cultural dialectic moves on [thriving on the growth and continuity of selected antinomic notions and values from all previous stages in cultural evolution.

Progress is a collective process in which the values of life, those that are concerned with man's biological and economic environment, and those belonging to the environment beyond the range of the senses, are shared among and appreciated and enjoyed by all men. The higher values of knowledge, art and character stand for a participation which increases its range until it comprehends the whole universe. Progress, permeated and directed at every turn by the spirit of social equality and democracy, brooks no boundaries, but in its scope of the organisation and expansion of life extends to the universe. It is the aim of the right type of education to facilitate and speed up social progress which means also world progress. A world view of progress and ethics, in which the fundamentals are social responsibility, solidarity and co-operativeness, can alone supply the sure moral foundation of world reconstruction of the future. Man's science, technology and economics have established one world for all, and created the demand of one morality for all, extending from the individual, the tribe and the nation to mankind, embracing more and more of those who were formerly strangers, barbarians and enemies. The one world is, however, a limited world that does not provide adequate living space and economic opportunity for all peoples. Thus there is perpetual strife between the nations due to unequal distribution of food, raw materials and scarce resources. The world is over-populated and chronically short of food and essential materials, without which there cannot be any progressive improvement of the standard of living, leisure and culture for all peoples. There also range bitter struggles between the economic classes and political parties within a nation. If the collective life of communities has tended to become insecure, barren and uncreative, so far as the mental life of the individual is concerned, his unremitting toil and fast tempo of life and interaction, his profound insecurity and his relegation to the role of a cog in a stupendous chain of complicated machine technology, which he can neither understand nor appreciate, greatly limit the interplay of his normal social, aesthetic and intellectual feelings and sentiments. In the crowded, impoverished and standardised world of today, it has become more and more difficult for great multitudes to enjoy more than a modicum of the intellectual, aesthetic and recreational values. Without these the opportunities for self-realisation become severely restricted for larger and larger sections of humanity. But the values of character, of good-will, love and communion can be unlimitedly appropriated and shared by the have-nots, whether whole peoples, classes or individuals. It is the cultivation and development of character and the moral values of self-discipline, co-operativeness and solidarity that accordingly can alone safeguard progress in the cramped and precarious modern world. Religion is the stimulus of the values of character that it raises to their highest potential, throwing open the possibilities of man's shared living with fellow-creatures of the universe in a measure not accessible to power, knowledge or art. It is the supreme value of the ordering and direction of progress, the grand passion and insight for a total engagement in the life of society through goodness, love and service which are essential for the survival of man's reason, and for its direction as a potent equipment for his evolutionary destiny. In the way in which it is conceived in some of the elevated impersonal types of mysticism, it brooks no boundaries between man and the rest of the world, and fashions his sharing of the common life after a pattern of the supra-human or transcendental group order and his progress as an episode of the grand symbiosis of the universe. There accordingly emerge one life, one form, one relationship, one value through nature and the processes and relationships of world and society. In the authentic religion of the mystic which with fanatical fervour and clear social insight revolutionizes the entire pattern of human relationships, goals and values, there is a sudden leap forward towards a new soul-stirring unity and solidarity of spiritual life, man and cosmos. Such wholeness is achieved through a more or less complete coordination and fusion of the largest number of polarities and contradictions in the individual and social dialectic. Mystical values through the epochs in human history fashion a fresh harmony and symbiosis of the cosmos—a virgin resolution of all polarities, tensions and conflicts, individual and social that normally beset human life, mind and society.

References

1. Selected Writings in Philosophy, p. 314.
2. See Moreno (Ed.): Group Psychotherapy; also his Who shall Survive?
3. See Juag : The Integration of Personality.
4. Diagnosis of Our Time, p. 135.

INDEX